STATE, LAW AND GENDER

State, Law and Gender

Debating the Age of Marriage in India, 1872–1978

SHREYA ROY

BOYDELL · MANOHAR

ISBN 978-81-19139-36-1 (Manohar Publishers & Distributors)
ISBN 978-1-83765-143-6 (Boydell • Manohar)

First published 2024 by
Ajay Kumar Jain for
Manohar Publishers & Distributors
4753/23 Ansari Road, Daryaganj
New Delhi 110 002

First published Worldwide excluding India, Sri Lanka, Nepal,
Bangladesh, Afghanistan, Pakistan and Bhutan, 2024 by Boydell • Manohar
A joint imprint of Boydell & Brewer Ltd and
Manohar Publishers & Distributors
PO Box 9, Woodbridge, Suffolk IP12 3DF, UK
and of Boydell & Brewer Inc.
668 Mt Hope Avenue, Rochester, NY 14620–2731, USA
website: www.boydellandbrewer.com

A CIP catalogue record for this book is available
from the British Library

Typeset by
Ravi Shanker
Delhi 110095

This publication is printed on acid-free paper

To My
Thamma (Grandmother)
KAMALINI ROY
who got married at the age of fifteen

Contents

List of Tables

Acknowledgements

The first person, to whom, I want to express my heartfelt gratitude, is my mentor, Sabyasachi Chattopadhyay of Department of History, University of Kalyani. From the beginning of my research, he has been by my side, despite all my childishness. Without his guidance and critical comments, this work most certainly would not have come through. I was sure of one thing that if I ever did research, I would do research on the histories of women and gender. While studying and writing on various topics of Women and Gender History, the thoughtful advice of Bimal Kanti Ghosh, a retired teacher of History at Jadavpur University and Sabyasachi Chattopadhyay opened a new horizon in my thinking and research work.

Sabyasachi Chattopadhyay suggested that I could explore the history of age of marriage in India from the historical perspective. He told me that the work would be extremely relevant in light of recent discussions and debates about raising the age of marriage for girls in India. In the initial phase, I started the work with some doubt. While looking for sources, I saw an immense wealth of information everywhere, from libraries to archives. Bimal Kanti Ghosh has bound me with gratitude by providing me with many valuable and rare documents; his well-thought-out advice has enriched me. I would like to thank both of them from the core of my heart.

Initially, I have discussed some aspects of this topic in my M.Phil. Dissertation, submitted to the Department of History, University of Kalyani, West Bengal. However, when I began revising my work for the present monograph, the comments from Mahua Sarkar, Department of History, Jadavpur University made me rethink the analytical framework within which I had so far laboured. I am also indebted to the anonymous reviewer who provided constructive comments and suggestions and to the team of Manohar Publishers & Distributors, New Delhi for their support.

Without academic, sensitive, and institutional support, this book would never have seen the light of the day. I take this occasion to express sincere gratitude to Bhaskar Chakraborty, Late Hari Shankar Vasudevan, Nirban Basu, Shireen Masood, Rachana Chakraborty, Suparna Gooptu, Ritwika Biswas, Amit Dey, Rajsekhar Basu, Shouvik Mukhopadhyay, Sarada Ghosh and Kingshuk Chatterjee of the University of Calcutta, where I did my Postgraduation, and Prabal Mukhopadhyay, Anasua Datta, Amrita Bagchi, Chirantani Das, Nivedita Chakraborty and Ishani Choudhury of Bethune College, where I did my Graduation, for helping me to develop as a researcher since my college and university days. I remain immensely grateful to Nirban Basu and Rachana Chakraborty, who have always relied on and given me infinite affection. Special thanks are owed to Alok Kumar Ghosh, Sutapa Sengupta and Anil Kumar Sarkar of University of Kalyani, where I did my M.Phil., for their words of encouragement regarding my work. The care and concern of my colleagues at Vivekananda College, Thakurpukur, Kolkata, Siddhartha Guha Ray, Aparajita Bhattacharyya and Amit Bhattacharyya (retired professor of Department of History, Jadavpur University) towards me has been heartening. Siddhartha Guha Ray has always treated me like his own daughter and encouraged me in my research. I am deeply indebted to Aparna Bandyopadhyay of Diamond Harbour Women's University for her rare scholarly insight on 'Women and Gender History'; her suggestion and critical comments on my topic helped me a lot. I extend my heartfelt gratitude to all my teachers of Begum Rokeya Smriti Balika Vidyalaya; I do not have enough words to thank them.

Prasenjit Mukherjee (Dada) of Department of History of Sankrail Anil Biswas Smriti Mahavidyalaya, has not only showered his affection but discussion with him on various topics has also inspired me a lot. I want to thank him for his affection.

This work would not have been possible without the support of my dear students, Shrabani, Saswata, Anirban, Rohan, Sagnik, Snigdho, Rupankar, Susmita, Souraditya, Baishali, Sudipta and

Sayak. I specially thank Shiv Shankar Banerjee, who is now more than a friend of mine, for our conversations on diverse issues, which have nudged me to think anew.

The extensive resources of several archives, the West Bengal State Archives, the Archives of Centre for Studies in Social Sciences, Calcutta and the National Archives of India played an important role in my research work. In addition to these, the immense treasury of various libraries, the National Library of India, the Ramkrishna Mission Institute of Culture Library, Golpark; Bangiya Sahitya Parishat Library, Library of Centre for Studies in Social Sciences, Calcutta; West Bengal State Library, and Central Library of Kalyani University helped me a lot throughout my research work.

Last but not the least, I am especially grateful to my family for being supportive of my academic ventures. The affection and constant encouragement of my grandmother (I call her Thamma), Kamalini Roy always make me happy. Mejo Didibhai and Dadabhai have always encouraged me in various subjects regarding my study. Dadabhai would have been really happy if he were alive today. Boro Maa, Mejo Maa, Chhoto Masi, Boro Pisi, Kakima, Boro Jethu, Mejo Jethu, Chhoto Mesho and Baba have always instilled confidence in me and stood by me in times of stress. I want to talk about two more persons – Kaku and Chhoto Pisi – I shall never have the opportunity to let you know about my book, but I have no doubt how happy you would be if you were with us. My two elder brothers (Barda and Mejda) are always more enthusiastic about my studies than their own. My two sisters-in-law (Boro Boudi and Chhoto Boudi), Didi and Jamaibabu have always been by my side like friends. Boro Boudi's words have inspired me a lot. My two younger brothers (I mention both of them as Bhai) and Bon have encouraged me a lot. The relaxed moments I had with my nephew (Babu) sustained me while I was writing this monograph. My acknowledgements would be incomplete without mentioning that my association with this work is inseparable from Maa and without her endless support, I could not have completed this work. So, I take this opportunity to record my love and sincere gratitude to Maa to understand and accept me as I am.

List of Abbreviations

AIWC	All India Women's Conference
CMRA	Child Marriage Restraint Act
CSWI	Committee on the Status of Women in India
IPC	Indian Penal Code
NCWI	National Council of Women in India
NFHS	National Family Health Survey
PCMA	Prohibition of Child Marriage Act
UCC	Uniform Civil Code
WBSA	West Bengal State Archives
WIA	Women's Indian Association

Introduction

Scholars of gender and jurisprudence have been studying legislative processes and laws in order to lay out the ways in which law can choose or oppose defined commands of power, as well as the modalities by which legal discourse facilitates and discovers cultural classifications. Many argue that the importance of the legal domain is best assessed in a broader socio-economic and political context.[1] The claim for statutory and legitimate power has turned out to be a pillar of the women's movement in Indian history. Women in the independence movement have struggled for their rights and legal reform. These claims for 'women's rights' and 'equal rights' have given the women's movement its political dimension in many ways. Despite legal achievements over the years, little has been improved in women's social, political, and economic status.[2] The social movement against child marriage and to involve the state in it was expressed for the first time in the second half of the nineteenth century, and the debate continues in the twenty-first century.[3] Despite the fact that this was one of the first legal campaigns, there are few insightful evaluations of what were the reasons that legal reforms have continued to fail to approach this issue. Although child marriage remains an obstacle, entrenched in socio-economic structures, a remedy is being looked for inside the realm of the legislation.[4] Girls are married at a young age all over the world, sometimes before they reach puberty and many times before they reach the age of eighteen. The practice of marrying girls as children is widespread in developing African, Asian, and Latin American countries. According to a survey conducted by the United Nations Children's Fund (UNICEF), 'a large percentage of girls between the ages of fifteen and nineteen are married in Sub-Saharan Africa.'[5] When viewed in a global context, India's situation is not dissimilar to that of these developing countries.[6] Child marriage of girls is a relatively ignored social problem in India, receiving little consideration from policymakers, law interpreters, scholars, law enforcement agencies, and academicians.[7] Child marriage is not an isolated practice forming sole sufferers out of children but is fundamentally tied up within the forms that compulsory marriage as a modern, dynamic and deeply hierarchical system is taking in contemporary Indian society. The challenge is far greater than the elimination of child marriage, given the differential forces shaping diverse women's life chances and future in India today.

According to Samita Sen and Anindita Ghosh (2021),[8] ongoing study on child marriage, or early marriage in India, as the case appears to be, is very unbalanced. This has become clearer in the context of the global campaign against child marriage over the last decade or so. Despite the fact that child marriage has been regarded as a social problem since the early nineteenth century, and despite a flood of didactic and creative writing in the nineteenth and early twentieth centuries, the problem tends to have quietly shifted from a contentious social issue to a consensus development agenda. This shift can be seen in the country's legislative activities in the 1970s and 1980s. The debate over child marriage has devolved into government policy rather than a public debate. 'This shift is related', Sen and Ghosh suggest, 'to the changing nature of child marriage.'[9] According to Flavia Agnes (2011),[10] 'the marriage of minors becomes a crucial question in a discourse on women's rights within marriage, since girls far outnumber boys in respect of child marriages. This is due to the fact that both customary practices and legal dictates sanction that brides should be younger than the bridegrooms. The issue of child marriage impacts both matrimonial and criminal law.'[11] Amidst reform, consciousness, strategy, and law, child marriage continues to exist on a scale that encourages the search for new or 'root' causes, or at the very least their reaffirmation. This structuring of the issue complicates another equally phenomenal 'reality'; while child marriage continues, the pattern has transformed. Samita Sen and Anindita Ghosh (2021)[12] have rightly pointed out that 'the shift from child marriage to early marriage means in effect that child marriage has declined. Indeed, the average age of marriage for women has increased from something like ten-twelve to nearly eighteen in the course of the twentieth century'.[13] Sen and Ghosh (2021) have assumed that child marriage should give way to adult marriage as part of the 'normal trajectory of modernization'. Nevertheless, turning the question around and paying some attention to the process of decline, which has so far been deemed void by the force of a presumed teleology of modernism, may be useful.[14]

It is remarkable that most of the social reform initiatives, which focused on women during the nineteenth century, were largely concerned with the girl child.[15] During this time, one can see how child marriage became not just the name of a problem but the most significant issue afflicting Indian society capable of capturing everything that was wrong with us as a people.[16] Furthermore, in the Hindu system, marriage was supposedly arranged by parents or guardians as part of a broader set of social collaborations and connections.[17] Samita Sen (2021) argued 'if there was no consent, then the question of child or adult was not legally relevant'. Rather, according to her, 'marriage is a life cycle ritual, which marks the transfer of women (with her productive and reproductive labour) from one family to another; it does not link directly with age, either physically (puberty) or legally (age of majority) and therefore, there was no word for "child marriage".' The term '*balyavivaha*' is a nineteenth-century translation of child marriage that arose in the midst of social reform, representing the reactions of the British, who were one of the very few population groups at the time to perform late and adult marriage for men and women.[18] Marriage is characterized as a union between a man and a woman; children born from this union are legal and acceptable in society. It denotes the socially identified 'institutional cohabitation of a man and a woman', which allows them to involve in sexual activities while also imposing certain responsibilities on them. However, one cannot reject the 'cultural construction of marriage' and its social and economic implications. Marriage is not only a legal union between two opposite sex, but it also creates cultural, social, and economic associations between families and kin-networks.[19] Marriage in India has traditionally been regarded as a religious ritual and sacred duty rather than a question of individual satisfaction and choice. Gooroo Dass Banerjee (1879),[20] M.K. Jabbi (1986)[21] and Werner F. Menski (2003)[22] stated that 'this custom of solemnizing the marriages of girl children is an entrenched social custom that has prevailed fairly widely, particularly amongst Hindus in India for several centuries'.[23] Werner F. Menski further discussed that 'the practice is integrally connected to the cultural heritage and tradition, which has its roots in the patriarchal social structure'. Legal writers have argued that marriages in the Vedic period were affected once the couples attained adulthood. The consent of the girls was invariably valued. Girls were free to select their own spouses.[24] This custom persisted until the sixth and seventh centuries. Following that, it began to decline as a result of the influence of Brahminical culture and patriarchy. Pre-puberty marriage was thought to be the best option for protecting women from sexual exploitation and preserving their chastity.[25] S.N. Agarwala (1962)[26] and K.M. Kapadia (1966)[27] affirm in their works that with the passing of time 'it became an institutionalized custom, the violation of which was met with social disapproval and disgrace'.[28] Kapadia identified different Brahminical sources and writers to try to determine when marriages occurred in ancient India and whether they changed over time. He also pointed out that 'Since marriage was all about the transfer of authority over a woman, from the father to the husband, it should hence take place before a girl reached the age when she might question it'.[29]

The issue of child marriage was raised for the first time in the early nineteenth century, in relation to the practice of *sati* (the immolation of the widow on the funeral pyre of her dead husband).[30] Most historians start their accounts of the period of social reform in India with the lengthy discussion over the practice of *sati* in colonial Bengal between the 1780s and 1820s. If one examines the three decades of debate over whether and how to ban *sati* as it unfolded between British colonial officials, Indian *pandits*, and reformers, one will notice that the women themselves were not involved in these discourses, which were instead about whether *sati* as an exercise was authorized in ancient religious texts.[31] The issue was 'whether a child widow could commit *sati* and if so, whether this could be seen as voluntary; could a child, already married, consent to suicide?'[32] These debates, which Lata Mani (1998)[33] has thoroughly discussed, were subsequently ended in 1829 with the Act prohibiting *sati*. The child widow, on the other hand, emerged as a more contentious figure in the remarriage debates.[34] *Sati* was practiced by a small number of people in specific parts of Bengal and to a smaller extent elsewhere, gaining enormous attention due to the extreme brutality associated with it. The less dramatic practice of ritually 'enforced widowhood' was far more common, especially among the upper castes.[35] As Janaki Nair (1994) has put it, 'the law against widow immolation may have saved them from the pyre, but condemned them to a living death'.[36] There was dissatisfaction with the role and position of young widows in a society that placed a high value on disciplining 'women's sexuality' within marriage. The emphasis on 'ascetic widowhood' was not a completely viable alternative.[37] Sumit Sarkar (2007), in one of his articles, argued that 'some of Vidyasagar's most passionate writings addressed the need to harness the sexuality of child widows within marriage and to recover their reproductive capacity.' It is also said that 'he witnessed the pain and difficulty of child widows in his own family'.[38] Uma Chakravarti believed that one primary objective of widow remarriage legislation was to bring the child (or the young) under the discipline of marriage. Thus, the 'child wife' and 'child widow' are corresponding images; the 'child wife' becomes the 'child widow' and, at times, the 'child wife' again.[39] Following the widow remarriage debates during the 1850s, B.M. Malabari's *Notes on Infant Marriage and Enforced Widowhood* (1884) once more brought up these issues and for the first time made a direct connection between 'child marriage and education'. Soon after that, there was the Rukhmabai case (1884-8), which has been widely demonstrated by historians. However, another case from more than ten years ago established the legal benchmark for child marriage. The 'Huchi case' has not received the attention it deserved in India's history of social reform movements. Gauri Viswanathan momentarily narrated the story in her book[40] and it has been discussed by Samita Sen (2009, 2012)[41] in more detail in two papers. The case involved child marriage, but it was in the context of religious conversion. The case was appealed to the Governor General, becoming an example for both 'child marriage and conversion marriage conflicts'.[42]

The contemporary debate and discussion must be reinterpreted within the context of ongoing structural shifts in the economic, cultural, and social structures. This issue was raised by nineteenth-century reformers inside the recently established 'colonial legal order', which was intended to culminate in modernization and the authority of the state. It was a hurdle to 'Brahminical patriarchy', that mostly placed a significant importance on the child brides' chastity.[43] The claim was to establish a statutory age of ten years below which intercourse, both in prostitution and marriage, was prohibited. This was objected by revivalists who questioned the colonial state's authority to intervene in local customs, norms, and religious convictions. The age of consent, however, was set at ten in the Indian Penal Code of 1860. After that, the subsequent death of a child bride, Phulmonee, as a result of brutal sexual intercourse by her husband, the age was raised to twelve in 1891 after a much publicized debate. Because the girl was over the age of consent at that time, the British courts ruled that 'her death could not be considered murder because the husband had a legal right to have sex with her.'[44] In the course of the first half of the twentieth century, when women's organizations arrived in the political ground, the emphasis moved to women's health, protection from early pregnancies and concern over women's education. The age for marriage of girls was raised from twelve to fourteen under the Child Marriage Restraint Act of 1929 (henceforth referred to as CMRA), when physically the body of the female would be more receptive to sexual intercourse and pregnancy. In 1949, 'the age of consent under the rape law was raised to fifteen years'.[45] However, the law did not make underage marriages illegal. It was partly related to the ideals of Hindu marriages seeming to be 'sacramental' and the serious social consequences of this kind of step might have on the children born of these marriages. In this framework, the CMRA was viewed further as 'rhetoric or an aspiration than a moral code or a legal mandate'. The socially authorized civic traditions and practices won out over the judicial and legitimate command.[46] Pratiksha Baxi (2009) in her *Habeas Corpus Juridical Narratives of Sexual Governance* has stated that 'The law on statutory rape of married female minors by their husbands is anchored in the colonial legal history of the prevention of child marriage and continues to be viewed as a deterrent to child marriage rather than as entailing the protection of married minors from sexual abuse in marriage.'[47] So, in spite of the protracted and extremely noticeable campaign prior to its passage, the Act was to some extent a debacle, with researchers in the late 1960s mentioning that there had barely been a hundred prosecutions under it in forty years, while millions of child marriages took place in the country. Numerous social aspects such as, urbanization improved chances for education of girls, a relaxation of the grip of conservative religious leaderships over communities, and westernization among the urban middle class have accorded to a steady rise in the average age of marriage. According to the suggestions of the *Committee on the Status of Women*, 'the minimum age for marriage was raised to eighteen for girls and twenty-one for boys' in the 1970s[48] and the law itself was changed to the Prohibition of Child Marriage Act in 2006 (henceforth referred to as PCMA) but the age limits remained the same. The steady rise in the age of consent for sexual intercourse and for marriage may be traced from Table I.1.

TABLE I.1: AGE OF CONSENT AND MINIMUM AGE OF MARRIAGE FOR GIRLS

Year	*Age of Consent under Section 375 (5) IPC*	*Age mentioned in the Marital Rape – Exception to Section 375, IPC*	*Minimum Age of Marriage under the Child Marriage Restraint Act (CMRA), 1929*
1860	10 years	10 years	
1891 (amendment of IPC)	12 years	12 years	
1925 (after the amendment of IPC)	14 years	13 years	
1929 (after the passing of the CMRA)	14 years	13 years	14 years
1949 (after the amendment of the Penal Code and the CMRA)	16 years	15 years	15 years
1978	16 years	15 years	18 years

Source: Flavia Agnes, *Family Law – Volume 2: Marriage, Divorce, and Matrimonial Litigation*, New Delhi: Oxford University Press 2011, p. 68.

With the establishment of a task force by the present Union Government of India, the issue of age at marriage for girls and women has resurfaced as a source of national apprehension. Since over fourteen decades, the age at marriage seems to have been a source of contention in India. In 2020, the government's proposal is to raise the marriage age for women entering marriage to twenty-one years.[49] The foremost justifications in giving approval of delaying the age of marriage for girls further than the present eighteen years are related to gender equality as well as health issue and demographic advantages. Gender equality can be addressed by lowering the age of marriage for boys, but this does not seem to be an advanced procedure. The advantage regarding health is supposed to accumulate because for girls teenage pregnancies are more dangerous than those over the age of twenty, but the risks are higher at fifteen or sixteen. The much more persuasive argument seems to be the demographic advantage derived from the adage that delaying marriage leads to delaying age of childbirth and the reducing number of pregnancies. This saying may have been right at one moment in time but it does not seem to express comprehensive sense in modern-day India. The fertility rates have hitherto deteriorated significantly and, in the states that are more progressive, they are now under the replacement level. During the 2015-16 National Family Health Survey (henceforth referred to as NFHS), about a quarter of all married women in the age-group of 20-24 years had been married before eighteen years of age. This was a significant development over the previous ten years, when approximately half of all married women in the same age group were married before the age of eighteen during the earlier session of the NFHS. Obviously, the age of girls at marriage is increasing steadily, and in most of the marriages throughout the country nowadays, the bride is over the age of eighteen. By the age of twenty-one, the large proportion of Indian women have not only had sex, but several have also had their first child. Now the question is, what advantages would be gained by legally delaying the marriage age of women? As a result, it could be said that the debate over the age of marriage for girls in colonial India has recently emerged with the idea of enacting a new law. And in this context, I have tried to probe the detailed history of 'age of marriage' of girls, especially focusing on the law reforms related to this issue in India. I found it moderately alarming and slightly discomfiting to delve into familiar histories with a different lens. Outlining concepts of 'marriage' and 'childhood' in further, less accustomed spaces has brought its own charms. The politics of feminism in relation to children and childhood has been developing on intricate (and sometimes on contradictory) ground. In recent years, it has perceived a polished interest. Twenty-first century observes huge efforts to remove 'child marriage'. India has noticeably a high number of women who have married before they turned eighteen.

Over the last century and a half, consecutive women's movements have started to turn to the law to secure their political aims. Social reformers, women's rights and feminist activists have effectively advocated for legal modifications in both the public and private spheres of lives and experiences of women, with the expectation that the law would therefore modify these facts. Despite this intense involvement, little appears to have changed in the lives of women on a daily basis. Is this due to the fact that the law is fundamentally conservative and traditional by nature and is intended to counter the liberal and radical ideologies of feminist thinkers? Is it because law is one of many narratives that work to maintain and normalize imbalanced power relations? Is the rule of law becoming too essential in our struggles for social and political change? These are just a few of the probing questions that this study has attempted to explore. I offer no easy solutions, but instead examine the contours of law in feminist struggles for social change. I hope to enhance feminist engagement with law by exposing the law's complex and contradictory nature. In my research, I have attempted to find a feminist theoretical framework. In India, feminist legal studies are evolving as an innovative and clearly significant area of study, analysis, and practice. It is a field of study that is yielding important new insights into how law performs in the context of women's lives.[50]

I have investigated how the law has been implicated in women's subordination. Many studies have been conducted to review the laws affecting women's status and to highlight those laws that continue to discriminate against women. I have aimed to explore the ideological expectations that underpin women's legal regulation, as well as the traditions in which law subjugates women – the multifaceted and elusive ways wherein law validates profoundly gender-based suppositions, relationships, and characters. Women have been constructed as gendered subjects in legal discourse – as 'wives and mothers', as 'passive and vulnerable', as 'subservient and in need of security'. It is a rhetoric that has made a significant contribution to the lesser position of women through its very development of women's roles and recognition. Simultaneously, law has been used as a site where these roles and identities have been contested. According to Ratna Kapur and Brenda Cossman (1996), 'it is a site where social reformers and feminist activists have sought to displace previously dominant understandings of women's appropriate roles and identities and sought to reconstruct women's roles and identities as more full and equal citizens'.[51] 'In place of an instrumentalist vision of law', as Kapur and Cossman (1996) argued 'that law needs to be re-conceptualized as a site of discursive struggle, where competing visions of the world and of women's place therein, have been and continue to be fought out. We believe that such a re-conceptualization of law can better capture both the possibilities and limitations of law, and law's contradictory nature in women's struggles for social change'.[52] Drawing on the insights of feminist legal studies, they also asserted that 'feminist engagement with law should be understood as a discursive struggle, where feminists seek to displace previously dominant understandings of women's roles and identities'.[53]

Within this framework, I set out my understanding of the role of law in feminist struggles for social change. Therefore, I have started by reviewing some of the different approaches to law that have been developed in the literature on women and law in India. During the colonial period, there was an intense public debate regarding child marriage. We find its appearance in novels and short stories in nearly every Indian language. Essays, pamphlets, satires, and writings of every genre were also available in Bengali. As a result, historians have paid close attention to these issues.[54] An assessment of the previous literature on this theme is therefore reasonably fundamental to understand the lacunae of earlier researches. Before reviewing the previous works, I would like to mention Ratna Kapur and Brenda Cossman's argument (1996) that 'there is no reason to think that either socialist feminism or poststructuralist feminism has provided all the answers to feminist inquiries into law'.[55] Despite these constraints in feminist legal erudition, theoretical discussions arising from the particular encounters of women engaging with the law may still have reverberations in India. The types of questions about the role of law that feminist theorists have begun to ask both inside and outside of India are remarkably similar, despite the fact that the specific perceptions of subjugation through and engagement with law may be worlds apart. A few fascinating and enlightening projects and research that have been published in the past from different fields apart from law. Scholars and historians of feminist history have taken the lead in developing a more nuanced understanding of the role of law in social reform and change. Tanika Sarkar (1993),[56] Lata Mani (1989),[57] Janaki Nair (1996)[58] and Prem Chowdhry (1993, 1994)[59] are among the feminist historians who have critically examined 'the complex relationship between law in colonial India and women's subordination'.[60] Feminist lawful scholarships, alongside feminist historians, have started to evolve within the social sciences and humanities much more broadly. In their pioneering expansive investigation of the Shah Bano case (1985), Zakia Pathak and Rajeswari Sunder Rajan (1989)[61] have studied legislation 'as discourse and the way in which this discourse constitutes subjects'.[62] More recently, economist Bina Agarwal's (1994)[63] research on women and land rights in South Asia has discovered 'the complex obstacles to women's land ownership and control, and provided an insightful analysis of both the importance and limitations of law, and land rights in particular, for women'.[64]

Recently, legal scholarship has initiated to advance these feminist standpoints. Do suggested reform efforts truly result in greater autonomy for women, or are women's issues simply the terrain on which political supremacy is tried to negotiate? Is the state's public patriarchy enhanced by laws that appear to limit domestic patriarchy? When laws resolve the needs of women, are women portrayed as a homogeneous faction with comparable aspirations? Which women are likely to suffer as a result of this homogenization? These issues have been investigated in relation to developed and developing countries, as well as colonial and post-colonial mechanisms. In a number of recent volumes, these matters have struck a chord with Indian scholars, such as Indu Prakash Singh's *Women, Law and Social*

Change in India (1989),[65] Vimal Balasubrahmanyan's *In Search of Justice: Women, Law, Landmark Judgements and Media* (1990),[66] Archana Parashar's *Women and Family Law Reform in India: Uniform Civil Code and Gender Equality* (1992),[67] Ratna Kapur and Brenda Cossman's *Subversive Sites: Feminist Engagements with Law in India* (1996a)[68] and Ratna Kapur's *Feminists Terrains in Legal Domains: Interdisciplinary Essays on Women and Law in India* (1996b).[69] These books have traced the evolution of legislation and questioned the efficacy of legal solutions. They have, however, largely focused on family law issues, which explicitly highlight gender issues.[70]

In her study of family law reform, Archana Parashar (1992) examined and analysed some of the perspectives of debates within feminist legal studies.[71] She has used the visions of these arguments to develop her compassion and concern regarding the responsibilities of law in social and cultural reform, although refusing certain facets of the arguments that do not appropriate the Indian framework. In order to improve her assessment of the influence of law and regulation in promoting gender equality, Parashar restructured 'the theoretical insights of feminist legal studies to better fit the specificity of the legal regulation of women in India'. While Parashar asserted for the significance of legislative changes in the struggling life of women, her understanding of the character of the role of law reform is notified by an evaluation of the confines of the law. She contends, for instance, that 'instead of dismissing law reform as a means of achieving equality for women, it is more productive to realize the limitations of law and have appropriate expectations that law reform by itself will be insufficient to change society and end women's oppression'.[72] Law, in her opinion, can have significant symbolic importance, 'Symbolic legislation can be of liberating value as it can provide a focus around which forces of change can mobilize.'[73] In this regard, Parashar's work represents a significant shift in feminist legal analysis, combining intensive and comprehensive legal analysis with a feminist perspective that considers both the constraints and potentialities of law.[74]

Possibly the most outstanding contribution of Janaki Nair's book, *Women and Law in Colonial India: A Social History*, is that she has contrasted family law alongside labour law on plantations and mines, questions of political representation of women, prostitution and traffic in women, transformation of female sexuality within or outside the family and is thereby able to show continuities in cultural constructions of gender and class in these different arenas. Nair has contended that the 'status of women is produced in and through structures of caste, class and community, and any solution must engage with this matrix of structures'.[75] Instead of recognizing colonialism as a unified problem or 'indigenous traditions' as serious hindrances, she traces the intersecting and intertwining layers of diverse patriarchal discourses and their associations with other systems of stratification such as caste, class and religion. The British reform agenda was portrayed as favourable to women, as a 'civilizing mission' that would liberate Indian women from inhumane practices. This justification provided the colonizers with a moral advantage over the male Indian elite, as well as an authority of racial superiority that could be used to establish political dominance. Despite this, British conceptions of women's equality were far from irrefutable fact; not only did stratified gender relations prevail in Victorian England, but Indian women were never regarded as equal to British women.[76] In the second chapter of her book, Nair briefly described some of the nineteenth-century controversies focused on colonial and early nationalist campaigns to prohibit certain practices, such as widow immolation (*sati*), female infanticide, and to reform other customs and norms, in particular, those related to widow and child marriage.[77]

Other scholars have begun to exacerbate feminist involvement with law in the same way.[78] Sudhir Chandra, in most of his works (1992, 1996, 1998)[79] managed to capture a social drama, which revolved around an exclusive incident in colonial India when a 22-year-old woman, Rukhmabai, disobeyed custom and the colonial legal commands by declining to be confined to a wedding ceremony, undertaken when she was hardly eleven years old.[80] Chandra's book *Enslaved Daughters: Colonialism, Law and Women's Rights* is a detailed examination of the Rukhmabai case, which framed a revolutionary challenge to orthodox Hindu and colonial views on women's rights and women's question.[81] She challenged 'what was expected to be natural, offering a subversive model of women asserting their urge as individuals in a realm governed by the family, community, and men'.[82] The text explored the implementation of Anglo-Indian law, though its contentions for the significant changes dominating the definition of women's issues in colonial courts were limited by the focus on a single case.[83] The Rukhmabai case was inextricably linked to the age of consent debates, because the issue of restitution of conjugal rights was intimately connected to the consummation of marriage. Rukhmabai's defiance, combined with the increasing boldness of Maharashtrian women, resulted in a clash of fears and hopes of 'contending conceptions of the desired social order'.[84]

In her work (2001),[85] Monmayee Basu has outlined the social and legislative history of the period spanning between two significant themes – the 'Hindu Widows' Remarriage Act of 1856' and the 'Hindu Succession Act of 1956'. Within these set of constraints, she has attempted 'to examine social realities and the impact of legislative reforms upon a particular section of women, namely the Hindu women of Bengal.'[86] The complications of child marriage and legislative efforts to end it are also briefly discussed. Her discussion essentially includes an introduction of the organizational background of legal reform. She emphasizes the role of Parliament and law reform directives in bringing about change by drawing an impact on public opinion. The discussions of controversies and parliamentary procedures that result in particular alterations provide a solid foundation for future critical assessments of how preferences are formulated and reflected through democratic institutions in colonial and post-colonial circumstances.[87]

Flavia Agnes' (1992) work has made a significant contribution to the advancement of more complicated and varied evaluations of feminist legal engagement. All across her writing, Agnes questions 'the implications of legal reforms on women and whether laws designed to advantage women have lived up to their promise'.[88] Through a comprehensive inspection of laws attempting to address 'rape, dowry, domestic violence, prostitution, indecent representation of women, *sati*, and sex determination tests', Agnes investigates the larger issues as to why the legislation has had such slight implications on the lives of the women or whether the social changes could even be achieved through law reforms. In her examination of laws regarding rape, for example, Agnes discloses the absolute disaster of the reform movement in the initial days of 1980s to effect a modification in the classification of rape.[89] Agnes' work (1992) on law has driven 'feminist analyses well beyond the either dichotomy of law as a mere instrument of social change, or an instrument of patriarchy'.[90] Her works (1990, 1994)[91] aim to evaluate some of the paradoxes in the role of law while also making constructive ideas for how law could be changed to better women empowerment.[92] Flavia Agnes' another major work (1999)[93] raises significant but relevant questions in the context of contemporary India's increasing expectation for a Uniform Civil Code (henceforth referred to as UCC.). Her insightful examination of the legal discourse on women in all significant religious sects illustrates the politics of law and the politicization of gendered roles developed from a communal viewpoint.[94] Her work judgementally estimates that 'Within a complex social, political and economic structure, the demand of gender equality cannot be confined within a linear mould of granting uniform rights to women of all communities. An all-encompassing UCC cannot be viewed as a magic wand, which will eliminate the woes and sufferings of Indian women in general and minority women in particular.'[95] In *Family Law Volume 1: Family Laws and Constitutional Claims* (2011), Agnes traces 'the legal history of diverse personal laws in colonial and post-colonial periods and women's claims within them as well as women's rights located within the Constitution of India'.[96] And in *Family Law Volume 2: Marriage, Divorce and Matrimonial Litigation* (2011)[97] she foregrounds three unique concerns – 'women's rights within the law of marriage and divorce', 'matrimonial rights and obligations', and 'the procedural aspect of the functioning of Family Courts in India'. Her book mirrors on the process around the legitimacy of marriage and actions for dissolving it; especially the chapter, titled 'Marriage and its Dissolution', addresses numerous complications that have constantly beleaguered society, such as, 'child marriage, registration of marriages and traditional notions of heterosexual marriages'.[98]

The historiography surrounding the Age of Consent debate is remarkable. Over the last fifty years, a vast body of scholarly literature on this topic has become available. In the 1960s, American cultural historians were enthusiastic to emphasize the significance of social legislation for the advent of nationalism in modern India.[99] Charles H. Heimsath (1962)[100] asserted that the material significance of the 'Bill' was in the footings of the nationalist movement and the widespread sustenance gained for 'Hindu' belief and orthodoxy; these components are being re-examined and re-established in considerable detail by the recent scholarly works which utilize post-colonial and post-structuralist theories.[101] Partha Chatterjee (1989, 1993),[102] on the other hand, perceives in the conservative reaction to the Age of Consent controversy and the exclusion of the 'women's question' from the outline of Indian nationalism after this, the 'coming of age' of the nationalist discourse. The discourse had effectively defined the interior frontier of the nation and positioned the home and the woman within it. While the discourse was prepared to admit the dominance of the colonial state in the 'outer', 'material sphere',[103] it was no longer ready to accept the colonial state's power to legislate on the 'inner cultural sphere'. The resolution of the 'women's question', therefore, was a daring assertion of the development of nationalism.[104] The writings and research work, utmost relevant to this discourse, however, are those which emerged from the 'second wave of feminism' in the 1970s. Therefore, it resulted in an innovative alteration in numerous fields of study, highlighting the 'exclusion of gender' as a classification in earlier works and demonstrating a commitment to rectify this through a fresh conduct of old questions.[105] Meredith Borthwick argued that 'the Age of Consent Bill provided a case-study in which Bengali women came to public prominence as symbolic objects rather than as a group speaking on their own behalf'.[106]

We have innovatory interventions on the age of consent controversy by Tanika Sarkar.[107] She surveys the explanatory frames[108] that define the limitations of public participation; the importance of gender in her approach is not restricted to an exclusively discourse or metaphoric ground for the upsurge of 'cultural nationalism', but is also focused on the subjectivity of 'women's bodies and agencies'. At the same time, the domestic realm and women in it, as the one remaining zone of self-government left to the colonized Indian male, became a foremost territory of contest. The body of Hindu woman itself became a site of the clash for emancipation against a foreign system of authority and wisdom.[109] Thus, for instance, Sarkar introduces fascinating interpretations of depictions of the physical pain and devastation of the bodies of women in discussions on acquainted controversies such as *sati* and child marriage.[110] For the better part of the nineteenth century, the Bengali middle class was preoccupied with the Hindu woman as well as her body, and its future as a wife and bearer of offspring, and later as a widow. The intense concern for the purity and chastity of the Hindu woman's body was also the impetus for a slew of significant laws – Sati Regulation XVII of 1829, Hindu Widows' Remarriage Act of 1856 and the Age of Consent Act of 1891. Tanika Sarkar[111] is specifically concerned for the Age of Consent Act and addresses different matters and debates rising around it at some length in some of her works.[112] In her recent work (2020), she claims that there were heated public debates, particularly in the Bengal and Bombay Presidencies, which remarkably shaped the Age of Consent Act and 'legal reform in the field of gender grew more out such debates than from colonial initiatives'.[113] Subsequent research, which are worthwhile modifications to modern Indian social history, assessed 'how the classification of woman was exploited as a symbol in the cultural contest for legitimacy between the colonizer and the colonized'.[114] Dagmar Engels (1985) made reference to the hostility between two gender systems in which the male control of female sexuality in Bengal was endangered by 'the dominant ideology of Victorian sexual values'.[115] Mrinalini Sinha (1989, 1995)[116] examines the controversy over the Age of Consent Act of 1891, which aimed at protecting young girls in India from the premature consummation of child marriage. By making noticeable the politics of colonial masculinity in the controversy over the Indian consent debate, she tried to show the role of the Indian opposition to the Bill in revitalizing nationalist politics.[117] She has argued that the assessment of Bengali masculinity was a vital component in the justification of empire.[118]

While Tanika Sarkar has principally focused on Bengal and the Phulmonee-Hari Maiti case regarding the age of consent issue, Meera Kosambi[119] identified the debates, which revolved around the Rukhmabai case in Maharashtra. Padma Anagol[120] looked at the same theme from the gendered perspective in the Bombay Presidency, giving special emphasis on the role of Maharashtrian women. Antoinette Burton's article (1998) also focussed attention on Rukhmabai case, especially on her journey from a child bride to a Hindu lady.[121] However, the noticeable irony about these examinations originating from gender studies is the limited consideration paid to women's observations and contribution.[122] In this context, we may mention the works of Leela Gulati (1976),[123] Geraldine Forbes (1979)[124] and Barbara Ramusack (1981)[125] who have provided an outline on age of marriage issue in India and also have explored women's participation for passing the Sarda Act.[126] Geraldine Forbes (1999) has argued that CMRA would not have been achievable without the assistance of All India Women's Conference (AIWC). It was the only time during the interwar period when women from across communities came together on women's issue.[127]

Another range of questions concerns with the construction of 'childhood' in contemporary India. Following the pioneering work of Philippe Aries (1960), some attempts have been made to understand this process in nineteenth-century India.[128] Ruby Lal (2013) attempted to reclaim girls' limited agency within patriarchal restrictions of seclusion and domesticity.[129] Ashwini Tambe (2019) has explored the definition of girls in terms of sexual preferences. Both of these works deal with the issue of agency in different ways.[130] Tambe in her articles (2009, 2013) reviews the raising of the age of consent for non-marital sexual relations in early twentieth-century India and explores the forces that led to the increase in the legal age of marriage in India in 1978.[131] Recent research also suggests that it is critical to investigate the intersection of marriage and sex work issues. Ashwini Tambe (2009) raises the relatively ignored issue of the age of consent for non-marital sex in India, 'which was higher than that for marriage, reaching the age of sixteen with the CMRA of 1929'.[132] Mrinalini Sinha shows in her works (1999, 2006)[133] that in the late 1920s, Indian feminists endorsed a new universal language of rights in order to build a cooperative political and legal subjectivity as women, arguing that they should be provided with legislative protections by the state rather than being subject to the regulations of caste and religious communities. The organized Indian women's movement exhibited their collective agency and used a political approach to enhance the social status of women in India by opposing Mayo's allegations and supporting the Sarda Act, thereby dissolving the segregation between the political and the social that had existed for a long time between nationalist and colonial patriarchies.[134] Sumita Mukherjee in her article (2006) has studied the Sarda Act by analysing 'how Indian reformers were ready to disobey hostility and utilize the new governing structures bestowed upon them to introduce legislation on a subject of national apprehension.'[135] Shahida Lateef (1990)[136] and Azra Asghar Ali (2000)[137] in their works, have dealt with the perspective of Muslim community towards the Sarda Act concisely. Besides these, Judy Whitehead (1995),[138] Andrea Major (2012),[139] Bhaswati Chatterjee (2016, 2021)[140] wrote on the passing of Sarda Act from different perspectives but historiographical analysis was missing in their writings.

Among the very few full-length studies of child marriage, Jaya Sagade's book (2005) examines the issue from the standpoint of human rights and also addresses with the social, religious, cultural and legal complications in forbidding the detrimental custom of child marriage in India.[141] She investigates the various laws prohibiting child marriage and the state's failure to enforce them. She also traces the conflicts between personal laws that resulted in a new law, the PCMA of 2006.[142] The age of consent was more about age and less about consent according to Radhika Singha (1998),[143] Himani Bannerji (2001),[144] Subhasri Ghosh (2014),[145] and Ishita Pande (2012, 2013, 2020).[146] Despite the compromises imposed on the colonial state, the Act was successful in focusing on age. This allowed the digital age to become a legal fact. Pande (2020) contends that the colonial state used the category of age to create the juridical subject of the child.[147] She goes on to argue that age became an epistemic contract, allowing a merge of a juridical category with the human by technologies of the body and the insertion of age and numbers into the governmental domain and the corresponding centering of the child as a seemingly transparent object of protection, constituted the newness of the Act of 1929.[148] Nevertheless, British Indian government made no attempt to confirm the execution of the registration of births, deaths and marriages. While age became extremely relevant in law, there was no simultaneous campaign to permit confirmation of age, an inconsistency that continues to plague the implementation of multiple laws even today.[149] Pande (2020) investigates how the digital age came to be associated with a judicial childhood, as well as its connection with the age of consent and child marriage. The child was created in colonial India through the merging of education, labour, and marriage. Despite the new work on a diversity of topics, there has been inadequate interest paid to this three-sided connection, which can assist us to comprehend 'the convergence of the problem of the child and the problem of marriage into a single social issue'.[150]

Two recent works demand important additions to this discussion. Samita Sen and Anindita Ghosh in their recent edited book (2021),[151] have tried to investigate the history of child marriage in India. The investigation is on the history of legislation with a focus on the Sarda Act, Prohibition of Child Marriage Act as well as the problems of child marriage in West Bengal. Biswajit Ghosh (2010, 2011)[152] has studied the relationship between the society, law and child marriage in rural West Bengal. Child marriage has been prioritized in agendas attempting to address 'harmful practises', as characterized by the United Nations Sustainable Development Goals. India dominates the world in the number of women marrying before the age of eighteen, making it of particular interest to international and national forums. Rejecting oversimplified tags like 'harmful practice', Mary E. John's work (2021)[153] delves into the multidimensional history of child marriage as a social and feminist issue in India covering diverse domains. It conducts a critical review of a wide range historical, demographic and legal scholarship on this theme. Principal ideas pertinent to child marriage – such as 'childhood', 'adolescence', the 'girl and marriage' – are examined in a comparative background that reveals the unnoticed presence of the practice in the USA and China. This book calls into question existing methods, examines the most recent data sources, and proposes a new concept of 'compulsory marriage'. It is an absolute study of child marriage in India in a changing global context.[154] But these above-mentioned works are based on mostly contemporary surveys. Appropriate historical study claims more than that.

At the end of the review of the above discussion and historiography, it can be said that although various studies have already been done on various issues related to social reform movements in India such as *sati*, widow remarriage, child marriage issue and the legal reforms related to these, each and every work focuses on a specific social-reform issue and region. So, an overall analysis has become particularly important in this regard. The detailed and thorough study on the evolution of the history of the age of marriage in India was lacking, which my research has modestly attempted. *State, Law, and Gender:*

Debating the Age of Marriage in India, 1872-1978 would give a wide-ranging historical and historiographical idea on this issue from an analytical and different standpoint, which is relevant in the context of raising the age of marriage for girls in India in recent times. It has been more or less confirmed by the previous historiography that child marriage in India is controlled by age-old socio-cultural and religious practices. In my research, I am not dealing with the problem of child marriage in India in detail rather I have emphasized on how the Indian legal system has dealt with the problem of child marriage. I start the argument with the historical advances that occurred before the implementation of the CMRA of 1929, which was enacted to control child marriages. Attempts to prevent child marriages commenced in 1880 with a modification in the Age of Consent for the crime of rape. According to Jaya Sagade (2005), 'Instead of laying down the minimum age of marriage, social reformers of that time thought of pushing those men who had sexual intercourse with their wives below a particular age. The change was intended to give protection to young girls from sexual abuse within the institution of marriage.'[155] An apprehension for the status of women in law has a long tradition and is not a recent phenomenon. The foundations of a collective attempt to legally remedy some of the most outrageous forms of discriminatory practices against women were laid during the period of colonial rule, when the modern legal system was being formulated. This period was distinguished by the continuous efforts of both colonial administrators and Indian nationalists to implement reforms aimed at improving the status of women in India.[156] In this study, I have examined the intense debate regarding the age of marriage for girls in India in which a transformation through legislations actually took place in that period. It is true that a large number of books and articles have already been written on movements for the rights of women, and any fresh attempt to write on such a topic, even for a select period, must involve some risk of repetition. Yet, much has been left out by previous writers and fresh research on the subject invariably brings to light new facts hitherto unknown. Most studies so far have been of a general character. I propose to deal exclusively with a particular section of women, namely, women belonging to the Hindu community. Moreover, among the unending problems of Hindu women, only those relating to their marriage are selected for study. I also propose to deal with the legal aspects of their marital problems. The remedial legislative measures, how these ultimately came up through long-drawn and tardy legislative procedures as well as the extent of their success will also be discussed at length. This, I hope, would contribute a new perspective to the subject. In short, *State, Law, and Gender: Debating the Age of Marriage in India, 1872-1978* attempts to examine the following interrogations – marital problems of Hindu women; how these were viewed by Hindu society in several phases of its development and what efforts were made by Indian reformers to advance the status of married Hindu women; whether the ventures made by Hindu society and its reformers succeeded in unfolding the marital problems of Hindu women; some attempts were made by the legislature to solve these problems and how far they succeeded in accomplishing their resolution.

I have elaborated my findings in the following chapters. After situating the study in this introductory chapter, my first chapter, titled, 'Hindu Women, Social Reform and Marriage in Nineteenth and Early Twentieth Century India' would give an overview regarding 'women's question' which became the centre of discussion during the mid-nineteenth century and would also bestow to the study of the condition of Hindu women in that period, which will serve as a background. It is necessary to discuss this separately to understand the history of the 'age of marriage' of girls in Indian context. Attention is centred on women's education and on their marriage practices – which were altered largely through new laws, in particular those that banned widow burning, allowed widow remarriage, and restricted child marriage. We do not survey the wider sphere of gender issues that consecrated immolation or prohibited widow remarriage when we study changes in widow immolation or widow remarriage practices, so I have made an effort to explain this along with the historiographical discussion on these social reform issues in India. I have described and analysed the practice of *sati* on the eve of its legal ban in 1829. This is followed by the argument on the thorny issue of child marriage and widow re-marriage, possibly the central theme in the history of reform through much of the nineteenth century. On the basis of contemporary literature and other writings, the true condition of the married and widowed women of the time has been depicted. Girls were married off at a very early age and were sent to their husband's homes as soon as they attained the age of puberty. And that time most of the families were joint family. I have also tried to address this factor. With no prospect of education or freedom, confined within the four walls of their homes, they were plunged into a hackneyed and tedious life of ceaseless domestic duties and of producing and rearing children. The plight of the widows was far worse. The condition prevailing in Bengal was, to a large extent, representative of the situation then existing in other parts of India. In every area of India, marriage and family history is not a modest account of historical advancement. The marriages among the Bengalis were a battleground for both liberal and narrow-minded conceptions of selfhood and family. As the extended joint family became a venerated, earliest social institution and arranged marriage became a signifier of culture and tradition of Indian society, new challenges arose to develop ideals of companionship, rights, and interests inside the framework of these constructions. Thus, through this chapter I have tried to give an account of the socio-legal reform movements in India, with special reference to *sati*, widow remarriage and child marriage; and also give an overview of the relationship between family, marriage and Hindu society in the nineteenth-century India.

The second chapter titled, 'Marriage and the Law: Brahmos and The Act III of 1872', and the third chapter, titled, 'Debates in History, Debates on History: The Age of Consent Act of 1891 and the Issue of Child Marriage in India' make an attempt to deal with two critical moments in marriage-related legislation in India. The second chapter is about Act III of 1872, the first civil marriage act, propagated in India. This was the consequence of the fight executed by a little nonetheless significant Bengali group or community ('the *Brahmos*'), that even without performing the sacramental rituals of Hindu marriages, their marriages had been sanctioned by the state. Nevertheless, few years after the passing of the law, in 1878, Keshub Chandra Sen, one of the significant contributors in the passage of this act, violated the majority of its provisions when he organized his younger daughter's marriage to a Hindu descendant of a princely state.[157] The exceptional popular uproar that accompanied this happening emphasized the connection between ceremonial representation and legitimacy in Indian marriage ceremonies. Rather than secularization of the law, most reformers urged that the law should be encompassed by ritual practices, which were inextricably linked to kinship, community, and religious and cultural identity. I have thrown some light on the background of the passing of the act and its implications on Indian society in a nutshell.

The third chapter revolves around the Age of Consent Act of 1891. In January 1891, the Law Member of India introduced a bill in the Legislative Council raising the age of consent for sexual intercourse with married and unmarried Indian girls from ten to twelve years. The bill was introduced in response to the death of a child-wife, Phulmonee, who died after her husband subjected her to violent sexual intercourse. The bill also proposed labelling sexual contact with girls under the age of ten as rape, punishable by ten years in prison. With Viceroy Lansdowne's final approval, the bill became an act on 19 March 1891. The Indian Penal Code and the Code of Criminal Procedure were amended to raise the age of sexual intercourse with girls from ten to twelve and to make its violation punishable by ten years' imprisonment or transportation for life. This act, according to an activist and historian of nineteenth-century India, 'was the last act as a measure of reform effected by influencing British public opinion and the first act where politics and reaction were successfully linked in India'.[158] The Age of Consent Bill and the Act sparked an enormous outrage and produced drastic opposition. Bengal, where the issue of premature consummation of child-marriage was deemed serious, acquired the lead in opposing the act. The fervent rejection of Bengali men persuaded the Viceroy, with the Lieutenant Governor of Bengal's prompting, to reach a compromise. Under the act, it became nearly impossible to bring cases of premature consummation of child marriages to trial.[159] The debates surrounding the Age of Consent gave women the chance to bring their apprehensions over domestic lives into the public domain and to express tensions produced by their newly acquired expectations for education, individuality, and a desire for a transition in conjugal relations and the unchangeable equilibrium of authority within household, family, and society. Behramji Malabari, a Parsi reformer from Bombay, published his *Notes on Infant Marriage and Enforced Widowhood* (1884), a few years before the Age of Consent

Bill was proposed, and requested the government to reform Indian domestic practices. Following the Revolt, colonial power supposedly regressed to non-interference in social and religious affairs, and Indian social reformers became ambivalent about the state's legal interference in the inner domain of the domestic life. And when reformers like M. G. Ranade did call for restricted interference, it was only to prevent the reproduction of a feeble race that would lead to India's economic ruin. Journals run by Maharashtrian women furiously mentioned Indian males' insensitivity to the plight of the female sex.[160] Rukhmabai, who became famous for a 'social drama' that developed from a case filed in 1884 in the High Court of Bombay for the restitution of conjugal rights by her husband Dadaji Bhikaji,[161] created a gendered appraisal of child marriage in a series of letters in *The Times of India* published under the pseudonym of *The Hindu Lady*. Women of Hindu, Muslim, Christian, and Jewish faiths rallied in support of the obstinate Rukhmabai, who had married at the age of eleven and had consistently denied to live with her husband upon reaching puberty, and had rejected to do so even after the court ruled that she would be imprisoned if she did not return to her husband. Rukhmabai insisted that she was not obligated to return to that man because she was married at an age when she was incapable of giving intelligent consent. While women blamed child marriage and arranged marriage for Indian wives' displeasure, male discourse avoided admitting the presence of uneasiness in child marriages. Indeed, for Tilak and huge sectors of orthodox men, Rukhmabai's defiance confirmed the negative consequences of English education,[162] which needed to be countered by convincing women to follow time-honoured tradition. Male insecurity was caused not by the colonial state's entrance into the private domain, but by women's increasing reliance on colonial structures, particularly the law, to restructure conjugal relations.[163]

Thus, I have explored the key facets of this complex controversy regarding the age of consent, especially focusing on the two cases – Dadaji Bhikaji *vs.* Rukhmabai case (1884-8) and Phulmonee-Hari Maiti case (1890) by analysing the proceedings of the council of the Governor-General of India and contemporary periodicals and newspapers. I have further assessed its implications for and effect on contemporary society by the portrayal of the socio-legal context. At the same time, I have also tried to explain the role that women had played in this debate. The growth of events from the early impetus in the mid-1880s to the final climax in 1891 has been demonstrated and the nature of the contention and the crucial subjects involved have also been defined and eventually, with a brief glance I have highlighted the political outcomes of the controversy. Therefore, in this chapter I argue that the collective endeavours of the colonial Government and challenges of the learned sections of the native society to fix the age of consent were essentially connected to the broader question of the history of raising the age of marriage for girls in India.

The problems of child marriage and efforts made for its eradication through legislation are dealt with primarily in the fourth chapter, entitled, 'The State, Age of Marriage and the Question of Social Legislation: The Sarda Act of 1929'. This chapter focuses on the legal discourse on the age of marriage in India. In the first part, I have discussed about the tragic situation that the girls had to face as a result of child marriage. Apart from this, I have highlighted how the Indian legal framework has dealt with the question of child marriage and the historical background that led to the implementation of the CMRA of 1929 by analysing the Census Report of India, Legislative Assembly debates and so on. The controversy over raising the age of consent culminated in the formation of two committees – the Select Committee and the Age of Consent Committee – to examine the issue of child marriage. I have critically analysed the Age of Consent Committee Evidences as well as the Report of the Age of Consent Committee from the feminist perspective, which may give another new dimension to this research. What was the perception and reaction of both the communities – Hindu and Muslim, towards the passage of this legislation, has also been highlighted in this chapter. It has been argued that the social reality of not giving room to or excluding women's experiences is also reflected when the law is formulated, applied, or enforced. In her article, *'What's Distinctive About Feminist Analysis of Law? A Conceptual Analysis of Women's Exclusion from Law'*, Denise Reaume's theoretical analysis of women's elimination from law is of excessive worth in understanding this state of affairs.[164] This feminist critique of law can be claimed at all levels of legal investigation of child marriage – 'legislative framework', 'judicial interpretation' and 'enforcement of rules regarding child marriages'.[165] Women's involvements, experiences and perceptions have not been taken into consideration solemnly by Indian society.[166] The exaggeration encompassing the Sarda Act signalled the manifestation of a different ideological fascination allowed specifically by the establishment of women's collective agency.[167] In this context, I have discussed the role of women and women's organization, especially the initiatives taken by All India Women's Conference (AIWC) and Women's Indian Association (WIA) in passing the Sarda Act by analysing their own writings, private papers, autobiographies, etc. And at the end I have examined whether the law came into force in Indian society at all in the next decade in short. I have mentioned the *Report of the Committee on the Status of Women in India*, titled '*Towards Equality*' in its published format. In addition to voicing apprehension about women's education, health, and population growth, the *Report* made a comment on 'age of marriage',

> When the legal age of marriage in case of a female is below the age of discretion, she cannot be expected to form an intelligent opinion about her partner in life. The policy of law, which permits the marriage of a girl before she is physically and mentally mature is open to serious question. As reported by the *Pushpaben Committee*, child marriage is one of the significant factors leading to the high incidence of suicide among young married women in India. Therefore, increasing the marriage age of girls to eighteen years is desirable.[168]

Wide-ranging issues, such as the traditional concept of Indian society about the contribution of women in their marital homes, the resulting problems experienced by women as a consequence of the dominant social thoughts, the contentious issue of the age of consent and marriage, how social reformers and legislators tried to address these problems through various legislative measures, and the changes brought about in the status of women in society as a result of these interventions have not yet found a satisfactory place in the attention of researchers of social sciences. Hence, I have chosen these issues as the theme of my study. The necessity for specific periodization, along with the selection of themes, dictated the choice of the chronological limits from 1872 to 1978. Not only do these years represent some significant events, but the prevailing period also exemplifies enormous transformations in the social history of India.

The fifth chapter, titled, 'Contemporary Concerns on the Age of Marriage', mainly focuses on the recent views regarding raising the age of marriage for girls. Finally, in the concluding chapter, some statistics regarding child marriage in India is presented from the perspective of the existing law. After the enactment of CMRA, the marriageable age for girls was fixed at fourteen and for boys at eighteen. Later, in 1949, an amendment to this act was introduced according to which the minimum age of marriage for girls became fifteen and the minimum age of marriage for boys remained eighteen. The law remained in force till 1978, when it was amended and the marriageable age for girls was raised to eighteen and for boys to twenty-one. In 2006, the old law was repealed by the new law, known as Prohibition of Child Marriage Act of 2006 (PCMA) and the emphasis was shifted from simple restraining of child marriages to that of prohibition. *State, Law, and Gender: Debating the Age of Marriage in India, 1872-1978* traces the history of these legal changes related to age of marriage in India after the post-Independence period and also links this issue with the present-day concern and Government's initiative for raising the age of marriage of girls to twenty-one.

TABLE 1.2: AGE AT MARRIAGE

Law in the Year	*Age at Marriage in Years*	
	Bride	*Bridegroom*
1929	14	18
1949	15	18
1978	18	21
2006	18	21

Because child marriage had declined in popularity among the middle classes, the laws prohibiting it were not opposed or even debated. Child marriage was now seen as a complication and problem of the poor and an agenda of development. It was no longer associated with the declaration of social and cultural rights. When the middle class stopped practicing child marriage or defending it in the name of 'tradition', the state was able to play a more dominant and interventionist role. State intervention, on the other hand, remained limited to passing laws; the magnitude of the problem prevented it from actually implementing them. Nonetheless, with the developing consensus on population control and the requirement to lessen fertility rates, policy intervention against child marriage gained new instrumentalist power. The United Nations and other international organizations may have sparked the first global movement against child marriage.[169]

NOTES

1. Janaki Nair, *Women and Law in Colonial India: A Social History*, Bengaluru: Kali for Women, published in collaboration with the National Law School of India University, 1996, pp. x-259, 'Review Essay' by Srimati Basu, *Gender & History*, vol. 11, no. 1, April 1999, pp. 173-6.
2. Ratna Kapur and Brenda Cossman, *Subversive Sites: Feminist Engagements with Law in India*, New Delhi/Thousand Oaks/London in associated with The Book Review Literary Trust: Sage Publications, 1996, pp. 19-20.
3. Flavia Agnes, 'Controversy over Age of Consent', *Economic and Political Weekly*, vol. XLVIII, no. 29, 20 July 2013, p. 11. Flavia Agnes, *Family Law Volume 2: Marriage, Divorce, and Matrimonial Litigation*, New Delhi: Oxford University Press, 2011, pp. 66-78.
4. Flavia Agnes, op. cit., 2013, p. 11.
5. Jaya Sagade, *Child Marriage in India: Socio-legal and Human Rights Dimensions*, New Delhi: Oxford University Press, 2005, p. xxiii.
6. Ibid., p. xxiv.
7. Ibid., p. xxv.
8. Samita Sen and Anindita Ghosh (eds.), *Love, Labour and Law: Early and Child Marriage in India*, New Delhi: Sage Publications India Pvt. Ltd.; Kolkata: Stree, 2021, pp. xi-xxxvi.
9. Ibid., p. xi.
10. Flavia Agnes, op. cit., 2011, p. 66.
11. Ibid., p. 66.
12. Samita Sen and Anindita Ghosh, op. cit., 2021, pp. xi-xxxvi.
13. Ibid., pp. xi-xii.
14. Ibid., p. xii.

15. Mary E. John, 'Some Historiographical Challenges in Approaching Child Marriage in India', in Samita Sen and Anindita Ghosh (eds.), *Love, Labour and Law: Early and Child Marriage in India*, New Delhi: Sage Publications India Pvt Ltd.; Kolkata: Stree, 2021, p. 8.
16. Ibid., pp. 9-10.
17. Samita Sen and Anindita Ghosh, op. cit., 2021, p. xii.
18. Ibid., pp. xii-xiii.
19. Ibid., p. xiii.
20. Gooroodass Banerjee, *Tagore Law Lectures-1878: The Hindu Law of Marriage and Stridhan*, Calcutta: Thacker Spink and Co., 1879, pp. 45-6.
21. M.K. Jabbi, 'Child Marriages in Rajasthan', *Social Change*, vol. 16, no. 1, 1986, pp. 3-9.
22. Werner F. Menski, *Hindu Law: Beyond Tradition and Modernity*, New Delhi: Oxford University Press, 2003, pp. 326-34.
23. Jaya Sagade, op. cit., 2005, p. 4.
24. Werner F. Menski, op. cit., 2003, pp. 326-34. Jaya Sagade, op. cit., 2005, p. 4.
25. Jaya Sagade, op. cit., 2005, p. 4.
26. S.N. Agarwala, *Age at Marriage in India*, Bombay: Kitab Mahal Publishing Ltd., 1962, pp. 1-5.
27. K.M. Kapadia, *Marriage and Family in India*, New Delhi: Oxford University Press, 1966, pp. 138-66.
28. Jaya Sagade, op. cit., 2005, p. 4.
29. Mary E. John, 'Some Historiographical Challenges in Approaching Child Marriage in India', in Samita Sen and Anindita Ghosh (eds.), *Love, Labour and Law: Early and Child Marriage in India*, New Delhi: Sage Publications India Pvt Ltd.; Kolkata: Stree, 2021, p. 5.
30. Samita Sen and Anindita Ghosh, op. cit., 2021, p. xvi.
31. Mary E. John, 'Some Historiographical Challenges in Approaching Child Marriage in India', in Samita Sen and Anindita Ghosh (eds.), *Love, Labour and Law: Early and Child Marriage in India*, New Delhi: Sage Publications India Pvt Ltd.; Kolkata: Stree, 2021, p. 10. Lata Mani, 'Contentious Traditions: The Debate on Sati in Colonial India', in Kumkum Sangari and Sudesh Vaid (eds.), *Recasting Women: Essays in Colonial History*, New Delhi: Zubaan Publishers Pvt. Ltd., 2003 (First published by Kali for Women, 1989), pp. 115-65.
32. Samita Sen and Anindita Ghosh, op. cit., 2021, p. xvi.
33. Lata Mani, *Contentious Traditions: The Debate on Sati in Colonial India*, Berkeley: University of California Press, 1998, pp. 1-9.

34. Samita Sen and Anindita Ghosh, op. cit., 2021, p. xvi.
35. Mary E. John, 'Some Historiographical Challenges in Approaching Child Marriage in India', in Samita Sen and Anindita Ghosh (eds.), *Love, Labour and Law: Early and Child Marriage in India*, New Delhi: Sage Publications India Pvt Ltd.; Kolkata: Stree, 2021, p. 11.
36. Janaki Nair, *Women and Law in Colonial India: A Social History*, New Delhi: Kali for Women and Bengaluru: National Law School of India University, 1996, p. 61.
37. Samita Sen and Anindita Ghosh, op. cit., 2021, p. xvi.
38. Sumit Sarkar, 'Vidyasagar and Brahmanical Society', in Sumit Sarkar and Tanika Sarkar (eds.), *Women and Social Reform in Modern India*, New Delhi: Permanent Black, 2007, pp. 172-214.
39. Samita Sen and Anindita Ghosh, op. cit., 2021, p. xvi. Uma Chakravarti, 'Whatever Happened to the Vedic *Dasi*? Orientalism, Nationalism, and a Script for the Past', in Kumkum Sangari and Sudesh Vaid (eds.), *Recasting Women: Essays in Colonial History*, New Delhi: Zubaan Publishers Pvt. Ltd., 2003 (first published by Kali for Women, 1989), pp. 35-114.
40. Gauri Viswanathan, *Outside the Fold: Conversion, Modernity and Belief*, New Jersey: Princeton University Press, 1998, pp. 98-9, 101-11.
41. Samita Sen, 'Religious Conversion, Infant Marriage and Polygamy: Regulating Marriage in India in the Late Nineteenth Century', *Journal of History*, vol. 26, pp. 99-145, 2009, cited in Samita Sen and Anindita Ghosh (eds.), *Love, Labour and Law: Early and Child Marriage in India*, New Delhi: Sage Publications India Pvt Ltd.; Kolkata: Stree, 2021, p. xvii. Samita Sen, 'Crossing Communities: Religious Conversion, Rights in Marriage, and Personal Law', in Flavia Agnes and Shoba Venkatesh Ghosh (eds.), *Negotiating Spaces: Legal Domains, Gender Concerns and Community Constructs*, New Delhi: Oxford University Press, 2012, pp. 77-109.
42. Samita Sen and Anindita Ghosh, op. cit., 2021, p. xvii.
43. Flavia Agnes, 'Controversy over Age of Consent', *Economic and Political Weekly*, vol. XLVIII, no. 29, 20 July 2013, p. 11.
44. Tanika Sarkar, 'Rhetoric against Age of Consent: Recasting Colonial Reason and Death of a Child-Wife', *Economic and Political Weekly*, vol. 28, no. 36, 4 September 1993, pp. 1869-79.
45. Flavia Agnes, op. cit., 2013, p. 11. A.S. Srinivasa Aiyar, *The Child Marriage Restraint Act (Act xix of 1929): with An Analytical Introduction, Critical Comments, Original Bill, Statement of Objects and Reasons, Reports of the Select Committees (with Minutes of Dissent) and Select*

Speeches in the Assembly, Madras: The Law Publishing Company, 1930, pp. 1-40.

46. Flavia Agnes, op. cit., 2013, p. 11.
47. Flavia Agnes, *Family Law Volume 2: Marriage, Divorce, and Matrimonial Litigation*, New Delhi: Oxford University Press, 2011, p. 68.
48. Flavia Agnes, op. cit., 2013, pp. 11-12.
49. http://thewire.in/women/india-new-law-age-at-marriage-women, accessed on 7 January 2021.
50. Ratna Kapur and Brenda Cossman, *Subversive Sites: Feminist Engagements with Law in India*, New Delhi/Thousand Oaks/London in associated with The Book Review Literary Trust: Sage Publications, 1996, pp. 11-12.
51. Ibid., p. 12.
52. Ibid.
53. Ibid., p. 15.
54. Samita Sen and Anindita Ghosh, op. cit., 2021, p. xvi.
55. Ratna Kapur and Brenda Cossman, op. cit., 1996, p. 35.
56. Tanika Sarkar, op. cit., 1993, pp. 1869-79.
57. Lata Mani, 'Contentious Traditions: The Debate on Sati in Colonial India', in Kumkum Sangari and Sudesh Vaid (eds.), *Recasting Women: Essays in Colonial History*, New Delhi: Zubaan Publishers Pvt. Ltd., 2003 (first published by Kali for Women, 1989), pp. 115-65.
58. Janaki Nair, op. cit., 1996.
59. Prem Chowdhry, 'Conjugality, Law and State: Inheritance Rights as Pivot of Control in Northern India', *National Law School Journal*, vol. 5, issue 1, 1993, pp. 95-116. Prem Chowdhry, *The Veiled Women: Shifting Gender Equations in Rural Haryana, 1880-1990*, New Delhi: Oxford University Press, 1994, pp. 1-23.
60. Ratna Kapur and Brenda Cossman, op. cit., 1996, p. 35.
61. Zakia Pathak and Rajeswari Sunder Rajan, 'Shahbano', *Signs: Journal of Women in Culture and Society*, vol. 14, no. 3, 1989, pp. 558-82.
62. Ratna Kapur and Brenda Cossman, op. cit., p. 36.
63. Bina Agarwal, *A Field of One's Own: Gender and Land Rights in South Asia*, Cambridge: University of Cambridge, 1994, pp. xv-xvi.
64. Ratna Kapur and Brenda Cossman, op. cit., 1996, p. 36.
65. Indu Prakash Singh, *Women, Law and Social Change in India*, New Delhi: Radiant Publishers, 1989, pp. 1-19.
66. Vimal Balasubrahmanyan, *In Search of Justice: Women, Law, Landmark Judgements, and Media*, Pune: Shubhada Saraswat Prakashan for

publisher not identified D.T. Research Centre for Women's Studies, 1990, pp. iii-vii.

67. Archana Parashar, *Women and Family Law Reform in India: Uniform Civil Code and Gender Equality*, New Delhi: Sage, 1992, pp. 17-22.
68. Ratna Kapur and Brenda Cossman, op. cit., 1996.
69. Ratna Kapur (ed.), *Feminist Terrains in Legal Domains: Interdisciplinary Essays on Women and Law in India*, New Delhi: Zubaan (first published by Kali for Women, 1996, E-book published by Zubaan Publishers Pvt Ltd.), 2020, pp. 150-83.
70. Janaki Nair, *Women and Law in Colonial India: A Social History*, Bangalore: Kali for Women, published in collaboration with the National Law School of India University, 1996, pp. x-259, 'Review Essay' by Srimati Basu, *Gender & History*, vol. 11, no. 1, April 1999, p. 173.
71. Archana Parashar, op. cit., 1992, pp. 17-22.
72. Ibid., p. 30.
73. Ibid., p. 33.
74. Ratna Kapur and Brenda Cossman, *Subversive Sites: Feminist Engagements with Law in India*, New Delhi/Thousand Oaks/London in associated with The Book Review Literary Trust: Sage Publications, 1996, p. 36.
75. Janaki Nair, op. cit., 1996, p. 3.
76. Janaki Nair, *Women and Law in Colonial India: A Social History*, Bangalore: Kali for Women, published in collaboration with the National Law School of India University, 1996, pp. x-259, 'Review Essay' by Srimati Basu, *Gender & History*, vol. 11, no. 1, April 1999, p. 174.
77. Janaki Nair, op. cit., 1996, pp. 9, 49-94.
78. Nivedita Menon, 'Abortion and the Law: Questions for Feminism', *Canadian Journal of Women and the Law*, vol. 6, no. 1, pp. 103-18, 1993, cited in Ratna Kapur and Brenda Cossman, *Subversive Sites: Feminist Engagements with Law in India*, New Delhi/Thousand Oaks/London in associated with The Book Review Literary Trust: Sage Publications, 1996, p. 36.
79. Sudhir Chandra, 'Whose laws? Notes on a legitimizing myth of the colonial Indian state', *Studies in History*, vol. 8, no. 2, n.s., New Delhi: Sage Publications, 1992, pp. 187-211. Sudhir Chandra, 'Rukhmabai: Debate Over Woman's Right to Her Person', *Economic and Political Weekly*, 2 November 1996, pp. 2937-47. Sudhir Chandra, *Enslaved*

Daughters: Colonialism, Law and Women's Rights, New Delhi: Oxford University Press, 1998, pp. 15-200.

80. Flavia Agnes, Sudhir Chandra and Monmayee Basu (eds.), *Women & Law in India*, New Delhi: Oxford University Press, 2004, Oxford India Paperbacks, 2016, p. ix.
81. Sudhir Chandra, *Enslaved Daughters: Colonialism, Law and Women's Rights*, Review by: Anupama Rao, *The Journal of Asian Studies*, vol. 58, no. 2, May, 1999, p. 543.
82. Sudhir Chandra, 'Enslaved Daughters: Colonialism, Law and Women's Rights', in Flavia Agnes, Sudhir Chandra and Monmayee Basu (eds.), *Women & Law in India*, New Delhi: Oxford University Press, 2004, Oxford India Paperbacks, 2016, p. 2.
83. Sudhir Chandra, *Enslaved Daughters: Colonialism, Law and Women's Rights*, Review by: Anupama Rao, *The Journal of Asian Studies*, vol. 58, no. 2, May, 1999, p. 544.
84. Sudhir Chandra, 'Enslaved Daughters: Colonialism, Law and Women's Rights', in Flavia Agnes, Sudhir Chandra and Monmayee Basu (eds.), *Women & Law in India*, New Delhi: Oxford University Press, 2004, Oxford India Paperbacks, 2016, p. 2.
85. Monmayee Basu, 'Hindu Women and Marriage Law: From Sacrament to Contract', in Flavia Agnes, Sudhir Chandra and Monmayee Basu (eds.), *Women & Law in India*, New Delhi: Oxford University Press, 2004, Oxford India Paperbacks, 2016, pp. xi-xvii.
86. Flavia Agnes, Sudhir Chandra and Monmayee Basu (eds.), *Women & Law in India*, New Delhi: Oxford University Press, 2004, Oxford India Paperbacks, 2016, p. ix.
87. Flavia Agnes, Sudhir Chandra and Monmayee Basu (eds.), *Women & Law in India*, Review by: Reena Patel, *Feminist Legal Studies*, vol. 13, 2005, p. 260.
88. Flavia Agnes, 'Protecting Women Against Violence? Review of a Decade of Legislation, 1980-89', *Economic and Political Weekly*, 25 April 1992, p. WS19, cited in Ratna Kapur and Brenda Cossman, *Subversive Sites: Feminist Engagements with Law in India*, New Delhi/Thousand Oaks/ London in associated with The Book Review Literary Trust: Sage Publications, 1996, p. 36.
89. Ratna Kapur and Brenda Cossman, *Subversive Sites: Feminist Engagements with Law in India*, New Delhi/Thousand Oaks/London in associated with The Book Review Literary Trust: Sage Publications, 1996, pp. 36-7.
90. Flavia Agnes, *Give Us this Day Our Daily Bread: Procedures and Case*

Law on Maintenance, Bombay: Majlis, 1992, cited in Ratna Kapur and Brenda Cossman, *Subversive Sites: Feminist Engagements with Law in India*, New Delhi/Thousand Oaks/London in associated with The Book Review Literary Trust: Sage Publications, 1996, p. 37.

91. Flavia Agnes, 'Fighting Rape – Has Amending the Law Helped?', *The Lawyers*, February 1990, p. 4. Flavia Agnes, 'Triple Talaq Judgement: Do Women Really Benefit?', *Economic and Political Weekly*, vol. XXIX, no. 20, 14 May 1994, p. 1169.
92. Ratna Kapur and Brenda Cossman, *Subversive Sites: Feminist Engagements with Law in India*, New Delhi/Thousand Oaks/London in associated with The Book Review Literary Trust: Sage Publications, 1996, p. 37.
93. Flavia Agnes, *Law and Gender Inequality: The Politics of Women's Rights in India*, New Delhi: Oxford University Press, 1999, ninth impression, 2012, pp. 1-7.
94. Flavia Agnes, Sudhir Chandra and Monmayee Basu (eds.), *Women & Law in India*, Review by: Reena Patel, *Feminist Legal Studies*, vol. 13, 2005, p. 259.
95. Flavia Agnes, Sudhir Chandra and Monmayee Basu (eds.), *Women & Law in India*, New Delhi: Oxford University Press, 2004, Oxford India Paperbacks, 2016, p. x.
96. Flavia Agnes, *Family Law Volume 1: Family Laws and Constitutional Claims*, New Delhi: Oxford University Press, 2011, pp. xxi-xxxi.
97. Flavia Agnes, *Family Law Volume 2: Marriage, Divorce, and Matrimonial Litigation*, New Delhi: Oxford University Press, 2011, pp. xxviii-xxxi.
98. Flavia Agnes, 'Family Law and Constitutional Claims; Marriage, Divorce and Matrimonial Litigation', Book Review by Anju Tyagi, *Journal of National Law University Delhi*, 30 July 2018, pp. 131-2.
99. Padma Anagol, 'Rebellious Wives and Dysfunctional Marriages: Indian Women's Discourses and Participation in the Debates over Restitution of Conjugal Rights and the Child Marriage Controversy in the 1880s and 1890s', in Sumit Sarkar and Tanika Sarkar (eds.), *Women and Social Reform in Modern India*, New Delhi: Permanent Black, 2007, p. 421.
100. Charles H. Heimsath, 'The Origin and Enactment of the Indian Age of Consent Bill, 1891', *The Journal of Asian Studies*, vol. 21, no. 4, August 1962, pp. 491-504.
101. Padma Anagol, op. cit., New Delhi: Permanent Black, 2007, p. 421.
102. Partha Chatterjee, 'The Nationalist Resolution of the Women's Question', in Kumkum Sangari and Sudesh Vaid (eds.), *Recasting*

Women: Essays in Colonial History, New Delhi: Zubaan Publishers Pvt. Ltd., 2003 (first published by Kali for Women, 1989), pp. 306-33. Partha Chatterjee, *The Nation and Its Fragments: Colonial and Postcolonial Histories*, New Jersey: Princeton University Press, 1993, pp. 116-34, 135-57.

103. Partha Chatterjee, op. cit., 1993, pp. 116-34.
104. Partha Chatterjee, op. cit., New Delhi: Zubaan Publishers Pvt. Ltd., 2003 (first published by Kali for Women, 1989), pp. 306-33.
105. Padma Anagol, op. cit., New Delhi: Permanent Black, 2007, p. 421.
106. Meredith Borthwick, 'The *Bhadramahila* and Changing Conjugal Relations in Bengal', in M. Allen and S.N. Mukherjee (eds.), *Women in India and Nepal*, Canberra: ANU, 1982, p. 116.
107. Tanika Sarkar, 'Rhetoric against Age of Consent: Recasting Colonial Reason and Death of a Child-Wife', *Economic and Political Weekly*, vol. 28, no. 36, 4 September 1993, pp. 1869-79. Tanika Sarkar, 'Hindu Conjugality and Nationalism: in Late Nineteenth-Century Bengal', in Jasodhara Bagchi (ed.), *Indian Women: Myth and Reality*, Hyderabad: Sangam Books, 1995, pp. 98-116. Tanika Sarkar, 'A Prehistory of Rights: The Age of Consent Debate in Colonial Bengal', *Feminist Studies*, vol. 26, no. 3, Autumn, 2000, pp. 601-22. Tanika Sarkar, *Hindu Wife, Hindu Nation: Community, Religion, and Cultural Nationalism*, Bloomington and Indianapolis: Indiana University Press, 2001, pp. 191-225, 226-49. Tanika Sarkar, 'Enfranchised Selves: Women, Culture and Rights in Nineteenth-Century Bengal', *Gender & History*, vol. 13, no. 3, November 2001, pp. 546-65. Sumit Sarkar and Tanika Sarkar (eds.), *Women and Social Reform in Modern India*, New Delhi: Permanent Black, 2007, pp. 1-18. Tanika Sarkar, 'Intimate Violence in Colonial Bengal: A Death, a Trial and a Law, 1889-1891', *Law and History Review*, vol. 38, no. 1, February 2020, pp. 177-200.
108. Tanika Sarkar, 'Rhetoric against Age of Consent: Recasting Colonial Reason and Death of a Child-Wife', *Economic and Political Weekly*, vol. 28, no. 36, 4 September 1993, pp. 1869-79. Tanika Sarkar, 'Hindu Conjugality and Nationalism: in Late Nineteenth-Century Bengal', in Jasodhara Bagchi (ed.), *Indian Women: Myth and Reality*, Hyderabad: Sangam Books, 1995, pp. 98-116. Tanika Sarkar, 'A Prehistory of Rights: The Age of Consent Debate in Colonial Bengal', *Feminist Studies*, vol. 26, no. 3, Autumn, 2000, pp. 601-22. Tanika Sarkar, *Hindu Wife, Hindu Nation: Community, Religion, and Cultural Nationalism*, Bloomington and Indianapolis: Indiana University Press, 2001, pp. 191-225, 226-49.

109. Jasodhara Bagchi (ed.), *Indian Women: Myth and Reality*, Book Review by: Samita Sen, *Indian Journal of Gender Studies*, vol. 4, no. 2, 1997, p. 278.
110. Tanika Sarkar, *Hindu Wife, Hindu Nation: Community, Religion, and Cultural Nationalism*, Book Review by: Leela Fernandes, *The Journal of Asian Studies*, vol. 62, no. 2, May 2003, pp. 683-4.
111. Tanika Sarkar, 'Rhetoric against Age of Consent: Recasting Colonial Reason and Death of a Child-Wife', *Economic and Political Weekly*, vol. 28, no. 36, 4 September 1993, pp. 1869-79. Tanika Sarkar, 'A Prehistory of Rights: The Age of Consent Debate in Colonial Bengal', *Feminist Studies*, vol. 26, no. 3, Autumn, 2000, pp. 601-22. Tanika Sarkar, *Hindu Wife, Hindu Nation: Community, Religion, and Cultural Nationalism*, Bloomington and Indianapolis: Indiana University Press, 2001, pp. 226-49. Sumit Sarkar and Tanika Sarkar (eds.), *Women and Social Reform in Modern India*, New Delhi: Permanent Black, 2007, pp. 1-18.
112. Tanika Sarkar, *Hindu Wife, Hindu Nation: Community, Religion, and Cultural Nationalism*, Book Review by: Malavika Karlekar, *Studies in History*, vol. 19, no. 1, n.s., 2003, p. 151.
113. Tanika Sarkar, 'Intimate Violence in Colonial Bengal: A Death, a Trial and a Law, 1889-1891', *Law and History Review*, vol. 38, no. 1, February 2020, p. 178.
114. Padma Anagol, op. cit., New Delhi: Permanent Black, 2007, p. 421.
115. Dagmar Engels, 'The Age of Consent Act of 1891: Colonial Ideology in Bengal', *South Asia Research*, vol. 3, no. 2, 1985, pp. 107-34.
116. Mrinalini Sinha, *Colonial Masculinity: The 'Manly Englishman' and the 'Effeminate Bengali' in the Late Nineteenth Century*, New York: Manchester University Press, 1995, pp. 138-80. Mrinalini Sinha, 'The Age of Consent Act: The Ideal of Masculinity and Colonial Ideology in Nineteenth-Century Bengal', in T. K. Stewart (ed.), *Shaping Bengali Worlds, Public and Private*, Michigan: Michigan State University, 1989, pp. 99-127.
117. Mrinalini Sinha, *Colonial Masculinity: The 'Manly Englishman' and the 'Effeminate Bengali' in the Late Nineteenth Century*, New York: Manchester University Press, 1995, p. 23.
118. Mrinalini Sinha, op. cit., 1989.
119. Meera Kosambi, 'Girl Brides and Socio-Legal Change: Age of Consent Bill (1891) Controversy', *Economic and Political Weekly*, vol. 26, no. 31/32, 3-10 August 1991, pp. 1857-68. Meera Kosambi, 'Gender reform and competing state controls over women: The Rakhmabai

case (1884-1888)', *Contributions to Indian Sociology*, vol. 29, no. 1&2, n.s., 1995. Meera Kosambi, 'Child Brides and Child Mothers: The Age of Consent Bill (1891) Controversy', in Meera Kosambi (ed.), *Crossing Thresholds: Feminist Essays in Social History*, New Delhi: Permanent Black, 2007, First Paperback Printing, 2011, pp. 274-310. Meera Kosambi, 'Resisting Conjugality: Rakhmabai's Protest', in Meera Kosambi (ed.), *Crossing Thresholds: Feminist Essays in Social History*, New Delhi: Permanent Black, 2007, First Paperback Printing, 2011, pp. 235-73.

120. Padma Anagol-McGinn, 'The Age of Consent Act (1891) Reconsidered: Women's Perspectives and Participation in the Child-Marriage Controversy in India', *South Asia Research*, vol. 12, no. 2, November 1992, pp. 100-18. Padma Anagol, *The Emergence of Feminism in India, 1850-1920*, New York: Routledge, 2016 (first published in 2005 by Ashgate Publishing), pp. 181-218. Padma Anagol, 'Rebellious Wives and Dysfunctional Marriages: Indian Women's Discourses and Participation in the Debates over Restitution of Conjugal Rights and the Child Marriage Controversy in the 1880s and 1890s', in Sumit Sarkar and Tanika Sarkar (eds.), *Women and Social Reform in Modern India*, New Delhi: Permanent Black, 2007, pp. 420-65. Padma Anagol, 'Feminist Inheritances and Foremothers: the beginnings of feminism in modern India', *Women's History Review*, vol. 19, no. 4, September 2010, pp. 523-46. Padma Anagol, 'Age of Consent and Child Marriage in India', in Nancy A. Naples (ed.), *The Wiley Blackwell Encyclopedia of Gender and Sexuality Studies*, 2016, pp. 1-5.
121. Antoinette Burton, 'From Child Bride to "Hindoo Lady": Rukhmabai and the Debate on Sexual Respectability in Imperial Britain', *The American Historical Review*, vol. 103, no. 4, October 1998, pp. 1119-46.
122. Padma Anagol, 'Rebellious Wives and Dysfunctional Marriages: Indian Women's Discourses and Participation in the Debates over Restitution of Conjugal Rights and the Child Marriage Controversy in the 1880s and 1890s', op. cit., 2007, p. 421.
123. Leela Gulati, 'Age of Marriage of Women and Population Growth: The Kerala Experience', *Economic and Political Weekly*, vol. 11, no. 31/32, August 1976, pp. 1225-34.
124. Geraldine H. Forbes, 'Women and Modernity: The Issue of Child Marriage in India', *Women's Studies Int. Quart.*, 1979, vol. 2, pp. 407-19.
125. Barbara Ramusack, 'Women's Organizations and Social Change: The

Age of Marriage Issue in India', in N. Black and A.C. Cottrell (eds.), *Women and World Change: Equity Issues in Development*', London: Sage Publications, 1981, pp. 198-216.

126. Geraldine H. Forbes, op. cit., 1979. Barbara Ramusack, op. cit., 1981.
127. Geraldine H. Forbes, op. cit., 1979.
128. Philippe Aries, *Centuries of Childhood: A Social History of Family Life*, New York: Alfred A. Knopf, 1962 (1960), pp. 9-11.
129. Ruby Lal, *Coming of Age in Nineteenth-Century India: The Girl-Child and the Art of Playfulness*, Cambridge: Cambridge University Press, 2013, pp. 1-31.
130. Ashwini Tambe, *Defining Girlhood in India: A Transnational History of Sexual Maturity Laws*, Urbana: University of Illinois Press, 2019, pp. 61-84, 85-100, 121-41.
131. Ashwini Tambe, 'The State as Surrogate Parent: Legislating Nonmarital Sex in Colonial India, 1911-1929', *The Journal of the History of Childhood and Youth*, vol. 2, no. 3, 2009, pp. 393-427. Rajani Bhatia and Ashwini Tambe, 'Raising the age of marriage in 1970s India: Demographers, despots, and feminists', *Women's Studies International Forum*, 2013, pp. 1-12.
132. Ashwini Tambe, *Codes of Misconduct: Regulating Prostitution in Late Colonial Bombay*, Minneapolis: University of Minnesota Press, 2009, cited in Samita Sen and Anindita Ghosh, op. cit., 2021, p. xxiii.
133. Mrinalini Sinha, 'The Lineage of the "Indian" Modern: Rhetoric, Agency and the Sarda Act in Late Colonial India', in Antoinette Burton (ed.), *Gender, Sexuality and Colonial Modernities*, London and New York: Routledge, 1999, pp. 209-24. Mrinalini Sinha, *Specters of Mother India: The Global Restructuring of an Empire*, Durham and London: Duke University Press, 2006, pp. 152-96.
134. Mrinalini Sinha, *Specters of Mother India: The Global Restructuring of an Empire*, Book Review by: Durba Ghosh, *Journal of British Studies*, vol. 46, no. 3, July 2007, p. 728. Mrinalini Sinha, op. cit., 1999.
135. Sumita Mukherjee, 'Using the Legislative Assembly for Social Reform: The Sarda Act of 1929', *South Asia Research*, vol. 26, no. 3, 2006, p. 219.
136. Shahida Lateef, *Muslim Women in India: Political & Private Realities: 1890s-1980s*, New Jersey: Zed Books Ltd., 1990, pp. 55-73, 74-94.
137. Azra Asghar Ali, *The Emergence of Feminism Among Indian Muslim Women 1920-1947*, Oxford: Oxford University Press, 2000, pp. 123-67.
138. Judy Whitehead, 'Modernising the Motherhood Archetype: Public

Health Models and the Child Marriage Restraint Act of 1929', *Contributions to Indian Sociology*, n.s., vol. 29, nos. 1&2, 1995, pp. 187-209.

139. Andrea Major, 'Mediating Modernity: Colonial State, Indian Nationalism and the Renegotiation of the "Civilizing Mission" in the Indian Child Marriage Debate of 1927-1932', in Carey A. Watt and Michael Mann (eds.), *Civilizing Missions in Colonial and Post-Colonial South Asia: From Improvement to Development*, London: Anthem Press, 2011, pp. 165-89.
140. Bhaswati Chakravarti (Chatterjee), 'The Second Social Reform Movement: Gender and Society in Bengal, 1930s-1950s', unpublished Ph.D. dissertation, Department of History, University of Calcutta, https://shodhganga.inflibnet.ac.in/handle/10603/211610, accessed on 31 January 2021. Bhaswati Chatterjee, 'Child Marriage and the Second Social Reform Movement', in Samita Sen and Anindita Ghosh, op. cit., 2021, pp. 29-62.
141. Jaya Sagade, *Child Marriage in India: Socio-legal and Human Rights Dimensions*, New Delhi: Oxford University Press, 2005, p. xxxvii.
142. Samita Sen and Anindita Ghosh, op. cit., 2021, p. xxvii.
143. Radhika Singha, *A Despotism of Law: Crime and Justice in Early Colonial India*, New Delhi: Oxford University Press, 1998, pp. vii-xviii.
144. Himani Bannerji, *Inventing Subjects: Studies in Hegemony, Patriarchy and Colonialism*, New Delhi: Tulika, 2001, pp. 72-98.
145. Subhasri Ghosh, 'Coming of Age in Colonial India: The Discourse and Debate over the Age of Consummation in the Nineteenth Century', in Kristine Moruzi and Michelle J. (eds.), *Colonial Girlhood in Literature, Culture and History, 1840-1950*, UK: Palgrave Macmillan, 2014, pp. 79-92.
146. Ishita Pande, 'Coming of Age: Law, Sex and Childhood in Late Colonial India', *Gender & History*, vol. 24, no. 1, April 2012, pp. 205-30. Ishita Pande, '"Listen to the Child": Law, Sex, and the Child Wife in Indian Historiography', *History Compass*, vol. 11, no. 9, 2013, pp. 687-701. Ishita Pande, 'Phulmoni's body: the autopsy, the inquest and the humanitarian narrative on child rape in India', *South Asian History and Culture*, vol. 4, no. 1, 2013, pp. 9-30. Ishita Pande, 'Sorting Boys and Men: Unlawful Intercourse, Boy-Protection, and the Child Marriage Restraint Act in Colonial India', *The Journal of the History of Childhood and Youth*, vol. 6, no. 2, Spring 2013, pp. 332-58. Ishita Pande, *Sex, Law and the Politics of Age: Child Marriage in India, 1891-1937*, Cambridge: Cambridge University Press, 2020, pp. 31-71,

72-120. Ishita Pande, 'Power, Knowledge, and the Epistemic Contract on Age: The Case of Colonial India', *American Historical Review*, April 2020, pp. 407-17.

147. Ishita Pande, *Sex, Law and the Politics of Age: Child Marriage in India, 1891-1937*, Cambridge: Cambridge University Press, 2020, pp. 31-71, 72-120.
148. Ishita Pande, 'Coming of Age: Law, Sex and Childhood in Late Colonial India', *Gender & History*, vol. 24, no. 1, April 2012, p. 205.
149. Samita Sen and Anindita Ghosh, op. cit., 2021, p. xxii.
150. Samita Sen and Anindita Ghosh, op. cit., 2021, p. xiv. Ishita Pande, *Sex, Law and the Politics of Age: Child Marriage in India, 1891-1937*, Cambridge: Cambridge University Press, 2020, pp. 31-71, 72-120.
151. Samita Sen and Anindita Ghosh, op. cit., 2021.
152. Biswajit Ghosh and Ananda Mohan Kar, 'Child Marriage in Rural West Bengal: Status and Challenges', *Indian Journal of Development Research and Social Action*, vol. 6, nos 1-2 (January-December), 2010, pp. 1-23. Biswajit Ghosh, 'Early Marriage of Girls in Contemporary Bengal: A Field View', *Social Change*, vol. 41, no. 1, 2011, pp. 41-61. Biswajit Ghosh, 'Child Marriage, Society and the Law: A Study in a Rural Context in West Bengal, India', *International Journal of Law, Policy and Family*, vol. 25, no. 2, 2011, pp. 199-219. Biswajit Ghosh. 'Child Marriage, Community, and Adolescent Girls: The Salience of Tradition and Modernity in the Malda District of West Bengal', *Sociological Bulletin*, Indian Sociological Society, vol. 60, no. 2, May-August 2011, pp. 307-26.
153. Mary E. John, *Child Marriage in an International Frame: A Feminist Review from India*, New York: Routledge, 2021, pp. 1-10.
154. Ibid.
155. Jaya Sagade, op. cit., 2005, p. 35.
156. Janaki Nair, op. cit., 1996, p. 8.
157. For a detailed discussion on the Cooch Behar Marriage Controversy, see David Kopf, *The Brahmo Samaj and the Shaping of the Modern Indian Mind*, New Jersey: Princeton University Press, 1979, pp. 313-35. Rochona Majumdar, *Marriage and Modernity: Family Values in Colonial Bengal*, Durham and London: Duke University Press, 2009, pp. 167-205.
158. Ishita Banerjee-Dube, *A History of Modern India*, Delhi: Cambridge University Press, 2014, pp. 201-2.
159. Ibid., pp. 201-4.
160. Ibid.

161. Sudhir Chandra, 'Enslaved Daughters: Colonialism, Law and Women's Rights', in Flavia Agnes, Sudhir Chandra and Monmayee Basu (eds.), *Women & Law in India: An Omnibus Comprising*, New Delhi: Oxford University Press, 2004, Oxford India Paperbacks, 2016, p. 1.
162. Ishita Banerjee-Dube, op. cit., pp. 201-4.
163. Ibid.
164. Denise Reaume, 'What is distinctive about feminist analysis of law? A Conceptual Analysis of Women's Exclusion from Law', *Legal Theory*, vol. 2, 1996, pp. 265-99.
165. Jaya Sagade, op. cit., 2005, p. xxxii.
166. Ibid.
167. Mrinalini Sinha, *Specters of Mother India: The Global Restructuring of an Empire*, Durham and London: Duke University Press, 2006, p. 153.
168. *Towards Equality: Report of the Committee on the Status of Women in India*, New Delhi: Government of India, Ministry of Education & Social Welfare, December 1974, p. 112.
169. Samita Sen and Anindita Ghosh, op. cit., 2021, p. xxiv.

CHAPTER 1

Hindu Women, Social Reform and Marriage in Nineteenth- and Early Twentieth-Century India

The 'women's question' in India, especially in Bengal, has had its share of eminent critics and activists. The frameworks of a temporally and spatially situated discourse of gender in society have already occurred and activities with the principal elements creating this emergent discourse have also been in prevalence for a while.[1] The period preceding the British rule in India had perceived several variations in the position and status of women. However, we all know that the condition of women did not become a foremost social reform issue until the nineteenth century. In nineteenth-century Bengal, the key momentum for social reform was a multifaceted reaction to the existence of British colonial rule.[2] However; the women's question in colonial India had its foundations in the first half of the nineteenth century in the curious symbiosis of the comforts of colonial and indigenous male elites.[3] Ramesh Chandra Majumdar observed in 1965 that 'it was somewhat singular that almost all the important social reforms of the nineteenth century should be centered on women.' Several others, after him, have noted in the same way the uniqueness of what is now generally identified as the woman question and a vast literature has since been constructed upon the issue by men and women speaking in different voices.[4] In Bengal, the fervour of ideological debate during the first half of the nineteenth century, as argued by Meredith Borthwick, had little perceptible effect on the condition of women.[5] In colonial India, a growing 'new elite' had seen the reconstruction of the women's social status as part of the reorganization of its class and caste identity. While the reform issue was being contested by the *bhadralok* (prosperous, well-educated people regarded as members of a social class) in public mediums and in the press, women sustained with their traditional domestic programme. Nevertheless, women's history in India commenced as an act of retrieval. Aparna Basu has aptly pointed out that 'since women had been *hidden from history*,[6] the aim was to have *Clio's consciousness raised*[7] by *liberating women's history*[8] from ignorance and neglect and in the resulting work, women in history were *becoming visible*.'[9] Despite the high perceptibility of women's subservience in Indian society, historical effort on the beginning and development of the patriarchal system does not hitherto prevail in an appropriate way. It is also being identified that women's history cannot be reviewed in segregation from the mainstream history.[10]

The history of women is not linear, nor does it have a well-organized form. It is actually an essential, however, mostly unseen part of the 'saga of civilization'. Its threads are thoroughly intertwined with those of culture, society, state and most importantly, with the lives of the people.[11] In the second half of the nineteenth century, the educated Indian elite faced unprecedented challenges. The advent of the British in India had brought not only a new form of government, but also new understanding, new notions as well as new technology. The section of the newly educated middle class realized to their distress that the society which had bred them and about which they often exaggerated was not the ideal one, but ridden with many evils. As social reformers began to examine the existing Indian social structure, they comprehended that 'women's question' in this context were important. The colonial context produced diverse reactions from the British ruling elite. The colonial rulers critiqued Indian society in a 'patronizing manner', and took upon themselves the 'role of patrons' attempting to advance a rigid Indian society.[12] An important instrument used by colonial ideology to prove the subservience of the subject population was the question of the status of women. The nineteenth-century socio-religious reform movement, a result of the clash and collaboration of British colonial rule with Indian culture, showed keen interest to the advancement of the situation and rights of women.[13] The moral inferiority of Indians, especially Hindus, was supposed to be demonstrated by the barbaric practices followed against women

– this was claimed by Christian missionaries as well as by historians like James Mill.[14] The higher morality of the imperial masters could be successfully recognized by emphasizing the low status of women among the subject population since it was a matter that could concurrently exhibit the moral inferiority of the subject population. As a result of this, the women's question became a significant tool in the colonial ideology.[15] Writing in the nineteenth century, in sharp disparity to the Orientalists who had proposed that the 'Hindus were a people of high culture' now in a state of decay, Mill considered 'Hindu civilization' as unpolished from its very early stages, plunging into the lowest depths of corruption and misdeed. Fundamental to the principle by which Mill refereed the level of civilization was the role it bestowed on its women.[16] Hindu women, he claimed, were in,

> a state of dependence more-strict and humiliating than that which is ordained for the weaker sex.... Nothing can exceed the habitual contempt which Hindus entertain for their women.... They are held in extreme degradation, excluded from the sacred books, deprived of education and (of a share) in the paternal property.... That remarkable barbarity, the wife held unworthy to eat with her husband, is prevalent in Hindustan.[17]

Mill's main supposition was that the practice of segregating women did not come with the Mohammedans; but moderately it was the result of the whole spirit of Hindu society in which women should be continuously defended for anxiety of their distinctive propensity close to 'infidelity'.[18] Therefore, colonial historians justified British rule in India by proclaiming that the defence and interference of the colonial state were required for Hindu women.

In response to this kind of classification of Indian or Hindu society, historians like Anant Sadashiv Altekar and Romesh Chunder Dutt, developed a school of nationalist history writing, who confronted colonial history writing by introducing the argument that the evils of Indian society were attributable to Muslim invasions. That is, the patriarchal structures of Hindu society were described completely as a reaction to external intimidations.[19] Women in ancient India have been the centre of academic attention since the nineteenth century. Both Indian and British scholars accepted to examine the position of women in early Indian society, although from different perspectives.[20]

Not all approved that gender relations required alteration. Tanika Sarkar[21] and Tapan Raychaudhuri[22] have argued that 'a number of Indian intellectuals praised their own culture's treatment of women or compared to the conditions of Indian women with those of European women and concluded that females in both countries suffered hardships.'[23] The 'woman question' had a similarly extended history in the conceptual work of elite proto-nationalism and nationalism in India. The form of the 'Aryan woman' of the ancient past, who was interpreted as superior to Western and westernized women as well as to lower caste or class women in India, had occupied a central place in the cultural nationalist project of reconstructing a 'golden past' from which contemporary Indian society had allegedly fallen.[24] Indian reformers utilized the frame of this perfect 'Aryan woman' to argue for modifications in contemporary Indian society and opponents of reforms used it to combat any change in the prevailing state of affairs.[25] Others who believed the notion that society's ills could be traced to the oppressed condition of women, identified women education as well as women emancipation by means of the first moves with regard to progress. Nevertheless, both sections of people, i.e. one group of people who eulogized gender relations and others who assured the matter regarding the need for reform – decided to share an ideological position, which was later connected with the nationalist project that segregated the 'home' from the 'world'.[26] As Partha Chatterjee has argued that 'the women's question by the second half of the nineteenth century had undergone a shift as it acquired a new political valence for an emerging cultural nationalist politics.'[27] According to him, Indians followed science, technology, rational economics and western political forms while regarding the 'home' as the source of true identity that needed protection and strengthening, not transformation.[28] A passage in Mahesh Chandra Deb's paper, 'A Sketch of the Condition of the Hindoo Women', presented by him at a meeting of the Society for Acquisition of General Knowledge, held at the Calcutta Sanskrit College Hall in the month of January of 1839, can guide us closer on the way to a clarification of the centrality of women's issues in the concerns of nineteenth century male reformers. Thorough criticism of the woman's sufferings – seclusion, arranged marriage, child marriage, polygamy, the ban on widow remarriage, were 'under their eyes every day and hour of their existence within the precincts of their own respective domiciles'.[29] He also said,

> Suffice it to say that every man who has carefully examined the condition of the Hindoo women cannot help pitying the benighted and miserable situation in which they are placed. Notwithstanding all their kind attention, their pious and dutiful conduct, their submissive behavior towards their husbands they frequently meet with severe scoldings and are even sometimes cruelly punished from ungrounded jealousy or a tyrannical whim.[30]

Inelegantly uttered through the newly acquired foreign tongue, Mahesh Chandra Deb's words yet pointed to firm severe problems of interpersonal adjustment within the family.[31] So as to convince his listeners that the 'woman question' required urgent consideration and recognition, he said, 'In whatever light, then, we view the situation of the Hindoo women – whether we look to their physical or mental condition – we shall find to our great mortification that it is truly deplorable.'[32] The subject matter of his speech reverberated among the western critics of Indian society and was persistent in speeches and essays throughout the century.[33]

Hindu women exhibited exceptional abilities as administrators and warriors, as well as in statecraft. For instance, Meerabai classified herself as the poet-queen of the fifteenth century. Ahalyabai of Central India's Holkar state and Rani Lakshmi Bai of Jhansi were rulers who demonstrated laudable courage and sporadic determination. Women made a name for themselves in a variety of fields in Bengal as well. Some like Rani Bhawani of Natore were exceptional estate managers, while some others flourished in education, passion, and thoughts. Hati Vidyalankar, a Bengali resident of Varanasi, and Shyammohini Devi, also from Bengal, were both renowned Sanskrit scholars.[34] But the subsequent political as well as economic discontent hindered the advancement and progress of Indian society in general and especially women. When invasion and war became a regular incident, the anxiety of insecurity, which troubled unmarried young women was accountable for the appearance of the system of early marriage. This undoubtedly contributed to the foundation of the harsh and inexcusable dowry system, which has existed for a long time. The fear of insecurity was predominantly responsible for the development and perpetuation of the system of *sati* (virtuous and chaste woman; the practice in Hinduism of a wife burning herself with the body of her dead husband).[35]

Contemporary feminist scholars have argued that the aforesaid history is 'the creation of the nineteenth century interaction between colonialism and nationalism'.[36] Historians like Uma Chakravarti (1993, 1989) and Kumkum Roy (1995) have interrogated this 'construction of the past' at several levels.[37] Uma Chakravarti has pointed out how Altekar and other historians were guided by nationalist ideas and the need to instill national pride at a time when Indians needed to build up their cultural self-confidence in face of attacks by western scholars.[38] These historians, therefore, twisted a picture of a 'golden age' in the ancient past when women occupied a very high status in society. A portrait of 'Hindu women' constructed on mythology, literature and history was projected by these nationalist historians. This 'idealized version' of the lives of 'Hindu women' gave a response to the critics of Hindu society about its consideration of women. They have pointed out that the evidence used by nationalist historians was exclusively drawn from Brahminical sources and was therefore, a partial history at best; even from the Brahminical sources alone, there was adequate evidence to display that the structure of institutions that ensured the subordination of women was complete long before Muslims as a religious community had even come into being. It has been commonly known that well-known women of Vedic and later Vedic age, like Gargi and Maitrayee were notable for their intellectual and spiritual accomplishments, as well demonstrated in the famous dialogues between 'Maitrayee and her husband, Yajnavalkya, in the Brihadaranyaka Upanishad iv.5 and Gargi Vachaknavi in Brihadaranyaka Upanishad III, 6.8'.[39] But regardless of this, stating precisely to the two features, which the nationalist argument has generally used – 'scholarship' and 'property' – contemporary feminist historians of ancient India have tried to detonate the myth of the superior position of women in the Vedic period. Regarding 'scholarship', they have pointed out specifically that less than 1 per cent of the one thousand hymns of the Rig Veda were attributed to women, which evidently shows the peripheral condition of women scholars. At the same time, Uma Chakravarti has pointed out that the well-known and common narrative about the controversy between Gargi and Yajnavalkya, marked as an instance of the education permitted to women, was an incident in which Gargi was eventually suppressed and removed from the competition by Yajnavalkya, not because of the power of his arguments, but because he frightened her – 'Gargi, do not question too much, lest your head fall off....'[40] Women had a steady limited appreciation only as wives and mothers within the patriarchal kinship structure.[41] Uma Chakravarti has asserted that 'for contemporary women this vision of the past has led to a narrow and preventive circle in which the image of Indian womanhood has become both a shackle and a rhetorical device that nevertheless functions as a historical truth'.[42]

As previously discussed, in reaction to the condemning critique of the West, male reformers envisioned a 'golden past' in which women were given special treatment and respect, and they tried to persuade reforms of those customs that they saw as misrepresentations or anomalies. Therefore, female infanticide was debarred, *sati* was eradicated and widow remarriage was legalized. In every occasion, such modifications were legalized by mentioning of the *shastras* (sacred scriptures of Hinduism) and no women were ever involved in the reform movements. It would be inaccurate to suggest that these male reformers lacked compassion or empathy for their female counterparts. However, they treated them as subjects of their 'modernizing project' and could not envisage them as conscious equals asserting agency because of their own emancipation.[43] The implications of this 'nationalist investment' on definite reforms for women advanced Hindu revivalists, specifically in the second half of the nineteenth century, with a nationalistic language through which they could be persuasive in their patriarchal resistance to legislative initiatives to enhance the condition of women. This was evident in the cries against colonial intervention that marked the aggressive Hindu resistance to the Age of Consent Act of 1891.[44] And this reformism sparked a virulent Hindu backlash when the Age of Consent Bill in 1891 pursued to raise the age for consummation of marriage for women from ten to twelve. By attempting to limit a husband's conjugal rights over his wife, the proposed reform invaded what was previously recognized as the only remaining site of autonomy for 'native masculinity'. As a result, the child bride became a symbol of Hindu glory; the control over her was an indigenous male privilege that could not be permitted to be tampered with by a foreign rule. Thus, the nineteenth century concluded in a shift from a modernizing project to a Hindu conservative assertion of patriarchal control over the women's domain, which now introduced a crucial part of the nationalist programme.[45] The additional sarcasm was that the removal of the 'woman question' as a subject to be contested with colonial rulers by the last half of the nineteenth century accorded satisfactorily with the political calculations of the colonial state. Notwithstanding the colonial state's interferences in the family, especially in its dealing with marginalized social groups and populations, familial matters, as Radha Kumar (1983) and Lucy Carroll (1983) argued, were characteristically entrusted 'outside the dominion of the unanimously applicable laws of the state to a separate body of personal laws dictated by religion'.[46] The colonial state, particularly in the repercussion of the rebellion of 1857, was eager to stimulate allegiance among conventional and orthodox segments of native society by granting indigenous communities sovereignty on specific issues. According to Radhika Singha (2003),

> The official policy of non-interference in religious and familial matters thus abdicated responsibility of domestic affairs to the reforming agency of the communities themselves. The result was that the female legal subject in colonial India was caught between the contradictory pulls of the state's drive toward administrative centralization and the political calculations that motivated an official policy of non-interference in religious and personal affairs of communities.[47]

There was no single uniform movement for social reform, but rather a variety of campaigns addressing local issues at various times. The colonial experience moulded these movements, as well as the opposition to such reform, in general. Both reformers and revivalists exchanged a misperception in some kind of a glorious pre-colonial and pre-Muslim past wherein women were venerated, and both used nationalist justifications, though mobilizing this representation of the past in different ways – reformers to show that Indians still had the capability to fulfil the enlightened excellence of the West and therefore was fit for self-government, and revivalists to claim that Indian or

Hindu traditions had the inner resources to cope with its problems and did not require foreign or imperialist intervention.[48] Partha Chatterjee has also argued that while the women's question was a key issue in controversies over social reforms in nineteenth-century Bengal, it had faded from the agenda of popular discourse by the end of the century. 'The reason for this', he stated, 'was the refusal of nationalism to make the "women's question" an issue of political negotiation with the colonial state.' It has been affirmed that the 'bourgeois leadership' of the nationalist movement determined to oppose colonial authority by concurrently identifying the citizen's 'public sphere' or 'outer world' as that where 'we' are the same as or equal to the imperialist masters and the *private* or *inner* domain as that where 'we' are different, in this way defending discriminatory practices against women.[49] His perceptive and significant analysis of the nationalist rhetoric has confirmed how the discussions and controversies over social reform and the condition of women allowed Indian men to gradually define the 'inner domain' – the 'interior frontier' – of national life from the 'outer space', the 'private' from the 'public', the 'spiritual' from the 'material', re-articulating them in innovative ways. And it was only after this domain had been established, and the position and role of women within it had been clearly defined, that nationalism, which had previously been indistinct and vague, acquired sufficient confidence to stake its claim in the open, to confront the colonial state's power to legislate over the 'inner life' of the nation.[50] Nationalist philosophy was founded on the construction of a perceived division between a 'outer' or 'material' domain, where European institutions were regarded as superior, and an 'inner' or 'spiritual' sphere, where the sovereignty and the real recognition of the nation situated. Women were representatively recognized with the 'inner' domain as the essence of the nation and where nationalists claimed autonomy from colonial intervention. The succeeding recognition of women with the accurate spirit of the nation reinterpreted the women's question in India. It underwrote the modernization of women as part of a broader regeneration of the nation; nonetheless it also established limits to that modernization in keeping with the supposedly authentic traditions of the nation.[51] This, however, was not solely the work of nationalists. Orthodox Hindu voices were also attempting to consolidate their own hegemonic positions by emphasizing the purity of Indian culture and the need for women to uphold it. These changes were also met with opposition from the administration and others. However, in her discussion of the age of consent debates, Tanika Sarkar (1993) has demonstrated how women's traditional roles were discussed and contested. Women's bodies and sexualities had become 'a site for the articulation and rearticulation of Indian culture'.[52]

The nationalist stance was based on the assumption that reforming women's lives was an area where the nation was behaving on its own, independent of the 'colonial state'. As a result, the new patriarchy established by nationalist discourse as a hegemonic construct differentiated from the West as well as from the majority of its own person, because its contention about retaining the contrast in the 'inner domain' was pertinent mostly to the fractions of the middle classes. The resolution of the women's question was definitely troublesome for the middle classes who were non-Hindu as well as certain other categories of Indian society who sensed alienated from the nationalist leadership's concept of the nation.[53] Even in Bengal, with its significant position in expounding a cultural nationalist politics in the second half of the nineteenth century, the re-evaluating of the women's question was not just part of an anti-colonial nationalist politics; it was also a indication of an increasing conventional indigenous backlash against societal difficulties from a variety of sources.[54] The era of social reform in the nineteenth century then, must be understood as enunciating multifaceted and debated inter-relationships between women on the one hand and on the other, the emerging notions of citizen, nation and community. The limited contours of the women's question, on the other hand, were from the beginning also vulnerable to innovative connotations generated by women's conversations. The cultural nationalist project had given women the skills to shape their own modern subjectivities, however limited, and it had also ushered in the arrival of elite and middle-class women into the public arena, whether it is through social reform or anti-colonial nationalist movements. Local women's associations sprouted up throughout the country, and some single women rose to prominence in a diversity of social reform and nationalist activities, but mostly under the leadership of men. The realm of women's actions, undeniably, was developed steadily to embrace, as it were, both *ghar/ andar* (home) and *bahir* (world).[55]

Law has long played a pivotal role in concerted initiatives to strengthen the status of women in India. Legal reform has been advocated in the nineteenth century by social reformers, by women in the freedom struggle as well as in the women's liberation movement of present-time. Despite the fact that the emphasis and purposes of every motion of reform varied in significant methods, every motion became law as a mechanism for upgrading social, economic, political, and cultural position of women, and as a result, at least certain expectation was placed in law's ability to bring about these kinds of social transformation. At about the same time, each wave of reform voiced scepticism about the role of law in this social transformation. Each subsequent women's rights movement expressed some concern about the law's limitations in bringing about social change. Despite this, each movement decided to use the law in their fights. It may be claimed that the contradictions within the perspectives and approaches of these social reformers and feminist activists cannot be completely comprehended within the instrumental considerations of law. The complicated function of laws in women's rights movements should be examined, and it may be claimed that social reformers and feminist activists have sought to utilize law as a 'subversive site' to challenge and alter conventional understandings of gender, tradition, and culture in many ways.[56]

Hindus, who constituted the largest community and population in British India, may be proven to be an essential factor in the approaches of modification. As to if correct or incorrect, the Hindus could claim an extensive and magnificent cultural heritage, which was bolstered by Orientalist scholarship in the late eighteenth and early nineteenth centuries. During the nineteenth century, the Hindus quickly realized that 'reform' meant more than just changing beliefs or practices; it also meant addressing underlying issues of 'self-identity'. They were able to compare 'the state of their own society and culture with that of the West' as well as acquire a strong self-reflexivity about their own tradition as their knowledge of modern subjects like history, anthropology, politics, and natural sciences developed.[57] The world of reform was distant from homogeneous or integrated into its goals.

Therefore, Raja Rammohan Roy (1772-1833) and Keshub Chandra Sen (1838-84) both classified idolatry and the worship of multiple gods and goddesses as concerns that should be prioritized in any reformist initiative. Pandit Ishwar Chandra Vidyasagar (1820-91) and Behramji M. Malabari (1853-1912) dedicated their existence, future and destiny to the emancipation of women. Jyotirao Phule (1827-90), E.V. Ramasamy Periyar (1879-1973) and Bhimrao Ambedkar recognized caste as the major stumbling block on the road to social progress. To some extent, such differences were undoubtedly driven by individual histories and the conventional social and cultural arrangements at any specified place. In any case, in the nineteenth century caste was never as sensitive an issue in Bengal as it was in parts of western and southern India. Though people also shifted from one zone of activity to another, mostly due to the pressure of changed circumstances. In Maharashtra, Rao Saheb V.N. Mandlik (1833-89) approached the subject of woman's emancipation after his attempt to bring about modification in caste rules was unsuccessful due to the opposition from orthodox *pandits* and *shastris*. In Bengal, after controversial attempts at marriage reform, Keshub Chandra Sen progressively stepped towards religious experimentation. Vidyasagar, who had sought state intervention during the widow marriage campaign, resisted it in 1891,[58] when the government was enforced to amend its own laws so as to further protect the interests of young women. For reasons not fully understandable, 'the conservative opposition to the amended age of consent (1891) in the Punjab was never as rabid as it was in Bengal and Maharashtra'. However, despite their differences and such alterations, social and religious reform movements in the nineteenth and early twentieth centuries shared a few characteristics in common. For one, they were mostly led by the new western-educated middle classes and henceforth, failed to notice the very distinct characteristics of lower-class problems. Remarkably enough, even those opposing reform itself were ready to seize upon these. In British India, the orthodox Dharma Sabha of Bengal, which opposed the move to abolish *sati*, was the first to use the method of petitioning and counter-petitioning higher authorities.[59] Sumit Sarkar in his essay 'The Controlled Emancipation of Wives', stated that

Rammohan's initiatives for the abolition of *sati*, Vidyasagar's campaigns for widow remarriage and against *kulin* polygamy, the daring radicalism of Young Bengal, the repeated splits within the *Brahmo* movement essentially on issues closely related to the women's question, the reassertion of traditionalist views in the movements for Hindu 'revival' towards the end of the nineteenth century, the memorable literary expression of conflicting values and contemporary debates in Bankim Chandra's *Bisha-Briksha* (The Poison Tree) and Rabindranath's *Chokher Bali* (A Grain of Sand or Eyesore) and *Gora* would be labouring the obvious.[60]

The Age of Reform began with a restructuring of the English East India Company's bureaucratic organization and was later explained by British and imperial historians as an 'era of transition' for the benefit of Indians as well as the British.[61] The utmost attainment that Lord William Bentinck is best known for was the prohibition of *sati* or self-immolation of widows on the funeral pyres of their dead husbands. It was a social custom predominant in India since the ancient period; though J.S. Hawley has confirmed, it has always been very much the exception rather than the rule in Hindu life. During the colonial era, in the late eighteenth and first half of nineteenth centuries, this custom was revitalized on a larger spectrum in regions that encountered the maximum percentage of expansion under colonial authorities, namely the city of Calcutta and its surrounding districts. 'There', according to Rajat K. Ray, 'the practice became popular not only among the upper castes, but also among the peasant families of lower and intermediary castes, who achieved social mobility and then sought to legitimize their new status by imitating their caste superiors'.[62] This was the period when 'upwardly mobile members of the middle and lower-ranking castes' forced their women to become *satis* in order to strengthen their newly earned economic growth and prosperity with social stature.[63] Besides this socio-cultural justification and the religious concept of an ideal wife who should obey her husband through life and death, the other factor, which was discussed by Ludo Roche, was the greed of the relatives, which the new prosperity of the families had possibly engendered. The practice had become most prevalent in certain places where the *dayabhaga school* of personal Hindu law was pertinent. In comparison to the *mitakshara school*, it permitted the widow relatively greater right to inherit her deceased husband's property. According to Ashis Nandy, Rammohan himself thought of economic reasons crucial for the practice. Tanika Sarkar has pointed out that, however, '*dayabhaga* as it prevailed in Bengal gave widows only usufruct rights on behalf of their minor sons'.[64]

Lata Mani has shown that '*Sati* had drawn the attention of Christian missionaries and had been outlawed in Calcutta, which was under the jurisdiction of English law, by the Chief Justice of the Supreme Court as early as 1798.' At the same time,

> Brahmin pundits were constantly called upon to interpret scriptural law in civil cases and their opinion on whether or not the practice of *sati* had a basis in *scriptures* had become vital in the debate on *sati*. This is what had inspired Mritunjay Vidyalankar of the Fort William College to argue against the practice of *satidaha* (burning of wives of dead husbands) before the cause was taken up by Rammohan Roy.[65]

Even though the Christian missionaries were the first to attack this practice, it was a robust 'abolitionist campaign' led by Raja Rammohan Roy that provided the activism actual political traction. Eventually in 1829, Bentinck, the then Governor General outlawed *sati* by a government regulation, that could not be repealed by a Hindu petition to the Privy Council from the anti-abolitionist Dharma Sabha in 1830. On the other side, Rammohan along with 300 residents of Calcutta, presented a petition to Bentinck supporting the prohibition.[66] The petition was envisioned to counteract the organizing efforts of those who opposed any interference in the practice of *sati*. Through the actions of the British and the reaction of the more orthodox forces that safeguarded the practice of *sati*, law became a site within a broader discursive struggle about the scriptural legitimacy of *sati*. The implementation of the regulation that prohibiting *sati* triggered a highly public debate, in which the proponents and detractors of social reform were involved in a contest over tradition; over the power to define and redefine tradition.[67] Nevertheless, while the occurrence of *sati* decreased moderately after passing of the order, the concept and the myth of *sati* remained consistent in prevalent traditions, in spite of the modernist critique of the middle classes influenced by the ideology of western education and the reformist fervor of the British

Government. From Ashis Nandy's writings, we come to know that 'the idea was continually reaffirmed through epics, ballads and folktales to reappear again in public life as late as in 1987 in the much publicised *"sati of Roop Kanwar"* at village Deorala in Rajasthan.'[68]

The debate on *sati* had begun in the 1780s, much before Bentinck's arrival. Anand A. Yang has mentioned that generally,

> a woman was burnt together with her deceased husband, a practice termed *sahamarana* or *sahagamanan* i.e., dying together with. But if concremation was not possible, such as when a husband died in a distant place or a woman's pregnancy required that she wait till after delivery, a *sati* conformed to the practice of *anumarana* or *anugamana*, i.e. burning with the husband's ashes or with some other memento representing him, for example, his sandals, turban, or piece of clothing.[69]

Lata Mani has stated that it still continued after the implementation of its abolition in 1829. 'Public debate on social reform', as Tanika Sarkar and Sumit Sarkar remind us, 'was a very new historical development of the time and requires understanding of how and among whom it took place.' In this case, the debate took place in the public domain between British officials and various strands of Indian literati, with Indian reformers engaging in prolonged contentions and discussions with one another and with their orthodox counterparts. It is important to keep in mind that the practice of *sati* pertained to the sphere of family or personal law as defined by Hastings, a domain in which the native Hindus were supposed to be governed by their own laws. The sensational portrayal of *sati* in British official discourse increased its significance. The prohibition of *sati* symbolized 'the noble implications of the reformist drive of liberals and evangelicals'; literally, a success story in which western, Christian sensibility, horrified by a cruel practice imposed on and carried out by Indian women put an end to it. In the years between 1815 and 1824, 6,632 cases of *sati* were reported for the three Presidencies of Bengal, Bombay and Madras. Of these, 5,997 (90.4 per cent) occurred in Bengal. In the 14 years between 1815 and 1828, a grand total of 8,134 cases of *satis* were reported for the Bengal Presidency. But as the data reveal, the practice was not uniformly observed across the region but predominated in specific areas. The division of Calcutta alone accounted for 5,119

Table 1.1: Sati Cases in Bengal Presidency, 1815-1828[72]

Division	*1815*	*1816*	*1817*	*1818*	*1819*	*1820*	*1821*	*1822*	*1823*	*1824*	*1825*	*1826*	*1827*	*1828*	*Total*
Calcutta	253	289	442	544	421	370	392	328	340	373	398	324	337	308	5,119
Dacca	31	24	52	58	55	51	52	45	40	40	101	65	49	47	710
Murshidabad	11	22	42	30	25	21	11	22	13	14	21	8	9	10	260
Patna	20	29	49	57	40	42	59	70	49	42	38	43	55	55	689
Banaras	48	65	103	137	92	93	114	102	121	93	64	70	49	33	1,153
Bareilly	15	13	19	13	17	20	15	16	12	10	17	8	18	10	203
Total	378	442	707	839	650	597	654	583	575	572	639	518	517	463	8,134

cases or almost 63 per cent of the Presidency total, followed by Banaras, Dacca, and Patna divisions in a distant second, third, and fourth position respectively.[70]

The legislative prohibition of *sati* was the outcome of a debate during which 8,134 instances of *sati* were documented, primarily, however, not exclusively, among 'upper caste Hindus' in the area adjacent to the city of Calcutta.[71] The debate, which was sparked predominantly by colonial administrators, was seen as exemplifying the anxiety for the position of women, which developed during nineteenth century. Though the controversy was fuelled by some deliberations that had very little to do with women. Radha Kumar (1993) has pointed out that *sati* was a bold and valorous practice and had become phenomenal.[73] Its socio-religious foundation laid in the notion of the wife as the true half of the husband, who followed him in life and death. The virtue of the practice derived from a religious logic that deemed a widow inauspicious for having outlived her husband; an unnatural circumstance caused by her 'sinful nature in this, or a previous life'.[74] It is difficult to trace the exact origin of the rite, although it is believed that *sati* may have been practiced by upper-caste Hindus for almost 2,000 years.[75] According to Yang, 'the *Puranas* (A vast genre of Indian literature about a wide range of topics) mentioned *sati* as an option for widows; they also prescribed a life of asceticism for them.'[76] According to studies, remarriage of widows was undoubtedly approved by ancient Hindu laws, and sacred texts were not favourable to the practice of *sati*. From the time of the *Puranas*, the rite obtained some credibility, and there was indication that *sati* was popular among Rajputs in Rajasthan during Mughal times, as well as among the upper castes in the kingdom of Vijayanagara in south India. However, by the seventeenth century, *sati* had become largely voluntary, and by the early eighteenth century, it was a rare occurrence.

The argument came to an end with the success of those who preferred the abolition of *sati*. Regulation XVII of the Bengal code defended the abolition, confirmed by the Governor-General in Council on 4 December 1829. The Regulation stated that 'the practice was revolting to the feelings of human nature' and was 'nowhere enjoined by the religion of the Hindus as an imperative duty'.[77]

Although this legislation characterized the accomplishment of Rammohan and his group, Rammohan's own position with regard to *sati* is fascinating. On the one hand, he assumed that the practice symbolized everything that was wrong with the subject matter of 'new Hinduism', that it was an anomaly and departure from the 'original'. Such a practice could only exist because the proponents of idolatry and their misdirected followers believed that such heinous crimes were part of their religious system. On the other hand, he did not deny that *sati* was sanctioned in scriptures. He argued against *sati* because

> it involved a desire for *sakam karma* (the fruits of one's action), in this case, the promise of heaven. This desire made the practice of *sati* less virtuous than that of *brahmacharya* (austere abstinence), which the widow was expected to carry out in *niskama karma* (a detached way) for the rest of her life. Widows, therefore, had to earn greater virtue by leading a desire-free life rather than aspire for easy access to heaven by committing *sati*.[78]

However, Rammohan Roy was anxious that any endeavours on the part of the colonial administration to outlaw the practice of *sati* would fail. He suspected that interference by the colonial administration in the sacred and religious customs of Hindu communities would trigger anger and vehement resistance.[79] By legislating against *sati*, the colonial state might only assist to incite an orthodox backlash, by generating anxiety that the British were determined on intruding in religious matters.[80] Despite his obvious difference of opinion with the colonial policy for abolishing *sati*, Rammohan Roy openly supported the regulation that prohibiting *sati* when it was enacted in December 1829 by the British administration.[81] Although Roy was shrewd enough to acknowledge the ways in which Indian patriarchy functioned to decrease women's status to such a miserable state that even death was not an option, he nonetheless exchanged much with colonial discourse by highlighting scriptural sanction, thereby admitting the religious foundation of Indian tradition.[82]

It has been argued that the battle over the abolition of *sati* by the British became 'less about women and their status and more about what constituted authentic cultural tradition'.[83] Lata Mani has pointed out that 'we must understand the practice of *sati* as well as the campaign against and for it, not simply in terms of attitudes to women, but in the larger, more complex context of the encounter between colonialism and the Indian elites.' This rendezvous fashioned *sati* as the archetype for Indian womanhood, so that the assault on the practice as well as its protection had little connection to its authentic occurrence or to faiths regarding the position of women and more to do with validations of colonial rule and various methods of confrontation to it, whether this struggle prompted tradition, i.e. 'We are different from you' or modernity, i.e. 'We are as civilized as you'.[84] Similarly, significant is the colonial essence of the modifications, as the positions of the Indian reformers in a noteworthy technique reflected the colonial attention and consequently, the contradiction of the imperial strategy organizers. The authoritative colonial supposition at that moment was that religious beliefs were the foundation of Indian society and this religion was encrypted in the sacred texts. This interpretation of the colonial government suspected that indigenous societies were completely submissive to the mandates of the scriptures. The colonial state's 'civilizing mission' was therefore viewed as returning to the indigenous people the realities of their very own slight read and much less recognized *shastras*. Lata Mani has contended that the entire discussion regarding *sati* was established on religious texts, and the British administration chose to outlaw this practice only after reaching the conclusion that the custom was not sanctioned by the scriptures. Because the colonial rulers placed such a high value on scriptures, both Indian reformers and their detractors relied on ancient religious texts to argue their corresponding incidences. The viciousness or absurdity of the practice, or the condition of women for whom the reform was destined, were secondary apprehensions in a debate that focused mostly on the concept of custom. According to Mani, 'women are neither subjects nor objects but, rather, the ground of the discourse on sati; .... women themselves are marginal to the debate'. Thus, the scriptures, which had recently been valorized by Orientalists, generated credibility for social reforms, while women were denied agency in their own liberation.[85]

In the first half of the nineteenth century, the term 'status of women' remained prominent in discourse concerning social reforms. Following the prohibition of *sati*, attention shifted to the issue of widow remarriage, as their plight was prominently mentioned in the writings of missionaries and liberals. In spite of the efforts by some persons like Rammohan Roy, Ishwar Chandra Vidyasagar, and others for reforms during nineteenth century, a vast segment of women who were widows by civil status were still being forced to live celibate and austere lives. According to the facts, while Rammohan Roy's venture was successful, Vidyasagar's purpose resulted in what has been characterized as an unavoidable defeat.[86] Lucy Carroll has shown that

> the problem of widows, especially of child widows, was largely a prerogative of the higher Hindu castes among whom child marriage was practiced and remarriage prohibited. On the other hand, the lower castes, (particularly *Sudra* and the Untouchables), were approximately 80 per cent of the Hindu population. They neither practiced child marriage nor prohibited the remarriage of widows.[87]

A child widow's situation was even worse; neglected and ill-treated from her very childhood, she grew up as a helpless being doomed to suffer. During this period, which was under consideration, the number of such child widows was extremely high. The renowned social worker, Kamaladevi Chattopadhyay in her book, *Indian Women's Battle for Freedom*, referred to a survey in Calcutta in 1891, which found 10,000 widows below the age of four in and around the city, which then had a total population of only four lakhs.[88]

Ishwar Chandra Vidyasagar, a renowned scholar who had devoted his life in promoting Bengali language and the printing of school textbooks, planned to prepare young minds ethically, took the lead in Bengal. Despite being influenced by William Carey, Vidyasagar's goal of morally educating young minds had nothing to do with evangelism but more to do with his own understanding of 'dharma' (path/way of rightness or duty). A scholar entrenched in the indigenous tradition, Vidyasagar was encouraged by the English responsiveness of associating 'life with reason', which bestowed upon him an untiring will for social action. He was drawn to the reasonable impact of western knowledge and humanism, but not to the alien styles of living.[89] Vidyasagar, like Rammohan, invoked the *shastras* to argue that widow remarriage was approved by the religious texts. However, his application of *shastras* varied from Rammohan's in that he used them to swipe into the root of popular support for social reforms and complement it with the authority of intelligence and the renewal of common Hindu sensibility.[90] According to Vidyasagar, the Hindu religion recommended laws that equally applied to men and women. Before arranging a marriage, Hindu scriptures asserted that it was necessary to research the boy's and girl's family roots and traditions. Just as 'a man could marry again if his wife was dead or barren, a woman had the same right in a similar situation. If it were shameful for a widowed woman to marry again, it should be just the same for a man'.[91] Vidyasagar was not a member of the Bengal Brahmo Sabha but he worked with that organization and with the Tattvabodhini Sabha to institute numerous written appeals for the reform of the institution of marriage, including the abolition of *kulin* polygamy. His public efforts winded up in the publication of a book *Marriage of Hindu Widows*, which tried to mention proper *shastric* authorities for the remarriage of widows.[92] He published an article in *Tattvabodhini Patrika*, highlighting the scriptural sanction of widow remarriage.[93] The marriage of child brides with infirm and aged *kulin* bridegrooms inevitably led to insufferable pain of celibate widowhood among upper-caste women. Vidyasagar in his two successive tracts of 1855 utilized a verse from *Parashara Samhita* to demonstrate that widow remarriage was sanctioned by the *shastras* and customary usage advising on the contrary should be overruled.[94] He pointed out that 'the *Parashara Samhita* was the scriptural authority of the Kaliyuga, so during the nineteenth century, we must follow its dictates sanctioning widow remarriage'. *Parashara Samhita* explicitly professed that 'on receiving no tidings of a husband, on his demise, on his turning an ascetic, on his being found impotent, or on his degradation, a woman could have another husband'.[95] Vidyasagar sent to Government a petition with approximately a thousand signatures demanding an appropriate enactment. Numerous memorials were received by the Council from all over India, both for and against the provisions of the Bill. The number of opponents was much larger, about 56,000 as against a few more than 5,000 who supported the Bill. Raja Radhakanta Dev of Calcutta arranged a petition of about 37,000 persons against the Bill. Tanika Sarkar has argued that

> It is significant that while official hesitation over abolishing widow immolation lasted sixty years, widow remarriage was decided upon fairly quickly. Though

the idea was rejected in 1837, it was revived in official circles again in 1855 when Vidyasagar approached Grant and Colville with a plea and a scriptural citation in favour of widow remarriage.[96]

The Act, legalizing the marriage of Hindu widows, was promulgated in July 1856.[97] During the nineteenth or the first half of the twentieth century socio-cultural realm of Bengal, women had not as hitherto appeared as sentient themes of history, attempting to proclaim their own authority. On one hand, *Bamabodhini Patrika*[98] epitomized the only 'feminine voice' addressed in favour of the reform, on the other hand, it also recognized in an acquiescent temper the ineffectuality of the exertion.[99]

The Report on the Census of British India 1881 observes that 'it was the discrepancy of age between the husband and wife that led to the increase in the number of widows'.[100] The statistics, given in Table 1.2, validates the wide-ranging incidence of widowhood in Bengal between 1881 and 1891.

TABLE 1.2: HINDU WIDOWS AMONGST WOMEN (IN PERCENTAGE) AGED 0-39 IN BENGAL, 1881-1891[101]

Age Group (in Years)	*Northern Bengal*	*Eastern Bengal*	*Western Bengal*
0-9	0.49	0.37	0.49
10-14	4.28	3.48	4.29
15-19	9.88	9.23	10.63
20-24	16.59	15.86	17.62
25-29	24.11	25.41	25.86
30-39	41.58	43.29	42.39

Sekhar Bandyopadhyay has aptly pointed out that '*Sati*, the eradication of which was on Rammohan's reform agenda, was abolished by Regulation XVII of 1829. Widow-burning was made a penal offence, any violation of which would immediately invite the regulating hand of the state.' According to Bandyopadhyay, 'Rammohan could thus save widows from being immolated with the help of the constant presence of state power and the law-enforcing apparatus.' Nevertheless, Vidyasagar did not witness many widows remarried, because in this case, the Act of 1856 only legitimized their marriage, but could not make it socially acceptable; nor was it possible to enforce it with the help of the police force. So that, in the climax, Vidyasagar had to depend on 'social consent' rather than 'state power', and 'his defeat was obvious'.[102] Lucy Carroll has argued that 'the legislation was intrinsically conservative in character, as on remarriage it disinherited the widow of her deceased husband's property, and thus endorsed the Brahmanical norm of rewarding only the chaste, prayerful widow'.[103] The Hindu Widows' Remarriage Act (Act XV of 1856), an act of statutory social reform that generated judicial controversies over its interpretation and application and set-in clear relief the three categories of 'Hindu Law, Customary Law and Statutory Law' utilized by the judicial branch of the Company's administration,[104] allowed widows to remarry. Its implications, on the other hand, was restricted and conflicting.[105] The circumstance was not unique in western India, where an unknown Maharashtrian Brahmin reformer favoured remarriage of infant widows as a means of controlling their sexuality and making their reproductive capability socially useful as early as 1841. In the 1860s, the movement to encourage widow remarriage spread among the Western educated middle classes, and the controversy between reformers and critics became more heated and resentful. In 1866, Vishnushastri Pandit founded a society to promote widow remarriage, while his adversaries established a competing organization. In 1870, the reformists suffered a major setback when Shankaracharya of Kabir Math found them to be at fault in a public debate in Poona, and a large number of them acknowledged the ritual of penance. Even though there were extraordinary widows, such as Pandita Ramabai, who left her trace in public life of Maharashtrian society and politics, the movement for widow remarriage ended with a sniffle, with only 38 widows remarried by the end of the century, and in those cases, the couples were compelled to immense social pressure and social exclusion.[106] In fact, the number of widows who remarried endured incredibly insignificant and as a consequence of this, social acceptance of the act was hard. Certainly, upwardly mobile middle and lower caste peasants who had the right to remarry attempted to prevent their widows from doing so. Vidyasagar was disappointed by the lack of enthusiasm for implementing the new measure. Indeed, in the years following the act's passage, he paid for so many widow remarriages until he was in debt. Worse still, Vidyasagar discovered that those who had married widows threatened to desert their wives unless he met their unreasonable demands.[107]

On the other hand, support for the cause of remarriage grew slowly after the passing of the act. The situation varied widely from region to region, for in Haryana, where 'the practice of widow remarriage was already in vogue at a large scale, the new act provided such marriages with legitimacy and further social acceptance.'[108] As Prem Chowdhry has shown, in the Haryana-Punjab region,

> where *karewa* (levirate marriage), in which the widow was accepted as the bride by one of the brothers of the deceased husband, was a common practice among the overwhelming majority of the landowning castes, the act vested greater power on the deceased husband's family to oblige the widow to marry again.[109]

Veerasalingam Pantulu, who established Society for Social Reform in the Telugu-speaking regions of Madras Presidency in 1878, spearheaded the reform movement in favour of widow remarriage. In the face of stiff opposition, he officiated the first widow remarriage in the region in 1881 in his hometown Rajahmundry. Preference for the reforms grew gradually, and a Widow Remarriage Association was established in 1891 with the patronage of the eminent people of the city.[110] However, according to Charles Heimsath, 'this enthusiasm notwithstanding, by this time only three such marriages had been arranged by the reformers. The colonial legislation for reform, in other words, had a very uneven impact on Indian society.'[111] The incompetence of Vidyasagar's campaign to produce significant results has been interpreted as a mismatch between his ongoing dedication and social consciousness and the accurate challenges of converting such commitment into practice due to the utter lack of a social milieu willing to carry it forward. However, women's own writings and testimonials from the late nineteenth century compel us to reconsider our assessments of legislative transformation. Many women did not see marriage as the solution to their problems and instead looked for educational and employment possibilities for widows, striving for financial stability rather than re-entering into the domestic fold.[112]

Vidyasagar proceeded his reform movement in Bengal, prompting it to oppose polygamy and child marriage, and eventually maintained a Age of Consent Act in 1860, which set the age of consent for the consummation of marriage at ten years for women. Another piece of legislation raised the age to twelve in 1891, but census figures suggest that in the twentieth century child marriage was still a common social practice among all castes irrespective of high or low.[113] Despite this, there were various institutions in Bengal attempting to improve social attitudes and accept widow-remarriage. Remarriages of widows have been reported in Pabna, Mymensingh, Bakargunge, Jalpaiguri, and Rajshahi as a result of their efforts. According to statistics from the Bengal Census Report of 1931, the third decade of the twentieth century saw a higher number of widow remarriages.

TABLE 1.3: NUMBER OF MARRIED AND UNMARRIED FEMALES AMONG HINDUS BY AGE-GROUPS TO NEAREST BIRTHDAY, 1931[114]

Age	*Married*	*Widowed*
4-6	47,106	3,711
7-13	613,402	19,905
14-16	536,094	30,261
17-23	1,355,654	149,949
24-26	628,750	131,555
27-33	857,504	306,953
34-36	301,864	187,791

It is to be noted from the above figures in Table 1.3, that the maximum number of girls got married when they were between 7 and 23 years of age, but surprisingly enough, the percentage of widowed girls was the minimum in this age group.[115]

It is, therefore, evident from the Table 1.4,[116] that the general ratio of widowed females had decreased in 1931 as compared with 1921 and widow remarriage was, to some extent, popular and the number of widows was also decreasing, even so, the improvement was not remarkable.[117]

The nineteenth-century social reformers did not have an unwavering faith in the power of the law to eradicate social practices.

TABLE 1.4: NUMBER OF MARRIED AND WIDOWED HINDU FEMALES PER 1,000 IN BENGAL IN 1931, 1921 AND 1911

Hindu Female Age	*1931*		*1921*		*1911*	
	Married	*Widowed*	*Married*	*Widowed*	*Married*	*Widowed*
0-5	26	2	7	1	5	1
5-10	260	9	85	6	120	6
10-15	505	22	584	38	671	34
15-20	866	83	867	94	874	93
20-40	739	248	713	276	724	266

Rammohan Roy acknowledged that a ban on *sati* was unlikely to end this violent exercise instantly, and he was concerned about the political ramifications of getting involved with the colonial state. The discrepancies of engaging with the colonial state were brought to a head at the end of the century in the debate over child marriage. Law, according to social reformers, had a role to engage in bringing about the transformation in perceptions and traditions that would be needed to eradicate these social practices. At the same time, it is critical to acknowledge that their primary focus was not solely on legislative reform. Social reformers positioned substantial position on the role of education in bringing about change and removing unjust social practices. However, in this discourse, law was a site on which competing visions of Hindu tradition and custom were fought out. Social reformers attempted to change this culture as well as norms even when looking for assistance for this restructuring in Hindu religious texts. Conservative and orthodox powers that objected to reform sought to validate the authority of their very differing perspectives of Hindu tradition and custom in Hindu scriptures. The conflict was primarily over who had the authority to define tradition and custom; it was fought on legal grounds. In these debates, law was once again a battleground for the much wider notions of social reformers and political nationalists. This time, however, the acceptability of the law itself was at stake. On one hand, social reformers were able to succeed because their claim to raise the age of consent was passed into law, on the other; political nationalists were tremendously effective in rearticulating the domestic realm as being beyond the reach of colonial intervention.[118]

The institution of child marriage was widespread throughout India, encompassing religious, caste and geographical boundaries. According to Padma Anagol, 'the long and impressive historical literature on the institution of Indian child marriage starting from the 1960s has unpicked the intimate relationships between sexual politics and sexual identities in the formation of new nationalist subjectivities both in the metropole (Britain) and the colony (India) displaying the power of the cultural realms in nationalist struggles.'[119] Law regarding child marriage has evolved as a result of long-term public campaigns that began during the colonial period and continued into the post-independence period. A. Kuppuswami has stated that 'the law givers, such as Manu, Yajnavalkya, Narada, etc., did not mandate child marriage and adult marriages were the norm during the Vedic period.' But later,

> during the post-*smriti* period, child marriages became the norm for the bride and girls were married between the ages of eight and twelve among the upper castes. But among the lower castes (which followed the custom of bride price, sanctioned divorce, and remarriage for women), consensual marriages between adults were accepted as the norm.[120]

The advancement of numerous national organizations formed by Indian women, their attempts to collaborate with each other, and their interrelations with Indian males, British officials, and British women in the second half of the 1920s can be seen through the subject of child marriage. The emphasis on this specific subject is especially noteworthy as it was the first social reform issue, in which structured women performed a significant character in both the advancement of justifications, in this situation against child marriage, and the effort for political petitioning.[121] During the nineteenth-century reform movements, one of the main considerations of the reformers was to raise the legal age for girls' marriage. Although the British persisted to emphasize the barbarism of child marriage, there was strong opposition among Hindus to raising the marriage age. Through

Brahmo endeavours, a Marriage Act was passed in 1872, setting the minimum marriageable age for non-Hindus at fourteen for girls and eighteen for boys. The Hindu community was ignorant because this act had no major impact on them. The government appraised a variety of measures to raise the marriageable age of Hindu girls.[122]

After the East India Company relinquished administrative power to the British Crown in 1858, the Age of Consent Act of 1860 was enacted as one of the first reforms, which established a minimum age of ten years for sexual intercourse.[123] The question resurfaced in the 1880s, and the criminal code was amended in 1891 to raise the age of consent to twelve years.[124] However, this legislation did not fix the problem of child marriage and the controversy raged on in the twentieth century, with social reformers such as Rai Saheb Harbilas Sarda spearheading a campaign to pass legislation prohibiting child marriages. Despite the fact that it was proposed to end child marriage, which was prevalent among Hindus, liberal Muslim women supported this Bill at local meetings and at national level through women's organizations like the All India Women's Conference (AIWC), Women's Indian Association (WIA) and the National Council of Women in India (NCWI). Notwithstanding the increasing fissure between Muslim and Hindu male politicians, feminists in the AIWC and WIA from both religion – Hindu and Muslim cooperatively condemned child marriage as an Indian tradition.[125] These women's organizations, with their focus on women's education and health, also struggled for this enactment as they sensed that marriage and child birth at a very young age is detrimental for women's physical and intellectual development. After a long campaign throughout the 1920s, the CMRA was finally enacted in 1929.[126] Feminist movements permitted Sarda's Bill to pass in the Central Legislative Council consisting of British and few Indian men. However, after independence of India in 1947, women finally became lawmakers, the principally male-dominated Indian Parliament accompanied this pattern of men's laws for women's welfare.[127] This controversial issue of marriageable age for girls demands special attention and is discussed in detail in the next two chapters.

However, in order to determine a woman's social status, her position in the family must first be examined.[128] Marriage was an irrevocable sacrament under customary Hindu law, but unlike a man, who could marry as many women as he wanted and desert his wife, a woman had no such rights. Marriage was not an option for a Hindu girl; it was the only goal in life; its satisfaction laid in having a son for the family. She was married by her parents as part of their religious responsibilities, along with a dowry. Arranged marriage and pre-puberty marriage for girls were mandatory.[129] The family was of chief reputation in the life of an Indian.[130] On marriage a bride was taken into her husband's family, which was usually joint.[131] Joint family – a term defined in different ways by different scholars[132] – characteristically meant joint residence, often joint ownership of property or business, of two or three generations related through males.[133] The modern perception of the nuclear family, comprising a husband, wife and children, borrowed from Western culture, had not developed then. There was so much bias against women that it was considered an act of immodesty if a husband happened to show any outward expression of attachment for his wife. She was, however, expected to show concern and care for all the members of the family without any discrimination. Marriage was a social institution and a couple's union was viewed as a social association between the brides' and bridegrooms' families. Three principal matters related to Hindu marriage were – *dharma* or religious duties to be performed by the couple, *proja* or procreation, and *rati* or conjugal love.[134] It may be understood from a Brahmo lady's memoir that a prospective mother-in-law, a Hindu, confessed her fears of damnation if her son married outside the Hindu fold and thereby lost his right to offer water to her thirsty soul after her death. The position of a wife in her in-laws' house and also in the wider kinship group was heavily reliant on her ability to give birth to a son.[135] Marriage had three distinct administrative levels, the first of which was a betrothal or engagement ceremony. The couple was irrevocably bound together the moment the ceremony was performed, regardless of whether or not the marriage was consummated. Even if the Hindu husband died before the second marriage was consummated or performed, the girl became a widow. The second ceremony involved the pre-pubertal girl being transported to her natal place, where she would stay until she reached puberty. The time when the bride reached puberty, it was determined the start of her married life. A third ceremony was then performed, which was known as *garbhadhan* ritual, consummation of marriage straight after the first menstrual flow.[136] In Bengal during the early nineteenth century, high-caste girls aged between eight and ten were married to men aged from fourteen to eighteen.[137]

It has been argued that the Hindu family was patrilineal in descent, patrilocal in residence and patriarchal in authority.[138] Child marriages, also known as *gouridan*, was considered an obscenity in Hindu society. Girls were frequently married off at the age of ten or even younger.[139] A huge age difference between husband and wife was the magnificent characteristic of Bengali marriages. The age of the bride at marriage was possibly the most important organizational factor of sentimental impacts in matrimony. The most heinous effect of the age gap between husband and wife was child widowhood, which provided many girls unacceptable guests in their husbands' and fathers' families, with no option to remarry or work elsewhere. Most narratives of pre-puberty marriage written by women, on the other hand, begin with stories of immature delight at the pomp and grandeur of the wedding ceremony. The wedding presents of expensive ornaments and sarees, the festivals, songs, and lighting fascinated the child brides, knowing that all this spectacle was for their advantage, their delight was still tempered by ambiguous insecurities.[140] The family structure was systematized under the eldest male member or *karta*, while his wife, *ginni*, was at the forefront of the domestic side of the household. A young bride had the lowest status in the family, she was almost always allocated the most difficult and burdensome household duties.[141] After her marriage, the young girl went to her husband's house and discovered that her life had become 'a crown of thorns'. She had no autonomy and was completely controlled by her husband's family. The young wife had to obey and satisfy her mother-in-law, who was the supreme authority in her new home.[142] Although all child brides were not handled so rudely, the emotional pain of leaving the house appears to have been a familiar component of their encounter. Rassundari Debi was married when she was twelve years old. She admired the marriage rituals; however as soon as they were finished, she eventually understood that she would have to leave her house. At that moment, she recalled, 'I clung to her (mother) and said, "Ma! Please don't send me away." The crowd around me began to weep and to comfort me. My mother put her arms around me and said, "You are my own little mother...don't be scared, the Great Lord is with you."...By then, I was petrified.... I was speechless.'[143]

Typically, a young girl was married off to a family rather than an individual. The institution's primary goal was clearly to provide happiness to the large family unit rather than to the individuals who she married. The perfect bride was one who won the approval of the enlarged family of her husband, particularly her in-laws.[144] The young bride's position enhanced slightly when she became the mother of a son, but she gained prominence only when she became the *ginni*, which was usually at an advanced age.[145] A young couple would never talk to each other in front of their elders. The wife never ate in front of her husband. If the husband appeared while she was eating, she had to stop immediately and he had no choice but to move out of sight into another room. Women were frequently neglected in Hindu families; no care was taken of their health, and they were expected to do a significant amount of household work even when they were ill. They were denied healthy food, and as a result of a lack of a proper diet and health care, they frequently suffered from serious diseases that worsened over time. During childbirth, a pregnant woman was isolated in a small thatched room, newly built or partially unpremeditated in an open area in the internal part of the house, and frequently damp, unnatural, and scratchy. Both mothers and infants died at a higher rate as a result of early marriage and childbirth. Many women did not live long in these conditions, and the death rate of young women was much higher than that of men.[146] With a few exceptions, a mother-in-law showed little compassion for her daughter-in-law, apparently because the latter posed a potential threat to a power that she herself had acquired after a long period of waiting and perseverance.[147] Nonetheless, the older generation of women remained to be important members of the traditional joint family. The grandmothers taught the new bride about the family's regulations and customs, frequently a friendship formulated between them that would not have been possible despite the generation gap.[148] Sarat Kumari Chaudhurani's short story *Didima* portrays a child wife who was treated with love and sympathy. The grandmother of the house and other women elders of the family poured love and warmth upon the young housewife, who was barely ten years old. They were apprehensive to provide her with adequate food and other comforts, and because she was a young girl, she was relieved of domestic duties. If she messed up the work, which she did, she was not chastised. Instead, the grandmother showed her how to do it and compassionately trained her. During the day, she was permitted to meet her young husband. Recognizing that the little girl might be homesick, the grandmother volunteered to arrange for her visit to her father's house. She also attended to the little girl's comforts, such as ensuring that the young bride was given an adequate amount of milk, which she was used to in her paternal home.[149] However, because the sacramental Hindu marriage was irreversible, the issue of 'individual agency', 'consent', or 'self-choice' was rendered ineffective within the system.[150] Rajendralal Mitra, at a meeting convened at the palace of the Rajas of *Shova Bazar*, asserted, 'In it (Hindu marriage) there is no selection, no self-choice, no consent on the part of the bride. She is an article of gift; she is given away even as a cow or any other cattle.... There is in Hinduism not the remotest idea of choice and whoever changed any small part of it was no Hindu'.[151] Nor did the bridegroom have any agency in the selection of the bride.

In this regard, we can mention the name of a renowned Bengali writer, Giribala Devi, who has narrated her life story,[152] providing a comprehensive description of the everyday tasks of a young housewife. Volumes of Bengali literature discuss the injustices and sufferings meted out to women in the second half of the nineteenth century. *Subarnalata,*[153] written by Ashapurna Devi, specifically addresses the evils of child marriage, and *Kari Diye Kinlam,*[154] written by Bimal Mitra, is also the story of an unhappy woman from a wealthy Bengali family. However, exceptional instances were always present. Giribala Devi openly admitted that it was primarily due to her husband's assistance and guidance that she was able to develop her literary potential. Giribala also had the support of her father-in-law, who was a patron of learning and was particularly interested in women's education. Giribala went on to become a well-known poet, receiving the Calcutta University's Lila Prize at a very old age in 1983.[155] According to Rani Chanda's account *Amar Ma'r Baper Bari*, there were a few families in Bengal at the time where women, even widows, were treated with love and respect. Her eldest aunt had lost her husband on the fourth day of their marriage, but she was still the most powerful woman in the family, second only to her mother-in-law. Despite her parents' entreaties, she refused to return home and instead spent her life freely and happily with her husband's family. Her brothers-in-law and sisters-in-law adored and admired her. They teased her, amused her, and always treated her as if she were one of them, holding her in high regard. She was upbeat in their company. She was a young girl when she was married, and she hardly remembered her husband; nonetheless, she had a deep affection for her husband's family.[156]

Purdah (the practice in certain Hindu and Muslim societies of screening women from men or strangers, especially by means of a curtain) was another major impediment for women, who were confined to the innermost part of the house and lived in complete seclusion, with little opportunity to widen their ideas and broaden their outlook. Young housewives were not even allowed to leave the house.[157] However, a shift in social norms in this regard had far-reaching consequences for the relationships between men and women. Satyendranath Tagore made headlines when he drove his wife, Jnanadanandini Devi, in an open carriage. Jnanadanandini had been a child bride who had grown accustomed to being fed by her mother-in-law. When the other women of the Tagore's household accompanied this model, the citizens of Calcutta regarded the situation as a major embarrassment and misconduct. However, other Brahmos soon challenged the 'seclusion' restrictions as well.[158] Women of the Tagore household, specifically, Jnanadanandini Devi, were effective and instrumental in bringing about groundbreaking sartorial changes, some of which blended components of western styles with the indigenous sari. In accordance with the leading patriarchal institution in upper-class homes of renaming a bride – Rabindranath's wife, Bhabatarini was renamed as Mrinalini and the young bride was educated at the Loreto Convent and skilled in numerous social and housewifely skills.[159] The palanquin was a popular mode of transportation for women in both villages and towns. It was considered a serious offence for a young husband to walk down the street with his wife openly. Keshub Chandra Sen, a member of an old Brahmo family, defied this convention in order to protest injustice to women. On 13 April 1862, Keshub accompanied by his wife in a *palki* (palanquin), descended from Kolutola to Jorasanko, an act that can be considered a major step towards the women's freedom movement.[160]

Upper caste Hindus practiced polygamy freely in the second half of the nineteenth century. The system was extensively prevalent among the *Kulin* Brahmins of Bengal, who frequently married more than a hundred wives. Ishwar Chandra Vidyasagar records in anguish,

> With the *Kulin* brahmin, the sacred rite of matrimony had been notoriously degraded to a system of shameful traffic. These men for the sordid gain of some paltry sum, visited village after village, accepting the hands of crores of maidens, the great majority of whom were destined never to enjoy the blessings of a wedded life.[161]

The *kulin* Brahmins were generally uneducated and since they were unable to earn a decent living, they took to the practice of marrying many wives as a means of subsistence, visiting their wives by turn mostly to collect gifts and money. In different publications, educated *bhadralok* started protesting against *kulin* polygamy. The *Calcutta Christian Observer* proposed in July 1841, 'Prostitution, abortion and infanticide are evils which we may venture to enumerate as immediately flowing from such a system'.[162] The editorial of the *Friend of India*, on 3 July 1856, remarked that 'a Brahman of any grade should marry an unlimited number of wives, that he should receive heavy douceurs with each, and that he should maintain none of them is a custom as offensive to Hinduism as to social policy'.[163] One of the explanations for the perseverance of the malicious custom was that 'the *Kulin* girls could not be given in marriage to anyone of a lower caste rank'. On the other hand, in accordance with social custom, they had to be married at an early age. Child marriage was unanimously practiced, with the exception of the *kulin* women who had to wait for a long time in life until a groom with appropriate sacramental rank had been discovered.[164] The *kulin* Brahmin men took advantage of the situation and demanded a large dowry. Because of these circumstances, poor girls were forced to marry old, diseased, or otherwise undesirable men, if they could marry at all. Many were murdered in secret to avoid scandals that would bring their families into disrepute. Dwarakanath Gangopadhyay, a pioneer of women's liberation, conducted personal investigations and discovered that within ten years, about 32 *kulin* Brahmin girls, who purportedly died of cholera, were in fact poisoned to death in his own village. Dwarakanath was so moved by their plight that he published a journal called *Abala Bandhab* (Women Friendly) to draw attention to the sufferings of these unfortunate women born in high *kulin* society.[165] However, there was little evidence of women's experience of polygamy who had to undergo it. The memoir or preferably the reminiscences of Nistarini Debi, an aunt of Brahmabandhab Upadhyay, the well-known revolutionary, was indeed a notable example. It has provided a different approach to the emotional effects of *kulin* polygamy as sustained by so many women. She referred with disrespect to her *kulin* grandfather, who had 54 wives; however, described her grandmother's first meeting with him, 'So long as her husband was there, she walked about near him, her veil properly drawn. It was as if she was trying to imprint the image of this handsome man on her mind the way one meditates on the image of one's deity.'[166]

In the nineteenth century, the procedures of conveying some kind of education to the daughters of middle-class families, either at home or in school, were introduced. During 1920s, educated families began to reject child marriage in favour of educating their daughters and ensuring their healthy development into adulthood. The large proportion of witnesses to the Age of Consent Committee: 1928-29, all from middle or upper-class backgrounds, supported raising the marriage age. Early marriage not only resulted in child-widowhood for many women, but it also meant the end of formal education in the majority of cases.[167] Most parents' principal intention was to make their daughters much more attractive as future brides. The reason behind this was that progressive men wanted wives who were enlightened and educated, if possible with some understanding of English, with the aim of having a help-mate in a professional career and a companion in their personal life.[168] Judith Walsh has argued that the nineteenth century reformations of Hindu domestic ideas grew out of the interactions of a hegemonic, transnational nineteenth-century domestic discourse and indigenous domestic concerns and practices and has juxtaposed nineteenth-century Bengali domestic manuals along with Euro-American domestic manuals. In her view, the issue of family was central to the discourse on women's education. Husband was the head of the household who worked outside the domestic space. His wife was supposed to provide him with companionship from home. She also needed to look after their children. Ideal of this new family life was drawn largely from the ideas of Enlightenment. Thus discipline, reason and science became essential features to organize a proper domestic life. A disciplined family became the equivalent for civilization for the bourgeoisie in the nineteenth century. A similar role was played by the domestic manuals in colonial Bengal in late nineteenth century.[169] In *Garhasthya Dharma* (Domestic Duties), Nagendra Bala Mustafi wrote,

> It is true that now steps are being taken to educate women, but that education is unsuitable for preparing women for household duties (*Garhasthya Dharma*).... A little learning does not bring wisdom, but it imparts a false sense of independence, women's nature becomes undisciplined and thus education causes unrest in society. Nowadays a little learning imparted to women has disturbed our society in many ways.... True education would prevent such problems.[170]

Priyanath Basu, in a chapter on 'The Awakening of Women' in *Griha Dharma* (Household Duties), said,

> Today we hear on all sides things about the awakening of women. Many men shudder to hear of it. Many women wonder what it is.... In conversation, behaviour and interactions, a sort of inversion (*ulta-britti*) has taken place. Men and women have lost their capacity to play their ordained roles (*dharma*); that is perhaps the reason why such a problem has arisen.[171]

There was a great deal of this sort of writing and it was simple to put it together to show how 'tradition' ruled the mind. However, there was also an attempt to negotiate with the challenge to tradition.

Kadambini Basu and Chandramukhi Basu were the first lady graduates of the University of Calcutta. After completion of her medical studies from the Medical College of Calcutta, Kadambini Basu (Ganguly) went abroad for her higher studies. She was the second wife of Dwarakanath Gangopadhyay and was the first woman doctor of Bengal. As a doctor, she moved about freely from place to place to treat her patients. She spoke English fluently as if it was her mother tongue, dressed in modern clothes and adorned her drawing room in a style that exhibited her excellent taste and imagination. Other girls of her family also had similar chances for a better life.[172] Girls of other enlightened families also had access to education as well. The 'new patriarchy' that sprang from colonial modernity was much different from older ideals of patriarchy. Of course, the new Western educated men did not want to deprive at least middle-class women from the benefits of a good education. However, a proper education was also not supposed to make women equal partners of men. In this context, it would make sense if one goes back to Partha Chatterjee's analysis of space. In the case of colonial Bengal, Chatterjee has argued that the construction of the 'public' and 'private' domains did not take place similarly as it did in Europe. Relatively, in colonial India, 'the colonized constructed the domains of the material and the spiritual as a way to mark themselves out from the colonizers'. He has also stated that 'this material or spiritual distinction further coalesced into the ideology of the outer or the world and the inner or the home.' Nevertheless, the more significant subject for the nationalists was the 'spiritual' sphere of family, which exemplified eastern spirituality. Chatterjee has matched this innovative interpretation of 'the home and the world dichotomy with the identification of social roles by gender'. Women became the symbols of this 'inner' realm of the 'spiritual'. However, this woman was also a product of colonial modernity. Thus, 'formal education' became a prerequisite for the 'new woman' and nationalist opinions demanded that women should attain 'cultural' modification through advanced education. Nevertheless, this 'new woman' would be the marker of an 'inner domain' where men could retain their full autonomy untrammelled by the colonial state. Bengali domestic manuals provide us with a comprehensive picture of this social history of nineteenth-century Bengal.[173] Census of India of 1931 had reported, 'In the traditional joint-family, vertically or horizontally extended, the elders among the women of the family would mould the young bride and fashion her personality to suit the wifely role. A substitute for that was needed when families began to nucleate with migration to the small towns.'[174] The traditional illustration of woman as wife and mother, merely augmented by education and some Victorian feminine notions taken from the West, was envisioned as the ideal for the good Indian woman in the emerging new phase 'construction of womanhood'. The same version was reproduced in the *Bamabodhini Patrika*.[175] The *Bamabodhini Patrika* in 1904 (1311 BS) penned, 'The wife, who like Goddess *Lakshmi* worships her husband as if he is a God Hari, will go to heaven after her death and will taste every happiness along with her husband just as God and Goddess, Hari and Lakshmi, enjoy eternal happiness'.[176] As Meredith Borthwick has mentioned, young men who became Brahmos faced social marginalization and they had a particular requirement for the backing of their wives in the 1850s and 1860s, and sometimes even after that. In order to choose between husband and family, women were required to understand something about their husband's beliefs. Jaganmohini Sen, Keshub Chandra Sen's wife, was enforced to select between her large house, friends, relatives, possessions, and her husband. He was chosen by her. Srinath Datta, Harasundari Datta's husband, married her when she was seven and he was fourteen. He organized for her to run away from his village in Bikrampur to attend him four years later, when he started to live his life as a Brahmo studying in Calcutta.[177]

Abala Bose (1865-1951), a prominent educationist argued that women required to receive a more comprehensive, extensive and prolonged education, 'not because we may make better matches for our girls…not even that the services of the daughter-in-law may be more valuable in the home of her adoption, but because woman like man is first of all a mind, and only in the second place physical and a body.'[178] Kamini Roy (1864-1933), in a speech given at a girls' school, demanded that the ultimate purpose of women's education was to provide some special rights and identity for their overall development.[179] Rani Chanda (1912-97), a student of Visva-Bharati, a Bengali writer and a close associate of Rabindranath Tagore and her sister attended Eden School of Dacca. Sarala Ray (1859-1946), the founder of Gokhale Memorial Girls' School (1920) of Calcutta; Abala Das (Bose), later Lady Abala who passed the entrance examination in 1881; Kumudini Khastagir (b. 1865), later Kumudini Das, who served as the Principal of Bethune College from 1902 to 1912, were all well-educated women of their times. Other girls were inspired by them to acquire learning. The Child Marriage Restraint Act of 1929, which

TABLE 1.5: NUMBER OF GIRLS UNDER INSTRUCTION IN RECOGNIZED INSTITUTIONS FOR GENERAL EDUCATION IN BENGAL[180]

	1937-1938	*1946-1947*
Primary Schools	6,84,758	7,57,806
Middle Schools	16,872	56,084
High Schools	24,610	47,197
Colleges	1,794	4,142
TOTAL	7,28,034	8,65,229

fixed the minimum age of marriage for a boy at eighteen and for a girl at fourteen made it possible for young women to understand their aspirations. The Table 1.5 provides a rough overview of the progress of women education from the late 1930s to the late 1940s.

Kusum Kumari Das (1875-1948) was mother of the great poet Jibanananda Das (1899-1954). She was another notable woman of the time who studied in Bethune School. She belonged to a middle-class family and lived the life of a typical housewife. Jibanananda writes, 'our home was full of people at Barisal. I saw my mother and aunt always engaged in domestic work. They were not spared of hard physical labour, nor did they want to be spared; indeed, they were not afraid of hard work. They were conscious of their duties and never thought of avoiding responsibilities'.[181] Kusum Kumari travelled to western India in search of a change of environment and better medical care for her sick son, Jibanananda. But her domestic responsibilities never stood in the way of her studies and writing habit. Kusum Kumari published *Kabita Mukul* (Poetry Buds), a collection of poems for children, around 1896. She was involved with the Brahmo Samaj, attended its meetings and gave short speeches at its gatherings. The essay, entitled 'Ideal Womenhood', revealed her thoughts on women's emancipation. She wrote that female power in this country was still stagnant, and thus the nation was 'half-dead'. She was engaged in social work and at the same time involved with women's organizations. She was also the secretary of the Barisal Mahila Samiti (Barisal Women's Association), an influential women's association. Simultaneously, skilled in literature, music and art, some of the women of Tagore's household were writers and poets who wrote stories, novels, poems, autobiographies also translated selected pieces of writings. Swarna Kumari Devi (1855-1932) and Jnanadanandini Devi (1850-1941) of the Tagore family were renowned for their dynamic attention and active involvement in women's emancipation. Jnanada brought about a fundamental change in ideas about the social condition of the women of Bengal. Swarna Kumari Devi had no interest in domestic responsibilities and she never lived the life of an ordinary housewife. Always engrossed in studies, she was a brilliant writer who contributed significantly to Bengali literature. The other girls of the Tagore family were also raised in an enlightened and rational environment with much care and attention paid to their education, which included music and art. Sarala, the daughter of Swarna Kumari and later known as Sarala Devi Chaudhurani (1872-1945) had received the Padmavati Gold Medal, donated by Rashbehari Ghosh, for passing the B.A. examination from the Bethune College in 1890. Indira, the daughter of Jnanadanandini, and later known as Indira Devi Chaudhurani was also bestowed the Padmavati Gold Medal for standing first in the B.A. examination in 1892. The men of the Tagore family made significant contribution to the advancement and enlightenment of the women of their family.[182]

However, the social and familial compulsion compelled girlchild towards early marriage. Dowry, as well, remained a recognized practice because marriage was challenging without it.[183] In a Hindu family, a daughter was a perpetual cause of burden because she had to be married at the appropriate age but it should be inside the recognized caste background. The girl's father had no choice but to agree to this high demand, which resulted in significant hardships for the bride's own family following her wedding.[184] The *Friend of India*, on 11 June 1868, had informed that in enlightened Bengal, the bridegrooms who have taken degrees are in high demand as husbands of young ladies who cannot spell. 'The price of a Bachelor of Arts is Rs. 2,500. A student who expects to get a degree is worth from Rs. 1,500 to Rs. 1,800, according to his chances of passing. Ordinary bridegrooms cost Rs. 1,000. Perhaps in the existing state of the market in Calcutta, arrangement might be made as regards the passed and unpassed bridegrooms.'[185] The parents were frequently embarrassed for failing to provide sufficient assistances and were repeatedly humiliated and mocked for not satisfying all the commitments of dowry. When her parents were unable to meet the demands of the husband's family, the girl was tortured by her mother-in-law and often by her husband as well. Sometimes she was sent back to her parent's house, never to be brought back. In his short story, *Dena Paona* (Assets and Liabilities),[186] Rabindranath Tagore had intensely depicted the evil effects of dowry and the connotation of the last line of this story is perhaps even deeper, *Ebare bish hajar taka pan ebong hate hate aaday* (This time a dowry of twenty thousand rupees was set and it was collected immediately). Nevertheless, one can differentiate the process of transformation in the attitudes of young women of Bengal towards marriage. The foremost aspect responsible for this was the raising of the age of their marriage. The generalization of marriage for women remained consistent between 1890 and 1930. Although statistics from before and after 1911 did not allow a correct juxtaposition, evidence has suggested that the percentage of married Hindu girls below the age of ten decreased until at least 1921 in some parts of India. On the contrary, an increasing number of girls were married after the age of fifteen. In 1911 more than 70 per cent of all girls were married or widowed before their fifteenth birthday, but by 1931 the proportion had dropped to just over 50 per cent.[187]

Table 1.6: Comparative Data Analysis of the Number of Married and Widowed Women in the Year 1911 and 1941[188]

	1911			*1941*		
1	*2*	*3*	*4*	*5*	*6*	*7*
Age	*Total number of women*	*Number of married or widowed women*	*Percentage of column 3 to 2*	*Total number of women*	*Number of married or widowed women*	*Percentage of column 6 to 5*
5-10 Years	1,000	126	12.6	31,164	2,151	6.9
10-15 Years	1,000	705	70.5	24,565	9,762	37.74
15-20 Years	1,000	967	96.7	22,102	18,469	83.54

It can be seen that the percentage of pre-fifteen-year-old girls being married off had been nearly halved, it is appropriate to conclude that significant numbers of urban middle-class girls were permitted to remain unmarried at least until the age of fifteen. The girls themselves expressed a clear preference for late marriage because it would provide them with better educational opportunities and a few more years of relative independence in their paternal homes.[189] The raising of the age of marriage, in conjunction with increased educational opportunities, occasionally allowed young girls to voice their own ideas about marriage and husband which their counterparts in the century had been incapable to do previously.[190] Supriya Acharya, Sarala Ghosh and Subhadra Sen revealed that their concept of husband was premised on the anticipation of companionship and romance and all three of these women formed nuclear households away from their own family homes.[191] In 1945, G.B. Desai's study on Gujarati girls discovered that 57.8 per cent of unmarried girls preferred marriage of choice, whereas in 1946, the study of educated Hindu girls in Bombay by C.A. Hate revealed that an overwhelming 74 per cent of unmarried girls preferred to choose their partners themselves.[192] Patterns of behaviour on the other hand, gradually transformed with time, precisely after the age of marriage for girls was raised. Brides were now older, stronger, to some extent educated and capable of developing a deeper bond with their husbands. They begrudged the domination and supremacy of the mother-in-law and attempted to state their own words, thus producing a new sort of conflict and tension in the traditional joint family structure. Education had nurtured their self-reliance, individualism and personal aspiration, all of these were incompatible with the atmosphere of the joint family and its ideals and not only that education had also made them eager to live in nuclear families, which would provide them with more time for themselves. Now the question is that whether the years surrounding the 1920s observed an effort to redefine the gender and sexual relationship. Since the nineteenth century, the trends in conjugal relations had been towards the formation of a companionship.[193] As a result of this, the notion of a married couple as a 'unit' began to emerge at this time. In Bengal, around the 1850s, some intellectuals began to seriously reconsider the nature of conjugal relations.[194] The companionate and supportive wife was supposed to act as a 'buffer' between the stresses of a fast-changing outer world with frequently conflicting expectations and the home. Increasingly, Indira Devi (1873-1960) and her husband Pramatha Chaudhury (1868-1946) shared responsibility for the prestigious journal *Sabujapatra* (The Green Leaf); Radharani Devi (b. 1904) and Narendra Dev were a renowned scholarly couple; C.R. Das (1870-1925) and his wife Basanti Devi (1880-1974) fought in the freedom struggle; Rama Chaudhury and Jatindra Bimal Chaudhury dedicated their lives towards education; Uma Guha and Biraja Sankar Guha cooperated each other at the Anthropological Survey of India; Dr Sarala Ghosh (b. 1904) and Dr P. K. Ghosh, both were doctors and practiced medicine. A partnership existed between husband and wife that brought them to a level of equality and reduced, to some extent, the gender discrepancy endorsed by tradition.[195] Attitudes had not remained constant. During this time, it is possible to say that a new mutual trust had developed in the way couples professed their marriages. Marriage had evolved into a conscious corporation. The feeling of companionship fostered an impression of equality in marriage. To some extent, women embraced the liberal paradigm that offered them a distinct but equivalent position. They also presumed in the worth of their roles as 'wives and mothers'. The powerful bond between husband and wife was an enjoyable characteristic of their conjugal lives. Sometimes, there was dissatisfaction, but it was not expressed most of the time. All outrage and dissatisfaction with the treatment of women was engaged at traditional Bengali as well as Indian society rather than at the reformed segment.[196] From time-to-time history displays certain contradictory trends. The colonial state legally sanctioned the remarriage of Hindu widows in 1856 but it did not initially obtain extensive popular acquiescence. The enactment of the Age of Consent Bill in 1891 made the consummation of a marriage with a bride younger than twelve to be a punishable offence; child marriage began to decline, albeit slightly from this time beyond, but there was a growing concern about a girl remaining unmarried for long after her early adolescence.

Female education and employment were on the rise, but women remained behind men in terms of progress.[197] These developments recommend that changes in the legal status of women did not essentially bring any transformation in their general social status. It is hard to envision how contemporary society could foster ideas about 'romantic love' and a 'nuclear couple form'. It is true that in the early twentieth century, Bengali male writers as well as some female writers portrayed romantic love in their novels and verses, yet simultaneously a convention of 'women's bhakti', or 'devotion' to husband was also being developed and valorized.[198] Photographs of the bride and bridegroom standing or sitting next to each other, frequently with their limbs touching, their bodies fixed in a gesture of togetherness, were relatively all-pervasive among the marriage souvenirs that persisted from the beginning of the twentieth century. Hitherto certain narratives appeared to imply that the feelings of 'coupledom' one might closely studied into these motions were much more debatable in daily situation.[199] But in literature, there was always a confrontation between old feelings and a new consciousness about love, whether conjugal or otherwise. Jyotirmoyee Ganguly (1889-1945), daughter of the Brahmo leader Dwarakanath Ganguly, questioned whether camaraderie or companionship in marriage was conceivable in a male-dominated society.[200] Nevertheless, there was a schism between two ideologies of men-women relationships, as well as an attempt to reconcile opposites. These transitional negotiations were equipped by women's participation in the public sphere, initially in social reform initiatives and progressively, in politics.[201]

However, not all educated families of Bengal accepted the waves of modernity, preferring to adhere to the conventional and orthodox ways of life. The family of Bhudev Mukhopadhyay (1827-94) was one of them. He was a student of Hindu College, had a great proficiency in English literature, including the works of Bacon, Shakespeare, Milton as well as the historical writings of Hume, Mitford, Fergusson, Gibbon, Elphinstone and Russell. His *Samajik Prabandha*[202] (Essays on Social Matters) and *Paribarik Prabandha*[203] (Essays on Family Matters) clearly represented his ideas and beliefs regarding social issues in India. He thought that women need not acquire knowledge by reading books and scriptures, but rather should focus on learning how to manage household duties because running a household in an efficient manner was their main concern. In his article *Stri Shiksha*[204] (Female Education), he expressed no inclination for school or college education for women. Bhudev's compassion for tradition and conservative stance strongly affected his talented granddaughter – Anurupa Devi (1882-1958) – well-known woman writer of that time. Concerned about the attack on Hindu culture and civilization, the sisters dedicated their works to the task of defending and protecting the traditions, customs and sacraments of Hindu religion and society. The key strengths or spiritual and social urge such as 'self-sacrifice', 'altruism', 'social wellbeing', 'love for God and religion', which characterized Hindu thought, were explicitly evident in all their writings. Nirupama Devi (1883-1951), famous woman author of her time, in her *Didi* (Elder Sister) and Anurupa Devi in her *Mantrashakti* (The Power of Chant or sacred utterance), both written in 1915, emphasized on the underlying strength of the sacramental Hindu marriage.[205]

In any case, the instances of enlightened women from educated and progressive families do not expunge the fact that the majority of Hindu women were submerged in extreme ignorance and distress. In comparison to the vast majority of unfortunate women who were forced to live in deplorable conditions, the number of emancipated women was still very limited, almost negligible. They were either glorified housewives or mere domestic workers or child-producing apparatuses.[206] Nevertheless, women became conscious about the prevailing gender discriminations in Indian society which fuelled a desire to liberate themselves from the shackles of prescribed belief – structural practices and roles that had accurately functioned against their interests.[207] It was less certain whether women's status had improved during the nineteenth century of Indian history. Certainly, the restructuring of women's positions was seldom at the forefront of the reform debate and one may say that there were several points where the arguments of advocates and opponents of social legislation regarding 'women's question' collided. In addition, expansive processes surrounding 'women's question' in colonial India propose strong links between the state, religion, and socio-legal actions. An analytical discussion of the historical backdrop of the Brahmo marriage and Age of Consent Controversy is, therefore, essential to grasp the evolution of forces that shaped the contours of the Act III of 1872 and the Age of Consent Act debate.

NOTES

1. Ipshita Chanda, 'Introduction: Women Writing Gender', in Ipshita Chanda and Jayeeta Bagchi (eds.), *Shaping the Discourse: Women's Writings in Bengali Periodicals, 1865-1947*, Kolkata: Stree, School of Women's Studies, Jadavpur University, 2014, p. xxi.
2. Meredith Borthwick, *The Changing Role of Women in Bengal, 1849-1905*, New Jersey: Princeton University Press, 1984, p. 26.
3. Mrinalini Sinha, *Specters of Mother India: The Global Restructuring of an Empire*, Durham and London: Duke University Press, 2006, p. 43.
4. Amiya P. Sen (ed.), *Social and Religious Reform: The Hindus of British India*, New Delhi: Oxford University Press, 2003, p. 38.
5. Meredith Borthwick, op. cit., 1984, pp. 40-1.
6. Sheila Rowbotham, *Hidden from History: 300 Years of Women's Oppression and the Fight Against It*, London: Pluto Press, 1973, pp. ix-x.
7. Mary S. Hartman and Lois Banner (eds.), *Clio's Consciousness Raised: New Perspectives on the History of Women*, New York: Octagon Press, 1976, pp. vii-xii.
8. Berenice A. Carroll (ed.), *Liberating Women's History: Theoretical and Critical Essays*, Urbana: University of Illinois Press, 1976, pp. ix-xiv.
9. Renate Bridenthal and Claudia Koonz (eds.), *Becoming Visible: Women in European History*, Boston: Houghton-Mifflin, 1977, pp. 1-10.
10. Aparna Basu, 'Women's History in India: An Historiographical Survey', in Karen Offen, Ruth Roach Pierson and Jane Rendall (eds.), *Writing Women's History: International Perspectives*, London: Macmillan Press, 1991, reprinted 1992, p. 182.
11. Neera Desai and Usha Thakkar (eds.), *Women in Indian Society*, India: National Book Trust, p. 1.
12. Ibid., p. 2.
13. Bharati Ray, 'Women of Bengal: Transformation in Ideas and Ideals, 1900-1947', *Social Scientist*, vol. 19, no. 5/6, May-June 1991, p. 6.
14. Nivedita Menon (ed.), *Gender and Politics in India*, New Delhi: Oxford University Press, 1999 (first edition), 2001 (Oxford India Paperbacks), p. 3.
15. Uma Chakravarti, 'Whatever Happened to the Vedic *Dasi*? Orientalism, Nationalism, and a Script for the Past', in Kumkum Sangari and Sudesh Vaid (eds.), *Recasting Women: Essays in Colonial History*, New Delhi: Zubaan, 2003, first published by Kali for Women, 1989, pp. 44-5.
16. Ibid., p. 45.

17. James Mill, *The History of British India*, with notes by H.H. Wilson, 5th edn., London: James Madden, 1840, pp. 312-13.
18. Uma Chakravarti, op. cit., 2003 (1989), p. 46.
19. Nivedita Menon (ed.), op. cit., 1999 (2001), p. 3.
20. Aparna Basu, op. cit., 1991 (1992), p. 183.
21. Tanika Sarkar, 'The Hindu Wife and the Hindu nation: Domesticity and nationalism in nineteenth century Bengal', *Studies in History*, vol. 8, no. 2, n.s., 1992, pp. 213-35.
22. Tapan Raychaudhuri, *Europe Reconsidered: Perceptions of the West in Nineteenth Century Bengal*, Delhi: Oxford University Press, 1988, p. 336.
23. Geraldine Forbes, *The New Cambridge History of India IV. 2: Women in Modern India*, New Delhi: Cambridge University Press, 1996 (first published), reprinted, 2015, pp. 14-15.
24. Uma Chakravarti, 'Whatever Happened to the Vedic *Dasi*? Orientalism, Nationalism, and a Script for the Past', in Kumkum Sangari and Sudesh Vaid (eds.), *Recasting Women: Essays in Indian Colonial History*, New Brunswick: Rutgers University Press, 1990, pp. 27-87.
25. Mrinalini Sinha (ed.), *Selections from Mother India: Katherine Mayo*, New Delhi: Kali for Women, 1998, p. 30.
26. Geraldine Forbes, op. cit., 1996 (2015), p. 15.
27. Partha Chatterjee, 'Colonialism, Nationalism and Colonized Women: The Contest in India', *American Ethnologist*, vol. 16, no. 4, November 1989, pp. 622-33; Partha Chatterjee, 'The Nationalist Resolution of the Woman Question', in Kumkum Sangari and Sudesh Vaid (eds.), *Recasting Women: Essays in Indian Colonial History*, New Brunswick, N.J.: Rutgers University Press, 1990, pp. 233-53. For a critique of Chatterjee's arguments, Himani Bannerji, 'Projects of Hegemony: Towards a Critique of Subaltern Studies' "Resolution of the Women's Question"', *Economic and Political Weekly*, vol. 35, no. 11, 11-17 March 2000, pp. 902-20.
28. Geraldine Forbes, op. cit., 1996 (2015), pp. 14-15.
29. Mahesh Chundra Deb, 'A Sketch of the Condition of the Hindoo Women', in Goutam Chattopadhyay (ed.), *Awakening in Bengal in Early Nineteenth Century (Selected Documents)*, vol. one, Calcutta: Progressive Publishers, 1956, p. 90.
30. Ibid., p. 93.
31. Sumit Sarkar, 'The Controlled Emancipation of Wives', in Amiya P. Sen (ed.), *Social and Religious Reform: The Hindus of British India*, New Delhi: Oxford University Press, 2003, p. 164.

32. Mahesh Chundra Deb, 'A Sketch of the Condition of the Hindoo Women', op. cit., 1956, p. 91.
33. Geraldine Forbes, op. cit., 1996 (2015), p. 15.
34. Monmayee Basu, *Hindu Women and Marriage Law: From Sacrament to Contract*, in *Women and Law in India: An Omnibus Comprising*, New Delhi: Oxford University Press, 2004 (first edition), 2016 (Oxford India Paperbacks), pp. 1-2.
35. Ibid., p. 2.
36. Nivedita Menon (ed.), op. cit., 1999 (2001), p. 3.
37. Ibid.
38. Uma Chakravarti, 'In Search of Our Past: A Review of the Limitations and Possibilities of the Historiography of Women in Early India', *Economic and Political Weekly*, vol. 23, no. 18, 30 April 1988, pp. WS2-WS10. Uma Chakravarti and Kumkum Roy, 'Breaking Out of Invisibility: Rewriting the History of Women in Ancient India', in S.J. Kleinberg (ed.), *Retrieving Women's History*, Oxford: Berg, UNESCO, 1988, pp. 319-37.
39. Monmayee Basu, op. cit., 2004 (first edition), 2016 (Oxford India Paperbacks), p. 1.
40. Nivedita Menon (ed.), op. cit., 1999 (2001), p. 4; Uma Chakravarti, 'Conceptualizing Brahmanical Patriarchy in Early India: Gender, Caste, Class and State', *Economic and Political Weekly*, 3 April 1993, pp. 579-85; Uma Chakravarti, 'Beyond the Altekarian Paradigm: Towards a New Understanding of Gender Relations in Early Indian History', in Kumkum Roy (ed.), *Women in Early Indian Societies*, New Delhi: Manohar, 1999, pp. 72-81.
41. Nivedita Menon (ed.), op. cit., 1999 (2001), p. 4.
42. Geraldine Forbes, op. cit., 1996 (2015), p. 16.
43. Sekhar Bandyopadhyay, *From Plassey to Partition and After: A History of Modern India*, New Delhi: Orient BlackSwan, 2004 (first published), reprinted 2016, p. 382.
44. Tanika Sarkar, 'Rhetoric Against Age of Consent: Resisting Colonial Reason and Death of a Child-Wife', *Economic and Political Weekly*, vol. 28, no. 36, 4 September 1993, pp. 1869-78; Tanika Sarkar, 'The Hindu Wife and the Hindu Nation: Domesticity and nationalism in nineteenth century Bengal', *Studies in History*, vol. 8, no. 2, n.s., 1992, pp. 213-35.
45. Sekhar Bandyopadhyay, op. cit., 2004 (first published), reprinted 2016, p. 382.

46. For some examples of state intervention in the family, especially among marginalized social groups, Radha Kumar, 'Family and Factory: Women in the Bombay Cotton Textile Industry, 1919-1939', *Indian Economic and Social History Review*, vol. 20, no. 1, 1983, pp. 81-110; Lucy Carroll, 'Law, Custom, and Statutory Social Reform: The Hindu Widows' Remarriage Act of 1856', *Indian Economic and Social History Review*, vol. 20, no. 4, 1983, pp. 363-88.
47. Mrinalini Sinha, op. cit., 2006, p. 46; Radhika Singha, 'Colonial Law and Infrastructural Power: Reconstructing Community, Locating the Female Subject', *Studies in History*, vol. 19, no. 1, January-June 2003, pp. 87-126.
48. Nivedita Menon (ed.), op. cit., 1999 (2001), p. 5.
49. Ibid., p. 6.
50. Ishita Banerjee-Dube, *A History of Modern India*, Delhi: Cambridge University Press, 2014, p. 189.
51. Mrinalini Sinha, op. cit., 2006, p. 44; Partha Chatterjee, *The Nation and Its Fragments: Colonial and Postcolonial Histories*, New Jersey: Princeton University Press, 1993, pp. 116-34.
52. Kavita Panjabi and Paromita Chakravarti (eds.), *Women Contesting Culture: Changing Frames of Gender Politics in India*, Kolkata: Stree, School of Women's Studies, Jadavpur University, 2012, pp. xix-xx.
53. Partha Chatterjee, op. cit., 1993.
54. Mrinalini Sinha, op. cit., 2006, p. 44.
55. Ibid., p. 47. 'The phrase has acquired an iconic status in accounts of gender in colonial India. It was also the title of Rabindranath Tagore's Bengali novel *Ghare Baire* (1916). It was translated as *Home and the World*.'
56. Ratna Kapur and Brenda Cossman (eds.), *Subversive Sites: Feminist Engagements with Law in India*, New Delhi: Sage Publications, 1996, pp. 43-4.
57. 'Introduction', in Amiya P. Sen (ed.), *Social and Religious Reform: The Hindus of British India*, New Delhi: Oxford University Press, 2003, p. 3.
58. Ibid., p. 5. Shaktisadhan Mukhopadhyay, 'Sahabas Sammati Bill O Vidyasagar Raay: Bekosur Khalas' (Age of Consent Bill and the Judgement of Vidyasagar: Acquitted), *Anustup*, vol. 54, nos. 3-4, 2020.
59. Ibid., pp. 5-6.
60. Sumit Sarkar, 'The Controlled Emancipation of Wives', op. cit., 2003, p. 162; Mahesh Chundra Deb, 'A Sketch of the Condition of the

Hindoo Women', in Goutam Chattopadhyay (ed.), *Awakening in Bengal in Early Nineteenth Century (Selected Documents)*, vol. one, Calcutta: Progressive Publishers, 1956, pp. 89-104.

61. Ishita Banerjee-Dube, op. cit., 2014, pp. 87-8.
62. Sekhar Bandyopadhyay, op. cit., 2004 (first published), reprinted 2016, p. 147.
63. Ishita Banerjee-Dube, op. cit., 2014, p. 94.
64. Ibid.
65. Lata Mani, 'Contentious Traditions: The Debate on Sati in Colonial India', in Kumkum Sangari and Sudesh Vaid (eds.), *Recasting Women: Essays in Colonial History*, New Delhi: Zubaan, 2003, first published by Kali for Women, 1989, pp. 115-65.
66. Ibid., citing 'Address to Lord William Bentinck', *English Works*, 16 January 1830, pp. 475-7.
67. Ratna Kapur and Brenda Cossman (eds.), op. cit., 1996, pp. 46-7.
68. Sekhar Bandyopadhyay, op. cit., 2004 (first published), rpt. 2016, pp. 147-8. Ashis Nandy, 'Sati as profit versus sati as spectacle: The public debate on Roop Kanwar's death', in J.S. Hawley (ed.), *Sati, the blessing and the Curse*, New York: Oxford University Press, 1994, pp. 131-49.
69. Anand A. Yang, 'Whose Sati? Widow Burning in Early-Nineteenth-Century India', in Sumit Sarkar and Tanika Sarkar (eds.), *Women and Social Reform in Modern India: A Reader, Volume 1*, New Delhi: Permanent Black, 2007, pp. 21-52. Bengal officials began to preserve a copious set of documentary evidence on burnings, on their numbers, family circumstances, and names of the *satis* and their husbands. Going by annual police reports sent to the *House of Commons* since 1815, '500 to 900 widows were burnt every year in the *Lower Provinces* of Bengal alone, while many more went unnoticed, according to missionaries and officials. Though Brahmans provided the single largest category of *satis*, *Shudra* castes came fairly close. Immolations, therefore, could well have been a path to upward ritual mobility for the "lower" castes. Although scriptures prescribed death by burning, Jugis buried their widows alive. The *satis*' recorded age ranged between four and hundred, though elderly widows constituted the largest group. They came from all classes – from substantial landowners to beggars. Since polygamy was widely practiced by Hindus, sometimes dozens of wives were burnt together on the same pyre.'
70. Ibid., p. 33.

71. Lata Mani, 'Contentious Traditions: The Debate on Sati in Colonial India', op. cit., p. 115.
72. *Compiled from Great Britain, Parliament, Parliamentary Papers, 1821, 1823, 1824, 1825, 1826/27, 1830*; Amitabha Mukhopadhyay, 'Sati as a Social Institution in Bengal', *Bengal Past and Present* Vol. 76, No. 142, 1957, p. 106, cited in Anand Yang, 'Whose Sati? Widow Burning in Early-Nineteenth-Century India', op. cit., 2007, p. 34.
73. Radha Kumar, *The History of Doing: An Illustrated Account of Movements for Women's Rights and Feminism in India, 1800-1990*, London/New Delhi: Verso/Kali for Women, 1993, pp. 7-31.
74. Anand A. Yang, 'Whose Sati? Widow Burning in Early-Nineteenth-Century India', op. cit., 2007, p. 29.
75. Ashis Nandy, 'Sati: A Nineteenth Century Tale of Women, Violence and Protest', in V.C. Joshi (ed.), *Rammohun Roy and the Process of Modernization in India*, Delhi: Vikas Publishing House, pp. 168-94; also, in Ashis Nandy, *At The Edge of Psychology: Essays in Politics and Culture*, Delhi: Oxford University Press, 1980, pp. 1-31.
76. Anand A. Yang, 'Whose Sati? Widow Burning in Early-Nineteenth-Century India', op. cit., 2007, p. 29.
77. Radha Kumar, op. cit., 1993.
78. Rammohan Roy, 'Sahamaran Visaye Pravartak O Nivartaker Sambad' (News of promoters and deterrents on dying together or burning oneself to death on one's husband's funeral pyre), in Ajit Kumar Ghosh (ed.), *Rammohan Rachanavali* ('Writings of Rammohan'), Calcutta: Haraf Prakashani, 1973, pp. 171-2, cited in Asoke Sen, *Iswar Chandra Vidyasagar and His Elusive Milestones*, Calcutta: Riddhi-India, 1977, pp. 74-5.
79. Radha Kumar, op. cit., 1993; Kumkum Sangari and Sudesh Vaid (eds.), *Recasting Women: Essays in Colonial History*, New Delhi: Zubaan, 2003, first published by Kali for Women, 1989, pp. 1-26.
80. Radha Kumar, op. cit., 1993.
81. Ratna Kapur and Brenda Cossman (eds.), op. cit., 1996, p. 4.
82. Sumit Sarkar and Tanika Sarkar (eds.), *Women and Social Reform in Modern India: A Reader, Volume 1*, New Delhi: Permanent Black, 2007, pp. 57-8.
83. Lata Mani, *Contentious Traditions: The Debate on Sati in Colonial India*, Berkeley/Los Angeles/London: University of California Press, 1998, pp. 1-9.
84. Nivedita Menon (ed.), op. cit., 1999 (2001), p. 6.

85. Sekhar Bandyopadhyay, op. cit., 2004 (first published), reprinted 2016, pp. 156-7; Tanika Sarkar, 'Changing Hindu Women: Bengal in the Long Nineteenth Century', in Sabyasachi Bhattacharya (ed.), *A Comprehensive History of Modern Bengal, 1700-1950, Volume II*, Kolkata: The Asiatic Society, in association with Primus Books, 2020, pp. 804-41.
86. Asoke Sen, *Iswar Chandra Vidyasagar and His Elusive Milestones*, Calcutta: Riddhi-India, 1977, p. 6, cited in Sekhar Bandyopadhyay, 'Caste, Widow-Remarriage, and the Reform of Popular Culture in Colonial Bengal', in Sumit Sarkar and Tanika Sarkar (eds.), *Women and Social Reform in Modern India: A Reader, Volume 1*, New Delhi: Permanent Black, 2007, p. 145.
87. Lucy Carroll, 'Law, Custom and Statutory Social Reform: The Hindu Widows' Remarriage Act of 1856', in Sumit Sarkar and Tanika Sarkar (eds.), *Women and Social Reform in Modern India: A Reader, Volume 1*, New Delhi: Permanent Black, 2007, pp. 114-15.
88. Monmayee Basu, op. cit., 2004 (first edition), 2016 (Oxford India Paperbacks), pp. 6-7; Kamaladevi Chattopadhyay, *Indian Women's Battle for Freedom*, New Delhi: Abhinav Publications, 1983, pp. 94-130.
89. 'Preface' in Asoke Sen, op. cit., 1977, pp. xiii-xiv.
90. Asoke Sen, op. cit., 1977, p. 75.
91. Monmayee Basu, op. cit., 2004 (first edition), 2016 (Oxford India Paperbacks), p. 6.
92. Janaki Nair, *Women and Law in Colonial India: A Social History*, New Delhi: Kali for Women, 1996, p. 61. Charles Heimsath, *Indian Nationalism and Hindu Social Reform*, Princeton: Princeton University Press, 1964, p. 80.
93. Extract from *Tattvabodhini Patrika*, February 1856, cited in Benoy Ghosh (ed.), *Samayikpatre Banglar Samajchitra, 1840-1905, Dwitiya Khanda: Tattvabodhini Patrikar Rachana Sankalan* (Social Representation of Bengal in Periodicals, Volume 2: Compilation of Essays of Tattvabodhini Patrika), Kolkata: Bikkhan Bhaban, Bengal Publishers Private Ltd., 1960, p. 145.
94. Ishwar Chandra Vidyasagar's 'Bidhaba Bibaha Prachalita Haoya Uchit Kina Etadbisayak Prastab' (A Suggestion on whether Widow Remarriage is to be Practiced) and 'Bidhaba Bibaha Prachalita Haoya Uchit Kina Etadbisayak Prastab: Dwitiya Prastab' (A Suggestion on whether Widow Remarriage is to be Practiced: Second Proposal), in Ishwar Chandra Vidyasagar, *Vidyasagar Rachana Samgraha: Dwitiya Khanda*,

(Collection of Writings of Vidyasagar: Volume 2), Calcutta: Vidyasagar Smarak Jatiya Samiti, 1972, pp. 11-33, 35-165. Ishwar Chandra Vidyasagar, *Marriage of Hindu Widows*, Calcutta: The Sanskrit Press, 1864, pp. 1-22.

95. Vidyasagar, 'Bidhaba Bibaha Prachalita Haoya Uchit Kina Etadbisayak Prastab' (A Suggestion on whether Widow Remarriage is to be Practiced), op. cit., 1972, pp. 23-5; Monmayee Basu, op. cit., 2004 (first edition), 2016 (Oxford India Paperbacks), p. 68.
96. Tanika Sarkar, 'Wicked Widows: Law and Faith in Nineteenth-century Public Sphere Debates', in Anindita Ghosh (ed.), *Behind the Veil: Resistance, Women and the Everyday in Colonial South Asia*, London: Palgrave Macmillan, 2008, p. 92; Legislative Council Proceedings: The Hindoo Widows' Remarriage Bill, November 1855.
97. Asoke Sen, op. cit., 1977, pp. 56-7.
98. The journal for women's enlightenment, published in Bengal by the enlightened and educated Brahmos between 1863 and 1922, functioned as an integral component of the novel solution worked out to resolve the thorny problem of accommodating the *antahpur* (inner space or home) with *bahir* (outer space). Bharati Ray (ed.), *Nari O Paribar: Bamabodhini Patrika* ('Women and Family: *Bamabodhini Patrika*'), Kolkata: Ananda Publishers, 2002 (1st edition), 2014 (3rd impression), pp. 1-16.
99. *Bamabodhini Patrika*, Sraban (July-August) 1277 BS (1870), cited in Sekhar Bandyopadhyay, 'Caste, Widow-Remarriage, and the Reform of Popular Culture in Colonial Bengal', op. cit., 2007, p. 166.
100. Maroona Murmu, *Words of Her Own: Women Authors in Nineteenth-Century Bengal*, New Delhi: Oxford University Press, 2020, p. 47.
101. C.J. O'Donnell, *Report on the Census of Lower Provinces of Bengal and their Feudatories 1891*, Calcutta: Bengal Secretariat Press, 1893, p. 186.
102. Sekhar Bandyopadhyay, 'Caste, Widow-Remarriage, and the Reform of Popular Culture in Colonial Bengal', in Sumit Sarkar and Tanika Sarkar (eds.), *Women and Social Reform in Modern India: A Reader, Volume 1*, New Delhi: Permanent Black, 2007, pp. 145-6.
103. Lucy Carroll, 'Law, Custom, and Statutory Social Reform: The Hindu Widows' Remarriage Act of 1856', op. cit., 1983, p. 379.
104. Ibid., pp. 363-88.
105. Ishita Banerjee-Dube, op. cit., 2014, p. 97.
106. Sekhar Bandyopadhyay, op. cit., 2004 (first published), reprinted 2016, pp. 148-9.

107. Janaki Nair, *Women and Law in Colonial India: A Social History*, New Delhi: Kali for Women, 1996, pp. 62-3.
108. Prem Chowdhry, 'Popular Perceptions of Widow-remarriage in Haryana: Past and Present', in Bharati Ray (ed.), *From the Seams of History: Essays on Indian Women*, Delhi: Oxford University Press, 1995, pp. 37-66.
109. Ibid.
110. Geraldine Forbes, op. cit., 1996 (first published), reprinted, 2015, p. 24.
111. Sekhar Bandyopadhyay, op. cit., 2004 (first published), reprinted 2016, p. 149.
112. Janaki Nair, op. cit., 1996, p. 63. 'Vidyasagar won the legal battle but lost the social one. The image of the chaste widow, lovingly embracing her deprivations and ever faithful to the husband's memory, continued to dominate Bengali Hindu imagination. Remarriages were ruthlessly disrupted, the couple disinherited and ostracized. They also faced obscene mockery in press. Weddings in Calcutta were performed under elaborate police protection, which was lacking in villages. Peasants supporting remarriage were evicted from their land, beaten up, and expelled from the village by their upper caste landlords and their 'low caste' musclemen. Reformist appeals for help were ignored by Hindu deputy magistrates and the police. Vidyasagar was threatened with death, which he managed to avert only with huge gifts to local brahmins. He had to fund most of the early remarriages himself, and also set up the new couple in the world. Sometimes, the husband abandoned the wife under unbearable family pressure. Widows, willing to marry, were abducted and kept under severe vigilance by outraged families, till their lovers could arrange counter-abductions', cited in Tanika Sarkar, 'Changing Hindu Women: Bengal in the Long Nineteenth Century', op. cit., 2020, pp. 825-6.
113. Sekhar Bandyopadhyay, op. cit., 2004 (first published), reprinted 2016, p. 149.
114. A.E. Porter (ed.), *Census Report of Bengal and Sikkim, 1931*, Census of India, vol. V, part I, chapter IV, Calcutta: Central Publication Branch, 1933, p. 201.
115. Monmayee Basu, op. cit., 2004 (first edition), 2016 (Oxford India Paperbacks), p. 73.
116. A.E. Porter (ed.), op. cit., 1933, p. 221.
117. Monmayee Basu, op. cit., 2004 (first edition), 2016 (Oxford India Paperbacks), p. 75.

118. Ratna Kapur and Brenda Cossman (eds.), op. cit., 1996, p. 51.
119. Padma Anagol, 'Age of Consent and Child Marriage in India', *The Wiley Blackwell Encyclopedia of Gender and Sexuality Studies*, 21 April 2016, p. 1.
120. Flavia Agnes, *Family Law: Volume 2: Marriage, Divorce, and Matrimonial Litigation*, New Delhi: Oxford University Press, 2011 p. 67.
121. Geraldine Forbes, op. cit., 1996 (first published), reprinted 2015, p. 83.
122. Meredith Borthwick, op. cit., 1984, p. 126.
123. Flavia Agnes, op. cit., 2011, p. 67.
124. Tanika Sarkar, 'Rhetoric against Age of Consent: Resisting Colonial Reason and Death of a Child-Wife', op. cit., 4 September 1993, p. 1870.
125. Sita Anantha Raman, *Women in India: A Social and Cultural History, Volume 2*, California: ABC CLIO, 2009, pp. 125-6.
126. Flavia Agnes, op. cit., 2011, pp. 67-8.
127. Sita Anantha Raman, op. cit., p. 108.
128. Monmayee Basu, op. cit., 2004 (first edition), 2016 (Oxford India Paperbacks), p. 3.
129. Bharati Ray, 'Women of Bengal: Transformation in Ideas and Ideals, 1900-1947', *Social Scientist*, vol. 19, nos. 5/6, May-June, 1991, p. 5.
130. Monmayee Basu, op. cit., 2004 (first edition), 2016 (Oxford India Paperbacks), p. 3.
131. Bharati Ray, op. cit., 1991, p. 5.
132. Irawati Karve, *Kinship Organisation in India*, Bombay: Asia Publishing House, 1968, p. 89, cited in Bharati Ray, op. cit., 1991, p. 5.
133. Ibid.
134. Monmayee Basu, op. cit., 2004 (first edition), 2016 (Oxford India Paperbacks), p. 4.
135. Tapan Raychaudhuri, 'Love in a Colonial Climate: Marriage, Sex and Romance in Nineteenth-Century Bengal', *Modern Asian Studies*, vol. 34, no. 2, May 2000, p. 351.
136. H.H. Risley and E.A. Gait (eds.), *Report on the Census of India, 1901*, Calcutta: Office of the Superintendent of Government Printing, 1903, pp. 249-50, cited in Maroona Murmu, op. cit., 2020, p. 38.
137. Meredith Borthwick, op. cit., 1984, p. 110.
138. Bharati Ray, op. cit., 1991, p. 5.
139. Monmayee Basu, op. cit., 2004 (first edition), 2016 (Oxford India Paperbacks), p. 4.
140. Tapan Raychaudhuri, op. cit., 2000, pp. 355-6.

141. Bharati Ray, op. cit., 1991, p. 5.
142. Monmayee Basu, op. cit., 2004 (first edition), 2016 (Oxford India Paperbacks), p. 4.
143. Tanika Sarkar, *Words to Win: The Making of Amar Jiban: A Modern Autobiography*, New Delhi: Kali for Women, 1999, p. 152.
144. Tapan Raychaudhuri, op. cit., 2000, p. 351.
145. Bharati Ray, op. cit., 1991, p. 5.
146. Monmayee Basu, op. cit., 2004 (first edition), 2016 (Oxford India Paperbacks), p. 9.
147. Bharati Ray, op. cit., 1991, p. 14.
148. Bharati Ray, 'Bengali Women and Politics of Joint Family, 1900-47', *Economic and Political Weekly*, vol. 26, no. 52, December 28, 1991, p. 3018.
149. Sarat Kumari Chaudhurani, 'Didima' ('Grandmother'), in Sri Brajendranath Bandyopadhyay and Sri Sajanikanta Das (eds.), *Sarat Kumari Chaudhuranir Rachanabali* (Writings of Sarat Kumari Chaudhurani), Kolkata: Bangiya Sahitya Parishad, 1357 (1950) Shraban (July-August), p. 233; *Bharati*, June-September, 1316 BS.
150. Maroona Murmu, op. cit., 2020, p. 41.
151. *Hindoo* Patriot, 19 September 1887, cited in Tanika Sarkar, *Hindu Wife, Hindu Nation: Community, Religion, and Cultural Nationalism*, Bloomington and Indianapolis: Indiana University Press, 2001, p. 51.
152. Giribala Devi, 'Raybari', in Bani Roy (ed.), *Giribala Devir Rachanabali*, Kolkata: Ramayani Prakash Bhaban, 1957, pp. 17-230.
153. Ashapurna Devi, *Subarnalata*, Kolkata: Mitra O Ghosh Publishers Private Limited, 1966.
154. Bimal Mitra, *Kari Diye Kinlam*, Kolkata: Mitra O Ghosh Publishers, 1961.
155. Monmayee Basu, op. cit., 2004 (first edition), 2016 (Oxford India Paperbacks), p. 13.
156. Monmayee Basu, op. cit., 2004 (first edition), 2016 (Oxford India Paperbacks), p. 14; Rani Chanda, *Amar Ma'r Baper Bari* ('My Mother's Father's House'), Kolkata: Visva-Bhararti Granthan Bibhag, 1384 (1977) Baishakh (April-May).
157. Rani Chanda, op. cit., 1384 (1977) Baishakh (April-May), p. 60.
158. Tapan Raychaudhuri, op. cit., 2000, p. 370.
159. Malavika Karlekar, *Re-visioning the Past: Early Photography in Bengal, 1875-1915*, New Delhi: Oxford University Press, 2005, p. 100.
160. *Desh*, 2 April 1983, p. 15 (article by Smt. Jhara Basu), cited in

Monmayee Basu, op. cit., 2004 (first edition), 2016 (Oxford India Paperbacks), p. 9.

161. *The Friend of India*, 30 March 1865, cited in Monmayee Basu, op. cit., 2004 (first edition), 2016 (Oxford India Paperbacks), p. 9.
162. *The Calcutta Christian Observer*, July 1841, cited in Swapan Basu (ed.), *Sambad-Samayik Patre Unish Shataker Bangali Samaj: Dwitiya Khanda* (Bengali Society of Nineteenth Century in Newspapers and Periodicals: vol. 2), Calcutta: Paschimbanga Bangla Academi, 2003, p. 172.
163. *The Friend of India*, 3 July 1856, cited in Benoy Ghose (ed.), *Selections from English Periodicals of 19th Century Bengal*, Volume III: 1849-56, Calcutta: Papyrus, 1980, p. 89.
164. Tapan Raychaudhuri, op. cit., 2000, p. 374.
165. Monmayee Basu, op. cit., 2004 (first edition), 2016 (Oxford India Paperbacks), pp. 10-11.
166. Tapan Raychaudhuri, op. cit., pp. 359-60.
167. Dagmar Engels, *Beyond Purdah? Women in Bengal 1890-1939*, Delhi: Oxford University Press, 1996, p. 44.
168. Bharati Ray, 'Women of Bengal: Transformation in Ideas and Ideals, 1900-1947', *Social Scientist*, vol. 19, nos. 5/6, May-June 1991, p. 8.
169. Utsa Ray, 'How to be a good wife? Some thoughts on 'new' domesticity in nineteenth-century Bengal', in Suparna Gooptu (ed.), *Writing Women in History: Glimpses from India's Colonial Past*, Kolkata: K.P. Bagchi & Company, 2019, pp. 82-3; Judith E. Walsh, *Domesticity in Colonial India: What Women Learned When Men Gave Them Advice*, USA: Rowman and Littlefield Publishers, 2004, pp. 1-10.
170. Sreemati Nagendra Bala Mustafi, *Garhasthya-dharma* (Domestic Duties), Burdwan: Shri Khagendranath Mustafi, 1904.
171. Priyanath Bose, *Griha-dharma* ('Household Duties'), Calcutta, 1934.
172. Monmayee Basu, op. cit., 2004 (first edition), 2016 (Oxford India Paperbacks), p. 12.
173. Utsa Ray, op. cit., 2019, pp. 83-4.
174. A.E. Porter, *Report on the Census of Bengal, 1931*, Calcutta, 1932, pp. 79-81, cited in Sabyasachi Bhattacharya, *The Defining Moments in Bengal, 1920-1947*, New Delhi: Oxford University Press, 2014, p. 51.
175. Bharati Ray and Aparna Basu (eds.), *From Independence Towards Freedom: Indian Women Since 1947*, New Delhi: Oxford University Press, 1999, p. 6.
176. Rachana Chakraborty, 'Women's Education and Empowerment in

Colonial Bengal', in Hans Hagerdal (ed.), *Responding to the West: Essays on Colonial Domination and Asian Agency*, Amsterdam: Amsterdam University Press, 2009, p. 88.

177. Meredith Borthwick, op. cit., 1984, p. 121.
178. Abala Bose, Report of Lecture in *Modern Review*, 1:2, cited in Bharati Ray, 'Women of Bengal: Transformation in Ideas and Ideals, 1900-1947', *Social Scientist*, vol. 19, nos. 5/6, May-June 1991, p. 8.
179. Kamini Roy, *Balikasikshar Adarsha* (The Ideal of Girls' Education), Calcutta: Sudhir Kumar Sen, 1918, cited in Bharati Ray, 'Women of Bengal: Transformation in Ideas and Ideals, 1900-1947', *Social Scientist*, vol. 19, nos. 5/6, May-June 1991, p. 9.
180. *Progress of Education in India, 1937-1947, Decennial review, 2: 362-9* cited in Bharati Ray, 'Women of Bengal: Transformation in Ideas and Ideals, 1900-1947', *Social Scientist*, vol. 19, no. 5/6, May-June 1991, p. 9.
181. Jibanananda Das, 'Amar Ma, Baba' (My Mother, Father), Uttar Suri, December-February, 1954, cited in Monmayee Basu, op. cit., 2004 (first edition), 2016 (Oxford India Paperbacks), p. 13.
182. Monmayee Basu, op. cit., 2004 (first edition), 2016 (Oxford India Paperbacks), p. 15.
183. Bharati Ray, 'Women of Bengal: Transformation in Ideas and Ideals, 1900-1947', *Social Scientist*, vol. 19, nos. 5/6, May-June 1991, p. 12.
184. Monmayee Basu, op. cit., 2004 (first edition), 2016 (Oxford India Paperbacks), pp. 7-8.
185. *The Friend of India*, 11 June 1868, cited in Benoy Ghose (ed.), *Selections from English Periodicals of 19th Century Bengal, Volume VI: 1861-1874*, Calcutta: Papyrus, 1981, p. 136.
186. Rabindranath Tagore, 'Dena Paona' (Assets and Liabilities), in *Galpaguccha*, Kolkata: Visva-Bharati Granthan Bibhag, Ashwin 1369.
187. *Census of India, 1931*, vol. 5, Part 1, p. 221; *Census of India, 1901*, vol. 6, part 1, p. 268.
188. *Census of India 1911*, vol. 1, Part 1 and *Census of India 1941*, vol. 4, cited in Bharati Ray, 'Women of Bengal: Transformation in Ideas and Ideals, 1900-1947', *Social Scientist*, vol. 19, nos. 5/6, May-June 1991, p. 13.
189. K.M. Kapadia, *Marriage and Family in India*, London: Oxford University Press (Indian edn.), 1958, p. 154.
190. Bharati Ray, 'Women of Bengal: Transformation in Ideas and Ideals, 1900-1947', *Social Scientist*, vol. 19, nos. 5/6, May-June 1991, p. 13.
191. Bharati Ray, 'Bengali Women and Politics of Joint Family, 1900-47',

Economic and Political Weekly, vol. 26, no. 52, 28 December 1991, p. 3016.

192. Ibid.
193. Bharati Ray, 'Women of Bengal: Transformation in Ideas and Ideals, 1900-1947', *Social Scientist*, vol. 19, nos. 5/6, May-June 1991, p. 15; Bharati Ray, 'The Three Generations: Female Rivalries and the Joint Family in Bengal, 1900-1947', in Rajat Kanta Ray (ed.), *Mind Body and Society: Life and Mentality in Colonial Bengal*, Oxford: Oxford University Press, 1995, pp. 364-90.
194. Sambuddha Chakrabarti, 'Changing Notions of Conjugal Relations in Nineteenth-Century Bengal', in Rajat Kanta Ray (ed.), *Mind Body and Society: Life and Mentality in Colonial Bengal*, Oxford: Oxford University Press, 1995, p. 301.
195. Bharati Ray, 'Women of Bengal: Transformation in Ideas and Ideals, 1900-1947', *Social Scientist*, vol. 19, nos. 5/6, May-June 1991, p. 15.
196. Meredith Borthwick, op. cit., 1984, p. 150.
197. Dagmar Engels, op. cit., 1996; Himani Bannerji, *Inventing Subjects: Studies in Hegemony, Patriarchy and Colonialism*, New Delhi: Tulika, 2001, pp. 72-98.
198. Judith E. Walsh, op. cit., 2004, pp. 1-10.
199. Rochona Majumdar, *Marriage and Modernity: Family Values in Colonial Bengal*, Durham and London: Duke University Press, 2009, p. 129.
200. Jyotirmoyee Devi, 'Narir Pratibha' ('Women's Talent'), *Bharati*, 1331 BS, pp. 796-801.
201. Barbara Southard, *The Women's Movement and Colonial Politics in Bengal*, New Delhi: Manohar, 1995, pp. 17-18.
202. Bhudev Mukhopadhyay, *Samajik Prabandha* (Essays on Social Matters), Chinsurah: Bishwanath Trust Fund, 1892, pp. 37-43.
203. Bhudev Mukhopadhyay, *Paribarik Prabandha* (Essays on Family Matters), Chinsurah: Published by Shri Kumardev Mukhopadhyay in Budhoday Press, 1882 (9th edn. 1919), pp. 1-5, 6-14, 18-23, 28-33, 34-38, 156-161.
204. Monmayee Basu, op. cit., 2004 (first edition), 2016 (Oxford India Paperbacks), p. 17.
205. Ibid., pp. 17-18. Samarpita Mitra, *Periodicals, Readers and the Making of a Modern Literary Culture: Bengal at the Turn of the Twentieth Century*, Leiden/Boston: Brill, 2020, pp. 176, 298-9.
206. Monmayee Basu, op. cit., 2004 (first edition), 2016 (Oxford India Paperbacks), pp. 16-18; Sabyasachi Bhattacharya (ed.), *A Comprehensive History of Modern Bengal, 1700-1950, Volume II*, Kolkata: The Asiatic

Society, in association with Primus Books, 2020, pp. 804-40; Sabyasachi Bhattacharya (ed.), *A Comprehensive History of Modern Bengal, 1700-1950, Volume III*, Kolkata: The Asiatic Society, in association with Primus Books, 2020, pp. 578-609, 630-63, 664-722.

207. Bharati Ray, 'Beyond the Domestic/Public Dichotomy: Women's History in Bengal, 1905-1947', in S.P. Sen and N.R. Ray (eds.), *Modern Bengal: A Socio-Economic Survey*, Calcutta, 1988, pp. 240-56.

CHAPTER 2

Marriage and the Law

Brahmos and The Act III of 1872

As agrarian relations were reconfigured, new sites of work appeared, displacing older ones and property relations were also re-gendered. Nevertheless, extensive debates on Hindu women captured the complications in our modernity. High caste women were rarely permitted to leave their homes or work outside the home and were compelled to enter into 'non-consensual, monogamous, indissoluble patrilocal' infant marriages to husbands who could have as many wives as they wanted. Marriage was a worthwhile 'profession' among the purest *kulin* brahmins. More or less all castes followed Brahmanical gender norms as claims to higher ritual status and social respectability increased among small sections of the lower castes. Census Reports obtained a comparatively serious form from 1881. Till 1901, each census registered the strong preference for sons among Bengali Hindus. The 1881 census cited the prevalence of female infanticide and attributed the skewed male-female sex ratio to it. The 1891 census specified, 'If a girl dies ... before she arrives at the age when caste custom demands that she should be betrothed, so much the better for the family resources. Many a girl is allowed to die unattended where medical aid would be at once called in if the son were attacked.' The 1901 census restated the 'universal desire amongst natives of India. ...for male offspring, and when the desire is fulfilled, the child is treated with much more care than it would be if it proved to be a girl, boys are better fed and better clothed'.[1]

In 1772, a colonial 'Judicial Plan' professed that 'all issues related to caste, marriage, divorce, succession, adoption, and inheritance would be regulated by Hindu and Muslim religious scripture and tradition, with each group having its own set of Personal Laws.' Only if pandits and maulvis could demonstrate that the latter were contravening authentic scriptural requirements, new laws would be imposed and old practises would be illegal. A Royal Edict of 1797 and an Imperial Decree of 1858 echoed the agreement. If there were any differences of opinion, the state acted as an adjudicator, adopting the most persuasive explanation.[2] As a result, personal laws provided an exclusive prospect for Indians to reawaken themselves on their own footing. Marriages had to be performed wholly within personal laws, inadvertently implanting a person within their community's rules and regulations. Intercommunity and intercaste alliances were thus ruled out. Personal choice was also buried under the weight of family and community expectations. A few petitions on remarriage had courageously proposed that marriage be removed from religious regulations and it would be made as a civil matter.

Initially known as the Calcutta Unitarian Committee in 1823, the Brahmo Sabha in 1828, and finally the Brahmo Samaj in 1843, this community was instrumental in the origin and advancement of every significant religious, social, and political movement in India from 1820 to 1930. Although the Brahmo Samaj was established at the house of Firingi Kamal Basu at Jorasanko in August 1828 on the initiative of Rammohan Roy, it was only the beginning. The real triumph of the Brahmo Samaj began after the establishment of the Tattvabodhini Sabha in 1839 and was accelerated on 21 December 1843 by Devendranath Tagore's conversion to Brahmo Dharma by Ramchandra Vidyabagish along with twenty other members of the Brahmo Samaj. Later, the Brahmo Samaj's radical-reformist wing, led by Keshub Chandra Sen, sought a separate set of marriage regulations in 1868, distinct from Hindu marriage rules, in order to assert their independence from Hinduism.[3] On the other hand, Adi Brahmo Samaj under Devendranath Tagore regarded their sect as a part of the Hindu community. This led to a schism in the Brahmo Samaj in 1866. As a result of a petition from Keshub Chandra Sen and the younger members of Brahmo Samaj ('Keshubites'), the Governor-General of India approved to an Act to Provide a Form of Marriage in Certain Cases, otherwise known as Act III of 1872. The Act III of 1872, which was essentially a law of civil marriage, constructively eliminated the significance of Hindu sacraments in the act and accomplishment of a marriage. Nevertheless, the 'Cooch Behar controversy' (1872), which emphasized the course of action, in which this law was disobeyed by the Brahmos under the leadership of Keshub Chandra Sen, who were the driving strength behind the passing of this act – was evident in the case of the flexibility of ritual adherence in Hindu marriages and to community distinctiveness during the nineteenth century.[4] Approximately 80 years after the first civil marriage act, alternative section of modern Indian administrators or representatives, most notably B.R. Ambedkar and Jawaharlal Nehru, managed to secularize Indian marriage once more through the Special Marriage Act of 1954 and specific procedures in the Hindu Code Bill of 1955-6. In the course of the 1860s and first half of the 1870s, there were two breaches, which split up Brahmo Samaj into three factions; the Adi Brahmo Samaj, the Brahmo Samaj of India, and the Sadharan Brahmo Samaj.[5] Marriage and marital law were significant matters in each of these schisms. It is hence significant to analyse the context of the debates around Brahmo marriage to understand fully the history of the passing of Act III of 1872, which was later linked with the history of raising the age of marriage of girls. The pursuit for substitutes to traditional marriage norms henceforth continued as an anxious and uncomfortable practice, generating successive splits within the Samaj. While conservative Brahmos thought that marriage became a medium for reconciling Hindu metaphysical thought; according to liberals, it was a device to forge new social and cultural identities. The development of new conceptions of conjugality portrayed a threat to established social conventions of gender inequality and women's confinement, making it one of the most contentious issues of the time.[6] The agenda of marriage reform was part of a greater women's issue within the Brahmo movement.

At first the split in the Brahmo Samaj (1866) into two groups – the Hinduized Brahmos (the Adi Brahmo Samaj) and radical Keshubites, over the marriage laws meant that the Council could not legislate for the group Brahmo Samaj marriages. Furthermore, the Council deemed it sensible to protect not only Keshub Sen's group of the Brahmo Samaj, but all those who opposed marrying in accordance with the religious laws of any of the native communities.[7] Act III of 1872 provided for the first time in India a law for civil marriage. One of the conditions of the act was a declaration of being above the age of eighteen for men and fourteen for women. This was an extremely sensitive issue, as proved by the Age of Consent debate nineteen years later. Opposition to the Age of Consent Bill came from orthodox and conservatives Hindus who sought to stop reformers from raising the age of consent for girls from ten to twelve years. Act III of 1872, on the other hand, succeeded to set a higher age for civil marriage. A clause in the Act increased the age of individual consent to twenty-one years, unless there was written consent of the parent or guardian.[8] Yet, its passage has been so broadly overlooked that even in an extensive work of Indian legal history – *Outlines of Indian Legal History* – from the seventeenth to the twentieth century, the first law to introduce civil marriage in India does not even merit a single mention.[9] In spite of the increasing academic attention in the relationships between reform movements and the law in the nineteenth century[10] there are only few works[11] that mention the history and significance of this very momentous and certainly emblematic legislation.

The crusade against child marriage began in Bengal during the middle of the nineteenth century. However, a few Bengali women from Chinsura had already expressed their dissatisfaction in the newspapers. Their grievances were engrossed in the structure of questions in the *Samachar Darpan* in 1835 as follows,

> Oh, father and brother: Why should you deprive us of the scope of education which the women of other countries do avail? Do you think that education would make us unfit for domestic duties? Why don't you allow us to live and move freely as women of other countries do? Why are we transferred like cattle at the tender age of 4, 5, 10 and 12 to unknown men who have no education, wealth or beauty? Why do you treat us so cruelly?[12]

In July 1847, the *Sambad Prabhakar* showed that early marriage was detrimental to the education of young boys.[13] The movement against child marriage obtained incentive throughout the 1860s and 1870s. The *Bamabodhini Patrika* published an article denouncing the evils of child marriage, highlighting numerous abuses originated by it.[14] The weekly paper, *Somprakash* was very critical of child marriage and polygamy and wrote strongly against it.[15]

The group that would be discussed here is the Brahmos – a reformist group of men and women who assembled confirmed claims to being distinct from practicing Hindus. As Rochona Majumdar has stated, 'Marriage was critical to the whole question of community identity' and eventually it has been established that 'the *Brahmos* leaned heavily toward defining themselves as a community with an identifiable set of marriage rituals, rather than as one whose weddings were a mark of secular individualism.'[16] Under the leadership of Keshub Chandra Sen, the younger members of Brahmo Samaj ('Keshubites') publicized marriage reforms during the 1860s. In 1866, Sen led a group of liberal Brahmos to break away from the conservative elders of the Samaj (Adi Brahmo Samaj) to form the Brahmo Samaj of India (Bharatbarshiya Brahmo Samaj) under his leadership. High-caste Brahmos detached their sacred threads as signs of a rejection of caste. Progressively, young Brahmos were being debarred by their castes and evicted from their families for their efforts at reforming Hinduism. Several Brahmos' biographical narrative and autobiographies gave evidence to their encounter of harassment by the Hindu community during the mid-nineteenth century in Bengal. A statement made by Devendranath Tagore reflected their lonely sufferings in the city of Calcutta, 'we Brahmos are situated amidst a community which views us with no friendly feelings' since 'we ourselves attack their Puranic and Tantric systems.' He argued that Brahmos show 'practical hostility' to Anglicized 'secularists' and to other 'denationalized' sorts such as the Christian converts. He went on to add, 'so long as our numbers are so small, our resources so limited and our enemies as powerful as they are now', the community would remain in a precarious position.[17] The orthodox backlash against Brahmoism was formidable. David Kopf has cited an incident of the 1860s, in which a Brahmo youth, Durga Mohun Das, fired up by the ideal of female emancipation, married off his widowed stepmother to a local medical practitioner. It was a love marriage. The result was social excommunication.[18] Sivanath Sastri has mentioned that the doctor's clients deserted him and he had to give up his practice. About Durga Mohun, men threw dust at him and abused him on the streets. Dirty stories were told about his stepmother. The Hindus would never hear the name of Durga Mohun uttered, but spit on the ground as a mark of their abhorrence.[19] Kopf also argues that 'by the time Sen submitted the petition regarding the marriage Bill, he was increasingly aware that while the Brahmo Samaj was viewed as a "religion" and an "ideology", he had to make it a full-fledged "community" in order to strengthen its ranks.' The Brahmo Samaj provided shelter to youths undergoing 'identity crises' and harassment. One of the most effective and practical ways early Brahmo leaders offered protection was to organize, institutionalize and legalize community solidarity.[20] Some like Durga Mohun Das and Dwarakanath Ganguly, went further to admit their wives and daughters into public life, strongly opposed by Hindus and elderly Brahmos.[21]

The year 1872 witnessed an important Reform Act, the earliest piece of legislation, which sought to deal with early marriage. Actually, Devendranath Tagore, the member of the earlier faction was the first to introduce a generalized and reformed Brahmo wedding ceremony that excluded the idolatry elements of conventional Hindu rituals in 1861.[22] While experimenting with alternative forms of life-cycle rituals, Devendranath innovated *Nirishwar Bibaha* (non-deist marriage), retaining the notion of a spiritual sacrament but rejecting Hindu *shastric achara* (scriptural services).[23] One of the earliest marriages in the Brahmo Samaj, which took place on 26 July 1861, according to the reformed rites was that of Sukumari Devi, the second daughter of Devendranath Tagore, to Hemendranath Mukhopadhyay. Sivanath Sastri decided to write regarding this marriage, 'Properly speaking, this was the first step taken by the two Brahmo leaders (Keshub Sen and Devendranath Tagore) conjointly in the direction of practical social reform.' It is remarkable that in framing the marriage ritual, Devendranath, in pursuance of his well-known conservative instincts, kept as close as possible to the rituals followed in orthodox Hindu marriages, excluding therefrom the idolatrous portions.[24] The rites carried out during the time of marriage comprised *arghopradan* (offerings to the Lord), *striachar* (women's rituals), *Brahmo worship*, *sampradan* (the gift of the daughter) and ministerial advice to the newlyweds.[25] This marriage was regarded as a significant move towards social reform, and therefore the Brahmo Samaj came to be recognized as a reforming body by the public.[26] In 1862, Devendranath's third son Hemendranath Tagore's marriage with the daughter of Joydeb Chattopadhyay of Santragachi took place according to the reformed rites.[27] The Keshubites contended that as a theist sect of reformist Hindus who wished to expunge from Hinduism the corruption of its later idolatry they hoped to introduce amongst themselves a legally valid form of marriage called the Brahmo Marriage. This would be celebrated with non-idolatrous rituals and between Brahmos who might or might not be of diverse Hindu castes.[28] Since before the split was formalized and the Brahmo Samaj of India was formed as a distinct entity, younger Brahmos of the new group had made some changes to their wedding ceremonies. Several old traditions were abandoned. In the place of *sampradan* (the Bengali term for *kanyadan*, i.e. gift of the bride), mutual vows were exchanged, the ceremony thus taking on a Western tinge. Instead of *sampradan*, they adopted the process of *kanya arpan*, which involved handing over the bride in a more participatory manner. In relation to this, when Brahmos gradually took vows in a somewhat more impressive way, a component of individualism was familiarized into ceremonial processes. As part of their marriage vows the younger party adopted declarations such as 'In the presence of the merciful lord and this spiritual assembly, I willingly and unhesitatingly accept my role as your husband (or wife).'[29] The decision for women's consent in marriage sparked debate about women's legal subjectivity, depicted an obstacle to child marriage, and commonly distorted the ongoing debates about Hindu marriage.[30] In 1864, the younger members of Brahmo Samaj made a daring modernization by getting Parvati Charan Das married to an accomplished widowed girl, Swarnamoyee of a different caste. This induced a dispute in the Samaj.[31] The progressive members of the Brahmo Samaj separated in November 1866. According to the newly revised rituals, another intercaste marriage took place in December between Babu Prasanna Kumar Sen and Srimati Raj Lakshmi Maitra.[32]

At the moment, predominantly after intercaste marriages became common among certain Brahmos, a proposal was forwarded to India's Advocate General, raising the question of whether or not Brahmo marriages were regarded valid in the eyes of the law. In 1868, the question of legitimacy of the changes concerning marriage ceremonies was brought up and the Advocate General acknowledged that the marriages which were conducted according to the Brahmo Samaj's rituals were legitimately unacceptable. He stated that 'Brahmo marriages not having been celebrated with Hindu or Mahomedan rites of orthodox regularity and not conforming to the usages of any recognized religion were invalid and the offspring of them illegitimate.'[33] The rejection of Brahmo marriages, which carefully avoided Hindu ceremonial procedures as well as the statement that the offspring of these weddings were also invalid, fuelled the movement for a Brahmo marriage act.[34] Perhaps encouraged by this decision, the issue was brought up again in front of a Brahmo congregation, and a decision was made to reach the government officially so that the proposed bill could be drafted.[35] As a result of this, Keshub Sen discussed the subject with the officials in charge of legislation, principally with Sir Henry Maine on 5 July 1868, who was then the Law Member of the Governor-General's Legislative Council.[36] Keen to promote this reformist urge, Henry Maine, best known for his anthropological speculation that 'societies moved from status to contract', determined not only to approve their proposal, but rather to bring a broad-reaching Bill to all of India that would allow any dissenting voices to marry anyone who they selected under a new civil marriage law. Maine unquestionably viewed the Brahmo petition as portraying a revolutionary advancement in which caste as well as kinship marriages would collapse to marriages grounded on individual contract.[37] In their appeal of 1868, the Keshubites had set forth a draft, which projected that 'a Brahmo in any of the provinces be chosen by the local government or Chief Commissioner who would sanction him to grant certificates of marriage between Brahmos.' The foremost settings for this kind of marriage were a minimum age of eighteen for a boy and fourteen for a girl.[38] If the girl was a minor, the permission of her father or guardian was to be acquired.[39] Neither party should have a living husband or wife, thereby upholding the ideals of widow remarriage and monogamy. Lastly, the oaths that was asked to take in front of the Brahmo registrar professed, 'I, A.B., am a Brahmo and I do declare in the presence of the Almighty God that I take thee C.D., to be my lawful wedded wife (or husband).'[40] The Keshubites successfully demanded the government to proceed for legislation designating them as a distinct community with the right to intermarry liberally according to the rituals of their principles.[41]

Henry Maine assumed that the Brahmo sect was new, and that its dogmas and principles, like those of all newly created religious bodies, were not well defined. He consequently, replied to the Keshubites' appeal by introducing a draft Bill before the Council entitled, 'A Bill to Legalize Marriages Between Certain Natives of India Not Professing the Christian Religion'.[42] This was the first draft among the three other drafts and it had been popularly mentioned as the Native Marriage Bill. This Bill's principal characteristic was that it was not restricted to the Brahmos and that it introduced civil marriage to India. As stated by this Bill, 'any two natives (crucially, not professing the Christian religion) who objected to be married in accordance with the rites of the Hindu, Muhammadan, Buddhist, Parsi or Jewish religion could legalize their marriages under this law.'[43] Previously, in the first draft one may perceive a shift in emphasis away from the Brahmo request to recognize them as a distinct community with legitimate rites of marriage, to a more individualistic conception of marriage based on the conjugal couple. The explanation by Henry Maine for broadening the Bill's pertinency to non-Brahmos was twofold. Primarily, he sensed that 'the Brahmos were an ill-defined group, whose formation as a sect was undergoing constant change. This made it difficult to define a Brahmo for legal purposes.'[44] Furthermore, he contended that 'increasingly, young educated Hindus who were approaching marriageable age were abandoning Hinduism and Hindu rites.' But all the citizens were not the members of factions like the Brahmo Samaj. If the Council limited the actions to the Brahmo Creed, those who were not conscientiously Brahmos but wanted to abandon their religious beliefs would have to apply for a new procedure.[45] On 18 November 1868, Maine presented the Bill and distributed it to the local government administrators and representatives for their opinions. The presented bill was defeated in the votes regarding opinions because it was to be expected to present comprehensive changes in native law and would intervene with indigenous social interactions.[46] The most considerable argument was that while Maine demanded it was a permissive act – it did not affect the rights of those to whom the Bill did not apply, the implementation of the Act was not limited to the Brahmos, but in its place contributed a much broader domain for people who desired to take advantage of its clauses and regulations. Considering this, it was eventually decided that 'the Bill should be introduced to a Select Committee and under a suspension of rules it should be published, so that public opinion might pronounce on it'.[47] The Bill was disapproved by the orthodox Hindus, the landholders of Bengal, and the Pandits of Varanasi, who were concerned about heterodox unions within their communities. As a result, the Bill was put on hold for two years. Maine's explanation for instituting a civil marriage registration was the purpose that as in several European countries, there would first be a civil and afterwards a religious marriage. This would permit factions such as the Brahmos to include regardless of what ceremonies they wished to perform; however, it would also allow people to tie the knot using rituals of their personal preference.[48] One of the challenging points in the controversy was the satisfactory marriageable age of Indian girls. In April 1871, Keshub Sen, as the President of the Indian Reform Association, sent a circular to well-known medical practitioners of the country and sought their view.[49] The medical authorities of Calcutta determined the age of fourteen as the minimum marriageable age for girls. Nevertheless, the Council sensed that all the Local Governments decided that restricting the Bill to the Brahmo Samaj would be inoffensive. After obtaining the report of the Select Committee in March 1871, Fitzjames Stephen (Sir James Stephen), who took the place of Maine as the Law Member, evaluated the hostility from the conservative Hindus and modified the Bill. Perveez Mody, who has investigated the consequences of this act in the context of 'love marriages' in modern Indian society, has constructed several important assumptions. She has drawn attention to the fact that 'only the second draft of the bill became one intended exclusively for the Brahmos under the name of the Brahmo Marriage Bill, 1871.'[50] The Bill's subject matter was nearly identical to what the Keshubites had initially requested. It encompassed 'a declaration prior to the solemnization of the marriage to the effect that both parties were members of the Brahmo Samaj, that they were unmarried and that the minimum age of marriage was to be eighteen for the boy and fourteen for the girl.'

The appellation Brahmo was not there in the first version, nor was it retained in the third and final edition,[51] which became law as Act III of 1872. Additionally, as the Brahmos had wanted, the Registrar came to be known as the 'Registrar for Brahmo Marriages', however it was vague whether he would necessarily be a Brahmo.[52]

This Bill elicited a far more venomous response in comparison with the first Bill, and at that moment, reactions came from other members of the Brahmo Samaj, apart from the Keshubites. By the year 1866, the Brahmo Samaj had been divided into two camps – the 'Conservatives' and the 'Progressives', which had already been mentioned. The former group called the Adi Brahmo Samaj, led by Devendranath Tagore, at once sent a deputation, which met the Law Member in the morning of the day on which the Bill was to be passed and pressed its objections against the measure. Following Maine's Bill, the Adi Brahmo Samaj appealed the Council in 1868, opposing to the consequence that members of the Brahmo Samaj were no more Hindus. According to them, their denial was not a refusal of Hinduism but simply 'an expunging from the latter of superstitious and non-essential marriage rituals'.[53] They further raised objections to the government intervening to legitimize the customs and conventions of the splinter group, as if it were a recognized power in Indian religious affairs. Stephen found a valid reason to postpone the Bill's passage until July. The same Adi Brahmo Samaj deputation travelled from Calcutta to Simla on 31 March 1871, and presented Stephen with a memorial opposing the Bill.[54] Adi Brahmo Samaj sent a petition to the Council, which was signed by 2,050 members, claiming that their '1868 memorial' defaming Keshub Chandra Sen had been completely overlooked. Stephen tried to defend himself by claiming that, despite signing a document stating that among other things, the petition of Adi Brahmo Samaj had been offered careful attention, but genuinely he had never noticed the document. He also asserted that he had no idea that the Brahmo Samaj had already been divided or that the Keshubites were a separate faction.[55] One of Keshub Chandra Sen's first problems was that his representation to the Council claimed to be on behalf of the Brahmo Samaj. There was no indication that he had previously initiated a split with another faction within the Samaj, and thus could only claim to represent one of the groups. The Adi

Brahmo Samaj petitioned the Council, vehemently rejecting Sen's claim that all Brahmos had broken away from the Hindu community. They argued,

> The *Brahmos*, notwithstanding that they have renounced certain opinions and practices which they look upon as superstitious and which are in no way essential portions of the Hindu religion, have always been recognised and treated even by the most orthodox Hindus as undoubted members of the Hindu community. … The reformed Hindu marriage ritual has in it all the essential elements which constitute a valid Hindu marriage.[56]

The first objection of the deputationists was that its application would extend to the whole body of Brahmos, although the majority of the members of the Brahmo Samaj did not feel the need for such an enactment, nor had they applied for any legislation on the subject of Brahmo Marriage. Second, they claimed that 'Brahmo marriages, by which they meant marriages celebrated under the rituals of the Adi Brahmo Samaj, were as valid as the marriages of other reformed Hindus.' Therefore, there was no question of seeking further validation from the state through a new law. Their objection was that such a law would tend to cut off the Brahmos from the general community of Hindus of which they formed an integral part. Their third argument was that 'the form prescribed by the Bill for registration of marriages would reduce it to a mere civil contract and consequently, the fact was that the parties to the marriage would not be mandatory to go through any religious observance was tremendously repellant to the feelings of the members of the Brahmo Samaj and it would be tough for them to reconcile themselves to the forms and practices enjoined in the proposed law.' Fourth, the provision with respect to the age of the parties contracting the Brahmo Marriage was inconsistent with the usages of the country, because the marriageable age of girls in India was considered to be below fourteen years. Fifth, the passing of the proposed law would lead to serious complications with regard to the question of succession and inheritance of the descendants of those who would avail of the provisions of the proposed enactment and marry out of the pale of Hindu society. There was nothing in the existing law to regulate the succession of the children of such a marriage to the property left either by the father or the mother.[57] The Keshubites' efforts to create a Brahmo community outside of Hinduism raised the prospect of complete alienation from the larger Hindu community, which the Adi Brahmo Samaj desired to avoid at all costs.[58] To gain support for the act, Keshub Sen sent a letter to the top medical professionals of the country, questioning for their opinions on the appropriate age of marriage for women.[59] The most of medical authorities, including, Dr Mahendralal Sircar, Charles, and Atmaram Pandurang, stated that 'sixteen should be the minimum age of marriage for girls'. The Table 2.1 mentioned in Miss Collet's *Brahmo Year Book*, would give a conception of these viewpoints.

TABLE 2.1: DOCTORS' OPINION REGARDING MARRIAGEABLE AGE OF INDIAN GIRLS DURING 1870S[60]

Name	*Minimum Age*	*Proper Age*
Dr Chandra K. Day	14	
Dr T. Charles	14	
Dr Nabin K. Bose	15	18
Dr A.V. White (Bombay)	15 or 16	18
Dr Mohendra Lal Sircar	16	
Dr Tumiz Khan Bahadur	16	
Dr Norman Chevers	16	18
Dr D.B. Smith	16	18 or 19
Dr Ewart	16	18 or 19
Dr J. Fayhar (Fayrer)	16	18 or 20
Dr S.G. Chakraverty	16	21
Dr Atmaram Pandurang	20	

The fact that Tumiz Khan did a lot of research to determine this age was evident by his letter to Keshub Chandra Sen. At the same time, Dr Khan considered the social, geographical, physical, and legal aspects. The letter was published in the *Calcutta Journal of Medicine* in 1871,

Experience and the laws both tend to establish the fact that in the tropical climates, this age is attained between the tenth and the thirteenth year.

Although a girl may become marriageable at the age, but dictates of observation, common sense, and lastly biological laws cannot but lead us to the conclusion, that a female cannot be sufficiently mature for the fulfilment of the serious duties of a wife, much less for those of a mother, at the extremely tender and early age, and that where forced to do so, her delicate and hitherto immature organization becomes rapidly impaired both in health and vigour, and thus before she is actually young, she gets old and decrepit. This exerts its baneful influences on her progeny. Speaking in a scientific and humane point of view, I might safely pronounce that in considering the proper age of marriage for a native girl of India, we should not look to the time when the signs of puberty show themselves generally, but make it a point that under no circumstances is a girl to be allowed to get married before she has attained the full age of sixteen years at least....[61]

Sen made this a ground to create support for the bill. He argued,

We contemplate the abolition of early marriages.... The medical authorities in Calcutta almost unanimously declared that sixteen is the minimum marriageable age of girls in this country.... In conformity with the suggestion and the opinion given by the other referees, we have come to the conclusion that for the present at least it would be expedient to follow the provision in the Bill which makes fourteen the minimum marriageable age of girls in this country; leaving it in the hands of time to develop this reform slowly and gradually into maturity and fulness.[62]

Keshub had thoroughly examined this issue in light of medical opinion, and it thus depicted a crucial facet of marriage reform for him.[63] It should be noted however that the objection letter sent to Simla by the Adi Brahmo Samaj, referred this as being 'too high'.[64]

Considering the Adi Brahmo Samaj's objections, the Bill was again postponed for a few months before being brought before the Council of the Governor-General of India on 16 January 1872, when Stephen moved the bill in the Council and explained the backdrop of the measure. He urged that the Bill be passed as soon as possible.[65] Inglis, a Council member, opposed the Bill on the premise that calculating people with nefarious intentions could use certain provisions of the Bill to entice lads from good families who were in love with dancing girls into marriages that would end in disgrace and ruin. As a result, he proposed that the Bill be re-circulated throughout the country and referred to local governments in order to gather public feedback on its provisions.[66] Cockerell, another Council member, agreed with the additional delay. Only Temple agreed with Stephen that the Bill should not be postponed. The motion by Inglis was put to vote, and it was carried by a vote of nine to two. The Bill was brought before the Council again on 19 March 1872.[67] Because native opinion did not support the measure, Inglis proposed that the bill be referred back to the Select Committee for necessary changes. He read letters from eminent people in high positions in the Government of the Madras Presidency. For example, V. Ramiengar, Additional Member of the Council of the Government of Fort St. George wrote on 28 February 1872 that 'It (Bill) appears to me to differ little from Sir Henry Maine's Bill, so universally condemned and withdrawn'. Sachish Sastri, the head *seristadar* (head governmental officer of a court) of the Madras Revenue Board, wrote on 12 February 1872 that it is highly injudicious on the part of the government to undertake to legislate on matters connected with the social and religious movement of the people. The Acting Collector of Madura, McQuhae said that 'a few Hindus objected to the Bill on the ground that it was founded on the same principle as the Act, which legalized the remarriage of Hindu widows and Act XXI of 1850'.[68] Stephen, on the other hand, highlighted that he had also gathered the opinions of a number of Indians, which were sufficiently favourable to justify the government's decision to press on with the Bill. Hannyngton, the Acting Collector of the Kistna District, accumulated the opinions of his district's 'native gentlemen' and wrote that 'the deduction, which may be drawn from their opinion, was that they consider the Bill not entirely necessitous, but on the whole a measure to be desired'. Mac Gregor, the Collector of Malabar wrote that 'he had consulted several Hindus of his district and they had no objection to the proposed measure'.[69] Stephen moved that the Bill as amended be passed. The motion was carried by eight votes, including those of the President and Commander-in-Chief to five. In estimation of the objection of the Adi Brahmo Samaj, the new Bill was, nevertheless, retitled as the 'Special Marriage Bill', and it became law, named as Act III of 1872 after three days. The Act abolished early marriage and made polygamy penal, sanctioned widow remarriage and intercaste marriage. It was similar to the first civil marriage bill proposed by Maine in many ways, but there were certain important changes that produced many compromises to the orthodox section that had objected it. Sivanath Sastri aptly pointed out that 'The passing of this act may be justly regarded as the crowning success of the prolonged efforts of the reformers for the amelioration of their social life.'[70] Initially, it allowed dissidents from Christianity to take advantage of its regulations.[71] Furthermore, the third Bill's Preamble stated unequivocally that 'those who availed themselves of the Act were no longer to be considered members of their respective religious communities'. It specified, 'It is expedient to provide a form of marriage for persons who are neither Christians nor Jews and who do not profess or who have renounced or been excluded from the communion of the Hindu, Muhammadan, Parsi, Buddhist, Sikh or Jain religion and to legalize certain marriages the legality of which is doubtful'.[72] The declaration that Maine had projected in the first Bill, '…I object to be married in accordance with the rites of the Hindu, Muhammadan, Buddhist, Parsi or Jewish religion' was exchanged in the ultimate Act III of 1872 with the statement 'I do not profess the Christian, Jewish, Hindu, Muhammadan, Parsi, Buddhist, Sikh or Jain religion'. This change was important because the 'law' was no longer intended to merely legalize marriages performed using unconventional sacred ceremonies. Instead, it attempted to legalise weddings for those who were enthusiastic to abandon their religious beliefs entirely.[73]

Usually mentioned in Bengali as *tin aain*, or 'three laws', Act III of 1872 had three foremost mechanisms; it necessitated the rejection of idolatry, it also stated a minimum age of eighteen for boys and fourteen for girls and endorsed intercaste matches. Besides that, boys and girls below the age of twenty-one years had to obtain the consent of their father or guardian before a marriage could be solemnized.[74] Remarkably, the third Bill advanced that consent be obtained if the boy were under twenty-one and the girl under eighteen. The mutual consent (*sammati*) of the bride and the bridegroom was also very much important. A further concession to the proceeding's traditional and conservative adversaries was the raising of the age from eighteen to twenty-one at which a girl might self-sufficiently negotiate a marriage of her preference. It should be acknowledged that the widely accepted and legitimate age of marriage for Hindu girls at that period was ten.

Suniti Devi, daughter of Keshub Chandra Sen, was married before she reached the age of fourteen, immediately after the legislation was enacted, causing yet another schism within the Brahmo Samaj. Saradasundari devotes a chapter to her granddaughter Suniti, whom she refers to as 'Maharani Suniti'. She played an important role in Suniti's controversial marriage to the twenty-first Maharaja of Cooch Behar, who was only fifteen years old.[75] Suniti Devi's marriage to Nripendranarayan Bhoop, Maharaja of Cooch Behar, on 6 March 1878, was unquestionably one of the most contentious matrimonial events that took place in late colonial India[76]. The 'wedding', or since some asserted, the 'betrothal', actually occurred six years after the enactment of the first civil marriage law in British India. Shortly after Act III of 1872 had been acknowledged by a sector of the Brahmo Samaj and at the cost of separating a huge section of the Brahmos under Devendranath Tagore, Sen supervised his daughter's marriage to the Raja, disobeying almost all of the provisions of the act.[77] On 9 February 1878, a protest letter signed by twenty-six Brahmos was sent to Keshub Chandra, but it went unanswered.[78]

The Act III of 1872 was evidently aimed at impulsive youth who, it was claimed, could take advantage of the Act without thinking about the repercussions. This issue was maintained to a degree in the 1954 amendment to Act III of 1872, when Nehru's government implemented the Special Marriage Act. The age of authorized permission for civil marriage in this scenario was twenty-one for men and eighteen for women. Remarkably, Act III of 1872 ruled that 'a widow of any age was not deemed to require the consent of her father or guardian, whereas widowers, unless over the age of twenty-one, still required consent to marry according to their own conscience'. As David Kopf demonstrated that Act III of 1872 was a foremost triumph for the reformist Keshubites. According to him, as soon as the Brahmo Marriage Bill was enacted by the government on 19 March 1872, the Brahmos who adhered to it were legally separate from the Hindu Samaj. The fact was momentarily ignored by the jubilant progressives all over India who hailed Keshub as a miracle worker. They pointed not to the provision on Brahmo identity, but to the provisions allowing for such reforms as intercaste and widow marriage, or prohibiting such social evils as child marriage and polygamy. Keshub had by means of memorials, letters, and visits to bureaucrats in Simla and by publicized consultations with doctors as to the proper marital age for young adults, convinced Lord Lawrence to sign into law 'a virtual social reform act'.[79] Perveez Mody has aptly pointed out that Kopf has misguidedly supposed that Act III of 1872 was called the Brahmo Marriage Bill and consequently 'at the stroke of a pen, in the eyes of the government, Brahmoism was no longer reformed Hinduism but a separate religion with a distinct legal identity'.[80] But it was precisely the reverse – the final Act did not actually make a specific mention to the Brahmos. 'It was clear' as Perveez Mody argued that 'Kopf was thinking of Stephen's "Brahmo Marriage Bill", which never saw the light of day.'

Supplementary inclusions were that it held bigamy to be punishable under the Indian Penal Code and made the provisions of the Indian Divorce Act (1869) applicable if any of the conditions of the Act were found to be violated. These circumstances were that neither partner should have a living spouse; that neither were related to each other in a nearer relationship than that of great-great-grandfather or great-great-grandmother and that a residence requirement of fourteen days (in the district where the marriage was to be registered) prior to the submission of notice was required. The proposal of notification would be recorded into the Registrar's Marriage Notice Book.[81] After the submission of the destined notice, another fourteen-day period was required before a marriage could be solemnized in the presence of the Registrar and three witnesses. Even before to Act III of 1872, Stephen's Bill proposed a much shorter five-day period of residence prior to notification and five days following entry of notice in the Registrar's Notice Book, after which the wedding could be performed.[82] The enhancement of this time frame to two weeks before and after registration in Act III of 1872 was yet another additional conciliatory gesture to the conservatives, who believed that enough time should be given to the relatives to move to the appropriate region and present their concerns to their children's marriages. The post-independence Special Marriage Act of 1954, on the other hand, increased the period from two weeks to thirty days prior and post-registration. The Act III of 1872 was a civil law that established a type of wedding that was to be performed by a state-appointed Registrar instead of a religiously appointed clergyman. Though, the chief precondition of Act III of 1872 was a declaration to the effect of a surrender of religious community. In a sarcastic turn, as Perveez Mody has rightly asserted, 'an Act born out of a petition that pleaded for legal recognition of marriages that could be solemnized in accordance to the "rights of conscience", made marriages under its provisions dependent on a denial of precisely some of those rights of conscience.'[83]

Now the question is that how significant was the women's question behind the passage of this Act III of 1872. The exciting point is that when it came to the question of expressive changes in the social position of the Hindu female, there was not much to distinguish the Adi Brahmo Samaj from the Keshubites group. It was only after much persuasion and intimidations of departure that radicals like Dwarakanath Ganguly, Ananda Charan Khastagir and Durga Mohun Das were able to push Keshub into permitting Brahmikas (female members of the Brahmo Samaj) to sit alongside males in Brahmo prayer-meetings.[84] Keshub was also opposed to the idea of University education among women[85] and one of his sermons of 1874 warned of the imminent social disaster, which would occur if women were not kept within their assigned place.[86] In his sermons, Keshub further encouraged orthodox practices, including female seclusion and modesty. One of the leading features of Sen's preaching, during this period, was to cry down attempts at women's emancipation. Upholding female seclusion and segregation, Keshub said, 'Where men are carnally panting for woman's company, and women are carnally panting for liberty, there I see the seed of great danger.'[87] Regarding the age of consent in marriage, he did not condemn early marriage, 'if these do not transgress the laws and limitations of nature' nor did he advocate late marriages 'when it is nothing but the love of animalism'.[88] At the meeting of the Arya Nari Samaj, Keshub Sen suggested 'a number of vows for Brahmo women, including *Savitri Brata*, *Draupadi Brata*, *Moitreyi Brata* and *Leelavati Brata* to promote wifely devotion and spiritual companionship with one's husband.' The non-idolatrous iconoclast Keshub glorified Hindu deities like *Durga*, *Saraswati* and *Lakshmi* as incarnations of chaste womanhood. In a number of sermons like *Patiprana Sati* (a wife intently devoted to her husband) and *Pati O Sati* (husband and chaste wife), Keshub invoked the Brahminic notions of chastity of wife while *Prem O Seba* (love and service), *Dasibrata* (slavery) and *Deeksha* (initiation) lauded chastity and unwavering devotion of women to their husbands.[89] Ishan Chandra Basu's *Nari Neeti* (principle of women) advised the Brahmo wife, 'you are the wife, the mother of his (your husband's) children, the keeper of this house... and the follower of your husband in his entire course of life'.[90] In *Streediger Prati Upadesh* (advice to the wives/advice for women), Ishan Chandra Basu articulated the dignity of a wife who was expected to attend her husband without expressing any sexual desires.[91] *Bamabodhini Patrika*, one of the principal woman's magazines edited by Brahmo liberals, published a series of articles endorsing the perfect ideal of a sacrificing, devotional and religious wifehood. A progressive voice supporting the companionate, empathetic and contract marriage was, nevertheless, uttered by Ananda Chandra Mitra. In 1899, he wrote a letter in which he questioned the gender disparity in marriage arrangements, 'the *Shastra* utters the woman is the living god of the home and poetry praises her as the soul mate of a man. In real life, the man becomes the real entity, demoting the woman into his simple shadow'. Mitra denounced the practice of *sampradan*. He claimed that this ritual ridiculed woman, as if she had been saved or encumbered by her husband.[92]

According to Perveez Mody, this act had three anthropological consequences. First, it has provided us with insight into the historical context in which colonial marriage legislation was drafted. This provided valuable information about how Indians perceived the relationship between the legal system and social reform, which was gaining traction around this time. It also allowed us to investigate the process by which the law unlocked a space, though half-heartedly, between the latter and practice of the law, representing that the law was only partially eager to support the personal right to marriage. Second, the debates surrounding the passage of this act demonstrated how the location of love and desire within marriage was perceived to be problematic and to jeopardize fame and prestige within the *biradari*, caste, or community. It also brought up obvious questions about how educated Indians and British colonial legislators considered marriage as a configuration between communities rather than individual people, as well as moral values as a realm beyond the colonial state's valid boundaries of involvement. Finally, it offered a range of debates about public morality in the particular context of multiple groups and communities objecting to the introduction of civil marriage and love marriages to India. Such responses to the legalization of love affairs revealed concerns about the probability of 'social mixing' between castes and ethno-religious groups, as well as the interpretation that anyone who had a civil marriage was blatant and extravagant.[93]

The Act III of 1872 was passed, but the uproar it caused within the Brahmo Samaj did not die away. For some Adi Brahmo Samaj members, the Marriage Act was an outrageous attack on Hindu subjects' private sphere. They argued against unjustified colonial meddling in Indians' personal affairs. Criticizing against the marriage reform at numerous public meetings and in editorials in the *National Paper* and the *Tattvabodhini Patrika*, they argued that, it was sufficient that the British had gained control of our government and administration. They could not be allowed to rule over our minds and manners, as well as our social, religious, and spiritual lives.[94] Rajnarain Bose, an eminent leader of the Adi Brahmo Samaj, circulated a pamphlet voicing agitated protests, entitled 'An Appeal to the Brahmos', in which he conveyed great regret that such a 'Godless' marriage could be implemented in the Samaj. He also voiced concern that the Brahmos had willingly surrendered their rights and liberties to a foreign government, allowing it to intervene in the country's social affairs. Babu Kali Prasanna Banarji argued that intercaste marriages would be viewed negatively by Hindus, who would regard them as heretics who would never be allowed to remain within the Hindu community. Banarji went on to praise the rigidity of caste in India, – 'India, as she now stands is proud of her unmixed blood, which would scarcely be found in any other part of the world; the chastity of her women is almost proverbial.' The fallacy of 'pure' and 'unmixed blood', remarkably connected to the chastity of India's women was utilized as an explanation to avoid intercaste as well as intercommunity marriages from being legitimized. All petitioners indirectly or openly utilize the specific instance of Brahminical and high-caste codes of purity, but generalize their impacts to all groups; in the aforesaid occasion, to all of India. Women of Indian society are seen as upholding the 'pure tradition' as reproducers of moral communities.[95] An article entitled *Nirishwar Bibaha* (Godless Marriages), which seemed in the *Tattvabodhini Patrika* of 1876 frankly stated that among other things, Act III of 1872 would certainly tend to encourage wives to forsake their husbands. A following article in the same periodical cautioned of the dreadful social revolution if the female liberated from her inferior condition of life were to somehow shift roles with the dominant male.[96]

Tattvakaumudi, on behalf of the younger Brahmos, defended the Marriage Act of 1872 on the ground that 'religious mediation was a vital feature of this new form of marriage'. The registration of marriage was only an extra act added to the existing rites, so it was wrong to suppose that this marriage system was devoid of the blessings of God. *Tattvakaumudi* also argued that 'there were different forms of marriages prevailing in India'. For example, the *Sudra* form of marriage was quite different from that of the *Brahmins* and in Bengal among the *Vaishnavas*, the exchange of garlands was the only rite observed in the marriage ceremony. All forms of marriages were equally accepted as valid in Hindu society, so what was wrong with the Act III of 1872 if it introduced a somewhat new pattern and different from the traditional one? Besides, the registration of a marriage was needed from another point of view. Since the presence of men was regarded as essential during a Hindu marriage, registration would only serve as testimony that the marriage ceremony had taken place. *Tattvabodhini*, however, refuted *Tattvakaumudi's* arguments and severely criticized the new Act. In its view, 'the marriage ceremony as envisaged in the Act of 1872 was definitely "Godless". Since registration was included as an essential part of marriage.'[97] Since the Bill provided that both the spouses must be Brahmos, the *Somprakash*, a weekly newspaper pointed out that 'this provision must be explicit and must clearly state that any person other than a Brahmo would necessarily be converted into a Brahmo a year before marriage, or else serious consequences might follow'. As, for instance, 'a shrewd prostitute with an evil motive might become a Brahmo a day before her marriage, and marry a young rich Brahmo. If the young-man died prematurely, the prostitute would inherit a large fortune and re-start her business, her purpose of marriage having been fulfilled.'[98] Second, according to the *Somprakash*, the age of marriage as prescribed in the Act was also to be opposed. It was argued that 'in India's tropical climate, girls attained puberty much earlier, so the girls' marriageable age should be lowered to twelve. As for doctors' opinions referred to by Keshub Chandra Sen, it was argued that eminent doctors like T. Charles, J. Fayhar and Mahendra Sircar looked at the problem from only one point of view and ignored the others.'[99] The argument continued that after puberty, girls felt an urge for cohabitation and that raising the age of marriage to sixteen would result in harm to the young girls due to suppression of their natural desires.[100]

However, during 1860s and 1870s, young members of Brahmo Samaj in different parts of Bengal rescued many *kulin* women and widows from forced marriages or enforced celibacy, causing a furore in society.[101] The Act III of 1872 granted women more rights than those sanctioned in the conventional construction of marriage. This Act prohibited a husband from marrying a second time during the lifetime of his first wife. When the husband died while married under the Special Marriage Act, his widow inherited his estates and her condition was not weak and pathetic. Furthermore, raising the marriageable age arrived as a relief to young girls who were saved partly from the dangers of early marriage. However, Act III of 1872 was unable to put an end to the evil practice of early marriage. The conservative Bengalis continued to support child marriage and objected strongly to Garrett's (the British government officer-in-charge of education) recommendation to the Director of Public Instruction that married boys should not be given permission to appear in the final examinations. The progressive section, on the other hand, supported Garrett's proposition because they assumed that child marriage was a harmful custom. Approximately 400 students gathered in Calcutta's Albert Hall in the month of August 1878, and decided that no student would marry before the age of twenty-one. The protest became stronger in the 1880s.[102] Yet, the marriage age increased significantly among Brahmos, particularly after the Marriage Act of 1872. In addition, the community developed a flexible system of facilitated rather than arranged marriages. Meredith Borthwick has given some instances of such marriages:

Nirmala Majumdar, whose parents were both Brahmo missionaries, met her future husband Nilratan Sircar at a Brahmo gathering. They were married when she was eighteen, in 1897. Hemantakumari Chaudhuri, editor of women's journals, met her husband at the home of her guardian, Brahmo Sibnath Shastri. He was supposed to be meeting another prospective bride, but she was also present and he preferred her.[103]

In 1876, sixteen-year-old Bhubonmohinee, daughter of a leader of East Bengal, Brajasundar Mitra, married Rajanikanta Ghosh in accordance with Act III of 1872. But Brajasundar was a staunch opponent of this act. Bhubonmohinee wrote a letter to him mentioning that she had chosen Rajanikanta as her husband and since Rajanikanta had decided to get married in accordance with this law, Brajasundar had to give his consent. At last, Brajasundar agreed to give his consent.[104] Krishna Kumar Mitra married Lilabati, fourth daughter of Rajnarain Bose, against her father's wishes, in 1881.[105] There were some photographic evidences of the emergent conjugal model increasingly common among Brahmos and reformist Hindu families. In 1883, another exciting marriage took place in obedience to the Act III of 1872. Dwarakanath Gangopadhyay married Kadambini Basu. It was unknown whether Kadambini's guardians had supported this marriage or not but none of Dwarakanath's close friends, Anandamohan Basu, Umeshchandra Dutt, Sivanath Sastri, attended the wedding.[106] In 1898, when Sisir Kumari Bagchi was twenty years old, she married a Brahmo geologist who was twenty years senior to her. Paresh Nath Sen, her professor and family friend, arranged this marriage.[107] Sarojini Chattopadhyay married Doctor Muthyala Govindarajulu Naidu in 1895; probably, Sarojini was able to get her father's consent, because she was not then twenty years old, otherwise this marriage would not have been possible, not only that, it was an intercommunity (linguistic) marriage and this incident was quite innovative in the context of that time.[108] Between 1872 and 1882, 149 Brahmo marriages were performed under the clauses of Act III of 1872.[109] Act III of 1872 opened up at least the possibility of love marriages. For a very limited circle, it took the institution of marriage out of the hands of the community and placed it with a state, which was neutral in religious terms. At the same time, it did so for far too few.[110] Leela Majumdar married Sudhir Majumdar, according to the amended form of Act III by Hari Singh Gour in 1923, without the consent of her father.[111]

A Brahmo marriage adhered to more or less the same norms as a

Hindu marriage – the bride's father paid all the marriage expenses as well as giving gifts to the groom. A few Brahmos saw this as a violation of their egalitarian principles and attempted to redress the balance.[112] Though Devendranath's opposition to an intercaste union put a stop to Surendranath Tagore's marriage with Sukriti, the daughter of Suniti Devi and Nripendranarayan of Cooch Behar, Sukriti was later married to Maharshi's maternal grandson, Jyotsnanath Ghosal, son of Swarnakumari.[113] In December 1902, Manika Sundari, the youngest daughter of Keshub Sen, married Subodh Chandra Mahalanabish, the son of liberal Brahmo, Gurucharan Mahalanabish, bridging the schism between the *Nababidhan* and the Sadharan Brahmo Samaj.[114] Nevertheless, the component of 'romance' constructed in European marriages was developing in the culture of Bengal in the late nineteenth century. Even though the idea had not yet received social consent, it must had provided the impetus of love and romance in marriage.[115] Marriages like that of Sucaru Debi, Keshub Chandra Sen's third daughter, satisfied this sort of 'romantic' anticipation, as Prabhat Basu described in *Maharani Sucaru Debir Jiban Kahini* (Life Story of Empress Sucaru Devi) that in 1889, when she was fifteen, her marriage to the 18-year-old maharaja of Mayurbhanj was arranged. His relatives were opposed to the match. They sent him to England for seven years, and on his return, he had to marry a Hindu girl. Sucaru vowed never to marry anyone else. The story had a happy ending, however. The Hindu maharani died, releasing the maharaja to marry his true love, Sucaru, in 1905, when she was thirty.[116] Change was also afoot in the Adi Brahmo camp, where the Vedantic marriages progressively gave way to unconventional marriages of widows and intercaste couples.[117] While ceremonial marriages ranged from excessive radicalism to severe orthodoxy, the ideal of the devoted wife remained relatively constant. None of the three factions of the Brahmos questioned the ideal of *pativratya* (faithful or loyal devotion of a wife to her husband). Though the lived encounters of some exceptional women definitely confronted the stereotype of a 'perfect wife', the emancipated 'new woman' remained an isolated dream in the face of reactionary Hindu nationalism. One may mention in this context the writings of Taslima Nasrin; she epitomizes the woman who goes beyond the limitations and is assaulted. Nasrin reveals the ways how patriarchal attitude encounters individuality and self-respect of women. One of the most significant feminist issues addressed in the writings of Taslima Nasrin is the conduct of women at the hands of several patriarchal establishments, such as 'family', 'society' and 'state', headed by a patriarch who either humiliates women or disregards them. Nasrin's writings characterize the question of 'gendered self-representation' in such a period when both Islamic fundamentalists and the modernizing nation-state deny it.[118]

The most notable aspect of Act III of 1872 was that, as one petitioner pointed out, even the Brahmos had not petitioned the state for a civil law of marriage. Despite this, it was passed, albeit with significant changes. Several concessions were written into the law, including an extension of the notice period and an increase in the age of majority. It demanded that people who wanted intercaste or inter-community marriages had to place themselves in a position of not-community through a categorical rejection of belonging to and professing any of India's main religions. If two people were keen to outcast themselves from the communities of their birth, the law would be willing to witness that choice and conduct a civil marriage. It could be argued then that the only difference to the situation prior to the passing of the Act was that those who contravened caste and community injunctions were excommunicated by their communities. Following the Act's passage, the same state of not-community was attained, but this time through a declaration of self-exile. Many Indians found the situation difficult to comprehend – how could anyone be of no religion?[119] The terms of Act III of 1872, as well as the orthodox reaction reflected in the petitions, promised severely to restrict its use by those seeking love marriages.[120] Act III of 1872 served as a precursor and the foundation for the Special Marriage Act of 1954, which established civil marriage law in independent India. It was amended in 1923 to allow Hindus, Buddhists, Sikhs, and Jains to marry without having to renounce their religions.[121] This was certainly a step toward allowing pan-Hindu alliances without demanding that Hindus inter-marrying should have to renounce Hinduism. Christians, Jews, Muslims, and Parsis, on the other hand, were still subject to the previous Act, as were any Hindus who wanted to marry these latter adherents. After 1872, there were legal challenges to the law, particularly in the areas of inheritance and succession. According to Hari Singh Gour, a legislator who championed the law's amendment in 1923, 'What is this; for one purpose (marriage) you say, I am not a Hindu, and for another purpose (succession) you claim to be a Hindu'. The law instituted 'self-excommunication a prerequisite, yet for the purposes of inheritance, persons could continue to avail of the benefits of their own personal laws'. The modification allowing inter-Hindu marriages was materially motivated in 1923, with the intention of replacing coparcenary rights and other rights pertaining to the Hindu undivided family with a position in which the person marrying would become a divided coparcener. The new clause stated, 'The marriage solemnised under this Act of any member of an undivided family who professes the Hindu, Buddhist, Sikh or Jain religion shall be deemed to effect his severance from such family.'[122]

Despite opposition in the Lower House of Parliament, the first Prime Minister of India, Jawaharlal Nehru, introduced a Bill into Parliament two years after India's independence, with Ambedkar as Law Minister, that subsequently amended Act III of 1872 into the Special Marriage Act of 1954.[123] The contentious declaration, portrayed by critiques of the law in the 1950s debate as stating, 'I am not a Hindu', was dropped in the new special law. According to Perveez Mody,

> The civil right to marry whomever one pleased was no longer conditional on a repudiation of religion and the Special Marriage Act thus constituted a properly civil and secular law of marriage. The Special Marriage Act was also extremely significant in Indian Statute Law because it was seen as an attempt to lay down a uniform territorial law for all of India.[124]

If India does obtain a Uniform Civil Code, as assured by the Indian Constitution,[125] the Special Marriage Act of 1954 would serve as the foundation for this future marriage law. The Special Marriage Act legalized intercommunity marriage in the wider sense of the term as it included all the religious communities residing in India. Further, there was also a provision for marriages already solemnized to be registered under it if so desired.[126] As a result of such a marriage or registration, the parties would limit the application of their personal law to their family affairs and the succession of their properties, without renunciation of their religion or sub-religious faiths.[127] The law in theory was effortlessly unresponsive to the religions of the parties utilizing in its provisions.

At the same time that the Lok Sabha was debating the Special Marriage Act, another bill was being debated. The Hindu Marriage Bill sought to make divorce and intercaste sacramental marriages between quasi-Hindu categories legal. Even before 1955, if such a Hindu desired to have a religious ceremonial intercaste marriage; he or she would have had to do so under the Arya Marriage Validation Act of 1937. This Act had been approved in favour of the Arya Samaj's constructive attitude towards intercaste marriage.[128] The Arya Samaj, like the Brahmos, sought to reform Hinduism, and one of their innovations was intercaste marriages. The Arya Marriage Validation Act was passed on the same grounds that Act III of 1872 had been confronted. The members of Arya Samaj who wanted to have intercaste marriages with other were unwilling to make the declaration of 'not-community' or 'no-religion' that Act III of 1872 necessitated, because they considered themselves to be Hindus. As a result, between 1937 and 1955, any Hindu who wanted to have an intercaste marriage without rejecting Hinduism could only do so by becoming an Arya Samaji. The Hindu Marriage Bill was introduced and passed in Parliament in 1955 to prevent such a situation from occurring and to assist Hindus who wished to have a religious marriage rather than a civil marriage.[129] This Act had three direct effects. First, it made religious marriages between Hindus, Buddhists, Sikhs, and Jains of any caste legal. Second, it introduced a provision for divorce that applied equally to men and women, and third, it enshrined the principle of monogamy for all Hindus irrespective of the forms of marriages. The discussions over the Hindu Marriage Act were far more heated and contentious than those of the previous year over the Special Marriage Act. This was because the latter was seen as catering to an urban westernized elite rather than attempting to enforce progressive ideas on conservative natives, whereas the Hindu Marriage Act affected a significant majority of the population. Many Members of Parliament (MPs) argued that on top of intercaste marriages destroying the fabric of social life, divorce would now definitively destroy the Hindu family. Furthermore, the debate brought up the issue of a civil code for all

Indians once more. The Hindu Marriage Act was deemed communal because it created unequal rights and privileges among the various communities and their personal laws. N.C. Chatterjee argued,

> this Bill is contrary to the Fundamental Rights laid down by the Constitution of India, because it discriminates by law against a community or a particular religion. What right have you to enact such a law? What right have you to say that monogamy must be made compulsory for all Hindus, for all Hindu men and for all Hindu women? If you honestly feel that this is a blessing and polygamy is a curse, then why not rescue our Muslim sisters from that curse and from that plight? What right have you to enact that this shall be compulsory only for one community and not for others?[130]

Khardekar, another Member of Parliament, initiated a vicious assault on Chatterjee's 'communalism'. He created a parody of Hindu right-wing politics of the post-independence period and contended that it was the politics of the Hindu Mahasabha and Jan Sangh (the predecessor of the Bharatiya Janata Party) that made them oppose the Bill on Hindu marriages rather than any true understanding of the spirit of Hinduism. The pressures between the state and the communities as political actors at the national level in India today are part of the identical historical development in which various ethno-religious communities have, on the one hand, struggled to retain their powers over their members and on the other hand, had to contend with judicial enactments that increasingly expanded the power of the civil state over their sacramental customs and beliefs. The process that Veena Das has defined in *Critical Events: An Anthropological Perspective on Contemporary India* as the state colonizing the life-worlds of communities as well as communities colonizing the life-worlds of individuals was as much in evidence in 1872 as it is in the post-independence period.[131]

Indeed, in *Individualism and Equality*, as Beteille has so ably shown, 'it was due to the insistence of Ambedkar that the "individual" was made the repository of rights in post-independence India.' Other parliamentarians attempted to make the village the basic unit, but he refused because he believed that this was the stronghold of caste and faction, which would inhibit individual accomplishment. The Special Marriage Act protects these democratic principles, and it is an example of the state shifting and directing the authority of ethno-religious communities in pursuit of individuals. The significance of 1872 to a work on love-marriages is that, while the Keshubites wanted to establish a Brahmo community, their dissent established a theoretical and, later, legal space for not-community. According to Perveez Mody,

> although both the Keshubites and the Council steadfastly avoided a discussion of 'love', the petitions saw all the three Bills as permitting an altogether new form of marriage in India. Those entering such marriages are represented as morally corrupt; a threat to 'native' religious and social values and the colonial state's legislation is viewed as 'making Indians into Europeans'.[132]

Nonetheless, the issue of Brahmo identity was inextricably linked with marriage reform. Notwithstanding, the section that succeeded the first civil marriage law in 1872 was split on the issue of its own identity even after the act was passed. Prasanta Chandra Mahalanobis wrote in the introduction to his book, *Brahmo Bibaha Bidhi* (Brahmo Marriage Rules), that the marriage act had been a source of great contention and strife among the Brahmos since it was enacted in 1872.[133] The Act III of 1872 became entangled in a slew of paradoxes, not the least of which was a colonial state interfering with communities' rights to organize marriages for their members. The deterrent path from Maine's original Bill to Stephen's Act demonstrated that there was a massive amount of accommodation that was made before the final enactment. Contradictorily, Nehru's government, the first independent government of democratic India, took a powerful political stance and did not need to recognize the demands of orthodoxy while enacting the Special Marriage Act. As a result, the Special Marriage Act is largely a secular law of civil marriage. Nevertheless, this does not imply that the passage of the Special Marriage Act had any effect on society. Rather, in the case of the Special Marriage Act of 1954, the accommodations occur after legislation in the exact way that the law is both administered and transformed to suit Indian exigencies. To summarize, Maine was partially correct when he stated that, in the absence of compensatory legislation, 'legal process would rigidify caste and religious divisions and empower communities at the expense of individuals.' Many opponents of the Bill were also primarily correct. A hierarchical, classified and discriminated caste society could only prosper in the modern world with the active support of state-endowing communities such as castes and religions with definite rights and entitlements at the expense of individuals. Both colonial and postcolonial governments were inconsistent, but the story of this Act has been reiterated many times in various realms, with the result that communities characterized by caste and religion are now more effective and comprehensible political identities and agencies than a century ago.

There was little evidence that widows agreed to marry whomever they chose under Act III of 1872. Despite the fact that this Act prohibited the role of guardian in their remarriage, the occurrence of a widow's 'love-remarriage' was relatively uncommon. According to an official report, 36 widow remarriages were held between 1872 and 1882 in accordance with the provisions of the Act III of 1872.[134] In 1905, Mrinalini Sen, a teenage widow, fled from her father-in-law's house to meet Nirmal Sen, son of Keshub Chandra Sen. She had been converted to Brahmo Dharma and married Nirmal Sen according to Brahmo rites.[135] Men and women had not been able to take full advantage of the possibilities of the Act III of 1872, as social and religious legitimacy had often been more important to them than legal recognition. Or, it may be said that the mind did not dare to deny allegiance to one's own religion. Sometimes, under the pressure of the family, legal recognition as well as religious atmosphere had to be organized. Nevertheless, we cannot deny that this act placed the idea of gender equality and individuality in an unprecedented position in the minds of Bengalis. And with the help of this law, some of the girls showed the courage not to follow the so-called prescribed path of patriarchy. Patriarchy never wanted to acknowledge the individuality of women. Act III of 1872 attempted to restore that entity. In this way, this act shattered the deceptive and double-edged chandelier of the inseparable divine blessing of marriage, which was built to maintain the absolute control of men over the body, mind and personality of women. By recognizing both men and women as individuals, this law gave them the right to marry with equal importance to the conscious consent of the two and to break the bond if necessary. The limitation of the Act III of 1872 was that one can take advantage of this law only by denying his/her religious identity. Act III of 1872 was the product of a liberal and rationalist thought regarding the male-female relationship. The Colonial government tried to print every draft of this law according to the expectation of the people and proceeded to legislate in an unprecedented democratic process by amending the provisions of the law as required by public opinion.

NOTES

1. J.A. Bourdillon, *Report on the Census of Bengal 1881*, Calcutta: Bengal Secretariat Press, 1883, pp. 122-4; J.A. Baines, *General Report on the Census of India, 1891*, London: HMSO, 1893, p. 247; and E.A. Gait, *Report on the Census of Lower Provinces of Bengal and their Feudatories, 1901*, Calcutta: Bengal Secretariat Press, p. 238.
2. J. Duncan M. Derrett, *Religion, Law and the State in India*, London: Faber and Faber, 1968, cited in Tanika Sarkar, 'Changing Hindu Women: Bengal in the Long Nineteenth Century', in Sabyasachi Bhattacharya (ed.), *A Comprehensive History of Modern Bengal, 1700-1950,* Volume II, Kolkata: The Asiatic Society, in association with Primus Books, 2020, p. 817. Mahua Sarkar has discussed the institutions, practices, and implementation of British colonial law and justice in relation to the making and remaking of the colonial state and society in Bengal by analysing the history of evolution of the Calcutta High Court. Mahua Sarkar, 'The Idea of Justice and Evolution of the Calcutta High Court, 1862-1915', in Sabyasachi Bhattacharya (ed.), *A Comprehensive History of Modern Bengal, 1700-1950,* Volume II, Kolkata: The Asiatic Society, in association with Primus Books, 2020, pp. 382-418.
3. Perveez Mody, 'Love and the Law: Love Marriage in Delhi', *Modern Asian Studies*, vol. 36, no. 1, 2002, pp. 223-56; and Nandini Chatterjee, 'English Law, Brahmo Marriage and the Problem of Religious Difference: Civil Marriage Laws in Britain and India', *Comparative Studies in Society and History*, vol. 52, no. 3, 2010, pp. 10–52.
4. Rochona Majumdar, *Marriage and Modernity: Family Values in Colonial Bengal*, Durham and London: Duke University Press, 2009, p. 168.
5. For a general history of the Brahmo movement, David Kopf, *The Brahmo Samaj and the Shaping of the Modern Indian Mind*, New Jersey: Princeton University Press, 1979; Sivanath Sastri, *History of the Brahmo Samaj*, Calcutta: Sadharan Brahmo Samaj, Volume 1 (1911), Volume 2 (1912), 2nd edn. 1974. In addition, there are a large number of tracts on particular phases of the movement as well as on important

individual members of the Samaj.

6. Aishika Chakraborty, 'Contract, Consent and Ceremony: The Brahmo Marriage Reform (1860-1930)', *Journal of History*, vol. 26 (2008-9), Department of History, Jadavpur University, Kolkata, 2009, pp. 1-32. https://www.academia.edu/6494083/Contract_Consent_and_Ceremony (Accessed on 31 March 2021).
7. 'The fact that Maine had to legislate for the whole of India, just because he could not define the Keshubites, was mocked in some "native" newspapers. One editor was alleged to have asked how Maine imagined he could define a "Hindu", "there being no judicial or legislative definition of that comprehensive term".' National Archives of India, Act III of 1872, no. 225, 'Summary of Opinions on the Native Marriage Bill', Vide Appendix O, 25 July 1870, cited in Perveez Mody, *The Intimate State: Love-Marriage and the Law in Delhi*, New Delhi: Routledge, 2008, p. 71.
8. Perveez Mody, 'Love and the Law: Love-Marriage in Delhi', *Modern Asian Studies*, vol. 36, no. 1, February 2002, pp. 223-56; Perveez Mody, *The Intimate State: Love-Marriage and the Law in Delhi*, New Delhi: Routledge, 2008, pp. 61-102; Rochona Majumdar, *Marriage and Modernity: Family Values in Colonial Bengal*, Durham and London: Duke University Press, 2009, pp. 167-205.
9. M.P. Jain, *Outlines of Indian Legal History*, Bombay: N.M. Tripathi Private Ltd., 1952, pp. ix-xiv.
10. For example, Partha Chatterjee, 'The Nationalist Resolution of the Women's Question', in Kumkum Sangari and Sudesh Vaid (eds.), *Recasting Women: Essays in Colonial History*, New Delhi: Kali for Women, 1989, pp. 233-53; Sudhir Chandra, *Enslaved Daughters: Colonialism, Law and Women's Rights*, New Delhi: Oxford University Press, 1998, pp. 1-13; Prem Chowdhry, 'Contesting Claims and Counter-Claims: Questions of the Inheritance and Sexuality of Widows in a Colonial State', in Patricia Uberoi (ed.), *Social Reform, Sexuality and the State*, London: Sage Publications, 1996, pp. 65-82; Geraldine Forbes, 'Women and Modernity: The Issue of Child Marriage in India', *Women's Studies International Quarterly*, 1979, vol. 2, pp. 407-19; Amiya P. Sen, *Hindu Revivalism in Bengal, 1872-1905: Some Essays in Interpretation*, Delhi: Oxford University Press, 1993, pp. 25-80, 363-400; Lata Mani, 'Contentious Traditions: The Debate on Sati in Colonial India', in Kumkum Sangari and Sudesh Vaid (eds.), *Recasting Women: Essays in Colonial History*, New Delhi: Kali for Women, 1989, pp. 88-126.

11. Tahir Mahmood, *Civil Marriage Law: Perspectives and Prospects*, New Delhi: Indian Law Institute, 1978, pp. 51-4; Monmayee Basu, *Hindu Women and Marriage Law: From Sacrament to Contract*, New Delhi: Oxford University Press, 2001, pp. 39-66; Perveez Mody, op. cit., 2002, 2008; Rochona Majumdar, op. cit., 2009; Aishika Chakraborty, op. cit.
12. *Samachar Darpan*, 21 March 1835.
13. *Sambad Prabhakar*, July 1847.
14. *Bamabodhini Patrika*, November 1864.
15. *Somprakash*, June 1868.
16. Rochona Majumdar, op. cit., 2009, pp. 170-1.
17. David Kopf, *The Brahmo Samaj and the Shaping of the Modern Indian Mind*, New Jersey: Princeton University Press, 1979, p. 103.
18. Ibid., p. 101.
19. Sivanath Sastri, *History of the Brahmo Samaj*, Volume II, Calcutta: Brahmo Mission Press, 1912, p. 367.
20. David Kopf, op. cit., p. 101.
21. Sivanath Sastri, *Ramtanu Lahiri O Tatkalin Banga Samaj* (Ramtanu Lahiri and The Then Bengal Society), Calcutta: New Age Publishers, first published 1903, repr. 1983, p. 246.
22. Monmayee Basu, *Hindu Women and Marriage Law: From Sacrament to Contract*, in *Women and Law in India: An Omnibus Comprising*, New Delhi: Oxford University Press, 2004 (1st edn.), 2016 (Oxford India Paperbacks), p. 40.
23. Aishika Chakraborty, op. cit., p. 4.
24. Sivanath Sastri, *History of the Brahmo Samaj*, Calcutta: Sadharan Brahmo Samaj, Volume 1 (1911), Volume 2 (1912), 2nd edn. 1974, pp. 85-6.
25. Rochona Majumdar, op. cit., 2009, p. 174.
26. Sivanath Sastri, *History of the Brahmo Samaj*, Calcutta: Sadharan Brahmo Samaj, Volume 1 (1911), Volume 2 (1912), 2nd edn. 1974, pp. 85-6.
27. Ibid., p. 156.
28. 'The National Archives of India, *Legislative Department*, May 1872, no. 148, Act III of 1872', cited in Perveez Mody, op. cit., 2002, p. 228.
29. Rochona Majumdar, op. cit., 2009, pp. 175-6.
30. Aishika Chakraborty, op. cit., p. 1.
31. Sivanath Sastri, *History of the Brahmo Samaj*, Calcutta: Sadharan

Brahmo Samaj, Volume 1 (1911), Volume 2 (1912), 2nd edn. 1974, p. 156.

32. Ibid.
33. *Gazette of India*, Supplement, 19 September 1868.
34. Amiya P. Sen agrees that 'the main reason behind the schism among the older generation of *Brahmos* (Devendranath Tagore and Rajnarain Bose) and the younger group led by Keshub Sen was the issue of marriage. In Sen's analysis the younger party's support of intercaste marriage and Tagore's opposition to it caused a meltdown in the relations between the two groups.' Amiya P. Sen, *Hindu Revivalism in Bengal, 1872-1905: Some Essays in Interpretation*, Delhi: Oxford University Press, 1993, pp. 37-48.
35. Ajit Kumar Chakrabarty, *Maharshi Devendranath Thakur*, Calcutta: Jignasa, 1958, p. 411, cited in Amiya P. Sen, op. cit., p. 40.
36. *Proceedings of the Council of the Governor-General of India, 1872*, p. 1820.
37. Perveez Mody, op. cit., 2002, p. 228.
38. In 1860, the age of consent had been fixed at ten for girls, so the age of fourteen years they proposed was substantially higher.
39. 'The Indian Majority Act, IX of 1875 was passed 8 years later and set majority at 18 years of age for men and women', cited in J. Duncan M. Derrett, op. cit., 1978, p. 295.
40. 'National Archives of India, Act III of 1872, no. 148, 11 September 1868', cited in Perveez Mody, op. cit., 2002, p. 229.
41. Perveez Mody, op. cit., 2002, p. 229.
42. 'National Archives of India, Act III of 1872, no. 151, 18 November 1868', cited in Perveez Mody, op. cit., 2002, p. 229.
43. 'National Archives of India, Act III of 1872, no. 173, 4 September 1868', cited in Perveez Mody, op. cit., 2002, p. 229.
44. 'National Archives of India, Act III of 1872, no. 150, 10 September 1868', cited in Perveez Mody, op. cit., 2002, p. 229.
45. Perveez Mody, op. cit., 2002, p. 229.
46. *Proceedings of the Council of the Governor-General of India, 1872*, p. 1820, cited in Monmayee Basu, *Hindu Women and Marriage Law: From Sacrament to Contract*, in *Women and Law in India: An Omnibus Comprising*, New Delhi: Oxford University Press, 2004 (1st edn.), 2016 (Oxford India Paperbacks), p. 41.
47. 'National Archives of India, Act III of 1872, no. 156, 27 November 1868', cited in Perveez Mody, op. cit., 2002, p. 230.

48. Perveez Mody, op. cit., 2002, p. 230.
49. Sivanath Sastri, *History of the Brahmo Samaj*, Calcutta: Sadharan Brahmo Samaj, Volume 1 (1911), Volume 2 (1912), 2nd edn. 1974, p. 158.
50. *Proceedings of the Council of the Governor-General of India, 1872*, p. 28, cited in Monmayee Basu, *Hindu Women and Marriage Law: From Sacrament to Contract*, in *Women and Law in India*, New Delhi: Oxford University Press, 2004 (1st edn.), 2016 (Oxford India Paperbacks), p. 41.
51. Rochona Majumdar, op. cit., 2009, p. 178.
52. 'Other conditions included the consent of the father or guardian if the girl was below 18 years of age and the prohibited degrees were to be degrees of consanguinity or affinity prohibited by the custom, which would have regulated marriages between them had the Act not been passed. Further, bigamous marriages under this Act were to be punished under the Indian Penal Code'; 'National Archives of India, Act III of 1872, no. 233, "A Bill to legalise Marriages between members of the Brahmo Samaja"', cited in Perveez Mody, op. cit., 2002, p. 231.
53. 'National Archives of India, Act III of 1872, no. 158, 26 November 1868', cited in Perveez Mody, op. cit., 2002, p. 231.
54. 'The Civil Marriage Bill', *Tattvabodhini Patrika*, Jyaistha 1794 Shak, June 1872, pp. 38-44.
55. 'National Archives of India, Act III of 1872, no. 237, 11 July 1871', cited in Perveez Mody, op. cit., 2002, p. 231.
56. 'Quoting from Thomas Strange's Hindu Law, they argue that these "elements" are the formal gifts for the bride, the acceptance of her hand in marriage and finally, the ceremony of *saptpadi* (Literally, seven steps)'. 'National Archives of India, Act III of 1872, no. 158, 26 November 1868', cited in Perveez Mody, op. cit., 2008, p. 70.
57. Monmayee Basu, *Hindu Women and Marriage Law: From Sacrament to Contract*, in *Women and Law in India: An Omnibus Comprising*, New Delhi: Oxford University Press, 2004 (1st edn.), 2016 (Oxford India Paperbacks), p. 42. Here is P.C. Mozoomdar's recollection of the Adi Brahmo opposition, 'But there was a real grievance which the Adi-Somaj pleaded. They said the form of Civil Marriage prescribed by the new law was revolting to their religious instincts, they could not conscientiously adopt the statutory form of registration before an official, and as they believed their marriage rites to be perfectly legal, it was needless oppression to compel them to appear before Marriage Registrars who might not be members of the Brahmo Somaj at all.

The formal renunciation of Hindu religion required by statutory declaration, was also against their conviction and conscience, they believed Brahmo religion was in essence Hindu religion', cited in P. C. Mozoomdar, *The Life and Teachings of Keshub Chunder Sen*, Calcutta: Baptist Mission Press, 1887, p. 249.

58. Perveez Mody, op. cit., 2008, p. 70.
59. Monika Mahalnobis, *Brahmananda Keshubchandrera Patrabali* (Letters of Brahmananda Keshubchandrera), Calcutta: Navabidhan Press, 1941, pp. 225-6, cited in Rochona Majumdar, op. cit., 2009, p. 179.
60. Sivanath Sastri, *History of the Brahmo Samaj*, Calcutta: Sadharan Brahmo Samaj, Volume 1 (1911), Volume 2 (1912), 2nd edn. 1974, p. 158.
61. Shankar Kumar Nath, *Unish Shataker Kayekjon Bangali-Gabeshak Chikitsak: Ramendrasundar Trivedi Smriti Pustakmala: 14* (Some Bengali Researcher Doctors of the Nineteenth Century: Ramendrasundar Trivedi Memorial Books: 14), Kolkata: Bangiya Bigyan Parishad, January 2019, pp. 56-7.
62. Keshub Chandra Sen, 'National Marriage Reform', speech (delivered on 13 September 1871) at the Town Hall of Calcutta, cited in Sivanath Sastri, *Ei Ki Brahmo Bibaha?* (Is this Brahmo form of Marriage?), Kolkata: Albert Press, 1878, pp. 17-19, cited in Rochona Majumdar, op. cit., 2009, pp. 179-80.
63. 'Marriageable Age of Native Girls', Circular of Babu Keshub Chunder Sen to certain medical men, dated 1 April 1871, cited in C. Yajnesvara Chintamani (ed.), *Indian Social Reform*, in four parts (Fourth Part: Miscellaneous Papers), Madras: Minerva Press, 1901, pp. 260-1.
64. Ajit Kumar Chakrabarty, *Maharshi Devendranath Thakur*, Calcutta: Jijnasa, 1958, p. 415, cited in Amiya P. Sen, op. cit., p. 43.
65. *Proceedings of the Council of the Governor-General of India, 1872*, pp. 15, 51-3, cited in Monmayee Basu, *Hindu Women and Marriage Law: From Sacrament to Contract*, in *Women and Law in India*, New Delhi: Oxford University Press, 2004 (1st edn.), 2016 (Oxford India Paperbacks), p. 42.
66. *Proceedings of the Council of the Governor-General of India, 1872*, pp. 53-6, cited in Monmayee Basu, *Hindu Women and Marriage Law: From Sacrament to Contract*, in *Women and Law in India*, New Delhi: Oxford University Press, 2004 (1st edn.), 2016 (Oxford India Paperbacks), p. 42.
67. *Proceedings of the Council of the Governor-General of India, 1872*, pp. 149-50, cited in Monmayee Basu, *Hindu Women and Marriage*

Law: From Sacrament to Contract, in *Women and Law in India*, New Delhi: Oxford University Press, 2004 (1st edn.), 2016 (Oxford India Paperbacks), p. 43.

68. Monmayee Basu, op. cit., 2004 (1st edn.), 2016 (Oxford India Paperbacks), p. 43.
69. *Proceedings of the Council of the Governor-General of India, 1872*, p. 187, cited in Monmayee Basu, *Hindu Women and Marriage Law: From Sacrament to Contract*, in *Women and Law in India*, New Delhi: Oxford University Press, 2004 (1st edn.), 2016 (Oxford India Paperbacks), p. 43.
70. Sivanath Sastri, *History of the Brahmo Samaj*, Calcutta: Sadharan Brahmo Samaj, Volume 1 (1911), Volume 2 (1912), 2nd edn. 1974, p. 159.
71. 'Despite Maine's legal justifications for the exclusion of Christians, the perceived inequity of the first Bill had been a particular cause of irritation because it was interpreted as meaning that marriages between Christians and non-Christians would still necessarily involve conversion in a Church', see, Perveez Mody, op. cit., 2002, p. 232.
72. 'National Archives of India, Act III of 1872, "A Bill to Provide a Form of Marriages in Certain Cases"', 21 December 1871, cited in Perveez Mody, op. cit., 2002, p. 232.
73. Perveez Mody, op. cit., 2002, p. 232.
74. Ibid., p. 233.
75. Saradasundari Debi, 'Atmakatha' (Autobiography), in Ahana Biswas and Prasun Ghosh (eds.), *Andarer Itihas: Narir Jabanbandi, Volume 2* (Inner History: Women's Testimony), Kolkata: Gangchil, 2013, 2016 (repr.), pp. 33-80.
76. Rochona Majumdar, op. cit., 2009, p. 168.
77. Ibid.
78. Saradasundari Debi, op. cit., pp. 33-80; Sivanath Sastri, *History of the Brahmo Samaj*, Volume I, published by R. Chatterji, Calcutta, 1911, pp. 274-94. 'A special correspondent of Cooch Behar appointed by the Brahmo Samaj Committee informed them that Hindu rituals were performed, a Hindu priest conducted Hindu rites, and no Brahmo officiated at the wedding. An attempt to conduct a Brahmo service failed, there was no mutual exchange of vows, the *homa* was performed by the maharaja. Keshub was deposed from the post of secretary of the Bharatbarshiya Brahmo Samaj and as the acharya or minister of the "Brahmo Mandir". The marriage designated as providential by

Keshub led to the formation of the Sadharan Brahmo Samaj on 15 May 1878 under Sivanath Shastri, Rajnarain Basu, Dwarakanath Ganguly, Durga Mohun Das, Anandamohan Bose, Shib Chandra Deb and Bijoy Krishna Goswami.'

79. David Kopf, op. cit., p. 104.
80. Ibid., p. 105.
81. 'The Office of the Registrar of Marriages under Act III of 1872 was initiated by the Act, and the Local Government was authorized to appoint one or more Registrars whose domain was the domain of the territory subject to its administration and was to be deemed his district.' 'National Archives of India, Act III of 1872, no. 332, 22 March 1872', cited in Perveez Mody, op. cit., 2002, p. 234.
82. 'National Archives of India, Act III of 1872, "A Bill to Legalise Marriages between certain Natives of India not professing the Christian Religion", 18 November 1868', cited in Perveez Mody, op. cit., 2002, p. 234.
83. Perveez Mody, op. cit., 2002, p. 234.
84. Amiya P. Sen, op. cit., p. 44.
85. Sivanath Sastri, *History of the Brahmo Samaj*, Calcutta: Sadharan Brahmo Samaj, Volume 1 (1911), Volume 2 (1912), 2nd edn. 1974, p. 163.
86. Amiya P. Sen, op. cit., p. 44.
87. Sivanath Sastri, *History of the Brahmo Samaj*, Calcutta: Sadharan Brahmo Samaj, Volume 1 (1911), Volume 2 (1912), 2nd edn. 1974, p. 211.
88. *Brahmo Public Opinion*, 1878, p. 98, Calcutta: Published for the proprietors by K.N. Dutt, cited in Aishika Chakraborty, op. cit., p. 24.
89. Keshub Chandra Sen, *Acharya Keshub Chandrer Baktrita* (Speeches of Acharya Keshub Chandra), Pyary Mohan Chowdhury, Calcutta, 1910; Keshub Chandra Sen, *Brahmikadiger Prati Srimadacharya Keshub Chandra Sener Upadesh* (Srimadacharya Keshub Chandra Sen's Advice to the women of Brahmo Samaj), Calcutta, Bidhan Yantra, 1885, cited in Aishika Chakraborty, op. cit., p. 24.
90. Ishan Chandra Basu, *Nari Neeti* (Principle of Women), Calcutta: Gurudas Chattopadhyay, 1884, pp. 32-3, cited in Sambuddha Chakraborty, *Andare Antare: Unish Satake Bangali Bhadramahila* (Domestic and Mental Spaces: Elite Women in Nineteenth Century), Calcutta: Stree, 1995, p. 120.

91. Ishan Chandra Basu, *Streediger Prati Upadesh* (Advice to the Wives/ Advice for Women), Calcutta: Victoria Press, 1884, p. 4, cited in Sambuddha Chakraborty, op. cit., p. 115.
92. Aishika Chakraborty, op. cit., p. 23.
93. Perveez Mody, op. cit., 2008, pp. 62-3.
94. Bipin Chandra Pal, *Memoirs of My Life and Times, in the Days of My Youth (1857-1884),* p. 3, Calcutta: Modern Book Agency, 1932, p. 262.
95. Perveez Mody, op. cit., 2002, pp. 236-7.
96. *Stree Shiksha ebong Stree Vidyalaye Streenibas* (Female education and the lodging of women in Female schools) T.P., Phalgun 1802 Shak (March 1881) in Benoy Ghosh, *Samayikpatre Banglar Samajchitra* (Social life in Bengal as depicted in Bengali periodicals), vol. 5, Calcutta: Deep Prakashan (rvd. edn.), 2020 (1963), p. 71.
97. *Tattvabodhini Patrika*, October 1879.
98. *Somprakash*, April 1871.
99. *Somprakash*, July 1871.
100. Monmayee Basu, *Hindu Women and Marriage Law: From Sacrament to Contract*, in *Women and Law in India: An Omnibus Comprising*, New Delhi: Oxford University Press, 2004 (1st edn.), 2016 (Oxford India Paperbacks), pp. 44-5.
101. 'Gurucharan, married to a high-caste widow; Baikunthanath Sen married widowed Bhabani. Even though the new Act had outlawed polygamy, Trailokyanath Chakraborty married thrice, in accordance with the Brahmo rite and two of his wives were widows from other castes. With the help of liberal Brahmos, Ramdurlabh Mazumdar married Sunila, the widowed niece of Sashibhusan Sarkar and Bhagaban Chandra Mukhopadhyay married Biraja Sundari, the widowed sister of Debiprasanna Roychaudhry. In 1868, Upendranath Das married a low-caste Hindu widow, which was celebrated as a significant event by the young Brahmo reformers. The marriage was performed, said Sivanath Sastri, in part, according to the ceremony recommended by Vidyasagar, and, in part, following the Brahmo divine service. In early 1868, Sivanath arranged the remarriage of his widower-friend, Jogendranath Bandyopadhyay with the widowed sister of Ishan Chandra Roy, Mahalakshmi. In this marriage too, a major part of the expenses was borne by Vidyasagar.' Sivanath Sastri, *Atmacharit* (Autobiography), Kolkata: Sadharan Brahmo Samaj, 1918, rpt. 2000, pp. 99-101; Gurucharan Mahalanabish, 'Atmakatha', in Naresh Jana,

Manu Jana and Kamal Kumar Sanyal (eds.), *Atmakatha,* 2, Calcutta: Ananya Prakashan, 1982 (1st pub. in 1974), pp. 41-5.

102. Monmayee Basu, *Hindu Women and Marriage Law: From Sacrament to Contract,* in *Women and Law in India: An Omnibus Comprising,* New Delhi: Oxford University Press, 2004 (1st edn.), 2016 (Oxford India Paperbacks), p. 45.
103. Meredith Borthwick, *The Changing Role of Women in Bengal, 1849-1905,* Princeton: Princeton University Press, 1984, p. 130.
104. Bankubihari Kar, *Purba Banglar Brahmo Samajer Itibritta* (History of the Brahmo Samaj of East Bengal), Kolkata: Sadharan Brahmo Samaj, 2003, p. 103.
105. 'Rajnarain was disturbed that the bridegroom intended the marriage to take place in the Sadharan Brahmo Samaj, not his own Adi Brahmo Samaj. He finally relented when, on asking the opinion of sixteen-year-old Lilabati, she expressed great eagerness for the marriage. He felt that she was of an age to make her own decision, and reluctantly gave his consent.' Krishna Kumar Mitra, *Atmacharit,* Calcutta: Bashanti Chakraborty, 1974 (1937), p. 291; 'Bibaha', *Tattvabodhini Patrika,* 457, Bhadra 1803 (1881), in Benoy Ghosh, *Samayikpatre Banglar Samajchitra* (Social life in Bengal as depicted in Bengali periodicals), part 2, Calcutta: Bikkhan Prakashak, 1963, p. 60, cited in Meredith Borthwick, op. cit., p. 130.
106. Prabhat Chandra Gangopadhyay, *Banglar Nari Jagaran* (Women's Awakening in Bengal), Kolkata: Sadharan Brahmo Samaj, 1352, Chaitra (1946), pp. 57-99.
107. 'The high moral tone of a Brahmo marriage, and the new outlook it represented, were evident in the kind of gifts she received on the occasion. Among these were the Revd F.W. Farrar's *Seekers after God,* from Professor Sen and the poetical works of James Russell Lowell from another *Brahmo* friend.' See, Meredith Borthwick, op. cit., pp. 130-1.
108. Makarand Paranjape (ed.), *Sarojini Naidu, Selected Letters, 1890s to 1940s,* New Delhi: Kali for Women, 1996, cited in Aparna Bandyopadhyay, 'Tin Aain Sambandhe Dui Char Katha' (Two or Four words about the Act III), in Shubhrakumar Mukhopadhyay, Pratapkumar Sen and Eeshita Chattopadhyay (eds.), *Nari: Andare Bahire* (Woman: Inside and Outside), Hooghly Mohsin College, 2014, pp. 36-47.
109. 'A full listing of Brahmo marriages from 1861 to 1882, with the age,

caste, and occupation of the parties as well as comments on any unusual features was given in the Register of Brahmo Marriages in the *Brahmo Year Book*, III, 1878; IV, 1879; V, 1881; VI, 1882', cited in Meredith Borthwick, op. cit., p. 131.

110. Tanika Sarkar, 'Changing Hindu Women: Bengal in the Long Nineteenth Century', in Sabyasachi Bhattacharya (ed.), *A Comprehensive History of Modern Bengal, 1700-1950,* Volume II, Kolkata: The Asiatic Society, in association with Primus Books, 2020, p. 829.
111. Leela Majumdar, *Pakdandi* (A Circuitous or Spiral Route that Leads to The Top of a Mountain), Kolkata: Ananda Publishers, 1986 (9th edn. 2010), p. 251.
112. 'In the marriage of Candraprabha Biswas and Binaycandra Gupta in 1896, it was first decided that the bride and groom would each look after his or her own expenses. Later a more generous agreement was reached, that each would take care of the other's expenses. This was, however, an exceptional case.' Meredith Borthwick, op. cit., p. 131; Srinath Chanda, *Brahmo Samaje Challis Bathsar* (Forty Years in Brahmo Samaj), Kolkata: Brahmo Mission Press, 1969 (1913), pp. 294-6.
113. Chitra Deb, *Thakurbarir Andarmahal* (Inner Space of Tagore Household), Kolkata: Ananda, first published 1980, repr. 1982, p. 205.
114. Aishika Chakraborty, op. cit., p. 25.
115. Meredith Borthwick, op. cit., p. 132.
116. Ibid., p. 133.
117. Aishika Chakraborty, op. cit., p. 25. 'Rabindranath arranged and officiated at the marriage of widowed Labanya (Guha Thakurta) with Ajit Kumar Chakraborty, his aide at Shantiniketan. While his son, Rathindranath married widowed Pratima in February 1910; almost a decade later an intercaste marriage was celebrated between Jayashri, daughter of Surendranath Tagore, with Kulaprasad Sen. Both these marriages were solemnised without registration. Another intercaste and intercommunity love marriage, held between Nandita (Gangopadhyay), Rabindranath's granddaughter, with Krishna Kripalani in 1936, was registered under Act III.' Chitra Deb, op. cit., pp. 244-5.
118. Taslima Nasrin, *Nirbachita Column* (Selected Column), Kolkata: Ananda Publishers Private Limited, 1992 (19th edn., 2012), pp. 9-17, 23-6. Taslima Nasrin, *Lajja* (Shame), Dhaka: Pearl, 1993, pp. 7-64.
119. 'National Archives of India, Act III of 1872 (no date given)', no. 193, Proceedings of Meerut Debating Society, cited in Perveez Mody, op. cit., 2008, p. 91.

120. Perveez Mody, op. cit., 2008, p. 91.
121. Government of India, 1974, *Law Commission of India, Fifty-Ninth Report on The Hindu Marriage Act, 1955 & The Special Marriage Act, 1954*. 'This was again amended in 1974. Hindus, Buddhists, Sikhs or Jains could intermarry without having to suffer any economic penalty so that they could continue to benefit from Hindu law for the purposes of succession, and so that their agnates would no longer be excluded from rights in joint-family property inherited by someone availing of the Act. To clarify the situation, if a person married under the Special Marriage Act, in the event of intestate succession, the Succession Act would apply (not the personal inheritance law). The changes brought about in 1974 ensured that if both parties to a marriage were "Hindu", then Hindu law would continue to apply both with regards to undivided property and divided property.'
122. Perveez Mody, op. cit., 2008, p. 92.
123. There is confusion over the name of the law. Mahmood implies that Act III of 1872 was already known as the Special Marriage Act by the time it came to be amended in 1923. However, in her archival work of 1872, Perveez Mody did not encounter this name other than the general description that the Act catered for marriages in 'special' instances. Even the final Act is entitled Act III of 1872; Perveez Mody, op. cit., 2008, p. 92.
124. Perveez Mody, op. cit., 2008, p. 92.
125. In recent years, the introduction of a Uniform Civil Code has taken on more sinister tones with Hindu nationalists having promised that when they have a clear majority in parliament, they will enact a new law for all Indians, thus displacing all personal laws. This has been a particularly contentious proposal, with feminists and civil rights activists arguing that any revision of the law by Hindu nationalists will be biased against women and minorities. Zakia Pathak and Rajeswari Sunder Rajan, 'Shahbano', in Judith Butler and Jean W. Scott (eds.), *Feminists Theorize the Political*, New York: Routledge, 1992, pp. 257-79; Flavia Agnes, 'Redefining the Agenda of the Women's Movement Within a Secular Framework', in Tanika Sarkar and Urvashi Butalia (eds.), *Women and the Hindu Right: A Collection of Essays*, New Delhi: Kali for Women, 1996, pp. 136-57; Susie Tharu and Tejaswini Niranjana, 'Problems for a Contemporary Theory of Gender', in Dipesh Chakrabarty (ed.), *Subaltern Studies IX*, New Delhi: Oxford University Press, 1996, pp. 231-60.
126. Tahir Mahmood, op. cit., p. 9.

127. Ibid., p. 14.
128. Perveez Mody, op. cit., 2008, p. 93.
129. Reba Som (1994) has argued that 'Nehru capitulated on many of the "progressive" elements of the Hindu Marriage Bill and allowed the orthodox opponents in parliament to limit its provisions. It was over this bill that Ambedkar resigned from Nehru's cabinet in September of 1951 because he felt that far too many concessions were being made to orthodox religion. It is noteworthy that the Special Marriage Act was also being debated in the house, and often the two acts were opposed together because they were seen as a threat to Hindu India', cited in Perveez Mody, op. cit., 2008, p. 93.
130. Perveez Mody, op. cit., 2008, p. 94.
131. Ibid., Veena Das, *Critical Events: An Anthropological Perspective on Contemporary India*, New Delhi: Oxford India Paperbacks, 1995, pp. 84-117.
132. Perveez Mody, op. cit., 2008, p. 95.
133. Rochona Majumdar, op. cit., 2009, p. 198.
134. Aishika Chakraborty, op. cit., p. 15.
135. For details see, Mrinalini Sen, *Knocking at the door (Lectures and Other Writings)*, Calcutta: Living Age Press, 1954, pp. 1-70.

CHAPTER 3

Debates in History, Debates on History

Age of Consent Act of 1891 and the Issue of Child Marriage in India

The legal age for an Indian woman to start conjugal life has been brought into socio-political discussions three times in less than a century. Yet this has usually been interpreted as proof of apprehension for women's emancipation, and a careful inspection and analysis of the historical indication advocates that this specific subject has functioned as a vehicle to accelerate a complete programme of socio-political perceptions. The Age of Consent controversy was redirected in 1891 from the issues such as child wives' despair to the question as to whether the British government had the power to intervene and participate in Hindu socio-cultural norms and practices. The Child Marriage Restraint Act of 1929 was struggled for by the progressive section of the Hindus and predominantly by the emergent women's organizations since it demonstrated that Indians were profoundly worried about and eager to modify firm social structures. The most recent rise in the age of marriage legally as a result of population policy occurred in the month of October in 1978. Preferring a later age of marriage has turned out to be identical with commitment to modernity, however, it does not always imply commitment to modifying the social position of women.[1] Initiatives to proscribe child marriage through legislative changes originated in India in the late nineteenth century. It converted into one of the major contentious public issues during the initial days of the twentieth century. Nevertheless, it is disappointing that the scenario has not significantly changed even at the turn of the century. Child marriages are however, common in many parts of the country, particularly in rural areas of the four major northern states – Uttar Pradesh, Bihar, Madhya Pradesh and Rajasthan – and in one southern state, Andhra Pradesh.[2]

Social reformers attempted to mobilize public support for legal sanctions against child marriage in the second half of the nineteenth century. The foremost purpose of preventing child marriages was to protect child brides who endured immensely as a result of forceful sexual intercourse with them by their husbands. Additional possible explanation for necessitating authorized approvals against child marriage was to limit a huge number of young widows. Men who were in their age of '30s and '40s, married young girls. As lifespan was low around this time, child wives had to accept the life of widows on a large scale after a few years of their marriage. The remarriage of a widow, especially a Hindu widow, was prohibited by law, religion, and society.[3] Such widows' lifestyles were appalling. The Age of Consent Bill, whose introduction practically began in 1891 and whose enactment was completed before the year completed its first quarter, was at the centre of the controversy. Today, a century later, the bill might indeed appear to be neither radical nor revolutionary sufficiently to have elicited such an unequal response unless it is weighed against contemporary social reality. The bill proposed to set a minimum age limit of twelve years for girls for cohabitation, giving girl-brides a protected childhood.[4] This proposal attacked at the very heart of the conservative Hindu marriage system and endangered its patriarchal ideological underpinnings by potentially stopping the compulsory performance of the *garbhadhan ceremony* (consummation ceremony) within sixteen days of the girl reaching puberty.[5] A regulation that announced 'rape an offence punishable with death when the girl was below eight years and imprisonment in other cases', was enclosed in the 'criminal justice code' managed in the cities of Calcutta, Madras and Bombay from the initial months of 1828.[6] The Law Commissioners who outlined the Indian Penal Code (IPC) first determined to strengthen the punishments of rape to husbands who consummated marriages with minor wives in the year 1846. As early as the mid-nineteenth century, Ishwar Chandra Vidyasagar and Keshub Chandra Sen expressed concern among Indians about establishing a legal minimum age of marriage both for men and women. Vidyasagar himself criticized the institution of child marriage for causing misery, blaming it on outmoded *shastras*.[7] The socio-religious essence was rapidly submerged in legal and political discourse, gaining relevance far beyond that warranted by its technical nature as a legal amendment to raise the earlier age of consent laid down by the IPC at ten years.[8] Reformers competently anticipated it as not a new law but a necessary amendment to the existing law that plugged a legal loophole, not as legislative interference but as damage control, because the Indian Penal Code of 1860 had specified different minimum legal ages. 'The discrepancy among these minimum age limits for consent', as Meera Kosambi argued, 'was the legal crux of an essentially social and religious controversy.'[9] This chapter discusses what could be described as the processes that enabled the first major legislation concerning child marriage, namely the Age of Consent Bill of 1891, to be enacted under colonial rule. The plan was unbelievably multifaceted, connecting characters from all over the country. It triggered substantial discussion because it set those eager to confront the colonial state for change in matters of social reform, explicitly 'consent' to 'sexual intercourse' (whether inside or outside of marriage), against those who supposed that nationalist expectations necessitated a break from such pleading to a foreign state. Scholars have decided to approach this juncture from multiple angles, and it is still being researched.

The crime of rape under the IPC was at first used to address the question of child marriage. The offence is explained in the IPC along these lines,

> A man is said to commit rape who, except in the cases hereinafter excepted, has sexual intercourse with a woman under circumstances falling under any of the following descriptions:
>
> *First: Against her will.*
> *Secondly: Without her consent.*
>
> . . .
>
> *Sixthly: With or without her consent, when she is under sixteen years of age.*
>
> Explanation: Sexual intercourse by a man with his own wife, the wife not being under fifteen years of age, is not rape.[10]

The issue of age of consent, the age at which a woman is regarded eligible to give permission to sexual intercourse, had set foot into the legal discourse in India with the promulgation of the IPC in 1860.

'Article 375' of the said Code defined the various circumstances under which sexual intercourse would be considered rape. One of the circumstances was 'the act of sexual intercourse with a woman with or without her consent, when she is under ten years of age'. The age of consent was ten years in the year 1860. In 1949, it was raised to sixteen years. Nevertheless, the exception to section 375 specified that sexual intercourse by a man with his own wife, the wife not being under ten years of age, is not rape. The implication was that if a wife was below the age of ten, her husband's act of sexual intercourse would be considered rape. The age of consent was thus fixed at ten and so was the age under the exception. This was ten years in 1860 and was raised to fifteen years in 1949.[11] When a severe movement to raise the age of consent was set in motion in the 1880s, a man was not held guilty of the offence of rape even if he had forcible sexual intercourse with his wife who was above ten years of age. When the campaign to raise the age of consent from 10 to 12 years old was initiated, it sparked a hot debate. The nationalists' strong political stance reiterated the general public's opposition. Through his editorials, Bal Gangadhar Tilak (1856-1920), a staunch nationalist, harshly condemned the credibility of the colonial government's authority to regulate on the intense domestic or internal affairs of the Hindus. He was opposed to the use of the law to change people's behaviour. Other social reformers, however, such as Behramji Malabari, Jyotirao Phule, and Gopal Ganesh Agarkar, supported this measure, i.e. using the law to prevent child marriages.[12]

The age of consent controversy established a crucial connection in the general, although largely unorganized, movement for women's liberation in the nineteenth century. Conventionally, the Hindu marriage sacrament was comprised of two parts. The first part was the wedding ceremony itself, which had to take place at any time during the girl's adolescence, from infancy to around the age of ten. The second stage was the consummation or *garbhadhan*, literally the impregnation ceremony – a name, which exactly connected sexual intercourse with the holy duty of reproduction. It had to be done within sixteen days of the bride's first menstrual cycle. This latter custom was jeopardized by the age of consent proposal due to the possible consequence of the bride's reaching puberty between the ages of ten and twelve. This possible danger sparked a debate that brought to light, for the very first time, a slew of women's issues intertwined with the marriage system. The foundation of patriarchal norms, which characterized nineteenth-century society and locked women into the life-long role of wife-mother, was set down centuries earlier in Hindu religious and socio-legal discourses. Consequently, the *garbhadhan* ceremony attained a fundamental position as the socio-religious authorization that transformed the girl into a legal tool of her husband's sexual satisfaction and a standard of reproduction.[13] It was written in *Indu Prakash*, a weekly journal of Bombay that

> according to the orthodox, the Hindu scriptures entitled a girl not to freedom, but to be given away as a sacred gift to her husband through *kanyadan*. By definition, after that, the person who gifted her away also bestowed her consent on her husband. In addition, the onset of puberty in a girl was construed as a clear signal given by nature for the commencement of married life, irrespective of her age at the time.

Post-pubertal marriages, according to nineteenth-century Bengali narratives, would damage the environment of the family because the moment a girl reached puberty, she would begin to desire men, resulting in a loss of honour and chastity. During a court case that served as the impetus for the Age of Consent Act in 1891, W.J. Simmons, Secretary, Public Health Society of Calcutta, wrote to the Government of Bengal that child marriage was an institution that the government could never tamper with, even if it leads to serious health hazards.[14] In stark contrast to this viewpoint, reformers continued to insist on a higher level of physical maturity in the girl-bride before beginning married life in order to avoid hurting her. In regards to social change, the reformist position sought to soften the harshness and extreme manifestations of the patriarchal system rather than to overthrow it entirely.[15]

Part of Vidyasagar's assertion was based on the belief that child marriage was disastrous for women's health and, as a result, harmful for the nation's health. If the Hindu Widows' Remarriage Act helped to mobilize reformers across the country, it was the Age of Consent bill that sharply divided the controversy on women and tradition the most vigorously.[16] Despite Vidyasagar's attempts, the issue of preventing child marriage was not simply settled and engrossed the spirit of Keshub Chandra Sen, a Bengali Brahmo, who sustained the hard work of Vidyasagar in the 1870s as well as 1880s. Specific endeavours were made to alter the marriage conventions of Brahmos concluding in the Act III of 1872, which introduced prohibitions against polygamy, a legal allowance for divorce, no reference to the caste of the marriage partner and instituted a minimum age for marriage of fourteen for girls and eighteen for men – all these issues has already been discussed in the previous chapter.[17] Sen's own dedication to women's education, (it was he, who inspired Pandita Ramabai to read the *Vedas*) and to the emboldening of widow remarriage was critically weakened when he permitted his daughter to marry the Maharaja of Cooch Behar, when both bride and groom were under the ages, he himself had suggested when drafting the Native Marriage Act. The disparity between reformers' public or political and private stance like Rammohan Roy (1772-1833), Keshub Chandra Sen (1838-84) or Mahadev Govind Ranade (1842-1901), was one of the tenacious sarcasms of the procedure of social reform and it was an appearance of the difference intrinsic within the social structure of the colonial system.[18]

Several Indians were particularly worried about what foreign missionaries referred to as the evils of Hindu society. They reacted by persuading social reform and predominantly by attempting to advance women's status. *Sati* (widow immolation), widow remarriage, polygamy, *purdah* (veiling, seclusion) and women's education demanded their consideration. Legislation was initially assumed to be the solution – the abolition of *sati* in 1829 and the Hindu Widows' Remarriage Act of 1856; however, it soon became evident that laws could not modify tradition and practice. However, it quickly became clear that laws could not change custom. Recognizing this, the reformers shifted their focus to educating society and modifying women through education and newly-developed women's organizations.[19] In the late nineteenth century, sections of the British press continued to advocate for reform, and articles portraying the sufferings of Indian child brides and widows heightened public concern.[20] The proposed Consent Bill aimed to establish an acceptable age requirement under which a girl was deemed to be incompetent of giving consent to cohabitation, even with her own husband, and thus to protect her childhood from physical compulsion. This was described chiefly and vehemently as an amendment to existing law, or as a way to close a legal loophole.[21] Social reformers' constant pressure on child marriage resulted in legislation in India in 1891. The heated debate over this legislation among Indians raised a number of significant issues.[22] The Act was one of the most debatable laws approved for the advantage of women in colonial India. It was supported by a segment of Indian intelligentsia and, while being opposed by many others. Opponents of the Act saw it as an unjustified intrusion into the intimate domain of conjugality. Child marriage, which had been conducted among the upper castes since the Christian era, became prevalent in the nineteenth century. This practice had *shastric* assistance and was endorsed by social norms and beliefs. Furthermore, female chastity was highly valued, and an unmarried female past puberty was considered vulnerable to rape or seduction. Besides that, a very young daughter-in-law could be slowly trained in the rules and system of her new family, significantly easing the pressure of accommodation.[23]

In 1884, a Parsi journalist from Bombay, Behramji M. Malabari sensed the necessity for legislation governing the age of marriage of Hindu girls. Just as others at that time were influenced that an All-Indian political campaign would meet with wide public approval, Malabari recognized that the stage could be set to make an India-wide issue of premature marriage and the related custom of enforced widowhood. He consequently disclosed *Notes on Infant Marriage and Enforced Widowhood* on 15 August 1884 and distributed the papers to the administrators and private individuals, both British as well as Indian, for their responses.[24] His main recommendations for preventing infant marriages were that, 'after five years, universities should prohibit married-students from taking examination'.[25] 'Government Institutions, particularly universities and the civil services should reward unmarried males and that school books would include information on the evils of child marriage.'[26] To improve the conditions of widows, Malabari urged the Government to enforce the provisions of the Hindu Widows' Remarriage Act of 1856 and provide channels for mistreated widows to complain to the authorities. Malabari was extremely concentrated about child marriage after recognizing the extreme complexity of implementing remarriage of widows, as some of his friends pointed out in response to such *Notes*.[27] In the years that followed, child marriage became the central focus of a crusade that emphasized physical weaknesses and moral degeneration instead of the complications of child widowhood.[28]

The Times, dated 15 October 1886, a reputed newspaper, reported that

> initially, the British Government was reluctant to act on this issue. They responded to Malabari's memorandum by consulting the Provincial Governors who in turn were to obtain the opinions of the most competent authorities representing the following groups – orthodoxy, liberals, Indians and Europeans. The majority of the Governors advised the Viceroy against interference and Lord Dufferin decided to postpone action until public opinion was sufficiently developed.[29]

The reactions of Indians to Malabari's *Notes* were far more important than the *Notes* themselves. Over two hundred formal responses were received by the government from social reformers, medical authorities, proponents of the conservative section, barristers, princes, intellectuals, colonial officers, and public authorities. The responses were overwhelmingly in favour of government action and included a variety of suggestions. The National Social Conference was formed by ardent supporters to serve as a dominant organization to promote this modification. Dr Mahendralal Sircar, president of the Conference in 1887, commented on the problems of child marriage,

> The Hindu race consists at the present day … by virtue of this very blessed [*sic*] custom, of abortions and premature births … every man and woman born of parents of such tender years as 10 or 12 years for a girl and 15 or 16 for a boy must be pronounced to be either an abortion or a premature birth (hear, hear). And are you surprised that the people of a nation so constituted should have fallen easy victims under every blessed tyrant that ever chose to trample upon them?[30]

Malabari's movement sparked widespread excitement throughout India. The leading Indian supporters of Malabari were Justice Mahadev Govind Ranade, the erudite scholar and thinker, also known as a prophet of the cultural renaissance in western India; Kashinath Trimbak Telang, a Judge of Bombay High Court and a thoughtful social reformer; Dayaram Gidumal, an Assistant Judge of Ahmedabad; Bipin Chandra Pal, the famous orator, freedom fighter and social reformer; Mahendralal Sircar, eminent in the field of medicine and others. Tilak organized a series of meetings in early January 1885, in which he staunchly argued that appealing to a foreign government to rectify an Indian social evil was humiliating. He did not deny that early marriage was harmful, but he believed that education, rather than legislation was needed to end this practice.[31] There had also been severe resistance in Bengal, where several vernacular newspapers harshly condemned Malabari. Though, the progressive Hindus championed his social crusade.[32] Malabari went on to say that child marriage had no religious sanction in the *shastras* and that the State should therefore treat it as an economic question as a source of over-population and consequent disturbances. In his revised *note*, dated 23 October 1884, Malabari beseeched for larger state cooperation.[33] Soon, there emerged a symposium of Hindu domestic reformers and anti-reformers from all over India (1889), compiled by Malabari's close associate Dayaram Gidumal, around the two issues dealt with by Malabari, namely, infant marriage and enforced widowhood. Being unsuccessful to awaken the Indian people or the Indian government to action, Malabari moved his ground to Britain in August 1890 and distributed a pamphlet on the same two issues, entitled 'An Appeal from the Daughters of India', conveyed to the British public and particularly British women. 'On its heels came the formation of a committee of concerned British elite, including the Earl of Northbrook, Lord Reay, the Marquis of Ripon, the Earl of Kinnaird, Professor and Mrs Max Muller, Mr and Mrs Ilbert, Cardinal Manning, Dadabhai Naoroji, and others' – it had been reported in *Indu-Prakash*.[34]

During Malabari's stay in England, several socialists and reformers in India attempted to transform the expanding political concern in social legislation into more reasonable proposals than those in the *Notes*. In his response to the *Notes* in 1884, K.T. Telang, who was a reformer and later became the Judge of Bombay High Court, asserted that 'reform is most urgently called for in regard to the time of consummation and not so much in regard to the time of marriage'. Undoubtedly, Telang was attempting to pacify the opponents by urging that delayed consummation of marriage be a reform from within

Hindu society and not imposed from without. Dayaram Gidumal who was Malabari's main supporter, backed Telang's suggestion for rational negotiation with the proposition that eventually became the Age of Consent Bill. Gidumal distributed a brochure that focused on the IPC rather than on caste and household traditions and practices. The Code incorporated an earlier Age of Consent Act, approved without much hostility in 1860 at the insistence of Vidyasagar, which recognized ten as the age of a girl below which sexual intercourse with her was regarded as rape. Gidumal suggested merely that the Penal Code be amended to raise the age of consent to twelve for both married and unmarried girls. Social activists and reformers recognized the worth of this kind of proposal; and it had the immediate benefit of not requesting the intervention of new government but instead functioning within prevailing legal provisions. As a result, hostility might be reduced.[35]

However, the orthodox section, especially in Bengal, vehemently opposed this move. The issue was also brought up at the Indian National Social Conference (1887). Ranade wholeheartedly endorsed Gidumal's amendment proposal. The third annual session of the Conference, held in Bombay in December 1889, determined that 'in order to prevent early consummation of marriage, which led to the impairment of the physical health of both husband and wife, cohabitation with wife below twelve years of age should be punishable as a criminal offence.'[36] The following resolution was passed at the fourth session of the Indian National Social Conference, assembled in Calcutta in December 1890,

> This Conference is of opinion that the practice of child marriage be discouraged by public sentiment and that within the sphere of the various caste and communities strenuous efforts be made to postpone the celebration of the marriage rites till 12 in the case of girls and 18 in the case of boys and the consummation of the marriage till after they attain the ages of 14 and 20 respectively and that the members of the various social reform activities in the country should, in their own cases, themselves see that those limits of age are realized in actual practice and public opinion educated to advance these limits still higher.[37]

On the legal front, the petition for consent legislation was significantly strengthened by two court cases, revealing diverse characteristics of the question of child marriage, which exploded on the national scenario. The first of these was the Rukhmabai Case in Bombay. Rukhmabai, 19 years old, from an educated non-Brahmin elite family of Bombay, had been married in her childhood, but rejected the offer to live with her husband on the grounds of socio-economic and personal incompatibility. Her husband filed a suit for the restitution of conjugal rights; the court case dragged on from 1884 to 1888, during which Rukhmabai was endangered with a prison sentence and ended in an out-of-court settlement in which he relinquished his claims on her. The outrage that erupted surrounding the case was fuelled by animosity between the largely traditional society and the reformers who sought to introduce the Western values of choice and compatibility in marriage, which presupposed adult marriage.[38]

Rukhmabai was born in 1864 in Mumbai, in the *Pachkalshi* sub-caste of Pathares. With the support of Mumbai's new academic and vocational advantages, a segment of this community had gained ground among the city's generous and pluralistic upper-class people. Rukhmabai belonged to this section, but not her husband, which was to have a significant impact on this case. Janardan Pandurang Save, Rukhmabai's father, was a successful building constructor. After his untimely death, his widow Jayantibai who was at that time nineteen-years-old, came back to the house of her own father, Rao Bahadur Harischandra Yadavji, an eminent personality in Mumbai, with her 3 years old daughter Rukhma. Jayantibai remarried three years later in 1870, as permitted by her caste. Her second husband Dr Sakharam Arjun Raut was a 29 years old widower and a Professor of Botany at Mumbai's Grant Medical College in 1883. Rukhmabai, then six years old, moved in with her stepfather, who motivated and assisted her in obtaining a better academic knowledge. When she was eleven years old, Rukhmabai was married to Dadaji Bhikaji Thakur and her mother and grandfather took this initiative. Dadaji, however, was not amenable to their efforts to educate and groom him, and grew to manhood with idle ways, barely eking out an income by occasional work and living with his maternal uncle, Narayan Dharmaji. At the beginning Rukhmabai sustained to live with her parents even after she reached the age of puberty because Dr Sakharam Arjun was opposed to early consummations of marriage and later because Dadaji was suspected of having contracted tuberculosis. Throughout this time, her irregular meetings with Dadaji eventually disclosed their socio-economic and cultural mismatch.[39]

Dadaji sent Rukhmabai a legal notice at the prompting of his family members and friends after trying to make unofficial but ineffective efforts to convince her to attend him. On her disregarding it, he filed a lawsuit in 1884 for the restitution of conjugal rights. The following year, while the case was sub judice, Rukhmabai published two letters on child marriage and compulsory widowhood in *The Times of India*, dated 26 June and 19 September of 1885 under the pseudonym 'A Hindu Lady', approving Malabari's feelings. The combativeness of Rukhmabai's opinions triggered a wide-ranging disruption and stimulated much antagonistic wonder regarding the identity of 'Hindu Lady', before *The Times of India* confirmed it, further firing up the anger of her adversaries. In September 1885, the case of Dadaji Bhikaji *vs.* Rukhmabai was heard in the Bombay High Court. Rukhmabai's reasons for unwilling to live with Dadaji, as stated by her lawyer, were – 'his inability to provide proper residence and maintenance for himself and his wife'; 'his poor health, eroded by asthma and consumption'; and 'the dubious moral character of Dadaji's maternal uncle, under whose protection he lived and expected Rukhmabai to live'. Rukhmabai's defence, directed by Advocate-General Latham and assisted by Mr Inverarity and Mr Telang, brought up the fundamental question of whether the restitution suit could be maintained in this case. Mr Justice Pinhey ruled in his decision, delivered on 19 and 21 September in the year 1885, that 'it was not maintainable because conjugal rights had not been established, and consent and consummation were both lacking'. Pinhey's decision, ostensibly based on solid legal grounds, adhered to the liberal British tradition, implicitly censuring the depraved attempt by an Indian man to enforce rights acquired through the palpably unjust and immoral custom of child marriage.[40]

Dadaji's attorneys contended that in this case, the reality of the marriage had been formed and the bride had reached the age of puberty. She had been permitted to live at her stepfather's house, but now she must be sent to her husband's house as he had requested. Nevertheless, Pinhey demanded that

> It is a misnomer to call this a suit for restitution of conjugal rights because the rights had not been established. The marriage was performed during the defendant's childhood but never consummated; and after the passage of eleven years, the plaintiff asked the court to compel her to join him that he may complete his contract with her by consummating the marriage.

Pinhey measured it to be barbarous, a cruel, a revolting thing to do to compel a young lady under these circumstances to go to a man whom she dislikes in order that he may cohabit with her against her will. He contended that neither the law nor the practice of our courts supported such a move, because the suits for restitution had no foundation in Hindu law but it had been transplanted from England into India, despite being refuted in England at that time. As a result, he ruled that 'the suit was not maintainable and that the plaintiff could not be granted the relief requested, while illuminating that the plaintiff's poverty was not one of the reasons for this decision'.[41] The decision sparked an outpouring of public outrage. For some, it was a daring statement of Indian women's privileges to individual independence and self-respect. Others saw it as an affront to the purity of Hindu marriage and family.[42] The case was heard in the High Court in early March 1887 before Mr Justice Farran (Pinhey had retired by then) and was made the decision in Dadaji's favour. The final judgement of the High Court seemed to have reiterated the Appellate Court's order. Newspapers, specially *Indu-Prakash*, dated 7 March 1887 reported that 'Rakhmabai was ordered to go and live with her husband within a month or face imprisonment for six months in a civil jail.'[43] Farran's decision formed an uproar among native newspapers in India and achieved the maximum levels of the British government, to a limited extent because the 'Matrimonial Causes Act had repealed that kind of penal provisions for English spouses in 1884.'[44] Rukhmabai made it clear that she would disobey the order, despite the proposed penalty; and also appealed against the judgement. The debate illustrates the idea in which British civil courts consistently, albeit silently, contributed to broaden the British state's judicial power over an unspecified, disputed social space in India. Tilak saw Rakhmabai's refusal to live with her uneducated husband as indicative of the dangers of female education. Accusing the reformers of using the case 'to fire bullets at our religion with the intention of castrating our eternal religion'.[45] During the course of Rukhmabai's trial, Muller wrote four letters to the *The Times* (London), which elicited a number of responses. However, he only tried to defend Hindu law in this case to support his belief that legal recourse was not the ultimate solution to the problems raised by Rukhmabai's case. Education was required, and Rukhmabai was the clear evidence of its accomplishment. For it was her acquaintance with Western education that had enabled her to become 'the best judge … herself of her own marriage choice', according to Muller.[46]

Dadaji publicly released 'An exposition of some of the facts of the case of Dadaji *vs.* Rukhmabai' on 24 April 1887, in order to dismiss Rukhmabai's allegations by demonstrating that his education matched hers, his health was good, and he could maintain her at a reasonable standard. He went on to say that he was stymied not by Rukhmabai's bias, but by her grandfather's avarice. Harishchandra Yadavji was blamed for preventing Rukhmabai's union with him in order to retain control of the paternal property (allegedly amounting to about Rs 25,000 in 1887) to which she was the sole heir.[47] Rukhmabai's response to this exposition denied the allegations concerning her inherited property and clarified that her refusal to unite with Dadaji was due to his living in objectionable surroundings with his maternal uncle.[48] As a consequence, Narayan Dharmaji, Dadaji's maternal uncle created a libel suit against Rukhmabai and her grandfather. In the meantime, following the High Court decree for restitution, which Rukhmabai chose to ignore, the Rukhmabai Defence Committee was formed on 3 April 1887, with prominent European and Indian women leaders as well as some compassionate men who thought of a liberal temperament, under the chairmanship of Professor Wordsworth, Principal of Elphinstone College, with the aim of saving her from the possible sentence of six months' imprisonment. The Committee was anticipated to advocate for the abolition of the practice of child marriage, however, Telang rejected, asserting that its only goal could be to make the penalty for disobedience milder, that is, to make imprisonment optional rather than mandatory.[49]

Attempts to awaken public opinion had also managed to reach in England. Latham, Rukhmabai's counsel, wrote about the Hindu law regarding the restitution of conjugal rights to the *London Times* and continued to say that English law was misguidedly interpreted to a case, which would not be acceptable in England.[50] Pinhey also wrote to *The Times*, defending the legal effectiveness of his initial decision and judgement.[51] It was furthermore revealed that English women were interested in Rukhmabai's case. According to another report, Rukhmabai decided to write a letter to a friend in England recommending that 'the Queen-Empress should announce all illegitimate marriages conducted before the ages of fifteen and twenty, for girls and boys, respectively', and that this letter was forwarded to *The Times* by this friend's brother, the Bishop of Carlisle.[52] Rukhmabai utilized the British press to compose her own justifications of what her case meant, what was wrong with the Hindu marriage system, and what needed to be done to ensure social and economic freedom for women of India.[53] British and American feminists raised funds to support her legal fees in the four-year-long case. The Queen was particularly interested in Rukhmabai's case in the 1880s. Rukhmabai pleaded straightforwardly to her 'Queen-Empress', as a 'poor afflicted Hindoo woman'.[54] This kind of humble attitudes were undertaken to extract the heart-strings of a monarch whom Rukhmabai and many women in India mentioned to as the mother. 'At such an unusual occasion will the mother listen to an earnest appeal from her millions of Indian daughters,' Rukhmabai asked, 'and grant them a few simple words of change into the books on Hindoo law'.[55] Queen Victoria afterward issued a special royal decree dissolving Rukhmabai's marriage and preventing her imprisonment.[56] Women's magazines enclosed Rukhmabai's case as well, depending profoundly on the reports of *The Times* communicator. Sudhir Chandra examines the course of action in which the Queen blamed both Dadaji and the orthodox Hindu community for Rukhmabai's troubles, but not without chastising the more progressive natives for bowing to the pressure of public meetings and agitations as well.[57] Rukhmabai became a gateway into the debate of progressive mission of Britain in India as a result of the British media coverage. As Antoinette Burton shows, 'the newspaper portrayal of Rakhmabai as an educated and refined (and also anglicized) lady, placed by fate and oppressive Hindu custom at the mercy of an ignorant, uncouth, and depraved husband, was calculated to win the sympathy of British readers.'[58] It is important to note that the discussion regarding child marriage sparked by the *London Times* did not emerge solely as a result of Rukhmabai's case. Discourses regarding good Hindu wife and her unconquered purity were central to a broad spectrum of revivalist and reformist controversy about politics, religion and the constraints of colonial rule in nineteenth-century India. Undeniably, Tanika Sarkar has estimated that, 'not only was the Hindu woman's body molded from her infancy by the *Shastric* regimen of non-consensual, indissoluble infant marriage, but her subjectivity and agency . . . [were] exhausted by this embodiment.'[59]

Finally, the Bombay High Court appeared reluctant to implement the restitution decree. In the meantime, in July 1888, a negotiated settlement managed to bring the momentous Rukhmabai Case to an anti-climactic end.[60] Recognizing that compromise was unattainable, Dadaji recommended a settlement, accepted Rs 2,000 from Rukhmabai and relinquished his rights over her. As Jim Masselos pointed out, 'his was a pyrrhic victory in that he obtained neither the body of his wife nor access to her fortune'.[61] The case was ultimately resolved in July 1888, but the social standing of marriage remained constant; it was not legally abolished, and it was considered legitimate and enforceable under Hindu law. Dadaji remarried shortly after that. In 1889, Rukhmabai decided to leave for Britain to learn medicine and came back to India with her medical degree in 1895. Indeed, she became the first woman doctor of Maharashtra to practice medicine. Afterward working for six months in Mumbai, she moved on to Surat Hospital, where she practiced till her retirement in 1917 and after that experienced a further fifteen years as a medical doctor at Rajkot. She lived her entire life as a single woman, dressing as a Hindu married woman as long as Dadaji was alive; after his death in the year 1904, Rukhmabai dressed as a widow. Rukhmabai decided to return to her native Mumbai at the age of nearly seventy, where she died in 1955 at the age of ninety-one.[62]

In Bengal, possibly the only paper to have steadily encouraged the Case of Rukhmabai was the Brahmo periodical, *Sanjivani*. A *Bombay Government Circular of 1887* evidently moved by the Rukhmabai Case received harsh condemnation when it projected that 'either spouse on reaching adulthood could obtain dissolution of marriage if so desired'.[63] Even *Somprakash*, the comparatively enlightened newspaper, was sceptical if Hindu marriages, being what they were, could be annulled with such recklessness.[64] The *Dainik*, on the other, claimed that Hindus unlike Englishmen were not legally or customarily barred from entering into multiple marriages and hence did not need any legal intervention for dissolving a previous marriage.[65] Surprisingly, as the potential of state intervention grew, the liberal-reformist components, or at least many of them, seemed to retreat. The prospect of the bureaucracy's taking the initiative not only outraged the orthodox but also nudged some former advocates of reform into the opposite site. The *Sahachar* for example was necessarily distressed 'to warn all provincial governments not to pay any attention to the Bombay Government's outrageous circular'[66] and the *Sulabh Samachar O Kusdaha*, truly a conservative paper, published an article 'with a long defence of the charms of an early marriage'.[67] The *Somprakash*, which in 1884, had observed positively Malabari's efforts, anticipating that 'the mitigation of early marriages would reduce the number of child-widows',[68] could not eventually support 'the idea of legislative interference, which was the very basis of Malabari's campaign'.[69] References were also formed to the low caste to which Rukhmabai supposedly belonged in order to emphasize the argument that the wife's defiance of her marital obligations was an incidence that could not occur in respectable upper-caste households. The *Burdwan-Sanjivani*, which in April 1887 had publicized some empathy towards Rukhmabai was contrived to remark only a couple of months later that 'since the *shastras* had strongly recommended the chastisement of women who had forsaken their husbands, it was only just that the likes of Rukhmabai be legally punished or at least be made to atone for their sins in keeping with *shastric* prescriptions.'[70] By the second half of 1887, Rukhmabai was a justifiably unpopular name in Bengali homes; on 30 May 1887, the men of the theatre organized a highly effective satire *Rukmini Rongo* (The Rukmini Comedy) to rejoice the growing opposition to reforms related to marriage.[71] The Rukhmabai episode of 1887 made it imperative at last to rewrite the narrative of love and pleasure in the language of force. Rajendralal Mitra insisted on attending a meeting at the *Shova Bazar Rajbari*, 'in it (Hindu marriage) there is no selection, no self-choice and no consent on the part of the bride. She is an article of gift; she is given away even as a cow or any other chattel'. Tanika Sarkar appropriately said that 'Rukhmabai's action violently foregrounded the sexual double standards and made a mockery of the notion of the loving heart of Hindu conjugality.'[72]

The Age of Consent Act in India represented a significant withdrawal from prior social reform policies, and the Government of India required an appropriate justification for its new effort.[73] 'Such an opportunity was afforded by the Hari Maiti case', wrote Lord Lansdowne, 'and we took advantage of it at once'.[74] Actually, this incident was the Calcutta child-wife murder case of 1889, involving 10 years old Phulmonee Dasi married to Hari Mohan Maitee who was over thirty years of age. Phulmonee died in pain, purportedly on her wedding night, and her husband was charged with murder. *Indu-Prakash* had mentioned that 'the much-publicized case led to the coining of the term "Harimaitism" to refer to the noxious practice of early consummation'.[75] Some contemporary witnesses have outmodedly called it a fatal case of marital rape. The government's advantage to approach the Consent Bill issue itself came only after the public outrage in India over the widely publicized case of Hari Mohan Maitee, who was committed for trial to the Sessions Court at Calcutta on 6 July 1890. Maitee, a 35 years old man, was accused of murdering his child-bride Phulmonee in 1889 through brutal sexual intercourse. Despite the fact that testimony from Phulmonee's mother revealed the brutality of Maitee's molest and Phulmonee's unbearable pain, he was not charged with rape.[76] Since, Justice Wilson, who presided over the case, stated that 'Phulmonee was eleven years old' and therefore, 'Maitee could not be tried for rape but only for the lesser charge of committing a rash and negligent act'; the 'Exception to the Fifth

Clause of Section 375 of the Indian Penal Code', introduced in 1860, declared that 'sexual intercourse by a man with his own wife not being under ten years of age is not rape'. The Phulmonee case brought to light other cases of 'Hari Maitism' in which husbands guilty of causing the death of their child-brides had been either acquitted by the Courts or else had been awarded relatively minor sentences for causing bodily harm.[77] Forty-four female doctors presented long lists of cases where child-wives had been maimed or killed because of rape.[78] The debate shifted from the potential impact of child marriage on future generations' health to the lives and protection of Hindu wives.[79]

Phulmonee was the daughter of late Kunj Behari Maitee. Kunj Behari belonged to the Oriya Kayastha caste group, and he worked as a bazar sircar at Bow Bazar Market. Her family members stated that, while they supported child marriage, they prohibited cohabitation before the girl menstruated, which Phulmonee had not done in this case.[80] According to their version, the newly-married couple had been kept apart according to caste rules, and that Hari, on a visit to his in-laws, had stolen into Phulmonee's room and had forced himself upon her, thereby causing her death. Hari Maitee, though, claimed that since the marriage she had spent at least a fortnight at his house and they had slept together all the time. He made no reference to caste regulations prohibiting pre-menstrual sexual intercourse. Despite Hari Maitee's insistence that they had not had sexual relations on the previous night, medical opinion was unequivocal that the girl had died as a result of violent sexual penetration. This incident was described in the pages of the *Nabyabharat.*[81] If the court agreed that Hari was correct and that he and Phulmonee had previously slept together, it could go a long way towards demonstrating that because nothing unusual had occurred previously, Hari would have had no motive to suspect that a more robust penetration would result in violent consequences on the deadly night in question. The English judge, Wilson, made it clear that he chose to accept Hari's version, thus exonerating him from the charge of culpable homicide. In any case, the charge of rape was not admissible because the Penal Code provisions barred the existence of rape by the husband if the wife was above the age of ten.[82] Phulmonee's case was by no means an isolated case. The report by Dr McLeod on child marriage made abundantly clear the severe repercussions of premenstrual cohabitation.[83] In court, an Indian doctor stated that '13 per cent of the maternity cases that he had handled involved mothers below the age of thirteen.'[84] Reformists contended that puberty was a prolonged process, and menarche was the sign of its commencement, not of its culmination. The beginning of menstruation did not indicate the girls' sexual maturity to sustain sexual penetration without serious pain or damage.[85] It was regrettable that all viewpoints decided on a definition of consent that was nailed to a purely physical capability, completely detached from certain issues like choice of partner, sexual, emotional or mental compatibility or other social considerations such as a girl's personal development.[86] The details of Phulmonee's death were reported by the contemporary press in Bengal and in other parts of India, thus bringing questions about child marriage into stark public view. *Nabyabharat* demanded that the Age of Consent of sexual intercourse of a girl should be raised to 14 years.[87] According to Tanika Sarkar, 'it was only the Phulmonee case of 1891 that dramatically ended the stalemate'.[88] Reformers insisted that the colonial state should pass legislation raising the legal age of consent in reaction to the controversy.[89]

On 9 January 1891 the Age of Consent Bill, drafted by Sir Andrew Scoble to amend Section 375 of the Indian Penal Code, was introduced by the Viceroy of India, Lord Lansdowne into the Supreme Legislative Council.[90] Scoble proposed that the 'age of consent be raised to twelve years in the case of both married and unmarried girls, though in the case of married girls the offence by the husband was made non-cognizable and the law was to apply to all religious communities'.[91] He also stated that, the objects of the Bill were twofold. Its purpose was to safeguard girl children – from premature prostitution and from premature cohabitation.[92] The Viceroy's council included eleven Europeans, two Muslims and two Hindu members. Of the last two, Sir Romesh Chunder Mitter of Bengal opposed the bill on several grounds, such as widespread discontent, the existing law being sufficient, departure from the wise policy of non-interference with religion and from the promises of the Queen's Proclamation, the law being a cause of annoyance and molestation, it being anomalous that a husband should commit a rape upon his wife, the marriage relations being unhappy in case of prosecution, reform being put back and agreement between the reformers and anti-reformers being made impossible.[93] *Indu-Prakash* mentioned that the other Hindu member, Rao Bahadur K.L. Nulkar of Mumbai, however, somewhat redeemed the name of educated India by taking a firm position in favour of the Bill, highlighting its defensive plea and he also said that any discontent that arose in certain sections of the society would only be temporary.[94]

Andrew Scoble, while describing the situation in Bengal, quoted an extract from Stewart Bayley, which ran thus, 'the custom appears to be universal … but it prevails generally over Bengal proper, especially over Eastern and Central Bengal'.[95] Scoble mentioned a document where Leyall, the Commissioner of Chittagong, had reported that the practice of consummating marriage with immature girls was universal in his division as it was in the whole of Bengal. The records of the criminal courts pointed to the same situation. In the Sessions Court in Rangpur, 'a man called Dhulamasga was tried in March 1890 for committing rape on his wife and was sentenced to three months' rigorous imprisonment.' On the basis of these cases, Andrew Scoble asserted that Phulmonee-Hari Maitee incident was not an isolated case and that the existing law needed further protective clauses. The Marquis of Lansdowne, the Viceroy and Governor-General of India and the President of the Council, declared, 'We justify our proposal on the ground that British Law would fail to provide adequately for the safety of the children of this country, if it failed to protect them from a particular form of ill usage infinitely more revolting and more disastrous in its direct as well as in its remote result than any form of ill treatment to which they are liable.'[96] The debate over the Age of Consent Bill erupted into a frenzy near the end of the year 1890. Fifty-five female doctors in India petitioned the Viceroy to pass legislation prohibiting consummation of marriages with girls under the age of fourteen.[97] Two thousand Indian women signed a similar petition to Queen Victoria.[98]

A select committee including both Hindu members reviewed the question and suggested minor amendments in its report presented on 6 March 1891; Mitter submitted a minute of dissent. The Age of Consent Act was finally passed on 19 March 1891 after a day-long debate. The age of consent specified in the IPC of 1860 was amended and raised from ten to twelve as a result of this Act.[99] The Act of 1891 redefined rape as an act of sexual intercourse with a woman, with or without her consent, when she was under twelve years of age. It also rewrote the exception, stating that sexual intercourse by a man with his own wife, the wife not being under 12 years of age, was not rape. By implication, sexual intercourse by a man with his wife under 12 years of age would be considered rape and was punishable by a maximum of 10 years imprisonment or transportation for life.[100] The legislation was enacted to defend young girls from premature and thus, supposedly hazardous, sexual intercourse. It was precisely this revised age of exception that triggered a serious controversy. Geraldine Forbes has commented that this was a compromise since it did not prevent families from forming a marriage alliance at an earlier age and then wait for its consummation when the girl was twelve.[101] Himani Bannerji observed that Consent had little to do with notions of a girl's right to choose; this was rather about the right of legal guardians to alienate a woman's body to a man, whether as husband or client.[102]

TABLE 3.1: TIMELINE FOR AGE OF MARRIAGE AND CONSENT FROM 1860 TO 1891

1860	Indian Penal Code makes all sexual intercourse below 10 years criminalizable as rape.
1884	Behramji Malabari's 'Notes' had been published in India.
1884-8	Dadaji Bhikaji *vs.* Rukhmabai Case
1891	Phulmonee Case (Queen Empress *vs.* Huree Mohan Mythee)
1891	Age of Consent Act was passed

However, neither the proponents nor the adversaries of the Act were bothered about the repercussions of this Act for unmarried women. Those who advocated for this Act were particularly worried about the physical security of married women. Those who objected it were concerned about the sexual prerogative of husbands and the absolute and unquestionable right over their wives' bodies that religion and custom had granted to them.[103] Although the instant impact of this Act was unfavourable, a silent shift in social mores slowly emerged. This could be attributed to improvements in education and, as a result, a subsequent shift in people's attitudes. Many prominent people noticed this shift. Manmohan Ghose (1869-1924), the elder brother of Aurobindo Ghose (1872-1950), asserted in his address at the meeting of the National Indian Association held in 1895, 'As regards child marriages, though I regret I cannot say that the practice has been discontinued, there has undoubtedly been a remarkable progress of late years.' Two Indian princely states receive special reference for approving actions to eradicate child marriage. In 1894, the Mysore Government passed the Infant Marriages Prevention Regulation to prohibit marriage of girls under the age of eight and to prevent marriage between men and women of very inequitable age, especially of girls under the age of fourteen.[104] In 1904, the Gaekwads of Baroda passed the Infant Marriage Prevention Act for their state, which prohibited the marriage of girls under the age of nine and permitted girls under the age of twelve and boys under the age of sixteen to marry, only if the parents first acquired the consent of a tribunal comprised of the local Sub-Judge and three assessors of the petitioner's caste.[105] The Census Report of 1911 proclaimed,

> The practice has been denounced by many social reformers since Malabari opened the campaign a quarter of a century ago; and the Social Conference, which holds its meeting, annually, in connection with the National Congress has made the abolition of child marriage, one of the leading planks in its platform. It is strongly discouraged by the Brahmos in Bengal and the Aryas in North India.[106]

Meera Kosambi has tried to state in one of her article[107] that the controversy itself was based on some fundamental issues – whether the ancient Hindu law prescribed child marriage and early completion of marriage as mandatory; whether contemporary practice, derived from hallowed tradition, sanctioned early marriage and consummation; whether child marriage resulted in harmful effects for the girl-bride, her family and society as a whole; whether, if reform should prove to be necessary, it should come through voluntary action or through government legislation; whether the proposed legislation violated the promise of non-interference into the socio-religious practices and customs, made by the Proclamation of 1858; and whether the proposed bill would indeed succeed in protecting girl-brides.

A nationwide public concern about the consent issue had resembled private measures and the legislative procedure. *The Mahratta,* an English weekly of Pune, asserted that the Bombay Presidency 'had no business to show any dissatisfaction' with the Act, that only Bengal exhibited any real feeling of dissatisfaction, while Madras wisely 'went in heartily for reform'.[108] However, the Bombay Presidency had also spearheaded protest movement alongside reform. An orthodox Hindu protest meeting at Madhavbag in Bombay in 1886 was one of the first responses to Malabari's campaign. The anti-reformers gathered in Tulsibag in Pune in October 1890 to protest against the formation of Malabari's English Committee, and again in Madhavbag in early February 1891 after the bill was introduced. In February 1891, the reformers launched a counter-offensive with public meetings at Javerbag in Bombay, and at Krida Bhuvan in Pune. The conveners of these and other related meetings dispatched a series of memorials to the Viceroy, to which was incorporated a widely publicized petition by several educated women of Mumbai urging the Queen-Empress for the reform of Hindu marriage customs.[109] *The Mahratta* wrote that protest meetings were also held at Jalgaon, Ahmednagar, Nagpur and Surat in the Bombay Presidency in February 1891. Even after the passage of the act, protests continued unabated. *Sudharak*, an Anglo-Marathi weekly newspaper of Pune, dated 30 March 1891, mentioned that 'a resolution was passed at Sholapur to send a deputation to Britain to enlist public opinion against the act, so that eventually the British parliament could be pressurized to direct the Indian government to repeal it'. We came to know from *The Mahratta*, dated 17 May 1891, that 'Bal Gangadhar Tilak moved a resolution at the Bombay Provincial Conference, blaming the government for complete disrespect of public opinion in passing the act.'[110] According to Kumari Jayawardena, Tilak, a *Chitpavan Brahmin* merged political extremism with conservatism on questions of social reform. Tilak's sort of revivalist Hindu nationalism was to show influential in assembling public opinion.[111] He was able to integrate nationalist political demands with religious and populist enthusiasm by appealing to mass attitude. Tilak collided with important reformers over the issue of Age of Consent and consistently criticized state intervention in social issues.[112] Dr R.G. Bhandarkar, a vociferous social reformer, was also embroiled in heated debates with Tilak. In *A Note on the Age of Marriage and its Consummation according to Hindu Religious Law* (1891), Bhandarkar stated that 'post-puberty marriages, deferment of consummation for three years after puberty and postponement of childbirth until after sixteen years of age were compatible with the sacred laws'.[113] However, in a long debate with Bhandarkar, Tilak sustained, among several other things, that 'the *prajapatya* and the *garbhadhan* ceremonies were to be performed in immediate succession (i.e. within twenty-four hours) on the conclusion of the girl's first menstruation'.[114]

The uproar in Bengal against such Act, it has been argued, marked an explicit denial of reformism and a return to conservative ideology. It was the first of its kind in colonial India that large crowds gathered in public places to protest against this Act. Hindu revivalist nationalism, a cultural and ideological movement that exploded in Bengal in the 1880s, is assumed to have outstretched its peak in 1891 with the counterblast against the Age of Consent Act.[115] 'The argument that the Consent Bill was the first real breach of Indian autonomy', as Tanika Sarkar has suggested,

> was the core of the revivalist-nationalist strategy against the Bill; it was grounded on the dubious claim that previous colonial legislations on *sati*, widow remarriage, and female infanticide were of much less significance for the autonomy of the Indian social fabric compared to the present legislation that interfered in marriage practices.[116]

The pioneers of this movement were proud of Hindu tradition and culture and they were against the colonial intervention in these regard. Anti-bill protests moved the city of Calcutta and established a momentous asset for the burgeoning extremist or militant nationalism, something which historians have so far overlooked. Chandranath Bose, one of the pioneers of orthodox Hindu thought, spoke in favour of child marriage in an article titled 'Bibaher Bayas O Uddeshya' (Age and Purpose of Marriage) in *Bangadarshan* (1880).[117] Akshaychandra Sarkar criticized the scientific argument, raised against child marriage.[118] The Age of Consent Bill, on the other hand, deviated from the established tradition of personal laws in two ways. It applied to all colonial subjects, regardless of religious faith. It went beyond the sphere of marriage because it applied to all girls under the age of twelve. Protests exploded in Bengal, nevertheless, specifically over the subject of Hindu wives. The incidence of Hindu infant marriages was the highest in Bengal; according to the 1881 Census, '14 per cent of Bengali Hindu girls were married off before they were ten, and they encompassed all castes except Adivasis. In Bombay, they amounted to 10 per cent and, in Madras, only 4.5 per cent.'[119] While highlighting the Hindu revivalist uproar, historians have neglected the numerous realms in which the issue regarding consent was discussed in Bengali society. The enthusiastic attitude of the Brahmo Samaj towards the Age of Consent Act for example, has not been sufficiently illustrated. The reactions of the Muslim community to the Act have also been overlooked in existing historiography. My investigation into contemporary newspapers and periodicals discloses that, while a large portion of the Muslim population conveyed discontent against this legal interference and criticized the Act as an attack on Muslim religion and social customs, a small but noticeable portion of the Muslim intelligentsia appreciated it.[120] It is thus necessary to outline the reformist fervour of a segment of Muslims, further complicating and nuanced societal acceptance of the Act in the context of the Bengali society.[121]

Sir Andrew Scoble's introduction of the Age of Consent Bill in the Viceroy's Legislative Council on 9 January 1891 sparked unprecedented public debate as well as widespread unrest in Bengal.[122] The adversaries of the Bill concentrated their disapproval on two subjects. Firstly, arguments placed surrounding the Bill's effect on women's status within Bengali society as well as the Hindu religion. Secondly, condemnation evolved into a safeguarding of Bengali society against the foreign culture of the West and its impact.[123] Whereas the practice of child-marriage among the upper-caste Hindus was relatively prevalent among various caste or class and religious groups throughout India, there was a universal agreement that the problem of premature child marriage was primarily found in the province of Bengal.[124] Two Bengali newspapers, the weekly *Bangabasi* and the daily *Dainik-o-Samachar Chandrika*, possessed and edited by Jogendro Chandra Ghosh and Krishna Chandra Banerjea, were critical of the Bill.[125] Acknowledging the fact that social cohesion as well as solidity was rooted on the joint family and the caste system, they were forced to protect the 'cultural heritage' of India against a liberal mindset, which was positioned entirely in the direction of social and intellectual ideologies of Western origin. Members of the British Indian Association, largely wealthy aristocrats[126] personified by Raja Peary Mohan Mukherjea, and a diverse group of men from the proficient and salaried groups endorsed this approach.[127] They attempted to devise an idea for India's future by examining the country's distinctiveness, which was connected to the Hindu religion. The Hindu religion, however, was to be represented as an ideologically-charged means of defending India against total control by the British. As a result, any intervention by a foreign ruler with Hindu society elicited the cry of 'Hindu religion and nation in danger'.[128] Jogendro Chandra Ghosh (1842-1902), one of the earliest Indian Positivists and later, the leader of the Indian Positivist Society, raised objections to the Act's attempt to impose the conjugal right as a privilege on moral grounds. 'The question of child marriage needed to be reviewed', Jogendro wrote and suggested that 'a committee of Brahmin priests and British jurists be commissioned to work out some enforceable marriage laws'.[129] Jogendro's antagonism to this bill was strikingly different from that of the extremists who raised the cry of 'Hinduism in danger'. The extremists would not accept foreign interference with Hindu customs, but Jogendro was more concerned with 'the viability of the measure', its 'compatibility with Hindu ethics' and its long-term 'impact on Hindu institutions'.[130]

Mrinalini Sinha wrote 'the entire country was sharply divided' over the passing of the Age of Consent Act.[131] Substantially, three staunch positions emerged from the extensive range of opinion, which was expressed during the entire controversy. At one end of the spectrum was the 'orthodox' or 'anti-reform section', which retained that 'the contemporary marriage practices posed no problem and need not be changed'. This group was represented mostly by *shastris* and *pandits*; it was indeed justifiable to mention the names of Ram Shastri Apte of Pune in the Bombay presidency and Pandit Shashadhar Tarkachuramani of Calcutta in the Bengal Presidency.[132] Ram Shastri Apte depended on evidence from fourteen *shastras* to demonstrate that 'the girl who sees her menses in her father's house (before marriage) is impure, and that by restricting her reproductive capacity her father incurs the charge of *bhrunahatya*, or killing the embryo.'[133] According to Pandit Shashadhar Tarkachuramani, 'The *garbhadhan* rite has to be performed on the first occurrence of that event (i.e. menstruation)....

This is the first *sanskara* enjoined upon the Hindoos and the non-observance of this first *sanskara* renders the performance of all other *sanskaras* of not much avail.'[134] The reformers, on the other hand, claimed that the ancient texts had been misinterpreted and must be interpreted correctly and accompanied, which would bring forth improvement, and that reform should be introduced, if required, through state legislation, for the welfare of women and society as a whole. The proponents of this section included Dr Ramkrishna Gopal Bhandarkar, Justice Ranade, Justice Kashinath Trimbak Telang, Prof Gopal Ganesh Agarkar, Rao Bahadur Krishnaji Laxman Nulkar and others in the Bombay Presidency and Dewan Bahadur Rai Raghunath Rao of Madras. The more humanitarian position of the reformers emphasized on the distinction between 'girlhood' and 'womanhood', which was based on criteria other than the mere onset of menstruation, and they attempted to make their point reliable by cloaking it in religious garb.[135] K.T. Telang, R.G. Bhandarkar, and Raghunath Rao, involved in widely publicized controversies with the religious orthodoxy to illustrate that the higher age of consent proposed by the Bill was compatible with Hindu religious practices.[136] Ganesh Srikrishna Khaparde, an Indian lawyer of Berar Province, applied this policy to persuade the people, 'If they accept the *shastras*, we accept them too, but interpret them in the light of the knowledge we have acquired, although without distortion.'[137] The Calcutta Committee in Support of the Consent Bill, which consisted of forty-four Hindus and eleven Muslims, published a pamphlet entitled, 'The Garbhadhan Vyavastha: Opinion on the Question in Hindu Religion Arising out of Consent' to reveal that the *garbhadhanist* argument against the Bill was unacceptable.[138] The *pandits*, led by Pundit (Pandit) Ram Misra, issued a factual statement stating the Consent Bill to be free from any religious objections. The reformers, such as, Ramnath Tarkaratna referenced ancient medical authorities such as Sushruta, Charaka and *shastra* like *Ayurveda Shastra* to demonstrate that contrary to modern interpreters of the *shastras*, ancient medical texts supported a higher age at which Indian girls first menstruated and hence became ready for sexual intercourse.[139] There was a third group, that of the reactionists, which advocated limited reform to be accomplished firmly and exclusively through persuading public opinion. The real fight, claimed *Indu-*

Prakash, was between reformers and reactionists. Bal Gangadhar Tilak and Professor Jinsivale of Pune were identified as belonging to this section. By the same motion, T. Madhav Rao and A. Sankariah of Madras and Romesh Chunder Mitter of Calcutta could be categorized as 'reactionists'. In practice, nevertheless, it was fundamentally a schism between the orthodox section and the reformers.[140]

However, the opponents of the Age of Consent Bill, under the leadership of Shashadhar Tarkachuramani became agitated. They presented their argument against the bill, entitled, 'Appeal to England to save India from the Wrong and Shame of the Age of Consent Act'. Romesh Chunder Mitter, Manmohan Ghose, Rajendralal Mitra, Raja Indra Chandra Singh, Chandranath Basu, Mahesh Chandra Nyayratna were in favour of this initiative. *Bangabasi*, *Dainik Amrita Bazar*, *Anusandhan*, *Hindu Ranjika*, *Dacca Prakash* were anti-reform newspapers and periodicals; on the other hand, *Nabyabharat*,[141] *Sahachar*, *Sanjivani*, *Bengalee*, *Indian Mirror* were pro-reform newspapers and periodicals. Whereas the numbers of publicity of *Bangabasi* were 20,000, the numbers of publicity of *Sanjivani* were only 4,000.[142]

The articles in *Bangabasi* issued on 10 January 1891 and 17 January 1891, *Dainik-o-Samachar Chandrika*, the pandits' reports to the government and various statements from meetings, mainly in the *mofussil* area (rural and urban Bengal outside Calcutta) asserted on the requirement of the *garbhadhan* ritual without consider to the wife's age.[143] Though orthodox sentiment opposed the issue, the proposal to raise the age of consent received widespread support from several sections of the society. Bipin Chandra Pal was vocal against child marriage in his articles titled, 'Bangalir Balyakrira O Tahar Bisamay Fal (Pratham Prastab)' (Childhood Sports of Bengali and Its Poisonous Results: First Proposal) and 'Bangalir Balyakrira O Tahar Bisamay Fal (Dwitiya Prastab)' (Childhood Sports of Bengali and Its Poisonous Results: Second Proposal) in *Aalochana*. For this, he had to suffer physical abuse after passing the bill.[144] According to the *Bandhab*, a journal of Dacca, if the law was enacted, educated Bengali youths might refrain from child marriage, but it would not change the social status of Bengali women.[145] The Brahmo Samaj fully supported the Bill. The Government and the Brahmo newspapers – *Sanjivani* among others, dismissed this interpretation of the *shastras* and the religious authority of Raghunandan by mentioning other ancient writers and in particular, to the convolution of the *shastras*, which stopped any 'unambiguous justification of a dubious social custom'.[146] On 15 February 1891, a public meeting at 12, Wellington Square in Calcutta constructed a committee that sent to the Government of India a memorial in favour of the Bill signed by 8,000 people. The eminent supporters of the Bill were the Nawab of Dacca, Narendra Nath Sen, editor of *Indian Mirror*; Sarat Chandra Roy, editor of *Saturday Herald*; Babu Krishna Kamal Bhattacharjee, Principal of Rippon College; and Peary Mohan Roy, grandson of Rammohan Roy. A group of 155 women of different religions – Hindu, Brahmo, Muslim, and Christian, worked for it.[147] Gynaecologists, further, asserted to have reviewed the age at which girls first started menstruating and concluded that 'it did not occur before the age of twelve, unless stimulated by "artificial" means such as the husband's company or a free attitude to the body.'[148] The Bengalis responded to this reprimand in two ways. Initially, they asked the basis of the results because Western doctors were hardly ever admitted to the women in a *zenana* (female quarters of the house). Furthermore, they set uncertainties on determining the age of menstruating girls, whose dates of birth had not been registered.[149] So, the frontrunners of the opposition planned to pay the British back in their own coin by seeking the medical advice of thirty-four doctors. They, on the other hand, claimed that 'premature intercourse hardly existed and never with fatal results'.[150] On 9 July 1890, *Sambad Prabhakar* reported that 'Indian brides were quite knowledgeable and accustomed to post-marital sex.'[151] In this context, Phulmonee's death was a rare exception, punishable under the criminal law and could not be taken to justify a change in the age of consent. The paper, *Sanjivani* associated with Sadharan Brahmo Samaj, set forth to demonstrate the reverse stance and accordingly, the desperate necessity for the law by uninterruptedly reported cases 'of barbarous behaviour of husbands towards their wives'.[152]

The Brahmos proceeded much farther, defending women's right as well as their autonomy and self-improvement through both justifications and initiative. The majority of the conservative section thus criticized the Sadharan Brahmos 'as the co-authors of the Bill and as completely alienated from Bengali society'.[153] In Calcutta, three formerly *kulin* Brahmins, who became Brahmo reformers – Shashipada Bandyopadhyay, Dwarakanath Gangopadhyay, and Ramananda Chattopadhyay – were at the forefront of the struggle. Ramananda was particularly energetic in his editorial role of explaining the facts in favour of the government bill. When a 10 years old girl died as a consequence of sexual intercourse in 1890, Chatterjee titled it 'murder' in an editorial of a Brahmo newspaper accusing early marriage among Hindus.[154] Dwarakanath Ganguli was a strong supporter of women's empowerment. He struggled against what he called the 'double standard' for males and females alongside Sivanath Sastri and Manmohan Ghose. Dwarakanath's (second) wife, Kadambini, was India's first fully-qualified woman physician, and she was likely the most accomplished and emancipated Brahmo woman of her time.[155] Almost 150 women in Calcutta, led by Kadambini Ganguly, appealed to the government in no undefined terms to protect the child-wives of India.[156] The Bengali Brahmo reformer, P. C. Majoomdar preferred the Consent Bill, but was antagonistic to adult marriages. Actually, he supported the Consent Bill specifically because it did not immediately encounter child-marriages.[157] On the other, the Bengali Christian inspector of girls' schools in Calcutta, Manhomini Wheeler opposed the Consent Bill, but supported legislation to proscribe or discourage child-marriage.[158] In March 1891, the Sadharan Brahmos introduced an systematized movement in opposition to the conventional Hindu antagonism to the bill and for the next year they engaged in a never-ending controversy with 'conservatives' and 'revivalists'. Ramananda himself desired that the age of consent be raised to sixteen, but age twelve was eventually recognized in the act's final enactment.[159] Despite the fact that Act III of 1872 raised the age of marriage for girls, the law had a limited constituency. Child marriage was not extensively debated in Bengali society until the Age of Consent agitation of 1890-1. The issue was openly discussed in both the English-language as well as vernacular newspapers, with the consequence that the reformist and progressive image of families came to be associated with their approval for marrying girls over the age of twelve and providing them with a basic education. The photographs basically reflected these changes. Most of the figures dated from the early years of the twentieth century. During 1890-1950, they discovered certain fascinating modifications how men and women introduced themselves, or were demonstrated by their family members, in public. The women in the photographs of that time definitely did not seem to be child brides, but the appearance of some of them did not resemble them being considerably older than thirteen or fourteen[160].

For supporting the Consent Bill, the Sadharan Brahmo Samaj, *Sanjivani*, Dwarakanath, Kadambini were attacked unnecessarily in the editorial of *Banganibasi* and *Anusandhan.*[161] The indecent language used in the case of Dwarakanath-Kadambini, however, had an indirect reason. Because, just a few days ago, on 19 March 1891, Lord Lansdowne signed the Age of Consent Bill. Ganguli consequently supported the Age of Consent Bill and approached the government in private, condemning the Bengali males' tyranny over their women and its religious rationalization. Referring to Dwarakanath, the *Banganibasi* wrote, 'You are known by your wife's name, your wife is known as *Nati* – you are known by that *Nati's* name; You're such an idiot.' Dwarakanath immediately filed a defamation suit against the editor of *Banganibasi*. Kadambini also filed a case in the Calcutta High Court in the name of the proprietor of *Banganibasi* demanding compensation of one lakh rupees. At this time, the periodical *Anusandhan* started fighting on behalf of *Banganibasi.*[162] On the other hand, individual associates of the Indian National Congress had different opinions on the Age of Consent Bill. Manmohan Ghose advanced a further way of thinking, which was also shared by the Sadharan Brahmos and several persons from the Congress, the majority of whom were members of the Indian Association.[163] They wished to keep them away from a choice whether to accept or reject the current recommendation and asserted in favour of a law raising the age of marriage which, appropriate or not at the time, would have cut the origins of the 'evil'. They contended that because the issue was less personal and easier to manage, such an interference would be encountered with very few criticisms. Of course, the Indian government emphasized the ritual importance of the marriage ceremony and blamed followers of this idea of being disconnected from Bengali sentiment.[164] Moreover, Manmohan claimed that since a child-wife was already sufficiently protected by the existing provisions of the Penal Code that held a husband criminally liable for various acts, which constituted an offence against his wife if she were under twelve years of age with or without her consent – such as for committing a rash and negligent act, for causing hurt simple and grievous, and for assault – there was no need to reinforce the provision of marital rape in the Penal Code.[165]

The issue was revisited by the *Bangabasi* after the law was passed. This particular argument raised the general question of whether legal intervention was conceivable within the sacramental agenda or not.[166]

Although *pandits* had previously gathered in August 1890 and yet again a day or two after the introduction of the bill in January to analyse the religious facets, the first massive public meetings were held on 20 and 21 January 1891. Newspapers reported that, up to 3,000 people assembled in Jan Bazar, Bagh Bazar and Shova Bazar in north Calcutta. They objected to 'religious interference and the upsetting consequences of the Bill, like police oppression, defamation and the medical examination of women'.[167] In Albert Hall, graduates from Calcutta University, voiced their cooperation with Indian cultural traditions.[168] Rajah Peary Mohan, chairman of the students' meeting, was unable to stop tussles with Brahmos and the meeting had to be adjourned after a short time. The newspapers conducted reports of daily protest meetings in the mofussil for the next two weeks. In Calcutta, on Sunday, 1 February 1891, the residents of the southern suburbs of Bhowanipur and Kalighat gathered and graduates assembled once more in the *Star Theatre*,[169] while the British Indian Association arranged a 'special meeting' on 11 February 1891.[170] One such meeting convened at Sealdah, Upper Circular Road on Sunday, 15 February 1891 was adorned by Pundit (Pandit) Shashadhar and Krishna Prasanna Sen.[171] About a week later, about 500 *pandits* from Nadia, Howrah, Hooghly, Burdwan, Midnapore, Murshidabad, Dacca, Rangpur and Jessore assembled at the Calcutta Town Hall.[172] The climax of public agitation, the mass meeting on the Calcutta Maidan on 25 February 1891, was organized by men from the British Indian Association, probably under the guidance of Peary Mohan Mookherjea (Mukherjea) and Krishna Chandra Banerjee and there were placards in the streets stating 'Abolition of second marriage, Abolition of the

Hindu religion, Protect us, Mother-Queen'.[173] On Thursday, 19 February 1891, they requested for the approval to operate a mass meeting on the Maidan between Dhurrumtollah and Government House on the following Wednesday. Four days were taken by the Government to make a decision to permit a meeting that was to be arranged miles away from the head office of British power, on the race course at the southern end of the Maidan.[174] 'The protest meetings', as Amiya Sen has demonstrated, 'were usually organized by local religious bodies that raised the cry of religion in danger to swell the numbers at the meetings but the meetings typically attracted crowds made up of different religious denominations, including Hindus, Jains and Buddhists, as well as Muslims from Calcutta and its surrounding suburbs.'[175] The Bengal Presidency that displayed the most vicious reaction was also recognized by the newspapers of Maharashtra. It was written in *Indu-Prakash* that 'Calcutta was swept by a mad fury and almost convulsed by an unseemly agitation.' Soon, the anti-bill agitation was spreading like wild-fire throughout Bengal.[176] *The Mahratta* wrote that a 'monster mass meeting' at the Calcutta Maidan in late February (25 February 1891) engrossed 'a vast assembly of Hindu, Mohammedan, Jain, Buddha and other communities of Calcutta and neighbourhood', reported a telegram. 'Even the blindest supporters of the bill admit Calcutta had never seen such spectacle.'[177] On the other hand, *Indu-Prakash* claimed that 'the opposition camp countered this mass mobilization by distributing pro-reform pamphlets and holding meetings.'[178] Apart from the male adversaries, some Indian women were also against the Consent Bill. The Bengal press documented the support for the resistance from 'ordinary housewives who lined the streets of Calcutta on the occasion of the *Mahapuja* (prayer ceremony) held at the Kalighat on 16 March 1891 to protest against the Consent Bill.'[179] The opposition categorized the reformist-nationalist faction in Bengal as a 'deracinated elite'. At a protest meeting against the Bill, once the Maharanee Swarnamoyee, a powerful female zamindar (landlord) of Cossimbazar and a renowned philanthropist and patron of a hostel for female medical students in Calcutta, determined to accuse Bengali reformers as 'an elite out of touch with their countrymen', who 'had been to England and returned to their mother country with new-fangled ideas'. Her accusation was very effective; it pointed out 'the limits in the social position of not just the nationalist supporters of the Bill' but, equally significantly, 'of the nationalist opponents who launched such critiques'. The Maharanee's telegram was delivered to the protest meeting arranged by the Shova Bazar Rajbari;[180] and another female zamindar, the Maharanee Bhivasundari of Dighapatia, also assembled protest meetings against the Bill.[181] In spite of the protests, the bill was passed into law because the Legislative Council was almost completely comprised British members. A section of the Bengali press presumed that the government was driven by the desire to plant the seeds of discord among the people throughout this consent act episode. Amritalal Basu's *Sammati Sankat* (Consent Dilemma) gave a dramatic expression to such fears and it was staged at the Star Theatre on 21 March 1891 and also in Harendralal Mitra's *Aain Bibhrat* (Legal Breaches).[182] Census statistics for 1891 and 1901 reveal a firm increase in the age of marriage. This inclination replicates a steady shift in social practice, but it could be attributed to the passage of the bill as well[183] (see Table 3.2).[184]

The nationalist surge of the Age of Consent agitation did not diminish with the passing of the Bill. Calcutta, on the other hand, persisted in a state of exhilaration throughout the summer of 1891. However, it is evident that the magnitude of the protest was caused by British intervention in a particularly sensitive space – the male Bengali's sexual control over women. Women's perspectives regarding this issue were not seriously taken into explanation at all. Women who defied the ideal explanation for complete female submission to father, brother, husband, or son and petitioned the Queen in support of the law relinquished their 'femininity' and 'Indian identity'. Arguing that 'our sex is solely dependent on the Government for the protection of our personal rights', women from all over India, including Calcutta and Mymensingh in Bengal, confronted the joint family, patriarchy and the guarantee of respect and protection they were expected according to Hindu religion.[185] There were two petitions from women's groups in favour of the bill. One was from the Aryan Ladies Association of Poona, which was signed by 65 Hindu ladies and 23 Bene Israelis. It stated

Table 3.2: Regional Distribution of Infant Marriages among Hindu and Muslims of Age Group 0-10 in Bengal between 1881 And 1901 (number per 1,000 who are married)

Division	*Hindus*						*Muslims*					
	Male			*Female*			*Male*			*Female*		
	1901	*1891*	*1881*	*1901*	*1891*	*1881*	*1901*	*1891*	*1881*	*1901*	*1891*	*1881*
Bengal	52	44	54	113	111	133	12	11	12	61	65	78
West Bengal	6	4	5	103	121	137	8	6	6	79	80	99
Central Bengal	7	6	6	87	102	122	9	6	5	87	81	95
North Bengal	9	6	6	54	61	66	8	7	7	72	75	77
East Bengal	6	5	6	52	64	78	7	7	7	39	45	60
North Bihar	143	115	134	222	191	226	40	36	41	88	92	110
South Bihar	80	70	89	144	127	156	37	33	38	76	74	84
Orissa	3	3	3	19	18	32	2	4	3	24	9	13

> We the women of India who number over 125,000,000, being immersed in ignorance, and kept almost all places in subjection by men are unable to open our lips and acquaint the government with our grievances. We, therefore, pray government will have mercy on us and pass a law whereby our little immature girls will be protected till at least 12 years from a horrible outrage.[186]

There was also a petition from Parsi and native Christian ladies of Poona on 23 February 1891. In a memorial addressed to Her Gracious Majesty, Queen Victoria, Empress of India, they demanded 'the age of consent be raised to at least 14 years.'[187] *The Times*, published an article about a petition from approximately 2,000 women living in India to Queen Victoria in support of raising the age of consent for Indian women. Members of the Legislative Council in India cited parallel petitions in favour of the Bill received by the Government of India from Indian women in Ahmedabad, Calcutta, Bombay, Lahore, Poona, and Mymensingh.[188] 'The Bengali female periodical literature', as Ghulam Murshid has confirmed, 'was curiously silent about the Bill throughout the Consent debate.' It was only in 1894 when the *Bamabodhini Patrika*, one of the foremost journals for women in Bengal, was rejoicing its thirtieth jubilee that Murshid has found a passing reference to the Consent Act. Mankumari Basu, in her article 'Bigata Shata Barshe Bharat Ramaniganer Abastha' (The Condition of Indian Women in the Last Century), recorded the Consent Act as one of the legislative activities that intended at improving the status of women in Bengal.[189]

Padma Anagol-McGinn's analysis of the Consent debate in the Bombay Presidency advocates that the nationalist opposition to the Bill also articulated male antagonism towards Indian women who planned meetings and public protests in support of the Bill.[190] The assertions referenced in Malabari's *Notes*, were utilized by many others in the successive campaign, varying from Jyotirao Phule to Pandita Ramabai[191] and also by a small number of the very first feminists of Maharashtra.[192] Women had stated that infant marriage was the most tenacious hindrance to the psychological development of the female sex, suppressing a woman's personality through the disavowal of higher education. Throughout the second part of the nineteenth century, women of Maharashtrian society were concerned with the issue of women's education.[193] An important style in the women's literature of that period involved a planned reorganization of the institution of marriage. Women of Maharashtra uncovered the issue of child-marriage to the financial considerations of the boy's parents, the anxiety of the girl-child's parents due to the low status accorded to the female sex as well as the psychological need for a woman to be a mother-in-law in order to gain access to power in a Hindu joint-family.[194] Another thread running through women's assertions was their emphasis that raising the marriage age for girls solely would not be successful in practice; the age of consent for boys needed to be raised as well. This debate positioned around the incapability of a young husband to meet the anger of the conventional members of his family despite his support for his girl-wife's education. Personal narratives and the biographical and semi-fictional writings of women, like Shevantibai M. Nikambe's *Ratanbai: A Sketch of a Bombay High Caste Hindu Young Wife* (1895), explored the financial reliance of young husbands on their enlarged family and how these connections successfully stopped them from defending their wives' labours to educate themselves. Autobiographical records of women, who contributed in the debate of age of consent, for example, *Ranade: His Wife's Reminiscences*,[195] clearly echoes about the conditions of women who were left to their own strategies in dealing with the hostility of in-laws without the sustenance of their husbands.[196]

Through the association of British feminists in Bombay as well as in London, a 'memorial' projected by women from the Bombay Presidency was completed. The efforts of a Women's Committee in Bombay to promote the positive aspects of the Age of Consent Bill were described in major newspapers in the middle of 1890. This Committee was made up of powerful English and Maharashtrian women.[197] The Women's Committee determined to send a 'memorial' addressing to the Queen with two thousand signatures of Maharashtrian women.[198] The memorial petitioned for 'the necessity for legislation in the interests of child-wives and other female minors'.[199] The petitioners contended that in India 'girls did not normally attain maturity before fourteen, basing their contention on the medical observations of European women doctors in India.'[200] At least eight women's meetings in western India and one in Bengal were identified to have taken place to discuss facets of the Bill, pass resolutions, and write new petitions.[201] The participation of Maharashtrian women in the widespread public unrest over the age of consent controversies of 1891 successfully pushed popular protests of Indian women back into the nineteenth century. But according to Meera Kosambi, 'women's participation in the mainstream discourse on the issue of "consent" was minimal.' Nevertheless, Pandita Ramabai summoned a meeting of her Arya Mahila Samaj in February 1891, in support of the Consent Bill. The Pune correspondent of *Indu-Prakash* encouraged that 'One hundred and fifty or more educated native ladies from the city and the camp attended the meeting. That Hindu ladies came together to consider the Bill favourably when a lot of Hindu gentlemen are opposing it, is an event without precedent in the annals of the Social Reform movement.' A draft memorial was read and unanimously adopted and signed by one hundred ladies on the spot.[202] *Kesari* provided a relatively changed sort of the meeting, asserting that many women were doubtful and that Kashibai Kanitkar, who spoke in support of Ramabai, was absolutely speechless when questioned whether she would admit a law that could send her own son-in-law behind the bars for breaching the age limit.[203]

Muslims, too, were assured that the proposed Bill would be detrimental to their community.[204] Muslims, like Jains and Christians, were frequently reported to have attended meetings in the mofussil, despite the fact that they were not among the opposition leaders.[205] It should be noted that the Indian Penal Code of 1860, whose amendment was advocated by this Act, was applicable to all communities, unlike the Act for the Abolition of Sati of 1829 and the Hindu Widows' Remarriage Act of 1856, which were statutory interventions in Hindu personal law. The Muslim elites of Calcutta organizations argued similarly to their Hindu equivalents, demonstrating that Bengal was more interested in a political question than a religious one.[206] Regarding some 'aristocratic' protectors of the law, the opponents had decent motives to spot to the Nawab's or the Maharajah's dependence on British kindness. They hoped to be praised with *honours* or, in the case of the Rajah of Sonbursa, with the benefit of *Private Entrée*.[207] The Maharajah of Darbhanga informed the government with the update regarding the opposition in the city of Calcutta[208] and worked hard to put an end to the opposition in Bihar.

He possibly introduced the telegram, which was supported by the Bihar Landholders' Association, the members of which were among the first to convey the government in this way. A skilled essayist and a renowned philanthropist, the third Nawab of Dacca, Khwaja Ashanullah (1846-1901) was an enthusiastic supporter of the Act. His attempts to retain the Muslims of Dacca away from the opposition was repaid certainly by the British officials.[209] He was endorsed by the honour of C.I.E. after having written the sincerest letter.[210] The *Hitakari* on 11 February 1891 wrote, 'The remarks of Nawab Khaja Ashanullah Khan Bahadur on the Age of Consent Bill are fully worthy of acceptance. The Nawab is the Head of the Mussulman community, the leader of the East Bengal Mussulmans, and an ornament of the society to which he belongs.'[211] Among the Muslim community, the Nawab did not have many followers. On 2 February 1891, the *Hindoo Patriot* was eager to declare that even the Nawab had to acknowledge that many Mussalmans were worried by the innovation and that among his co-religionist girls frequently reached puberty between the ages of ten and eleven.[212] The Nawab, though, was accompanied by his brother-in-law, Yusuf Jan Miya. At a public meeting assembled in Dacca on 1 February 1891 to denounce the Age of Consent Bill, Yusuf Jan Miya objected against the motion and said that there could be no harm in marrying girls after twelve. According to reports, Yusuf Jan Miya and three or four others left the meeting as soon as the pleader, Osmanuddin Saheb, rose to point out the error.[213] Maulvi Abdul Jabbar, Deputy Magistrate and Deputy Collector, Alipore, wrote to the Chief Secretary, Government of Bengal, 'The existing law has already introduced a change in the penal system of Mohammedans.... age of consent provided in section 375 of Indian Penal Code raised the limit to 10 years. The Mohammedans will, therefore, not regard the amendment as a novelty.'[214] An earnest champion of the Age of Consent Act was the Mohammedan Literary Society. Nawab Abdul Latif founded the society in Calcutta in 1863 with the objective of boosting English education among Muslim youth and persuading the British government to address to the educational needs of India's Muslim community. According to newspaper reports, the society played a key role in campaigning for a higher age of consent. Abdul Latif on the behalf of Mahomedan Literary Society published a pamphlet entitled 'A Practical View of the Age of Consent Act, for the Benefit of the Mahomedan Community in General, by the Committee of the Mahomedan Literary Society of Calcutta' (1891) to guarantee the Muslim community that the Bill did not transform Muslim religious beliefs and traditions. The pamphlet was written in the vernaculars of the country and was spontaneously distributed. 'The Society', it was reported, 'advocated the cause of the supporters of the measures, thus hoping to win Mahomedan society to its cause'.[215] The Muslim members of the Viceroy's Legislative Council supported the Consent Bill, but the *Sudhakar*, *Ahmadi*, the Muslim vernacular newspaper in Bengal as well as the Central National Mahomedan Association in Calcutta, voiced disapproval of the Muslim members of the Council and of Muslim organizations that favoured the Bill.[216]

Muslim women in Bengal were among the first to use this legal tool to rectify the acts of sexual violence committed by spouses. Several historians have noted that Bengali women remained silent on the issue of consent, whereas their Maharashtrian counterparts were outspoken supporters of a higher consent age.[217] As a result, it is critical to highlight the entity of Bengali Muslim women and their desire to enjoy the benefits of the Act, challenging preconceived notions about their passivity. Following the Act's implementation, Muslim women in Bengal were among the first to utilize it to protect themselves from rude husbands. The Muslim woman, detained within the confines of the home and exposed to the engaged tyranny of patriarchy and community, was said to be incompetent of protest. Meaningfully, though, Muslim women in Bengal were among the first to situate this Act for punishing men for their acts of sexual violence within marriage. The *Dacca Prakash* on 3 January 1892 reported that 'one Darya Sheikh was charged before the Magistrate of Mymensingh with having committed rape on his wife Bheki Bibi, a girl below the age of twelve. In the absence of satisfactory evidence of rape, the Magistrate found the accused guilty of having voluntarily caused grievous hurt.'[218] On 17 January 1892, the *Dacca Prakash* claimed that the Consent Act had begun to bear fruit. It has been reported that a Muslim woman of the Rupgunj Thana in the Dacca district charged her son-in-law with having committed rape upon her daughter who was less than twelve years old. Upon medical examination the girl was pronounced to be much older than twelve, and the accused was discharged.[219] The preceding legal battles, while not entirely successful, demonstrate that Muslim women were evolving as stakeholders and legally conscious representatives who were eager to fight for justice in courts of law.

Historical research on the social reform movement in Bengal has chiefly concentrated on reforms orchestrated by high caste Hindu men to improve the conditions of high caste elite Hindu women. Lower castes and Muslim women were not included in the proposals of the renowned Bengali reformers or in the discussions among historians writing about them. What was once a limited Hindu high caste elite affair was viewed as an essential and beneficial aspect of the Bengal Renaissance! In effect, what was upheld in historiography as a Bengali phenomenon was based on a series of omissions – the exclusion of lower castes, non-elites, and non-Hindus, particularly Muslims. The Hindu revivalist uproar against the Age of Consent Act has been cited as an indicator of not only the Act's incompetence to gain momentum in Bengal, but also the dramatic reduction of the women's question in this area.[220] It is essential to examine such viewpoints by mentioning, first, that the Age of Consent Act was a legislative interference by the colonial state that was intended for the first time for all religious communities, including Muslims, and, second, that the Act had some staunch supporters among Muslim men. Muslim women's institution has been particularly denied, with scholarly work dominated by the generalization of the veiled and subdued Muslim woman. As a result of this discussion, the exclusionary politics underpinning the creation of historical knowledge in relation to the Age of Consent controversy and the total reformist initiative in colonial Bengal were naked.

In November 1890, in the Madras Presidency, Raja Sir T. Madhav Rao, once a keen supporter of the women's cause, who had wholly overturned his stance on all the associated reform issues, planned a public protest meeting, at which an open confrontation took place between him and Rai Raghunath Rao, Dewan of Indore and an Indian Independence activist.[221] A. Sankariah, the president of the Madras Hindu Sabha and a former judge and magistrate, stressed that this act was virtually a missionary attack on the modesty, virtue and holy sacraments of the native females. Some influential residents of the south encouraged his protest.[222] Statistical data collected from the 1881 census showed that the percentages of ever married Hindu girls and boys under ten years, respectively, were as follows – in Berar 21.7 and 4; in the Bengal Presidency 13.9 and 5.6; in the Bombay Presidency 10.5 and 2.5; in the Central Provinces 8 and 2.6; in the North-Western Provinces 5.4 and 2.4; in the Madras Presidency 4.5 and 0.8; and in Punjab 3.5 and 1.1.[223]

Dr Mahendralal Sircar emphasized that 'while early maternity results in giving birth to short-lived or unhealthy children, it at the same time seriously compromises the health of the mother also.... A host of complaints from which our females suffer life-long, or to which they fall early victims, arise from the evils of early marriage – namely, early pubescence and early maternity.'[224] British medical doctors who advocated for reform brought Western medicine into the debate with a vengeance. The difference between puberty and nubility was highlighted in Dr Peechy-Phipson's talk in Bombay on 'The Physiological Effects of Early Marriage'. She said that at first, she sensed that Indian women gained youth before European women. But when she came here, she saw that the 15 years old Indian girl did not enter into the phase of womanhood. Phipson also clarified that although the conventional notion of puberty was based on the first menstruation, the 'true' or 'complete' puberty was reached by a girl only by about her 20th year when the body and mind were fully developed and when alone a woman attains the capacity for maternity.[225] A group of fifty-five British woman doctors made possibly the most staggering and surprising contribution to the discussion by revealing the viciousness to which girl-wives were confined. *Sudharak* revealed that in a petition, which was sent to government, they presented as evidence 13 cases for medical treatment that they had collected.[226] The *Sanitary Commissioner's Report of 1890* added an incentive revealing the fact that children under the age of five accounted for 43 per cent of the total number of deaths in Mumbai. *Indu-Prakash* mourned the evils arising from early marriage, which were exacerbated by our flawed child-rearing system.[227] Even the reformist sections were at first reluctant to allow the government into the Hindu domestic realm fearing that it would be used as the narrow end of a pernicious section. Bhandarkar admitted, 'I would not avoid the evil (of child marriage) and secure the good, by a legislative measure.'[228] Khaparde agreed that such reforms should spring from the people and should not be forced on them; for the appearance of force disinclined people to all reform and this made matters worse.[229] However, the reformers demanded that the Age of Consent Act was possibly desirable even more than the Abolition of the *Sati* Act, because the former dealt with circumstances of wider intimidation as well as immoral and monstrous attitudes.[230] Eventually, reformers validated the state's power to intervene in family issues by claiming that marriage was a social concern on equal ground with other social relations. The bill was seen as a protective measure and it is a function of the government to afford protection to any of its subjects who may need protection.[231] According to Meera Kosambi, 'This ideology of raising wives from their subordinate status to equality with men, and entitled to equal protection, was perhaps the bill's most important contribution.'[232]

The Age of Consent Bill elicited significantly opposing views on its legal status. The orthodox argued that it was a new British law that resulted in undue intrusion in Indian family affairs; reformers saw it as a British amendment to an established but imperfect British law that had already been enforced on Indian society. Gidumal's pamphlet summarizing the existing statutes of the IPC regarding the age of consent and comparing them to those of English Criminal Law laid the groundwork for the reformist argument.[233] According to English law, 'intercourse with a girl under thirteen, with or without her consent, was punishable with penal servitude for life; and intercourse with a girl over thirteen and below sixteen, with or without her consent, was punishable with ten years' rigorous imprisonment'. Gidumal called this, 'a crying inequality'. The concept of consent in this discourse was totally theoretical and inoffensive, because if even a bride was matured enough to give 'intelligent consent' to her marriage, it was not acknowledged the right to refuse her consent from an arrangement established by her parents and elders.[234] The noticeable conventional oppositions were offered by Romesh Chunder Mitter during the debate in the legislative council, that the existing law was adequate for protecting girl brides; that puberty was a far more reliable criterion of physical maturity than a numerical age limit; that the husband whose wife reached puberty before the age of twelve was faced with the dilemma as to whether to go to prison (for breaking the British law) or 'to go to hell' (for violating Hindu sacred law); that if the husband was sentenced for breaking the British law and sent to prison, or transported for life, it would lead to the almost civil death of a Hindu wife, so that there was the hardship of the law punishing the wife for the guilt of her husband.[235]

Finally, the bill was enacted in March 1891 and epitomized the first step towards protecting girl brides from sexual coercion. The complementary measure to protect girls from becoming girl brides had to wait another four decades, when the Child Marriage Restraint Act of 1929 (also known as Sarda Act), which went into effect in 1930, set the minimum age at marriage for girls and boys at fourteen and eighteen, respectively. Another difficult issue was the definite implementation of the Consent Act. It was argued that determining a girl's age was difficult due to the defective birth registration system, and that a physical examination of girls by medical doctors was unappealing. Furthermore, a wife (of any age) was extremely doubtful to file a complaint or testify against her husband. Ultimately, it was suggested that antagonistic family members or neighbours might take advantage of the situation to make false accusations. The reformers addressed the last two objections by emphasizing the possibility of enacting certain provisions, such as making the offence non-cognizable (as was eventually done) and allowing bail in situations where the offence did not lead to severe crimes.[236]

The socio-political climate of the closing decades of the nineteenth century facilitated the marginalization of women's issues by publicizing them as 'social issues'. On the one hand, anti-reformers claimed that the government had introduced the act under pressure from British pro-reform opinion, which had been misled by Indian reformers. On the other hand, reformers expressed an equal and opposite reaction, making political reform contingent upon social reform. While the day was won by the social reformers, who rejoiced in the passage of the Age of Consent Act in 1891, the days and years to come were claimed by the champions of political reform, who succeeded in stalling further social change. The Consent Act ensured legal protection for girl brides and the related controversy introduced a more humane perspective on their condition, but the cause of women's emancipation was nevertheless relegated to the background over the next few decades. Whatever the outcome, however, Bengal's urban, educated middle-class intelligentsia found its way to a collective protest centred around the Consent Bill, and the protest was largely against the legal recognition of Indian women's rights. Society had no longer a way of denying the rights that had already been reserved for women in the wake of nineteenth-century social reform. But at the moment, when the field of women's rights began to transcend issues in terms of education and earning money, and in married life also began to speak for themselves and for their survival; the urge for social control became very urgent. The oppositions against 'Rukhmabai case', Phulmonee-Hari Maitee Case or the Age of Consent Bill in the late nineteenth century were a prime example. Nevertheless, in the face of this opposition, the tendency of the Indian people to protest against the colonial rule was also strong. Thus, the establishment of women's rights and the raising of awareness of the rights of the Indian people were not complementary. So, with the development of Indian nationalism, the extent to which the consciousness of Indian women had been spread, is a matter of debate.

Nonetheless, the women's movement formulated a link between Indian nationalism and conjugality that was structurally different from the aggressive revivalism of the 1890s. Instead of just supporting child marriage as a symbol of national cultural superiority, as defenders of Dadaji Bhikaji and Hari Mohan Maitee did in the late nineteenth century, Indian feminists urged its exclusion as 'a symbol of national respectability and progress'. The route towards home rule essentially preferred the modification of an Indian household structure.[237] With a few exceptions, social reformers who fought for amendments in the age of consent controversy were not the promoters of women's rights or women's equality.[238] They were attempting to secure the lives of young girls from being exploited by men by excluding women's experiences. They never genuinely inquired about the implications that patriarchal social structures had on women. According to Sathe, 'There was no consciousness about the oppressive character of the patriarchal system.'[239] Women were generally expected to be wives and mothers. The authoritarian cultural and conventional processes that were objectionable to women fuelled the social reform movement at the time. The Age of Consent Act, which raised the age of consent for girls to twelve while abandoning the preparation and presentation of marriage unhindered, was a signal of the negotiations that had been shaped by adversaries of the bill. In March 1891, both the Indian Penal Code and the Criminal Procedure Code were amended to raise the age of consent to twelve for married and unmarried girls; sexual intercourse with girls below that age was punishable with up to ten years in prison or transportation for life. The real significance of the act was not in the effects it had on marriage ceremonies and rituals, but in organizing a national clash between two ideas for social and political transformation that were thought to be reciprocally contradictory. Even though it was long assumed that women were virtually absent from discussions on the Age of Consent during the 1880s and 1890s, new research has demonstrated that this was not the case, as previously discussed. This chapter has introduced some of the issues that have emerged in thinking about child marriage in India. There was substantial evidence that child marriage became known during the colonial era, when it became one of the most contentious issues for reformers and nationalists alike. However, in the first half of the twentieth century, not only women were articulating critiques of legislation, at the same time, they were claiming advanced rights and safety. They lost their timidity by the 1920s and 1930s and became vocal participants in the debate leading up to and following the passage of the Child Marriage Restraint Act of 1929. Child marriage had fully appeared in the public spotlight by the time the women's organizations were constructed in the early twentieth century, and it had come to obtain an immense international appeal. This was a watershed moment in the history of child marriage in India.

NOTES

1. Geraldine Forbes, 'Women and Modernity: The Issue of Child Marriage in India', *Women's Studies International Quarterly*, vol. 2, no. 4, 1979, p. 407.
2. S. Bhavan, 'Demographic profile and future strategies for development of the girl child in India', *Social Change*, vol. 25, nos. 2-3, June-September 1995, pp. 24, 29, cited in Jaya Sagade, *Child Marriage in India: Socio-legal and Human Rights Dimensions*, New Delhi: Oxford

University Press, 2005 (first published), 2012 (Oxford India Paperbacks), p. 37.

3. Tahir Mahmood, 'Marriage-Age in India and Abroad – A Comparative Conspectus', *Journal of Indian Law Institute*, vol. 22, no. 1, 1980, pp. 38-80.
4. Meera Kosambi, 'Girl Brides and Socio-Legal Change: Age of Consent Bill (1891) Controversy', *Economic and Political Weekly*, vol. 26, no. 31/32, 3-10 August 1991, p. 1857.
5. Meera Kosambi, *Crossing Thresholds: Feminist Essays in Social History*, Ranikhet: Permanent Black, 2007, 2011 (Paperback), p. 276.
6. Janaki Nair, *Women and Law in Colonial India: A Social History*, New Delhi: Kali for Women, 1996, p. 71.
7. Geraldine Forbes, op. cit., 1979, p. 408.
8. Meera Kosambi, 'Girl Brides and Socio-Legal Change: Age of Consent Bill (1891) Controversy', op. cit., August 3-10, 1991, p. 1857.
9. Meera Kosambi, *Crossing Thresholds: Feminist Essays in Social History*, Ranikhet: Permanent Black, 2007, 2011 (Paperback), p. 277.
10. Section 375 of the Indian Penal Code, cited in Jaya Sagade, op. cit., p. 38.
11. The Table 1.6, mentioned in Flavia Agnes, *Family Law: Volume 2: Marriage, Divorce, and Matrimonial Litigation*, New Delhi: Oxford University Press, 2011, p. 68.
12. S.P. Sathe, *Towards Gender Justice*, Bombay: S.N.D.T. Women's University, 1993, p. 25, cited in Jaya Sagade, op. cit., p. 38.
13. Meera Kosambi, 'Girl Brides and Socio-Legal Change: Age of Consent Bill (1891) Controversy', op. cit., 3-10 August 1991, p. 1857.
14. Proceedings File nos. 105-6, File J C/172, Government of Bengal, Judicial Department, June 1893 cited in Tanika Sarkar, 'Changing Hindu Women: Bengal in the Long Nineteenth Century', in Sabyasachi Bhattacharya (ed.), *A Comprehensive History of Modern Bengal, 1700-1950,* Volume II, Kolkata: The Asiatic Society, in association with Primus Books, 2020, p. 829.
15. Meera Kosambi, 'Girl Brides and Socio-Legal Change: Age of Consent Bill (1891) Controversy', op. cit., 3-10 August 1991, p. 1857; Meera Kosambi, 'Women, Emancipation and Equality: Pandita Ramabai's Contribution to Women's Cause', *Economic and Political Weekly*, vol. 23, no. 44, 29 October 1988, pp. WS38-WS49.
16. Janaki Nair, op. cit., p. 71.
17. Charles Heimsath, *Indian Nationalism and Hindu Social Reform*, Princeton: Princeton University Press, 1964, pp. 92-3.

18. Janaki Nair, op. cit., p. 72.
19. Geraldine Forbes, op. cit., 1979, p. 408.
20. Kumari Jayawardena, *The White Woman's Other Burden: Western Women and South Asia During British Colonial Rule*, London and New York: Routledge, 1995, p. 92.
21. Meera Kosambi, 'Girl Brides and Socio-Legal Change: Age of Consent Bill (1891) Controversy', op. cit., 3-10 August 1991, p. 1858.
22. Kumari Jayawardena, op. cit., p. 92.
23. *Towards Equality: Report of the Committee on the Status of Women in India*, New Delhi: Government of India, 1974, pp. 81-2 cited in Geraldine Forbes, op. cit., 1979, p. 408.
24. Charles Heimsath, 'The Origin and Enactment of the Indian Age of Consent Bill, 1891', *The Journal of Asian Studies*, vol. 21, no. 4, August 1962, p. 492.
25. Ibid.
26. Geraldine Forbes, op. cit., 1979, p. 409.
27. K.T. Telang, *Selected Writing and Speeches*, Bombay: K.R. Mitra, 1916, pp. 241-51 cited in Geraldine Forbes, op. cit., p. 409.
28. K.M. Kapadia, *Marriage and Family in India*, Calcutta: Oxford University Press, 1966, pp. 148-9 cited in Geraldine Forbes, op. cit., 1979, p. 409.
29. *The Times*, 15 October 1886, p. 8, cited in Geraldine Forbes, op. cit., 1979, p. 409.
30. C. Yajnesvara Chintamani, *Indian Social Reform, In Four Parts*, Part III, Madras: Minerva Press, pp. 140-1.
31. D.V. Tahmankar, *Lokamanya Tilak: Father of Indian Unrest and Maker of Modern India*, London: John Murray Publishers, 1956, p. 46.
32. Monmayee Basu, *Hindu Women and Marriage Law: From Sacrament to Contract*, in *Women and Law in India*, New Delhi: Oxford University Press, 2004 (1st edn.), 2016 (Oxford India Paperbacks), pp. 46-7.
33. Dayaram Gidumal, *The Life and Life-Work of Behramji M. Malabari*, Bombay: Education Society's Press, 1888, pp. 38-42.
34. *Indu-Prakash*, 1 September 1890: 3, cited in Meera Kosambi, 'Girl Brides and Socio-Legal Change: Age of Consent Bill (1891) Controversy', op. cit., 3-10 August 1991, p. 1858.
35. Charles Heimsath, 'The Origin and Enactment of the Indian Age of Consent Bill, 1891', op. cit., August 1962, p. 497.
36. *Report of the Third Annual Session of the Indian National Social Conference, 1889*, Appendix G, Bombay, cited in Monmayee Basu, op. cit., p. 47.

37. *Report of the Fourth Annual Session of the Indian National Social Conference, 1890*, Appendix A, Bombay, cited in Monmayee Basu, op. cit., p. 47.
38. Meera Kosambi, 'Girl Brides and Socio-Legal Change: Age of Consent Bill (1891) Controversy', op. cit., 3-10 August 1991, p. 1858.
39. Meera Kosambi, op. cit., 2007, 2011 (Paperback), pp. 244-5.
40. Ibid., pp. 245-6.
41. *Indian Law Reports, Bombay Series*, vol. IX, pp. 533-4 cited in Meera Kosambi, 'Resisting Conjugality: Rakhmabai's Protest', in op. cit., 2007, 2011 (Paperback), p. 247.
42. Jaya Sagade, op. cit., p. 39.
43. *Indu-Prakash*, 7 March 1887 cited in Meera Kosambi, 'Resisting Conjugality: Rakhmabai's Protest', in op. cit., 2007, 2011 (Paperback), p. 249.
44. Sudhir Chandra, 'Rukhmabai: Debate Over Woman's Right to her Person', *Economic and Political Weekly*, 2 November 1996, p. 2937.
45. Uma Chakravarti, 'Whatever Happened to the Vedic *Dasi*? Orientalism, Nationalism, and a Script for the Past', in Kumkum Sangari and Sudesh Vaid (eds.), *Recasting Women: Essays in Colonial History*, New Delhi: Kali for Women, 1989, p. 75.
46. Max Müller, Letter to the Editor, *The Times* (London), 22 August 1887, cited in Antoinette Burton, 'Conjugality on Trial: the Rukhmabai Case and the Debate on Indian Child-Marriage in Late-Victorian Britain', in George Robb and Nancy Erber (eds.), *Disorder in the Court: Trials and Sexual Conflict at the Turn of the Century*, London: Macmillan, 1999, p. 43.
47. *The Mahratta*, 24 April 1887 cited in Meera Kosambi, 'Resisting Conjugality: Rakhmabai's Protest', in *Crossing Thresholds: Feminist Essays in Social History*, Ranikhet: Permanent Black, 2007, 2011 (Paperback), p. 249.
48. *Indu-Prakash*, 4 July 1887 cited in Meera Kosambi, 'Resisting Conjugality: Rakhmabai's Protest', in *Crossing Thresholds: Feminist Essays in Social History*, Ranikhet: Permanent Black, 2007, 2011 (Paperback), pp. 249-50.
49. *The Mahratta*, 29 May 1887 cited in Meera Kosambi, 'Resisting Conjugality: Rakhmabai's Protest', in *Crossing Thresholds: Feminist Essays in Social History*, Ranikhet: Permanent Black, 2007, 2011 (Paperback), p. 250; Padma Anagol, *The Emergence of Feminism in India, 1850-1920*, London: Routledge, 2016, 2005 (1st published), p. 202; Sudhir Chandra, 'Enslaved Daughters: Colonialism, Law and

Women's Rights', in *Women and Law in India: An Omnibus Comprising*, New Delhi: Oxford University Press, 2004 (1st edn.), 2016 (Oxford India Paperbacks), pp. 126, 128, 144, 162, 169.

50. *Indu-Prakash*, 11 April 1887 cited in Meera Kosambi, 'Resisting Conjugality: Rakhmabai's Protest', in *Crossing Thresholds: Feminist Essays in Social History*, Ranikhet: Permanent Black, 2007, 2011 (Paperback), p. 250.
51. Antoinette Burton, 'From "Child Bride" to "Hindoo Lady": Rukhmabai and the Debate about Sexual Respectability in Imperial Britain', *American Historical Review*, vol. 103, no. 4, October 1998, p. 1131.
52. *The Mahratta*, 8 May 1887, cited in Meera Kosambi, 'Resisting Conjugality: Rakhmabai's Protest', in *Crossing Thresholds: Feminist Essays in Social History*, Ranikhet: Permanent Black, 2007, 2011 (Paperback), p. 250.
53. Antoinette Burton, 'Conjugality on Trial: the Rukhmabai Case and the Debate on Indian Child-Marriage in Late-Victorian Britain', in George Robb and Nancy Erber (eds.), *Disorder in the Court: Trials and Sexual Conflict at the Turn of the Century*, London: Macmillan, 1999, p. 35.
54. Antoinette Burton, op. cit., October 1998, p. 1142.
55. Ibid., p. 1141.
56. Helen Rappaport, *Queen Victoria: A Biographical Companion*, California: ABC-CLIO, 2003, pp. 429-30.
57. Antoinette Burton, 'Conjugality on Trial: the Rukhmabai Case and the Debate on Indian Child-Marriage in Late-Victorian Britain', in George Robb and Nancy Erber (eds.), op. cit., p. 44.
58. Antoinette Burton, op. cit., October 1998, pp. 1119-46.
59. Tanika Sarkar, 'Bankimchandra and the Impossibility of a Political Agenda', *Oxford Literary Review*, vol. 16, 1994, p. 183.
60. Sudhir Chandra, 'Enslaved Daughters: Colonialism, Law and Women's Rights', op. cit., 2004 (1st edn.), 2016 (Oxford India Paperbacks), p. 162.
61. Jim Masselos, 'Sexual Property/Sexual Violence: Wives in Nineteenth-Century Bombay', *South Asia Research*, vol. 12, no. 2, November 1992, p. 86.
62. Meera Kosambi, 'Resisting Conjugality: Rakhmabai's Protest', in *Crossing Thresholds: Feminist Essays in Social History*, Ranikhet: Permanent Black, 2007, 2011 (Paperback), p. 251.
63. Amiya P. Sen, *Hindu Revivalism in Bengal, 1872-1905: Some Essays in Interpretation*, Delhi: Oxford University Press, 1993, p. 374.

64. *Somprakash*, 27 June 1887 in *Report on Native Papers (Bengal)*, week ending 2 July 1887 cited in Amiya P. Sen, op. cit., p. 375.
65. *Dainik O Samachar Chandrika*, 26 June 1887 in *Report on Native Papers (Bengal)*, week ending 2 July 1887 cited in Amiya Sen, op. cit., p. 375.
66. *Sahachar*, 29 June 1887 in *Report on Native Papers (Bengal)*, week ending 9 July 1887 cited in Amiya Sen, op. cit., p. 375.
67. *Sulabh Samachar O Kusdaha*, 22 July 1887 in *Report on Native Papers (Bengal)*, week ending 30 July 1887 cited in Amiya Sen, op. cit., p. 375.
68. *Somprakash*, 22 December 1884 in *Report on Native Papers (Bengal)*, week ending 27 December 1884 cited in Amiya Sen, op. cit., p. 375.
69. *Somprakash*, 1 November 1886 in *Report on Native Papers (Bengal)*, week ending 6 November 1886 cited in Amiya Sen, op. cit., p. 375.
70. *Burdwan Sanjivani*, 5 July 1887 *Report on Native Papers (Bengal)*, week ending 16 July 1887 cited in Amiya Sen, op. cit., p. 375.
71. Ibid., p. 375.
72. Tanika Sarkar, 'Conjugality and Hindu Nationalism: Resisting Colonial Reason and the Death of a Child-Wife' in *Women and Social Reform in Modern India: A Reader*, Volume I, Ranikhet: Permanent Black, 2007, p. 398; Tanika Sarkar, 'Rhetoric against Age of Consent: Resisting Colonial Reason and Death of a Child Wife', *Economic and Political Weekly*, 4 September 1993, p. 1873.
73. India Office Library and Records, London, Lansdowne to Northbrook, 6 September 1890, MSS. Eur. D 558/12, cited in Dagmar Engels, *Beyond Purdah? Women in Bengal, 1890-1939*, New Delhi: Oxford University Press, 1996, p. 102.
74. India Office Library and Records, London, Lansdowne to Bailey, 10 October 1890, MSS. Eur. D 558/19, cited in Dagmar Engels, op. cit., 1996, p. 102.
75. *Indu-Prakash*, 6 October 1890: 3 cited in Meera Kosambi, 'Girl Brides and Socio-Legal Change: Age of Consent Bill (1891) Controversy', op. cit., 3-10 August 1991, p. 1858.
76. Geraldine Forbes, op. cit., 1979, p. 410.
77. Mrinalini Sinha, *Colonial Masculinity: The 'Manly Englishman' and the 'Effeminate Bengali' in the Late Nineteenth Century*, Manchester and New York: Manchester University Press, 1995, p. 143.
78. Charles Heimsath, *Indian Nationalism and Hindu Social Reform*, Princeton: Princeton University Press, 1964, pp. 147-75.
79. Tanika Sarkar, 'Colonial Law-making and Lives/Deaths of Indian

Women: Different Readings of Law and Community', in Ratna Kapur (ed.), *Feminist Terrains in Legal Domains*, New Delhi: Kali for Women/ Zubaan, 1996, 2020 (e-book), pp. 210-38.

80. 'Hari Mohan Maiteer Danda o Samaj' ('Penalty of Hari Mohan Maitee and Society'), *Nabyabharat*, vol. 8, no. 4, 1297 Shraban (July-August), 1890, p. 215.
81. Ibid.
82. Tanika Sarkar, 'Conjugality and Hindu Nationalism: Resisting Colonial Reason and the Death of a Child-Wife' in Sumit Sarkar and Tanika Sarkar (eds.), op. cit., pp. 400-1; Tanika Sarkar, op. cit., 4 September 1993, p. 1873.
83. Bengal Government Judicial, McLeod's Medical Report on Child Wives NF J C/17 Proceedings 104-17, June 1893, cited in Jaya Sagade, op. cit., p. 40.
84. Ibid.
85. Jaya Sagade, op. cit., p. 41.
86. Tanika Sarkar, 'Colonial Law-making and Lives/Deaths of Indian Women: Different Readings of Law and Community', in Ratna Kapur (ed.), op. cit., New Delhi: Kali for Women/Zubaan, 1996, 2020 (e-book), p. 231.
87. 'Hari Mohan Maiteer Danda O Samaj' (Penalty of Hari Mohan Maitee and Society), *Nabyabharat*, vol. 8, no. 4, 1297 Shraban (July-August), 1890, p. 216.
88. Tanika Sarkar, *Hindu Wife, Hindu Nation: Community, Religion, and Cultural Nationalism*, Bloomington/Ranikhet: Indiana University Press/Permanent Black, 2001, pp. 191-225, 226-49.
89. Mytheli Sreenivas, *Wives, Widows, and Concubines: The Conjugal Family Ideal in Colonial India*, Bloomington and Indianapolis: Indiana University Press, 2008, p. 71.
90. Monmayee Basu, op. cit., p. 48, Meera Kosambi, 'Girl Brides and Socio-Legal Change: Age of Consent Bill (1891) Controversy', op. cit., 3-10 August 1991, p. 1858.
91. *Indu-Prakash*, 12 January 1891, cited in Meera Kosambi, *Crossing Thresholds: Feminist Essays in Social History*, Ranikhet: Permanent Black, 2007, 2011 (Paperback), p. 279.
92. Monmayee Basu, op. cit., p. 48.
93. Meera Kosambi, *Crossing Thresholds: Feminist Essays in Social History*, Ranikhet: Permanent Black, 2007, 2011 (Paperback), p. 279; Meera Kosambi, 'Girl Brides and Socio-Legal Change: Age of Consent Bill (1891) Controversy', *Economic and Political Weekly*, vol. 26, nos. 31/32,

3-10 August 1991, p. 1859; *The Statesman*, 7 March 1891, cited in Monmayee Basu, op. cit., p. 49; Mahua Sarkar, *Justice in a Gothic Edifice: The Calcutta High Court & Colonial Rule in Bengal*, Calcutta: Firma KLM Private Limited, 1997, p. 83.

94. Meera Kosambi, op. cit., 1991, p. 1859; *Proceedings of the Council of the Governor-General of India, 1891*, p. 119, cited in Monmayee Basu, op. cit., p. 49.
95. *Proceedings of the Council of the Governor-General of India, 1891*, p. 11, cited in Monmayee Basu, op. cit., p. 50.
96. Monmayee Basu, op. cit., p. 50.
97. *The Times* (London), 8 October, 7 November 1890, cited in Charles Heimsath, 'The Origin and Enactment of the Indian Age of Consent Bill, 1891', op. cit., p. 501.
98. *The Times* (London), 29 November 1890, cited in Charles Heimsath, op. cit., 1962, p. 501.
99. Proceedings of the Council of the Governor-General of India, 1891, p. 154, cited in Monmayee Basu, op. cit., p. 51.
100. *Abstract of the Proceedings of the Council of the Governor General of India, assembled for the Purpose of Making Laws and Regulations*, 1891.
101. Geraldine Forbes, op. cit., 1979, p. 410.
102. Himani Bannerji, *Inventing Subjects: Studies in Hegemony, Patriarchy and Colonialism*, New Delhi: Tulika, 2001, pp. 72-98.
103. Aparna Bandyopadhyay, 'Muslim Voices and Historiographical Silences: The Age of Consent Controversy in Colonial Bengal', The Docket, *Law and History Review*, vol. 3, no. 2, June 2020: Age of Consent Laws in Historical Context. https://lawandhistoryreview.org/article/aparna-bandyopadhyay, accessed on 1 March 2021.
104. Janaki Nair, op. cit., pp. 75-9.
105. Census Report of India, 1911, vol. 1, part 1, chapter VII, p. 272.
106. Ibid., p. 271.
107. Meera Kosambi, 'Girl Brides and Socio-Legal Change: Age of Consent Bill (1891) Controversy', *Economic and Political Weekly*, vol. 26, no. 31/32, 3-10 August 1991, p. 1860.
108. *The Mahratta*, 10 May 1891, cited in Meera Kosambi, op. cit., 2007, 2011 (Paperback), p. 280.
109. *The Mahratta*, 5 October, 14 December 1890, cited in Meera Kosambi, op. cit., 2007, 2011 (Paperback), p. 280.
110. Meera Kosambi, op. cit., 2007, 2011 (Paperback), p. 281; Meera Kosambi, 'Girl Brides and Socio-Legal Change: Age of Consent Bill (1891) Controversy', op. cit., 3-10 August 1991, p. 1859.

111. Tilak pioneered 'the use of religious orthodoxy as a method of mass contact' through his emotive attacks on reformers as anti-Hindu and, therefore, unpatriotic. He acquired a mass base by resorting in the 1890s to Hindu religious symbolism and appeals to past glory. He launched a 'patriotic-cum-historical cult' of the Hindu warrior-king Shivaji, who fought the British and was made into a 'central symbol of nationalism'. Sumit Sarkar, *Modem India: 1885-1947*, Madras: MacMillan India Ltd., 1983, p. 99.
112. Kumari Jayawardena, op. cit., p. 92.
113. Ibid., p. 93.
114. Meera Kosambi, op. cit., 2007, 2011 (Paperback), p. 284.
115. Tanika Sarkar, 'Rhetoric against Age of Consent: Resisting Colonial Reason and Death of a Child Wife', *Economic and Political Weekly*, 4 September 1993; 'Hindu Conjugality and Nationalism in Late Nineteenth-Century Bengal', in Jasodhara Bagchi (ed.), *Indian Women: Myth and Reality*, Hyderabad: Sangam Books, 1995, pp. 98-115.
116. Tanika Sarkar, 'Rhetoric against Age of Consent: Resisting Colonial Reason and Death of a Child Wife', *Economic and Political Weekly*, 4 September 1993, p. 1876.
117. Chandranath Basu, 'Bibaher Bayas O Uddeshya' (Age and Purpose of Marriage), *Bangadarshan*, 1880.
118. Akshaychandra Sarkar, 'Hindu Parinay Pratha' (Hindu Marriage Custom), *Bharatbarsha*, 1352 Bangabda, repr., *Akshaychandra Rachanabali* (Collection of Writings of Akshaychandra), vol. 1, Kolkata, pp. 178-81.
119. Tanika Sarkar, 'Changing Hindu Women: Bengal in the Long Nineteenth Century', op. cit., p. 830.
120. Mrinalini Sinha, 'Potent Protests: The Age of Consent Controversy, 1891' in *Handbook of Gender*, Raka Ray (ed.), New Delhi: Oxford University Press, 2012, p. 227.
121. Aparna Bandyopadhyay, 'Muslim Voices and Historiographical Silences: The Age of Consent Controversy in Colonial Bengal', The Docket, *Law and History Review*, vol. 3, no. 2, June 2020: Age of Consent Laws in Historical Context. https://lawandhistoryreview.org/article/aparna-bandyopadhyay, accessed on 1 March 2021.
122. S. Natarajan, *A Century of Social Reform in India*, Bombay: Asia Publishing House, 1959, p. 82.
123. Dagmar Engels, 'The Age of Consent Act of 1891: Colonial Ideology in Bengal', *South Asia Research*, vol. 3, no. 2, 1 November 1983, p. 115.

124. Mrinalini Sinha, op. cit., 1995, p. 138.
125. Shyamananda Banerjee, *National Awakening and the Bangabasi*, Calcutta: Amitava-Kalyan Publishers, 1968, pp. 19-21, 74-6, 93, 222-38. In 1891 the *Bangabasi*, a weekly, had 20,000 subscribers, the daily *Dainik-O-Samachar Chandrika* had 1,500. They were thus the largest selling Bengali newspapers, both of which were founded in 1881; *Reports on Bengal Native Press, 1891*.
126. Rajat Sanyal, *Voluntary Associations and the Urban Public Life in Bengal (1815-1876): An Aspect of Social History*, Riddhi-India, 1980, p. 121.
127. Pradip Sinha, *Nineteenth Century Bengal: Aspects of Social History*, Firma K.L. Mukhopadhyay, 1965, pp. 91-143.
128. *Reports on the Bengal Native Press, 1891*, cited in Dagmar Engles, 'The Age of Consent Act of 1891: Colonial Ideology in Bengal', *South Asia Research*, vol. 3, no. 2, 1 November 1983, p. 115.
129. J.C. Ghosh, *Age of Consent: Remarks on the Bill of 1891*, Calcutta, 1891, pp. 1-32, cited in Geraldine Hancock Forbes, *Positivism in Bengal: A Case Study in the Transmission and Assimilation of an Ideology*, India: Minerva Associates Private Limited, 1975, p. 87.
130. Geraldine Hancock Forbes, op. cit., 1975, p. 88.
131. Mrinalini Sinha, op. cit., 1995, p. 138.
132. Meera Kosambi, 'Girl Brides and Socio-Legal Change: Age of Consent Bill (1891) Controversy', op. cit., 3-10 August 1991, p. 1859.
133. Meera Kosambi, op. cit., 2007, 2011 (Paperback), p. 283.
134. Meera Kosambi, 'Girl Brides and Socio-Legal Change: Age of Consent Bill (1891) Controversy', op. cit., 3-10 August 1991, p. 1860.
135. Meera Kosambi, op. cit., 2007, 2011 (Paperback), p. 284.
136. Mrinalini Sinha, op. cit., 1995, p. 147.
137. Meera Kosambi, op. cit., 2007, 2011 (Paperback), p. 284; Meera Kosambi, 'Girl Brides and Socio-Legal Change: Age of Consent Bill (1891) Controversy', *Economic and Political Weekly*, vol. 26, nos. 31/32, 3-10 August 1991, p. 1861.
138. The pamphlet by Ramnath Tarkaratna and Nilmani Mukherjee was reprinted from the Reis and Reyyat; *Tracts on Indian Marriage Customs 1887-1891*, no. 12, British Museum (BM), London, cited in Mrinalini Sinha, op. cit., 1995, p. 147.
139. Mrinalini Sinha, op. cit., 1995, p. 147; Biswanath Mukhopadhyay, 'Sahabas Sammati Bill (1891) Sediner Samajik Andolon' [Age of Consent Bill (1891) The Social Movement of that Day], *Desh*, vol. 53, no. 30, 31 May 1986, p. 16, cited in Shaktisadhan

Mukhopadhyay, 'Sahabas Sammati Bill O Vidyasagar/ Raay: Bekasur Khalas' (Age of Consent Bill and the Judgement of Vidyasagar: Acquitted), *Anustup*, vol. 54, nos. 3-4, 2020, p. 379.

140. Meera Kosambi, 'Girl Brides and Socio-Legal Change: Age of Consent Bill (1891) Controversy', op. cit., 3-10 August 1991, p. 1860.
141. Sri Maheshchandra Sen, 'Sahabas Sammati O Samaj' (Consent to Sexual Intercourse and Society), *Nabyabharat*, vol. 10, no. 2, Jyaistha (May-June), 1299 (1892), pp. 85-90; Sri Maheshchandra Sen, 'Sahabas Sammati O Samaj' (Consent to Sexual Intercourse and Society), *Nabyabharat*, vol. 10, no. 8, Agrahayan (November-December), 1299 (1892), pp. 401-5; Sri Maheshchandra Sen, 'Sahabas Sammati O Samaj' (Consent to Sexual Intercourse and Society), *Nabyabharat*, vol. 10, no. 12, Chaitra (March-April), 1299 (1892), pp. 620-5.
142. Biswanath Mukhopadhyay, op. cit., pp. 15-18, cited in Shaktisadhan Mukhopadhyay, 'Sahabas Sammati Bill O Vidyasagar/ Raay: Bekasur Khalas' (Age of Consent Bill and the Judgement of Vidyasagar: Acquitted), *Anustup*, vol. 54, nos. 3-4, 2020, p. 379.
143. *Bangabasi*, 10 January 1891, *Report on Bengal Native Press*, p. 57; *Bangabasi*, 17 January 1891, *Report on Bengal Native Press*, p. 108, cited in Dagmar Engels, 'The Age of Consent Act of 1891: Colonial Ideology in Bengal', *South Asia Research*, vol. 3, no. 2, 1 November 1983, p. 116.
144. Sri Bipin Chandra Pal, 'Bangalir Balyakrira O Tahar Bisamay Fal (Pratham Prastab)' (Childhood Sports of Bengali and Its Poisonous Results: First Proposal), *Aalochana*, vol. 1, 1806 Shakabda (1884), Kolkata, pp. 111-22; Sri Bipin Chandra Pal, 'Bangalir Balyakrira O Tahar Bisamay Fal (Dwitiya Prastab)' (Childhood Sports of Bengali and Its Poisonous Results: Second Proposal), *Aalochana*, vol. 1, 1806 Shakabda (1884), Kolkata, pp. 134-41.
145. 'Balyabibaha Sambandhe Malabarir Mantabya' (Malabari's Comments on Child Marriage), *Bandhab*, vol. 8, no. 8, 1291 Bangabda, p. 374-81.
146. *Abstract of the Proceedings of the Council of the Governor-General of India, 1891*, p. 83; *Sanjivani*, 24 and 31 January 1891, *Report on Bengal Native Press*, pp. 158-9.
147. *Journal of Indian History*, vol. 49 (April, August and December), The University of Kerala, Trivandrum, 1971, p. 295 cited in Monmayee Basu, op. cit., p. 48.
148. Legislative Proceedings of the Council of the Governor-General of

India, 1891, p. 51 cited in Dagmar Engles, 'The Age of Consent Act of 1891: Colonial Ideology in Bengal', *South Asia Research*, vol. 3, no. 2, 1 November 1983, p. 117.

149. *Shakti*, 20 January 1891, *Report on Bengal Native Press*, p. 157.
150. *The Statesman*, no. 4, 24 January 1891, p. 4; *The Statesman*, no. 6, 7 February 1891, p. 1, cited in Dagmar Engels, 'The Age of Consent Act of 1891: Colonial Ideology in Bengal', *South Asia Research*, vol. 3, Issue: 2, 1 November 1983, p. 117.
151. *Sambad Prabhakar*, 9 July 1890.
152. *Sanjivani*, 21 February 1891, *Report on Native Papers, Bengal*, 1891, p. 261, cited in Dagmar Engels, 'The Age of Consent Act of 1891: Colonial Ideology in Bengal', *South Asia Research*, vol. 3, no. 2, 1 November 1983, p. 117.
153. *Dainik*, 11 January 1891, *Report on Native Papers, Bengal*, p. 60; *Dainik*, 4 March 1891, *Report on Native Papers, Bengal*, p. 292 cited in Dagmar Engels, 'The Age of Consent Act of 1891: Colonial Ideology in Bengal', *South Asia Research*, vol. 3, no. 2, 1 November 1983, p. 119.
154. Ramananda Chatterji, 'Frequent Cases of Suicide among Young men and Women', *Indian Messenger*, VII, 8 June 1890, p. 313 cited in David Kopf, *The Brahmo Samaj and the Shaping of the Modern Indian Mind*, Princeton: Princeton University Press, p. 127.
155. David Kopf, op. cit., pp. 124-6.
156. Mrinalini Sinha, op. cit., 1995, p. 145.
157. Quoted in *Pioneer*, 19 March 1891, p. 359 cited in Mrinalini Sinha, *Colonial Masculinity*, p. 169.
158. Mrinalini Sinha, op. cit., 1995, p. 169.
159. David Kopf, op. cit., p. 127.
160. Rochona Majumdar, *Marriage and Modernity: Family Values in Colonial Bengal*, Durham and London: Duke University Press, 2009, pp. 132-3.
161. 'Sammatir Bill O Brahmo Samaj' (Consent Bill and Brahmo Samaj), *Anusandhan*, 31 Baishakh (April-May), 1298 (1891), vol. 4, no. 19, pp. 456-8.
162. 'Bibidha Prasanga' (Miscellaneous Context), *Anusandhan*, 32 Ashar (June-July), 1298 (1891), vol. 4, no. 23, p. 555.
163. Manmohan Ghose, 4 February 1891, *Proceedings of the Council of the Governor-General of India, 1891*, Appendix U, cited in Dagmar Engels, 'The Age of Consent Act of 1891: Colonial Ideology in Bengal', *South Asia Research*, vol. 3, no. 2, 1 November 1983, p. 120.
164. Dagmar Engels, 'The Age of Consent Act of 1891: Colonial Ideology

in Bengal', *South Asia Research*, vol. 3, no. 2, 1 November 1983, p. 120.

165. Mrinalini Sinha, op. cit., 1995, pp. 163-4.
166. Dagmar Engels, 'The Age of Consent Act of 1891: Colonial Ideology in Bengal', *South Asia Research*, vol. 3, no. 2, 1 November 1983, p. 120.
167. *The Statesman*, no. 4, 24 January 1891, p. 5, cited in Dagmar Engels, 'The Age of Consent Act of 1891: Colonial Ideology in Bengal', *South Asia Research*, vol. 3, no. 2, 1 November 1983, p. 121.
168. *Bangabasi*, 24 January 1891, *Report on Native Papers*, p. 160, cited in Dagmar Engels, 'The Age of Consent Act of 1891: Colonial Ideology in Bengal', *South Asia Research*, vol. 3, no. 2, 1 November 1983, p. 121.
169. Ibid.
170. *The Statesman*, no. 4, 24 January 1891, p. 4, cited in Dagmar Engels, op. cit., 1983, p. 121.
171. *Indian Mirror*, 15 February 1891; *Hindu Patriot*, 23 February 1891, cited in Amiya P. Sen, op. cit., p. 380.
172. *Hindu Patriot*, 2 March 1891, cited in Amiya P. Sen, *Hindu Revivalism in Bengal, 1872-1905: Some Essays in Interpretation*, p. 380.
173. Meredith Borthwick, *The Changing Role of Women in Bengal, 1849-1905*, Princeton: Princeton University Press, 1984, p. 129.
174. *Bangabasi*, 25 February 1891, *Report on Native Papers*, p. 264, cited in Dagmar Engels, 'The Age of Consent Act of 1891: Colonial Ideology in Bengal', *South Asia Research*, vol. 3, no. 2, 1 November 1983, p. 121.
175. Amiya P. Sen, op. cit., p. 380.
176. *Indu-Prakash*, 19 January 1891, p. 4; 2 February, 1891, p. 4, cited in Meera Kosambi, op. cit., 1991, p. 1859.
177. *The Mahratta*, 1 March 1891, p. 4, cited in Meera Kosambi, op. cit., 1991, p. 1859.
178. *Indu-Prakash*, 16 February 1891, p. 3; 9 March 1891, p. 3, cited in Meera Kosambi, op. cit., 1991, p. 1859; Meera Kosambi, op. cit., 2007, 2011 (Paperback), p. 281. For detailed information on important protest meetings held during the Age of Consent Bill agitation in different parts of India, Amiya P. Sen, *Hindu Revivalism in Bengal, 1872-1905: Some Essays in Interpretation*, pp. 415-25.
179. 'The procession started from the junction of Kansaripara and Russa roads, about three kilometres from the temple premises and was led by leading Pundits and orthodox spokesmen like Khettragopal

Smritiratna, Rajkumar Nyayratna, Nilkrishna Deb, Kaviraj Ganga Prasad Sen and Raja Inder Chunder Singh of Paikpara. The absence of Pundit Sasadhar and Krishna Prasanna was rather striking but on its way to the shrine, the rally nonetheless impressed everybody with passionate cries of *Haribol* and *Makali Dharma Raksha Karo* (O Mother Kali, save our religion)', cited in Amiya P. Sen, op. cit., p. 381; Mrinalini Sinha, op. cit., 1995, pp. 169-70.

180. *The Statesman*, 24 January 1891, p. 4; for her role, Paramanda Dutt, *Memoirs of Motilal Ghose*, Calcutta: Amrita Bazar Patrika Office, 1935, pp. 74-5, cited in Mrinalini Sinha, op. cit., pp. 149-50.
181. Mrinalini Sinha, op. cit., 1995, p. 176.
182. Amritalal Basu, 'Sammati Sankat' (Consent Dilemma), Harendralal Mitra, 'Aain Bibhrat' (Legal Breaches), in Dr Jayanta Goswami (ed.), *Samajchitre Unabingsha Shatabdir Bangla Prahasan* (Bengali Farce of Nineteenth Century in Social Representation), Kolkata: Sahityashree, pp. 424-32.
183. Meredith Borthwick, op. cit., p. 129.
184. Census Report, Bengal (1901), pp. 268-9, cited in Amiya P. Sen, op. cit., p. 426. ('The figures cited in the table supported the interesting conclusion that the incidence of child-marriages, especially among Hindu males seemed to have increased in most parts of Bengal by 1901 after a brief setback between 1881 and 1891. Among females, whether Hindu or Muslim, however, the practice suffered a decline to some extent.')
185. *The Times*, 29 November 1890, quoted by Charles Heimsath, 'The Origin and Enactment of the Indian Age of Consent Bill, 1891', p. 501; *Dainik-O-Samachar Chandrika*, 4 February 1891, *Report on Native Newspapers, Bengal*, 7 February 1891; Abstract, 1891, pp. 80-2, cited in Dagmar Engels, *Beyond Purdah? Women in Bengal, 1890-1939*, pp. 109-10.
186. Act X, 1891, p. 32, cited in Shahida Lateef, *Muslim Women in India – Political & Private Realities: 1890s-1980s*, London and New Jersey: Zed Books Ltd, 1990, p. 64.
187. Ibid., p. 64.
188. Mrinalini Sinha, op. cit., 1995, p. 154.
189. Ghulam Murshid, *Reluctant Debutante: Response of Bengali Women to Modernization, 1849-1905*, Rajshahi: Rajshahi University Press, 1983, pp. 184-5.
190. Padma Anagol-McGinn, 'The Age of Consent Act (1891) Reconsidered: Women's Perspectives and Participation in the Child-Marriage

Controversy in India', *South Asia Research*, vol. 12, no. 2, November 1992, pp. 100-18.

191. Ramabai Sarasvati, *The High-Caste Hindu Woman*, Philadelphia: J.B. Rodgers Printing Company, 1888, pp. i-xxiv.
192. Padma Anagol, 'Rebellious Wives and Dysfunctional Marriages: Indian Women's Discourses and Participation in the Debates over Restitution of Conjugal Rights and the Child Marriage Controversy in the 1880s and 1890s', in Tanika Sarkar and Sumit Sarkar (eds.), *Women and Social Reform in Modern India*, vol. 1, India: Permanent Black, 2007, pp. 420-65.
193. Padma Anagol-McGinn, 'The Age of Consent Act (1891) Reconsidered: Women's Perspectives and Participation in the Child-Marriage Controversy in India', *South Asia Research*, vol. 12, no. 2, November 1992, p. 104.
194. Ibid., p. 107.
195. Translated by Kusumavati Deshpande from Ramabai Ranade's Marathi original, *Amchya ayushatil kahi athavani*.
196. Padma Anagol-McGinn, 'The Age of Consent Act (1891) Reconsidered: Women's Perspectives and Participation in the Child-Marriage Controversy in India', *South Asia Research*, vol. 12, no. 2, November 1992, p. 108.
197. Ibid., p. 112, Lady Reay and Dr Pechey-Phipson were the British representatives; the Indian women were Rakhmabai Modak, Pandita Ramabai, and Dr Rakhmabai.
198. Ibid., p. 113.
199. Ibid.
200. 'Memorial of Lady Doctors in India, signed by Monelle Mansell and forty-nine others', 22 September 1890, *Proceedings*, Appendix A15, cited in Padma Anagol-McGinn, 'The Age of Consent Act (1891) Reconsidered: Women's Perspectives and Participation in the Child-Marriage Controversy in India', *South Asia Research*, vol. 12, no. 2, November 1992, p. 113.
201. 'Mrs Ghosal of Calcutta, under the pseudonym of "Srimati" informed the Statesman that at a private meeting of middle-aged Hindu ladies, a unanimous verdict was passed in favour of Sir Andrew Scoble's Age of Consent Bill'. She said, 'Trustful of the government, the ladies hail any legislation that aims at an amelioration of the nameless doom to which among others, the married girlhood of India are subjected', *Indu-Prakash*, 16 February 1891, p. 3, ibid., p. 113.

202. *Indu-Prakash*, 2 March 1891, cited in Meera Kosambi, op. cit., 2007, 2011 (Paperback), pp. 296-7.
203. *Kesari*, 24 February 1891, cited in Meera Kosambi, op. cit., 2007, 2011 (Paperback), pp. 296-7.
204. *Sudhakar*, 13 February 1891; *Ahmadi*, 12 February 1891; *Bangabasi*, 31 January 1891; *Report on Native Papers, Bengal*, cited in Dagmar Engels, 'The Age of Consent Act of 1891: Colonial Ideology in Bengal', *South Asia Research*, vol. 3, no. 2, 1 November 1983, p. 118.
205. *The Statesman*, no. 6, 7 February 1891, p. 2; *Shakti*, 3 February 1891, Report on Native Papers, Bengal, p. 209.
206. 'The Mahomedan Literary Society of Calcutta shared the doubts of the moderate Hindus'; Nawab Abdul Luteef Bahadur, CIE, Secretary to the Mahomedan Literary Society of Calcutta, 6 February 1891 in Proceedings: Appendix U, cited in Dagmar Engels, 'The Age of Consent Act of 1891: Colonial Ideology in Bengal', *South Asia Research*, vol. 3, no. 2, 1 November 1983, p. 118.
207. Elliott to Lansdowne, 17 March 1891, *Lansdowne Papers Correspondence India*, vol. V, no. 255 cited in Dagmar Engels, 'The Age of Consent Act of 1891: Colonial Ideology in Bengal', *South Asia Research*, vol. 3, no. 2, 1 November 1983, p. 118.
208. Maharajah Lakshmiswar Singh of Darbangha to J.A. Ardagh, Private Secretary to the Viceroy, 16 February 1891, *Lansdowne Papers Correspondence India*, vol. V, no. 174, cited in Dagmar Engels, 'The Age of Consent Act of 1891: Colonial Ideology in Bengal', *South Asia Research*, vol. 3, no. 2, 1 November 1983, p. 118.
209. Nawab Ashanullah Khan Bahadur to Lansdowne, 28 February 1891, *Lansdowne Papers Correspondence India*, vol. V, no. 219, cited in Dagmar Engels, op. cit., 1983, p. 118.
210. Dagmar Engels, op. cit., 1983, p. 118. The Most Eminent Order of the Indian Empire is an order of chivalry founded by Queen Victoria in 1 January 1878. The Order includes members of three classes: Knight Grand Commander (GCIE), Knight Commander (KCIE) and Companion (CIE).
211. *Hitakari*, 11 January 1891, *Report on Native Papers*, week ending 21 February 1891.
212. *Hindoo Patriot*, 2 February 1891.
213. *Shakti*, 3 February 1891, *Report on Native Papers*, week ending 14 February 1891.
214. Act X, 1891, p. 16 cited in Shahida Lateef, *Muslim Women in India – Political & Private Realities: 1890s-1980s*, p. 64.

215. *Sudhakar,* 10 July 1891, *Report on Native Papers,* week ending 18 July 1891.
216. Mrinalini Sinha, op. cit., 1995, p. 152.
217. Meredith Borthwick, 'The Bhadramahila and Changing Conjugal Relations in Bengal', in *Women in India and Nepal,* M. Allen and S.N. Mukherjee (eds.), Canberra, 1982, p. 116; Padma Anagol, *The Emergence of Feminism in India, 1850-1920,* New York: Routledge, 2005, p. 15.
218. *Dacca Prakash,* 3 January 1892, *Report on Native Papers,* week ending 9 January 1892.
219. *Dacca Prakash,* 17 January 1892, *Report on Native Papers,* week ending 23 January 1892.
220. Partha Chatterjee, 'The Nationalist Resolution of the Women's Question', in *Recasting Women: Essays in Colonial History,* K. Sangari and S. Vaid (eds.), New Delhi: Kali for Women, 1990, pp. 233-53. Aparna Bandyopadhyay, 'Revisiting the Women's Question in Late Colonial Bengal' in *The Other Universe: An Anthology of Women's Studies,* Aparna Bandyopadhyay and Krishna Dasgupta (eds.), Kolkata: Setu Prakashani, 2015, pp. 286-306.
221. *The Mahratta,* 23 November 1890, 14 December 1890, cited in Meera Kosambi, op. cit., 2007, 2011 (Paperback), p. 281.
222. *The Mahratta,* 10 May 1891, cited in Meera Kosambi, op. cit., 2007, 2011 (Paperback), p. 281; Meera Kosambi, op. cit., 1991, p. 1859.
223. Dayaram Gidumal, *The Status of Woman in India, or A Handbook for Hindu Social Reformers,* Bombay: Fort Printing Press, 1889, p. 18.
224. Ibid., p. 246.
225. 'Sammatir Bayas O Swadeshiyadiger Nikat Abedan' (Age of Consent and Appeal to the Natives), *Nabyabharat,* vol. 8, no. 4, Poush (December-January), 1297 (1890), pp. 466-9.
226. Meera Kosambi, op. cit., 1991, p. 1863.
227. *Indu-Prakash,* 7 July 1890, cited in Meera Kosambi, op. cit., 2007, 2011 (Paperback), p. 289.
228. Dayaram Gidumal, op. cit., 1889, p. 22.
229. C. Yajnesvara Chintamani, *Indian Social Reform, in Four Parts, Being a Collection of Essays, Addresses, Speeches, etc., with an Appendix,* Madras: Thompson & Co., 1901, p. 143.
230. *Indu-Prakash,* 21 July 1890, cited in Meera Kosambi, op. cit., 2007, 2011 (Paperback), p. 292.
231. *Indu-Prakash,* 19 January 1891, cited in Meera Kosambi, op. cit., 2007, 2011 (Paperback), pp. 292-3.

232. Meera Kosambi, op. cit., 2007, 2011 (Paperback), p. 293.
233. Dayaram Gidumal, op. cit., 1889, pp. 281-8.
234. On a more general level, feminists, like Jane Gallup, have argued that 'the institution of marriage is located in a society of unequal power relations between men and women, so that a woman's consent is always to some extent coerced'. Jane Gallop, 'Feminist Accused of Sexual Harassment (excerpt)', in Elisabeth Bronfen and Misha Kavka (eds.), *Feminist Consequences: Theory for the New Century*, New York: Columbia University Press, pp. 18-37.
235. Meera Kosambi, op. cit., 2007, 2011 (Paperback), p. 300.
236. *The Miscellaneous Writings of the Late Hon'ble Mr Justice M.G. Ranade*, published by Mrs Ramabai Ranade, Bombay: The Manoranjan Press, 1915, p. 102.
237. Mytheli Sreenivas, op. cit., p. 74.
238. Meera Kosambi, 'Girl-Brides and Socio-Legal Change: Age of Consent Bill (1891) Controversy', *Economic and Political Weekly*, vol. 26, nos. 31/32, 3-10 August 1991, p. 42.
239. S.P. Sathe, *Towards Gender Justice*, Bombay: SNDT Women's University, 1993, p. 25, cited in Jaya Sagade, op. cit., p. 42.

CHAPTER 4

The State, Age of Marriage and the Question of Social Legislation

The Sarda Act of 1929

Anti-colonial struggles against the British rule, which continued for a long period, have been hardly explained in relation to autonomy for equal rights in the political and economic domains in the construction of self-governing, independent nation-states. However, since the 1960s, an extensive and remarkable historical literature on the agency of Indian child marriage has left untouched the intimate relationships between sexual politics and sexual identities in the creation of new nationalist perspectives both in Britain and India, demonstrating the power of cultural spheres in nationalist hardships. A careful inspection of arguments produced over child marriage, which was also linked up with the age of consent issues in late nineteenth-century India discloses obstacles and eventually, the space of feudal male-controlled kinship practices in colonial India. The practice of child marriage is familiar all over India, regardless of the lines of religion, caste, and geography.[1] The passage of the Child Marriage Restraint Act (CMRA) in 1929 marked the climax of eight years' campaign, action and movement in the Legislative Assembly to raise the age of consent inside and outside of marriage.[2] The CMRA of 1929 was the first segment of extensive social restructuring approved by the Legislative Assembly, which was formed in 1921. The period was that when India saw historic transformations, with the devastation of World War I and its consequences for colonial subjects within the British Empire, the rise of political nationalism and, growing Hindu-Muslim communal turmoil, a pivotal moment in anti-caste movements and the position of Ambedkar in that movement, and the emergence of communism on Indian soil with labour and peasant agitation.[3] A new generation of Indian politicians was now able to debate and pass legislation on issues that directly concerned them, due to the power granted to them by the Montagu-Chelmsford Reforms of 1919. The subsequent legislation regarding child marriage demonstrates that these members of the Legislative Assembly recognized how to exercise political freedom while also showing apprehension regarding social issues. With some restricted authorization, the members were representatives from the upper-class section of Indian society, drawn from various sections of society, trying to represent diverse areas, religious faiths, and professions.[4] The modifications in British imperial policy towards India in the 1920s had generated new circumstances for the strategic mobilization of the 'woman's question' in India in broadening the imperialist agenda. The significant announcement of E.M. Montagu, the Secretary of State for India, in 1917 had signalled a radical transformation in expansionist and colonial thought processes regarding India.[5] On 20 August 1917, Montagu announced in the House of Commons that henceforward British policy in India would be directed towards advancing self-governing institutions that would ultimately bestow self-rule on India as an integral part of the British Empire,[6] though the character and intensity of this change remained firmly in the hands of the government. The political reforms suggested in the Government of India Act of 1919 were intended to personify this new imperial order[7] while also promoting the cause of responsible self-government by giving provincial autonomy and introducing the mechanism of 'diarchy'. Specific functions of provincial governments, such as those relating to education, health, agriculture and local bodies, were handed over to ministers answerable to legislative assemblies, that is, they were given some executive powers.[8]

The 1920s were the beginning of the defining moment for Indian nationalism, which seemed to claim a new formation of the 'woman's question' in India. In 1919, the advent of Gandhi in the all-India political context as well as the Indian National Congress's acceptance of Gandhi's Non-Cooperation Movement in 1920, with its aim of *Swaraj*, had given a fresh impetus to the India nationalist movement.

Nevertheless, following the sensational days of the Non-Cooperation Movement, Gandhi unexpectedly resigned from the vigorous political skirmish in pursuit of social reform effort. In reality, most of the time of 1920s was monopolized by the apparently further humdrum concerns of Indian politicians of various perspectives and generally they were involved in accommodating and sorting out their relationship with the Congress, and to each other, within the latest constitutional and legislative outline of the Government of India Act of 1919. Within the wide-ranging anti-colonial movement, this period also saw the amalgamation and exasperation of diverse competing politics premised on dissimilarities between class, caste, religion, and area. In this context, the Indian National Congress, under the influence of a section of young activists directed by Jawaharlal Nehru, interested for the first time in December 1927, a proposal favouring the notion of 'complete freedom' for India. Although still it was the demand from the minority section of the Congress, it would become the authorized forum of the Indian National Congress by 1929, despite strong opposition from the large proportion of the Congress Party that preferred dominion status for India within the British Empire.[9] In some of the works in the field of gender history nowadays, there is possibly an explanatory and informative propensity, presenting a relatively monotonous depiction of the nineteenth and early twentieth century rhetoric on the 'woman's question'. At the same time, there is no denying the fact that the representation is absolutely correct in concentrating on the prevalent and leading patriarchal norms and values, the realities of the 1920s and 1930s are identified by dynamic controversy, and on the other hand, uncertainties on the part of those in confrontational roles discussing the 'woman's question', must be taken into consideration.[10]

However, the 1920s also witnessed the formation of the first major women's organizations in India, varying from the All India Muslim Ladies Conference based in Lahore (1914), the Women's Indian Association (WIA) based in Madras in 1917 and the succeeding network-based All India Women's Conference (AIWC) in 1926 with branches throughout the country. The women's movement headed the struggle to have the CMRA of 1929 passed through the legislature;

the subsequent debate helped to educate public opinion and also further politicized the issue of women and their position, as political parties and community leaders sought to exploit the issue for political determinations.[11] Besides the Hindus, according to Shahida Lateef, this politicization was visible when Muslim Legislators pursued to legislate on the *Shariat* rights of Muslim women and were held up by the women's movement.[12] She also argued that the arguments surrounding each legislative changes were symbolic of the social, political and economic changes taking place in society. A comparison of various legislative initiatives as well as the subsequent debates and Government action, revealed the intrinsic political and social burdens that Government faced when dealing with women's issues.[13] Some of the educated women began to participate in the country's public matters. They had gained the franchise through the votes of the local Legislatures in several Provinces. One of the first queries that they discussed about was the state of their sex and the means by which it should be enhanced. Though the number of such ladies was undoubtedly very small, but they had exercised a significant impact in moulding such legislation.[14]

The practice of early marriage existed to a very large amount in diverse parts of India.[15] The Punjab addressed fewer challenges than most other Provinces in India. However, early marriage was not as uncommon among both Hindus and Muslims as one might expect. The Census of 1921 disclosed that '70 Hindu, 26 Muslim and 25 Sikh girls aged between five to ten were married out of every thousands. The number of Hindu, Muslim and Sikh girls was respectively 367, 187 and 223, who were married between the age period of ten to fifteen.'[16] On the other hand, in the Himalayan region, where 'there were only 30 Muslims per thousands of the population compared to 642 Hindus, the Muslim population emerged to be motivated to go a phase more than even the Hindus. There were 415 Muslim girls, who were married between the ages of ten and fifteen in comparison with 390 Hindu girls, out of every thousands of the population.'[17] The practice of child marriage was not at all widespread in the North-West Frontier Province. It has been reported that 'no child under five years of age got married either among Hindus or Muslims. In the age period 5-10, only 2 out of every 1,000 Muslim, 11 Hindu and 17

Sikh girls were in a married state. In the age period 10-15; 121 Muslim, 190 Hindu and 306 Sikh girls out of every 1,000 were found married.'[18] The custom of early marriage differed significantly by district, with Kohat having the highest prevalence and Dera Ismail Khan having the lowest. This practice was more widely observed by a few religious groups and castes than by others. The *Rangrez* (Dyer sect of Muslims), however a small group, married off most of their girls at an early age.[19] There were no early marriages among the Amils in Sind, with the average marriage age for girls being sixteen and above.[20] The Province of Delhi was occupied by several different communities. Marriage was not practiced at such a young age. Marriages of girls among Hindus generally took place between the ages of ten and eighteen, more generally at twelve. In the case of Muslims, it appeared that their girls were married at about the age of thirteen or fourteen. Child marriage, on the other hand, was common among the lower classes, and was sometimes performed at the ages of three, four, seven, and eight.[21] As a result, child marriage as a standard occurrence could be found throughout Indian society without discernment of caste as well as creed. The practice of child marriage was extensively predominant in Bombay and Bengal.[22] Girls were married at a very early age in the Bombay Presidency. In 1921, there were 1,666 girls, married or widowed, under one year of age, 1,671 girls married or widowed between one and two years of age, 4,378 girls married or widowed between two and three years of age, 7,219 girls married or widowed between three and four years of age, 12,834 girls married or widowed between four and five years of age, 1,93,582 girls married or widowed between five and ten years of age and 4,98,706 girls married or widowed between ten and fifteen years of age. Muslims had a slightly better situation.[23] It may be recalled that it was too late for the legislation raising the age of Consent in 1891 to come into effect, nearly completely to the thoughtful and significant state of affairs, which was exposed in Bengal. However, there were minor differences between Hindus and Muslims, but both practiced child marriage.[24] Although the tendency of child marriage had started to decrease a bit, but the 1911 and 1921 Census Report (Tables 4.1 and 4.2) had confirmed how prevalent it was in India.

TABLE 4.1: DISTRIBUTION BY CIVIL CONDITION OF 1,000 FEMALES, OF ALL RELIGION AND MAIN AGE PERIOD AT EACH OF THE LAST FOUR CENSUSES[25]

Age	Married				Widowed			
	1911	1901	1891	1881	1911	1901	1891	1881
Females	483	476	485	490	173	180	176	187
0-5	14	13	13	75	1	1	1	2
5-10	105	102	123		4	5	3	
10-15	430	423	495	500	15	18	14	19
15-20	800	777	833	834	37	44	35	44
20-30	884	868	893	882	82	92	81	96
30-40	784	765	779	764	200	214	208	225
40-60	487	484	477	476	501	503	513	517
60 and over	158	163	143	149	830	825	849	846

TABLE 4.2: THE PROPORTION OF UNMARRIED, MARRIED AND WIDOWED PER 1,000 GIRLS IN INDIA, 1921[26]

Age	Unmarried Females	Married Females	Widowed Females
0-5	988	11	1
5-10	907	88	5
10-15	601	382	17
15-20	188	771	41

The Report of 1921 census also recorded that 'for every 1,000 girls between the ages of 5 and 10, 88 were married and 5 were widowed; between the ages of 10 and 15, 382 were married and 17 were already widowed'.[27]

TABLE 4.3: NUMBER OF MARRIED PER 1,000 OF EACH SEX IN INDIA, 1921[28]

Age	Hindus		Muhammadans		Christians	
	Males	Females	Males	Females	Males	Females
0-5	7	14	3	6	2	3
5-10	42	111	14	50	7	15
10-15	144	437	66	344	26	85
15-20	339	814	241	815	133	510
20-30	677	871	656	901	548	841
30-40	831	755	858	799	856	815

By religion, out of every 1,000 Hindu girls between the ages of 5 and 10, 111 were married and between the ages of 10 and 15, 437 were married. Out of every 1,000 Muslim girls, between the ages of 5 and 10, 50 were married and between the ages of 10 and 15, 344 were married. Christians in India also performed child marriage, as 3 in every 1,000 Christian girls under the age of 5 were married, though the Census Report of 1921 attempted to claim that 'these marriages probably took place before conversion'.[29] The issue of early marriage was one of substantial interests and it was thoroughly addressed in the 1911 Census report. The Census explained that 'the custom of child marriage, i.e. marriage before the age of ten, was most prevalent in Bihar and Orissa, Bombay, Baroda, the Central India tract and Hyderabad. It was rare in Assam, Burma, the North-West Frontier Province and the States of Southern India.' The Census Report also argued that 'it was not exclusively a Hindu custom and of the Hindus who were most addicted to the practice, it was among the lower rather than the higher castes that the custom is most rigidly observed.' Child marriage had two practical consequences; first, it implied cohabitation at an immature age, sometimes even before puberty and practically always immediately on the first signs of puberty, resulting in grave physical effects upon the girl and in all the evils of premature child-birth and secondly, in the event of the husband dying, the child-wife was, in the case of the castes in which the re-marriage of widows was prohibited, left a widow for life.[30] In the immediate wake of the Swadeshi movement in Bengal, the issue of infant and maternal mortality took on national significance, eliciting conflicting reactions from nationalists and colonial authorities.[31] The British administrators and western witnesses directly condemned the moribund Bengali social customs of child marriage, and bad midwifery for infant and maternal mortality. The census as well as annual reports of the Calcutta Municipal Corporation and Public Health Department recognized the 'official' viewpoint. The Census of 1911 accredited high infant mortality to premature birth, debility at birth, bad midwifery and 'tetanus neonatorum due to the umbilical cord being cut with dirty instruments'.[32] In 1914, H.M. Crake, the Health Officer of the Calcutta Corporation, recognized equivalent causes attributing 'tetanus neonatorum to ignorance and defective midwifery practices and attributing debility at birth and premature birth to the economic and social conditions of the people, particularly poverty, insanitary conditions, child marriage and the purdah, a baffling group of causes.'[33] The well-known women's magazine *Bharati* in 1919, assessed 'child marriage and early maternity leading to maternal mortality as the chief factors facilitating the decline in national health and deterioration of race'.[34] During a Legislative Council debate, the Government of Bengal evidently stayed away from taking any special action to lessen the high percentage of child deaths, contending that 'the deaths had a lot to do with the domestic life and social customs of the Bengalis and hence could not be eradicated easily'.[35] According to the Bengali health magazine *Swasthya Samachar*, 'if social customs were the main reasons behind infant mortality, both the communities (Hindu and Muslim) would have ceased to exist long back'.[36] Considering upon how child marriage was associated with the question of health, an article published in 1901 in *Swasthya* stated, 'It is usually seen that children of healthy parents are strong and healthy, whereas weak children result from a marriage between parents in poor health ... it needs no great effort to show that the primary reason for the weak constitution of Bengalis lies in the custom of child marriage practiced by them.'[37] While deficiency of healthy food and physical exercise were also documented as important issues, child marriage was regarded as a much more significant issue in the production of weak and unhealthy children.

The range of the complication can be seen from Tables 4.4 and 4.5 of the civil status of little girls in different provinces of India.

TABLE 4.4: FEMALE POPULATION UNDER THE AGE 5 AND THEIR CIVIL STATUS IN DIFFERENT PROVINCES IN 1921[38]

Province and Religion	*Married*	*Unmarried*	*Widowed*	*Total*
ASSAM				
All Religions	81	532,013	12	532,106
Hindus	49	273,195	0	273,250
Mussalmans	18	158,855	4	158,877
BENGAL				
All Religions	23,246	3,057,696	2,819	3,083,761
Hindus	7,747	1,175,935	1,404	1,185,086
Mussalmans	15,209	1,794,017	1,390	1,810,616

Province and Religion	Married	Unmarried	Widowed	Total
BIHAR & ORISSA				
All Religions	40,665	2,013,142	2,510	2,056,317
Hindus	30,311	1,629,157	2,099	1,667,567
Mussalmans	3,710	236,869	887	240,966
BOMBAY				
All Religions	26,287	1,180,148	1,501	1,207,938
Hindus	23,740	917,711	1,312	942,763
Mussalmans	1,689	223,816	130	225,635
C.P. & BERAR				
All Religions	17,514	909,125	547	927,186
Hindus	16,396	757,157	477	774,030
Mussalmans	206	35,942	16	36,164
MADRAS				
All Religions	20,192	636,933	2,298	2,659,423
Hindus	10,206	317,841	1,194	2,338,241
Mussalmans	484	190,403	41	190,878
NWFP				
All Religions	Nil	153,595	Nil	153,595
Hindus	Nil	7,645	Nil	7,645
Mussalmans	Nil	144,865	Nil	144,865
PUNJAB				
All Religions	1,882	1,398,665	Nil	1,400,547
Hindus	1,014	418,027	Nil	419,041
Mussalmans	763	798,193	Nil	798,956
UP				
All Religions	18,663	2,753,446	1,202	2,773,311
Hindus	16,355	2,314,092	1,033	2,331,480
Mussalmans	2,176	411,710	150	414,038

TABLE 4.5: FEMALE POPULATION BETWEEN THE AGES 5 AND 10 AND THEIR CIVIL STATUS IN DIFFERENT PROVINCES IN 1921[39]

Province and Religion	Married	Unmarried	Widowed	Total
ASSAM				
All Religions	11,256	610,635	578	622,469
Hindus	6,788	313,165	348	320,301
Mussalmans	3,657	201,658	199	205,514

Contd.

TABLE 4.5 (*Contd.*)

Province and Religion	*Married*	*Unmarried*	*Widowed*	*Total*
BENGAL				
All Religions	246,462	3,335,493	16,086	3,616,041
Hindus	117,040	1,256,314	8,470	1,381,824
Mussalmans	127,582	1,097,977	7,466	2,133,025
BIHAR & ORISSA				
All Religions	426,830	2,198,747	22,561	2,648,138
Hindus	387,677	1,754,246	20,376	2,162,299
Mussalmans	85,358	266,751	1,964	304,073
BOMBAY				
All Religions	184,025	1,186,269	9,557	1,379,851
Hindus	169,648	894,591	8,604	1,072,843
Mussalmans	10,996	250,738	706	262,440
C.P. & BERAR				
All Religions	172,665	927,815	6,649	1,107,129
Hindus	164,646	747,127	6,092	917,865
Mussalmans		39,498	128	41,573
MADRAS				
All Religions	122,991	2,766,058	7,101	2,896,150
Hindus	119,410	2,428,659	5,651	2,553,720
Mussalmans	1,877	198,899	198	200,974
NWFP				
All Religions	324	163,825	13	164,189
Hindus	72	7,017	4	7,093
Mussalmans	232	155,435	8	155,675
PUNJAB				
All Religions	50,960	1,395,526	1,717	1,448,203
Hindus	27,012	402,918	764	430,694
Mussalmans	20,008	810,645	730	831,383
UP				
All Religions	306,618	2,721,133	12,223	3,039,974
Hindus	272,892	2,273,067	10,953	2,556,912
Mussalmans	32,484	418,589	1,200	452,273

Child marriage was not unique to India, but it became a notably contentious subject as Hindus tried to validate the exercise through the path of religion. Concern about child marriage reached its height in the 1920s, when political activists assumed that improving this practice would not only abolish a 'social evil', but would also exemplify to the rest of the world the ability of Indians to follow them.[40] The League of Nations convened a conference in 1921 to consider the problem of traffic in women and girls. The outcome was a recommendation that participating countries raise the minimum age of consent for single females to twenty-one years. Members of the Conference were primarily concerned with female trafficking and did not recognize the age of consent within marriage. However, the Indian representative to the League projected that age sixteen be substituted for age twenty-one and apply within marriage.[41] Ashwini Tambe has shown that 'a focus on child marriage reform alone would yield a distorted account of the interlocking workings of the age or sex system that shaped notions of childhood and more specifically of girlhood in the colonial context.'[42]

The Age of Consent Act of 1891 had stated that the minimum age of consent within marriage for girls should be twelve years. In 1922, Rai Bahadur Bakshi Sohan Lal recommended that the age of consent should be raised from twelve to fourteen. This motion was defeated. After that in 1924, Sir Hari Singh Gour, a barrister from the Central Provinces, introduced a Bill 'to amend Section 375 to the Indian Penal Code so as to raise the age of consent from twelve to fourteen.'[43] Amar Nath Dutt, a member of Legislative Assembly from Burdwan Division, said that he was opposed to

> the raising of the age of consent in the case of marital relations to 14 or to any figure than what is to be found already in the Indian Penal Code, for the simple reason that this Legislature, constituted as it is by an alien Government, whose faith and religious, moral and social ideas are quite different from those of the children of the soil, has no right to legislate or thrust its will upon an unwilling people.[44]

On 1 September 1925, another Bill was introduced by Sir Alexander Muddiman, the Home Member – the Bill was the measure to amend the Penal Code by raising the age of consent from 12 to 13 in the case of a wife and to 14 in the case of a girl outside the marital relationship. The Home Member explained that he was the stepfather of the Bill; the credit for the measure must go to Sir Hari Singh Gour.

The natural impulse of every Englishmen, Sir Alexander Muddiman affirmed, was towards progress, but as Home Member he must hold the balance and the Bill went as far as was justified by the opinions of the Local Governments. M.K. Acharya, a member of Legislative Assembly, objected to Penal legislation for social reform and denounced the authors of the Bill as busy bodies.[45] Shanmukham Chetty, another member of Legislative Assembly, accused the Government of being slow in social reform. 'If the state of the law of a country', he said heatedly, 'was the index to a country's civilization, then the position of the law in this matter was a slur upon the civilization of India.'[46] After a long debate, Sir Hari Singh Gour moved that the age be raised to fifteen and strongly specified a state of affairs, which caused misery and death to helpless Indian women and children. But his amendment was rejected by 63 votes to 42.[47] Another member of the Legislative Assembly, Dr S.K. Datta, on 3 September 1925, moved that the age of consent for married girls be raised to fourteen years instead of thirteen as provided by the Bill. He stated that his amendment was for educating the community; he mentioned the unhealthy growth of children in Calcutta, realizing that the low age of marriage was responsible for this and the real solution was to raise the age of consent.[48]

On 27 August 1925, Gandhi wrote in the pages of *Young India* that 'Mrs Dorothy Jinarajadasa had issued a circular letter upon a Bill before the Legislative Assembly, whose object was to raise the age of consent at least to fourteen.' Gandhi admitted that he had no knowledge regarding the Bill, but he was firmly in favour of raising the age of consent not merely to fourteen, but even to sixteen. He could say 'nothing about the text of the Bill' but he would 'heartily endorse any movement whose object was to save innocent girls of tender age from man's lust.' He observed, 'the ruin of the health of many a child mother and when to the horrors of an early marriage was added enforced early widowhood, human tragedy became complete'. 'Any sensible legislation in the direction of raising the age of consent' would positively have his support. He also wrote, 'I wish every success to those who are engaged in the noble task of rescuing Indian girls from premature old age and early death, and Hinduism from being responsible for bringing into being rickety weaklings.'[49]

Gandhi, under the caption 'Curse of Child Marriage' in *Young India* on 26 August 1926, stated about an incident, which he came to know from Margaret E. Cousins, who had sent him notes of a tragic case

that appears to have occurred in Madras and has arisen out of a child marriage, the girl being 13 years and the 'husband' 26. Hardly had the pair lived together for 13 days when the girl died of burning. The jury has found that she committed suicide owing to the unbearable and inhuman solicitations of the so-called husband. The dying deposition of the girl would go to show that the 'husband' had set fire to her clothes.

'This custom of child marriage', Gandhi wrote

is both a moral as well as a physical evil. For it undermines our morals and induces physical degeneration. By countenancing such customs, we recede from God as well as Swaraj.... Fight for Swaraj means not mere political awakening but an all-round awakening – social, educational, moral, economic and political. Legislation is being promoted to raise the age of consent.... But it is not legislation that will cure a popular evil; it is enlightened public opinion that can do it. I am not opposed to legislation in such matters, but I do lay greater stress on cultivation of public opinion.... Ordinarily a girl under 18 years should never be given in marriage.[50]

On 7 October 1926, in *Young India*, Gandhi brought out the news of another incident under the title 'Sorrows of Girl Wives'. The incident was basically written by a Hindu lady from Bengal. That lady wrote,

The Madras case is not a singular one. One year ago, a similar incident took place in Calcutta. The girl was only 10 years old. After living two nights with her husband, she refused to go to him at all. One day, however, she was sent by her mother to give some *paan* to the man. Perhaps the poor girl thought that she could return as soon as she had handed it over to the husband. But the man shut the door and she could not get out of the room. After a while pitiable groaning was heard. The girl's mother ran up to the room. When the door was opened the girl was found dead – so severely was she struck on the head by the husband.[51]

A significant number of people, however, actively supported child marriage even in the twentieth century, arguing that early marriage was a common practice of Hindu society and that it was inappropriate to say that the Hindu *sastrakars* (an author of a scripture) were completely wrong in recommending child marriage. Early marriage, in their opinion, was not the reason for feeble health. Rather, they believed as *Young India* stated that 'as the marriageable age continued to rise, the race was becoming weaker. The argument was that fifty or a hundred years ago men and women were stronger by far, so early marriage could not be condemned.'[52] But on the other hand, on 31 December 1925, the All India Social Conference was held in the Albert Institute Hall, Calcutta, presided by Sarala Devi Chaudhurani and this conference, while recording with satisfaction the rise in the age of marriage, emphasized the need for further raising the age both for boys and girls in view of physical degeneration and other evils resulting from early marriage.[53] Several Muslim women, including Begum Hamid Ali, Lady Abdul Qadir, Asif Ali, Begum Aziz Rasul, Akhtar Husain, Kazi Mir Ahmed, Begum Hamida Momin and I.F. Hasan actively participated in the endeavours of the All India Women's Association. From its very inception, it aimed at removing the evil of child marriage.[54] Two years later, the first AIWC was held at Poona on 5 January 1927 and the presidential address was given by Maharani of Baroda; voicing on the problem at the Poona session, Maharani Chimnabai told the delegates of the AIWC,

> The age of consent should be made by law a minimum of 16.... It is also now known that Sir Hari Singh Gour, to whom the women of India owe a great debt of gratitude for his very valuable services, is going to bring the question of raising the age of consent inside and outside marriage to 16 in the next assembly. We have not merely to pass a resolution giving our wholehearted support to the proposed resolution of Sir Hari Singh, but we have to organize a regular campaign of propaganda throughout the country in favour of the resolution with a view to getting it accepted both by the assembly and the Government of India.[55]

On 7 January 1927, the Conference criticized the effect of early marriage on education and appealed to the Government to pass legislation to make marriage below the age of sixteen a penal offence. It also demanded that the age of consent be raised to sixteen; not only that it wholeheartedly supported Gour's Bill and resolved to send a deputation to the Legislative Assembly to convey to its members the demands of women on this vital subject.[56] In this context, Dr (Mrs) Muthulakshmi Reddy, an Indian Medical Practitioner, a lawmaker and also a woman activist, wrote in the *Social Service Quarterly*[57] that she could convince the government that there was no text in their religion, which gave support to this suicidal custom and child sacrifice. She also pointed out that

> as women constitute more than half the population, even if the Government desires to be impartial if it wants to do justice and not provoke criticism it ought to take into consideration the unanimous resolution of the All India Women's Conference and give its verdict in favour of Dr Gour's Bill, especially in the absence of women representatives in the Legislative Assembly, … a measure concerning the health and happiness of the womanhood of the country and the future race.

As soon as, the third Legislative Assembly met on 28 March 1927, Sir Hari Singh introduced his bill to amend Section 375 of the Indian Penal Code, raising the age of Consent in marital cases to 14 and in extra-marital cases to 16.[58] During the development of the controversy, the Government, while articulating overall consideration with the purpose of the bill, specified that

> detailed reports had been called for on the operation of the amended law of 1925 from the local Governments, and that the Government intended to appoint a strong Committee to undertake a comprehensive survey of the whole question with a view to taking further action, if the reports of the local Governments appeared to render such a course necessary.[59]

The motion to take into account the bill was not pushed as a result of this statement, and the House passed an amendment to circulate it for public comment. This resulted in the appointment of the Age of Consent Committee on 25 June 1928.[60] The Committee as finally constituted consisted of Sir Moropant Vishwanath Joshi (as Chairman), late Home Member of the Executive Council of the Governor of the Central Provinces; Rai Bahadur Pandit Kanhaiya Lal, late Judge of the Allahabad High Court; Mr A. Ramaswami Mudaliyar, lately a Member of the Madras Legislative Council; Khan Bahadur Mahbub Mian Imam Baksh Kadri, lately a District and Sessions Judge in the Bombay Presidency; Mrs M. O'Brien Beadon, Superintendent of Victoria Government Hospital of Madras; Mrs Brij Lal Nehru (Rameshwari Nehru), a social worker; Mr Satyendra Chandra Mitra, Advocate of High Court of Calcutta; Pandit Thakur Das Bhargava, Advocate of High Court of Lahore; Maulvi Muhammad Yakub, Deputy President of Legislative Assembly; Mian Mohammad Shah Nawaz from Lahore and Mr M.D. Sagane (as Secretary).[61] On 1 February 1927, Rai Sahib M. Harbilas Sarda, an elected member from Ajmer-Merwara in Rajasthan, introduced a Bill to regulate marriages of children amongst the Hindus.[62] It was hereby enacted as follows – 'Notwithstanding any provision to the contrary existing anywhere, no marriage of a Hindu girl … shall be valid, unless she has, on the day of her marriage, completed her twelfth year and no marriage of a Hindu boy shall be valid unless he has, on the day of his marriage, completed his fifteenth year'.[63] The Bill was called the Hindu Child Marriage Bill, popularly called the Sarda Bill. Born in 1867, Sarda married at the age of nine, and when he was twenty-two years old, his wife died. After the death of his wife, Sarda remarried. He had Arya Samajist sympathies. This backdrop and events and conditions of his personal life were significant in persuading him of the prerequisite of proposing legislation that would advance the lives and position of Hindu women. Therefore, ultimately the Sarda Act set the minimum age of marriage at fourteen for girls in India.[64] According to Harbilas Sarda, the primary object of the Bill was 'to put a stop to child widowhood' and 'to remove the principle impediment to the physical and mental growth of the youth of both sexes and the chief cause of their premature decay and death.'[65] He also felt that if the Bill would pass, it would give a 'real and effective protection to girls, which the Age of Consent Act does not do'.[66] Ramananda Chatterjee in the *Modern Review* invoked the image of civilizing mission grinding to a halt in the face of sinister imperial imperatives, saying,

> The abolition of child marriage and child mortality and the raising of the age of consent within and outside marital relations would tend to make Indians a physically, intellectually and morally fitter nation. But British bureaucrats have all along been very unwilling to help Indian social reformers in affecting these reforms by direct and indirect legislation. They had no

objection to abolish suttee, probably because it was mainly a question of humanity; – the abolition of suttee was not expected to promote the building up of a stalwart nation. But the abolition of child marriage is indirectly and almost directly, a political as well as a social remedy. So in these matters our British bureaucrat friends fall back on the cant of neutrality and non-interference in religious and socio-religious matters. As if suttee, hook swinging, etc., were not such things, which the British Government have stopped by legislation.[67]

Therefore it is necessary to explore and analyse the criticisms and controversies that have taken place specifically within the Legislative Assembly relating to child marriage and age of marriage for girls until the Sarda Act, also called as Child Marriage Restraint Act (CMRA) was passed.

Discourses on the age of marriage in India in the 1920s were exceptionally distinct from those on the age of consent in the 1890s, when many Indians significantly felt aggrieved regarding British intervention into personal sexual affairs. In disparity to the controversies concerning the Age of Consent Act of 1891, passed by the imperial legislature, there were severe public deliberations in the decades of the 1920 in India among Indians and the British regarding the protection of the young girls through raising the minimum age of marriage. The period was a dynamic time for Indians as nationalist movements developed and Indians were able to endorse legislation for the first time through the newly formed Central Legislative Assembly. Marriage at an early age became a major concern for social reformers who were particularly worried about the physical and emotional implications upon girls married as children. Although the age of consent was a major source of concern, the matter of marriage had broader effects. Girls who married at an early age gave up most of their liberties, and generally the burden of childbirth was too much for their fragile bodies. Those associated in the controversies had to deal with the religious and social implications of child marriage. The 'evil' practice of child marriage sparked outrage among educated Indians. The subject was frequently discussed and quite a few requests were made to upgrade the condition by the implementation of the law.[68] *Mother India*, a hostile charge against Indian self-rule written by Katherine Mayo, an American white Nationalist and author, has obtained somewhat of a renowned position amongst students of colonial India and especially among Indian women.[69] The publication of *Mother India* by Katherine Mayo in 1927, which criticized the sexual depravity of Hindu men, generated a defensive tension among Indians.[70] For, in response to Mayo's rhetorical argument in *Mother India*, the leaders of India's nationalist movement and the autonomous women's movement laid the groundwork for a collaboration that provided modern Indian nationalism its exclusive spirit, as encapsulated in the popular nationalist expression of the time, 'India cannot be free until its women are free and women cannot be free until India is free'. Thus, the debate over *Mother India* marked a watershed moment in the history of modern nationalism and feminism in late colonial India.[71]

However, *Mother India* was written after Mayo and her friend and collaborator, Moyca Newell, made a three-month tour of India in the winter of 1925-6. This book carried a solid accusation of demands of Indian self-rule as well as an argument in favour of continued British rule over India, supported by plentiful citations to various official and non-official source materials on India. *Mother India* provided a comprehensive examination of the numerous evils that Mayo believed plagued Indian society, 'the heinous treatment of women, untouchables, and animals; the filthy living conditions of Indians; and the insincerity and emptiness of educated Indians, particularly the new sort of nationalist Indian politicians in the 1920s.' Mayo's core argument was that the sexual agency of Hindu society was at the heart of all of India's difficulties. She had written, 'The whole pyramid of the Indian's woes, material and spiritual … rests upon a rock-bottom physical base. This base is, simply, his manner of getting into the world and his sex life thenceforward.'[72] She described in graphic detail some of the atrocities committed against Indian women in support of this argument, including child marriage and widowhood, premature consummation and pregnancy, female infanticide, *purdah*, temple prostitution and *sati*.[73] The book thus highlighted an extremely exaggerated representation of uncontrolled sexuality and its repercussions in India – 'masturbation, rape, homosexuality, prostitution, venereal diseases and most importantly, early sexual intercourse and premature maternity.'[74] Mayo believed that the problems of Indian society were inherent in Hinduism and as such, were actually tolerated by Hindu religion and culture. Her argument that India's backwardness developed not from political or economic causes but it was due to religious and cultural factors represented two significant motives – it refuted nationalist Indian assertion of Indian superiority in the domain of culture and spirituality over the positivist West; and it released colonial rule from any accountability for the backwardness of India, evoking instead compassion for the reform work of the innumerable British men and women who struggled generously against such odds.[75] Although in the 1920s and 1930s, leaders of both the nationalist and the women's movements in India, had harshly criticized *Mother India*, the book continued to have an huge impact in moulding understandings about India and Indian women, specifically in Mayo's home country.[76] Despite Manoranjan Jha's *Katherine Mayo and India*, the only full-length scholarly treatment of the '*Mother India* controversy', which illustrated the political motivations underneath Mayo's book and reconstituted Mayo's linkages to the official British imperial propaganda machine, the myth of Mayo as a feminist warrior has persevered.[77] The influence of *Mother India*, indeed, required to be understood in the various contexts of the United States, British, and Indian politics.[78] Mayo herself stated repeatedly that her goal in writing *Mother India* was to give the American public with the 'true' picture of Indian Civilization as a counter to the advantageous advertisements that was being engulfed by India-lovers in the United States.[79]

The detailed complexion and scope of the British government's official engagement in Mayo's project remains shrouded in mystery. Even though there is no doubt that *Mother India* was created with the full understanding and endorsement of the pertinent colonial authorities concerned with India, government representatives were forced to concede any official interference in Mayo's project on several occasions in reaction to questions raised in the British Parliament and the Central Legislative Assembly in India. The government's representatives asserted to have offered Mayo with nothing other than just what foreign traveller in India would have received. However, the official story was undermined when Mayo began to refer to her correlation with the British government in a very positive direction. Disregarding the disavowal, she had written in *Mother India*, Mayo made the political mistake of later publicly acknowledging her enormous indebtedness to the British authorities, without whose assistance she now admitted she could not have written her book. This blunder put British officials and diverse government agencies in India in a bind.[80] The greatest irony possibly is that, despite *Mother India's* successive stardom as a book exposing India's problems with child marriage and premature maternity, Mayo had originally planned to write a very different type of book on India. Mayo's primary intention was to concentrate on public health in India, particularly on epidemics such as cholera, which were undoubtedly man-made.[81]

According to Mrinalini Sinha, 'Mayo's horrific description of the actual conditions of child birth – presided over by the allegedly filthy, louse-infested, unscientific *Indian-Dai* or midwife – presented in the book, together with the terrible consequences of child marriage on Indian women and children, were generally agreed to constitute the main contribution of the book.'[82] Eleanor Rathbone, a British feminist who had been a strong supporter of *Mother India* and had been influenced by the book to take on the responsibility of alleviating the suffering of India's child brides, could not help but chastise Mayo for deliberately misinterpreting evidence on child marriage in Volume II. According to Rathbone, the later book had lost its effectiveness because Mayo was too eager to demonstrate that the horrors of child marriage were a uniquely 'Hindu' phenomenon. The government decided to ban *The Face of Mother India* from India on its own initiative because, as one official clarified, the 'whole thesis of it is Hindu-Muslim antagonism'. Cornelia Sorabji, Mayo's friend and confidante and one of the few prominent Indian women to write a favourable review of *Mother India*, had already made the decision against having her photograph used in *The Face of Mother India*, fearing that its extreme bias against Hindus would estrange her from her orthodox and conservative Hindu friends and clients in India.[83] The myth of *Mother India* that followed was the result of a long history of the use of the 'woman's question' in India's struggle between imperialism and nationalism. Many other scholars have highlighted that the 'woman's question' had already become an ideological battlefield between Indian nationalists and British imperialists in colonial India long before *Mother India* was authored.[84] *Mother India* focused solely on British men and women's contributions for the betterment of Indian women. Mayo was indifferent regarding the colonial government's repeated opposition to a number of reform measures, including bills sponsored by Indian legislators to raise the age of consent and abolish child marriage, or the numerous reform initiatives for women undertaken by Indian men and women themselves.[85]

The debate over *Mother India*, on the other hand, accorded with the continued integration of more elite and middle-class Indian women into the public life of the new nation-in-the-making. Through the middle of the 1920s, Indian women, albeit in small numbers, had gained the right to vote and the right to be elected to provincial legislatures from the body of new Indian legislators across most of British India's provinces.[86] Despite the fact that the first two women candidates who stood for election to the newly formed legislative councils were defeated, a representative of the WIA was assigned to the Madras Legislative Council. Dr Muthulakshmi Reddi, the first Indian woman legislator, also became the first woman to be elected as a legislative body's deputy president.[87] At that time, women's organizations themselves were becoming more energetic on an all-India level in support of numerous reforms for women. Throughout the 1920s, the WIA and its various branch organizations held meetings and passed resolutions on behalf of multiple private bills across the country that were consecutively introduced in the Central Legislative Assembly in Delhi to raise the age of marriage and consent for girls in India.[88] In the Madras Legislative Council, Reddi introduced related reform bills for women. Geraldine Forbes has described the importance of women's organizations in the passing of this Act, including their composition of problems, campaigns through day and night, synchronizing across all types of groups from different parts of the country, and their untiring petitioning of the government as a rite of passage into a world where every act had political significance.[89] Thus, when presenting their claims to Indian legislators and the colonial state, the WIA and the AIWC used propaganda from both of nationalism and women's rights. Besides that, activists maintained that conjugal reform was a critical aspect for the refurbishing development of the Indian nation. In the words of WIA member Muthulakshmi Reddy, 'If we want to grow into a strong, robust and self-respecting nation, if we want to reach our full physical and mental height, the system of child marriage must go.'[90]

Between 1922 and 1927, the Indian Legislative Assembly contested a number of Bills aimed at raising the age of consent, or the age at which intercourse was legally acceptable. It has been already discussed that in 1927, Rai Saheb Harbilas Sarda introduced the Hindu Child Marriage Bill, which according to him, 'struck at the heart of the problem'.[91] The AIWC in Poona laid the groundwork for what would become one of India's most ambitious 'all-India organizational structures' to depict women's views on social and educational reforms. The new pattern of engagement of Indian women in Indian national life was noteworthy enough to draw the consideration of tire Simon Commission, which remarked on this advancement in its report on the political and constitutional evolution in India.[92] In a speech delivered at the AIWC session in Delhi in 1928, the Begum of Bhopal denounced child marriage, stating that it was 'incumbent upon us to stop this evil, as far as possible'. The Rani of Mandi proposed a resolution that was unanimously passed, strongly condemning the impact of child marriage on education.[93] The AIWC's stance was that, the religion of the child was insignificant. It had been demonstrated that child marriage was widespread in all communities; therefore, the Act should apply to all communities. On February 1929, at the Hyderabad session of the All India Muslim Ladies Conference, the Honorary Secretary Abru Begum encouraged women to join the movement to raise the age of consent for marriage.[94] Sinha has highlighted that women's organizations made an opinion to include everyone along in their programme, including Muslim organizations. As a result, women became legitimately universal subjects under the CMRA, transcending the harsh realities of separate personal laws based on religion.[95] Mrinalini Sinha wrote, 'On 11 February 1928, a delegation of nineteen members of the AIWC led by the Rani of Mandi met the viceroy and leaders of all the major Indian political parties to urge the passage of the Sarda Bill in the Legislative Assembly.'[96] It has also been written by Sinha that the delegation was also able to acquire the appointment of one of its members, Rameshwari Nehru, to the government-appointed Age of Consent Committee on 25 June 1928. Rameshwari Nehru later wrote that 'it was in dealing with private bills on age of marriage and consent that the government had appointed this committee'.[97] In the history of the AIWC, 11 February 1928 was a red-letter day. According to AIWC's Annual Report (1928), a deputation comprising almost all provinces in India waited on various political parties in the country to pursue their collaboration in enacting legislation to end the practice of child marriage. The first deputation included Mrs. S.R. Das, Rameshwari Nehru, Sarala Devi Chaudhurani, Mrs. Ambalal Sarabhai, Begum Hamid Ali, Kamaladevi Chattopadhyay, Margaret Cousins and eleven others. A second deputation led by Indira Bhagwat met the non-official European members of the Imperial Legislative Assembly and leaders of political parties including Mohammed Ali Jinnah, Pandit Madan Mohan Malaviya, Motilal Nehru, Srinivasa Iyengar, Lajpat Rai, M.R. Jayakar and the Raja of Mahmudabad. A third deputation comprised of Sushma Sen, Kamaladevi Chattopadhyay and Srirangamma and others met with the Age of Consent Committee to advance their opinions and challenge the contentions raised by the adversaries of the Bill constructed on the basis of religion and popular sentiment.[98] On behalf of the AIWC, Kamaladevi Chattopadhyay wrote the work of obtaining support for the bill from Indian legislators in Delhi. As secretary of the Child Marriage Abolition League, Dhanvanthi Rama Rau worked among the wives of British government officials, urging them to motivate their husbands to support child marriage legislation.[99] The Mysore Ladies Conference steadfastly urged women of state to benefit from legislation that would elevate their social status. It demanded at one of its meetings, presided over by Lady Ismail, the wife of Sir Muhammad Ismail, the Dewan of Mysore, that 'the enactment of legislation on the lines of the Sarda Bill should be immediately introduced in the state by fixing the minimum age of marriage for girls at sixteen and for boys at twenty-one'.[100]

At both the first and second session of AIWC, members damned the practice of permitting young boys and girls to become parents and urged the central government and the provincial legislatures to go after the pattern established by the states of Baroda, Mysore, Rajkot, Kashmir, Gondal, Limbdi and Mandi, which had raised the legal age of marriage. They started demanding that the legal age for both girls and boys be raised to sixteen and twenty-one years old, respectively.

They revealed the sheer inequity of child marriage; its terrible effects on women's health; the tragedy of premature widowhood; the bearing of unfit children by immature and uneducated women; and lastly, the utter impossibility of affecting any successful far-reaching plans of education as long as girls were to be claimed, at an early age, by marriage. The members suggested: (1) 'The conference should elect a small standing committee to watch and report on the progress of the Child Marriage Bill, to coordinate and direct the activities of the provincial committees and to urge their views upon the legislatures.' (2) 'The delegates should urge their provincial constituent bodies to form similar provincial and local committees to carry on an intensive educational campaign against child marriage and to bring their views urgently and constantly to the attention of the provincial and central legislative bodies.' At the same time, proposals for the movement comprised (a) Propaganda meetings and lectures, (b) Writing literature and posters, (c) Petitions, (d) Postcard campaign urging people to sign postcards or write to their representatives in the legislative assembly demanding passage of the Child Marriage Bill, and (e) Allocation of some part of the finances for this purpose and seeking of special donations to the campaign fund.[101]

A significant occasion of AIWC was a meeting of Bengali women at Albert Hall on College Street in Calcutta. Among those who addressed the meeting were Lady Abala Bose (1864-1951), the wife of Acharya Jagadish Chandra Bose; Sneha Sheela Chaudhuri (1886–1955), a prominent Congress activist in Jessore since 1921; Sucharu Devi (1874–1961), the wife of the Maharaja of Mayurbhanj and more generally known as daughter of Keshub Chandra Sen and Kamaladevi Chattopadhyay.[102] Lady Abala Bose was the secretary and Maharani Sucharu Devi was chairman of the Reception Committee. The gathered Bengali women passed resolutions in support of the Sarda Bill and against the foundation of child marriage. Sneha Sheela Chaudhuri's statement was perhaps similarly noteworthy and more impressive, 'Love is not born in the mind of a girl at the age of twelve or thirteen.... Do the makers of laws (*shastras*) look upon women as manufacturing machines?'[103] What the reactions were went unreported, but it was a momentous statement from a woman, demanding 'love in conjugal relationship'. The structured attempts to promote the women's cause into the public sphere, especially in terms of legislation and franchise, were supported by ongoing efforts by the nationalist political leadership to take over that cause. 'If India is to win freedom the women must be awakened' and so on.[104] There were two different versions of this. The weak version advocated for women to play a constructive role within the restrictions of the home rather than direct participation in politics, 'India's wives and mothers will ... raise the future soldiers for *Swaraj*' in their homes, which remain 'their principal realm'. The strong version argued that this was insufficient, and that women should not be restricted to domestic duties, and they must 'carry the flag and enter the freedom struggle like their husbands and sons'.[105] Members of the AIWC persevered in their demand for legislation, and refused to let religion interfere. They would make no exceptions to the rule they wanted to have enacted as law. The Act was welcomed by reformist view all over the country. Recognizing the significance of such an Act, many princely states took on the task of enacting similar legislation within their borders. Child marriage was already prohibited in the states of Baroda and Kotah. However, there were orthodox and backward sections of Hindus and Muslims who were hostile to the Act, according to the Annual Report (1932) of AIWC reported.[106] The AIWC advocated for the inclusion of Muslims and other communities in the limits of the Child Marriage Act.[107] Apart from Albert Hall meeting, there was another meeting of women in Rammohan Hall in Calcutta, which took resolutions passionately supporting the Sarda Bill.[108] The Saroj Nalini Memorial Association supported the Bill, and tried to implement the reform in villages where they had established women's groups.[109] Even women from the conservative Marwari society of Bengal organized an All India Marwari Women's Conference in Calcutta at University Institute Hall under the presidentship of Janaki Debi Bajaj and took a resolution against seclusion or purdah and the evil effects of child marriage.[110]

By passing a marriage legislation, the Government was now intruding with the religious ceremony of the wedding, preferably than simply the private act of consummation. Marriage was a necessary ceremony for achieving 'religious maturity and bearing children, as well as a community-involved project'.[111] As J.T. Marten clarified in the Census Report of 1921, 'For a Hindu, marriage is a sacrament, which must be performed regardless of the fitness of the parties to bear the responsibilities of a mated existence'.[112] M.K. Acharya from South Arcot, told on 26 March 1928,

> I am very strongly opposed on principle to penal legislation coming in to the aid of social reform.... Perhaps the most important sacrament in a Hindu's religious life is the sacrament of marriage; and there is a large section of Hindus who regard that this sacrament must be administered to the girl before she attains puberty.... I consider this (Sarda's Bill) even more dangerous than Sir Hari Singh Gour's Age of Consent Bills.[113]

From Lucknow, Munshi Iswar Saran argued in response that 'this Bill does not seek, to make the marriage of Hindus a civil contract.... What it says is that instead of performing this religious sacrament at a particular age, you will perform it after a certain age.'[114] Amidst the pressure created by Mayo's book, Harbilas Sarda presented 90 petitions, signed by 2,700 women from Bombay in favour of the Bill.[115] On 8 September 1928, before the Assembly, he moved that the Bill be recommitted to a select committee and also pointed out that the Bill had been before the country for about two years and he wanted that the select committee should report within three days. Lala Lajpat Rai supported this move and at this stage, Sir Moropant Joshi and the Rani of Mandi and a large number of supporters of the Bill were present in the gallery.[116] On the same day, ladies of all shades of opinion and representing every woman's society of Bengal accorded unanimous support to the Child Marriage and Age of Consent Bills in a crowded meeting in Calcutta under the presidency of Lady Mukherjea.[117]

The Bill was brought before the Assembly on 29 January 1929 after being amended by the select committee. The first amendment that the select committee made to the original Bill was that the Bill was to be applicable to all classes and communities in British India. Second, clause 6 of the original Bill, i.e. the conscience clause, was completely eliminated. Third, originally the intention was to declare all objectionable marriages of boys or girls below a certain age to be invalid; instead, the select committee introduced a provision to make it penal. Finally, not only the substance of the Bill, but also the very title and preamble were altered.[118] Harbilas Sarda gave a powerful speech in the house. He claimed that marriage had a far greater impact on a woman's life than it did on a man's life. Then it was her turn to bear the responsibility of motherhood. Society and the state should consequently, assign much greater weight to her assessments and her considered opinion in the issue of marriage.[119] According to Sarda, hundreds of ladies' meetings had been held in the country; district and Provincial Ladies' Conferences had taken place, ladies associations and sabhas representing different communities met and passed resolutions on this Bill. Three All India Ladies' Conferences in different parts of the country had met, discussed and passed resolutions regarding this matter. He further questioned whether the members of that Assembly found a single instance of such a public meeting of women protesting against the Bill. Women all over the country demanded that this Bill be passed as soon as possible, with remarkable, almost astounding agreement. Even the Rajputana Provincial Ladies' Conference, was predominately made up of Marwari women, which met on 19 November 1928, ardently claimed that this Bill be passed immediately.[120] The women of Madras supported it, as evidenced by the women's meetings conducted throughout the Presidency. The majority of the Brahmins of Madras favoured the Bill, which was evident from the report of Williams who said, 'I have received the opinions of 22 persons of standing in Berhampur. Of these 22, 13 are Brahmins and nine non-Brahmins. Of the 22, sixteen support the Bill. Of these sixteen, 10 are Brahmins. Thus, of the thirteen Brahmins consulted, ten support the Bill and only three oppose it.' Sarda also stated that the Sub-Collector of Kumbakonam said, 'At a meeting of the ladies of Kumbakonam town', – which was a seat of Brahmins, 'the Bill was unanimously supported'.[121] Mrs Gomathi Ammal, speaking for the WIA, Veerargaupuram, told that the Child Marriage Bill has not come a minute earlier and cannot be postponed for a minute later. Child marriages must be prevented.[122] Mrs Lakhshmi Ekambaram for the Ladies' Association affectionately supported the Bill. The Hindu Patit Pavan Mission, Ganjam and the Hindu Dharam Paripalan Sabha, the Madras League of Youth and the Indian Women's Association in Madras wholeheartedly supported the Bill.[123] Child marriage resulted in child widowhood, and it occasionally resulted in the death of girl victims during the first childbirth. Dr Campbell, Lady Principal of the Lady Hardinge College, Delhi, confessed before the Age of Consent Committee on 10 October 1928, about the impact of child marriage on girls, describing how girls were condemned to slow deaths by becoming mothers. She told that, she had attended more than one thousand Hindu girls for child births at the ages of from 12 to 16 years. And the evil effects seen in them and in others under observation or treatment as a result of early child bearing could be hardly exaggerated. Tuberculosis was very often developed during pregnancy or lactation as the resistance of the tissues was lowered by the strain, unnatural at so early an age. This was the reason why tuberculosis was much more common in girls than in boys. About 40 per cent of the children of girl mothers died in the first year and those who survived were weaklings.[124] And, according to Dr Campbell, 'there was no other way to check early consummation but by fixing the marriageable age of girls sixteen'.[125]

M.S. Sesha Ayyangar completely opposed the Bill on the basis of that the original Bill, which was introduced had been undergone so much of vital change both in form and substance, that the Parliamentary practice was to withdraw the present Bill and to reintroduce a new Bill. According to him, 'the original Bill is to apply to Hindus, Jains, Sikhs, Brahmos, and Arya Samajist. Now it is made to apply to all communities and classes in British India'. In the first report of the select committee, it was said that 'The Bill has been so materially altered by us that in our opinion it requires republication'.[126] M.K. Acharya said that the consideration of the Bill should be postponed till the report of the Age of Consent Committee became available to the Members of the House.[127] His motion was put to vote and was carried by 53 against 34.[128] Harbilas Sarda pointed out that hundreds of ladies' meetings, district and provincial ladies' conferences had been held, ladies' associations and *sabhas* on behalf of diverse communities had met and passed resolutions on this Bill.[129]

The Age of Consent Committee told that 'taking the age period five to ten, it was found that among Hindus, 126 per 1,000 were in a married state in 1911 as against 91 in 1921, and among Muslims 11 were found married in the former year as against 64 in the latter.' These statistics from Census Reports provided a relatively general evidence of the scale to which the age of marriage for girls has increased, either through voluntary attempt or as a result of surrounding situation.

TABLE 4.6: NUMBER OF MARRIED AND WIDOWED GIRLS BETWEEN THE AGES 10 AND 15 FOR ALL RELIGIONS, HINDUS AND MOHAMMEDANS TO THE TOTAL POPULATION OF GIRLS OF THAT AGE PERIOD FOR ALL-INDIA AND FOR DIFFERENT PROVINCES[130]

	Total Number of Girls between 10 and 15	*Number of Girls married*	*Number of Girls widowed*
ALL-INDIA			
ALL RELIGIONS			
1901	15,566,718	6,584,768	275,862
1911	15,222,701	6,555,424	223,042
1921	16,570,526	6,330,207	279,124
HINDUS			
1901	11,028,381	5,166,687	227,367
1911	10,491,997	5,117,635	181,507
1921	11,327,411	4,947,266	232,147
MUSSALMANS			
1901	3,185,372	1,244,352	39,091
1911	3,203,754	1,258,842	36,264
1921	3,487,589	1,200,722	39,873
ASSAM			
ALL RELIGIONS			
1901	287,769	83,811	4,027
1911	298,017	86,006	3,115
1921	383,550	95,747	3,528
HINDUS			
1901	154,961	48,393	2,547
1911	155,960	49,875	1,908
1921	201,480	52,445	2,004
MUSSALMANS			
1901	78,779	28,840	1,202
1911	84,511	30,776	990
1921	114,638	37,527	1,301
BENGAL			
ALL RELIGIONS			
1901	3,778,010	2,212,394	100,056
1911	2,172,105	1,302,687	52,234

Contd.

TABLE 4.6 (*Contd.*)

	Total Number of Girls between 10 and 15	*Number of Girls married*	*Number of Girls widowed*
1921	2,325,989	1,199,856	59,228
HINDUS			
1901	2,315,655	1,433,117	73,564
1911	918,851	619,191	31,370
1921	941,214	552,184	35,428
MUSSALMANS			
1901	1,294,340	748,082	25,296
1911	1,195,153	672,675	20,475
1921	1,312,414	636,287	23,129
BOMBAY			
ALL RELIGIONS			
1901	1,002,757	484,202	31,041
1911	894,522	484,678	16,672
1921	969,652	472,618	26,088
HINDUS			
1901	795,832	428,972	27,682
1911	698,368	434,479	15,243
1921	771,445	425,504	24,311
MUSSALMANS			
1901	173,909	46,059	2,241
1911	164,144	41,019	1,098
1921	163,335	39,674	1,337
CP			
ALL RELIGIONS			
1901	566,929	223,182	9,583
1911	577,689	331,098	8,096
1921	750,230	386,959	16,138
HINDUS			
1901	464,486	200,996	8,341
1911	479,449	304,357	7,511
1921	621,959	356,107	14,956

MUSSALMANS			
1901	15,767	4,079	182
1911	24,135	7,466	223
1921	29,007	8,558	242
BIHAR AND ORISSA			
ALL RELIGIONS			
1911	1,763,410	939,047	47,015
1921	1,827,533	861,210	46,348
HINDUS			
1901	140,457	102,582	5,088
1911	1,432,203	817,289	42,471
1921	1,497,004	951,088	41,717
MUSSALMANS			
1901	12,094	2,679	87
1911	182,422	93,527	3,555
1921	191,286	86,373	3,465
MADRAS			
ALL RELIGIONS			
1901	2,210,030	516,337	18,961
1911	2,295,029	580,380	19,297
1921	2,438,224	534,649	23,486
HINDUS			
1901	1,957,753	488,063	18,015
1911	2,030,910	548,498	18,251
1921	2,151,441	505,833	22,209
MUSSALMANS			
1901	151,295	20,342	646
1911	160,799	22,489	765
1921	171,181	20,286	715
NWFP			
ALL RELIGIONS			
1911	98,969	11,328	275
1921	100,722	12,325	379
HINDUS			
1911	4,982	936	16
1921	5,514	1,003	41
MUSSALMANS			
1911	92,897	10,154	251
1921	94,122	11,003	333

Contd.

TABLE 4.6 (*Contd.*)

	Total Number of Girls between 10 and 15	*Number of Girls married*	*Number of Girls widowed*
PUNJAB			
ALL RELIGIONS			
1901	1,112,780	287,032	4,284
1911	931,615	258,190	6,474
1921	1,040,026	241,746	4,767
HINDUS			
1901	401,655	152,922	2,449
1911	312,065	120,977	3,333
1921	317,227	110,418	2,377
MUSSALMANS			
1901	638,575	113,256	1,609
1911	521,582	110,503	2,460
1921	584,428	103,354	1,950
UNITED PROVINCES			
ALL RELIGIONS			
1901	2,475,207	1,338,007	28,951
1911	2,316,499	1,208,174	32,170
1921	2,196,089	1,087,379	34,785
HINDUS			
1901	2,107,321	1,184,093	25,871
1911	1,960,423	1,059,900	28,849
1921	1,844,042	955,117	31,418
MUSSALMANS			
1901	358,508	150,557	3,000
1911	337,022	141,067	3,139
1921	328,592	124,782	3,163

Among the Brahmins, 4 in every 1,000 girls were married before the age of five, according to both Census Reports of 1911 as well as of 1921. In the age-period five to twelve, 160 girls were found married in 1911 and 108 in 1921 out of every 1,000. The rise in the age of marriage was therefore understood to be very slow throughout the period. It could be argued that pre-puberty marriage was prescribed by religion among these groups. In Bengal, the *Chasi Kaibarta* class was the huge caste groups among the Hindus. The members belonged to the depressed classes and could not be influenced so much by texts of Manu, Parashara or Raghunandan and still the practice of child marriage was more widespread among them than even among Brahmins. In 1911, 12 out of every 1,000 girls were found married before the age of five as against 11 in 1921. Again 259 and 216 girls between five and twelve out of 1,000 were in a married state in 1911 and in 1921 respectively. The practice was predominant to almost the same range among the Namasudras, who were the next largest class in the province.[131]

Among the Muslim factions of Bengal, the *Saiyads*, who were the most learned and knowledgeable segment of the community, practiced the custom of child marriage, which was roughly very close to those of Brahmins. In 1911, 7 out of 1,000 girls below five years, were married and in 1921, the figure went up to 12. Census Reports have confirmed that 'Between the ages of five and twelve, 123 girls were found married in 1911 as compared with 105 in 1921 while at the age-period twelve to fifteen, 707 were in a married state in 1911 and 553 in 1921.' Other groups were more likely to engage in this practice. According to the census of 1911,

> 20 girls below the age of five and 314 between five and twelve, out of every 1,000 were in a married state among the Ajlafs (Muslims). Among the Jolahas, the respective figures were 11 and 277. Among the Kulus, 5 girls were married before five years and 194 between five and twelve. Even the Moghuls and Pathans were not far beyond the reach of the custom as 136 and 161 girls were married between five and twelve years of age in each of these sects.

The Sheikhs who made up the majority of the population numbering nearly 23 million were closer the Jolahas than the Moghuls or Pathans in perceiving this practice.[132] The evidence presented to the Committee revealed that early marriage was commonly observed throughout Bengal, both among Hindus and Muslims. The evidence also established that pre-puberty consummations were prevalent and that contraventions of the Law of Consent took place on many occasions. The practice of *Gaona*, according to which the girl-wife was not sent to the husband's family till sometime after marriage and generally after puberty, did not exist in Bengal, as a consequence of this, soon after marriage, at any age, the girl lived with her husband and consummation invariably followed on attainment of puberty irrespective of the age of the girl.[133]

On the other hand, among the orthodox section of the Muslim community, Hajee Ismail Chowdhury stated that 'puberty was the only test and consummation took place irrespective of the age of the girl.' He was personally in favour of checking the evil having a Law of Marriage, but would not support it even if medical opinion regarded sixteen as the proper age of consummation, as the opinion of the community was against it. Quazi Zahirul Haq of Dacca admitted that girls were married at all ages, even at two and three, among the lower class of Muslims, that immediately after puberty, which happened at eleven or twelve, the girl was sent to the husband's house and that he was aware of girls who became mothers at thirteen or fourteen, but he would oppose all Consent and Marriage legislation as it interfered with the liberty granted by God's law.[134] Khan Bahadur K.A. Siddiqui, Khan Bahadur Maulvi Ekramul Huq were also against any legislation, though Ekramul Huq admitted that 'girls below thirteen did not escape the consequences of marriage'.[135] Khondkar Ali Taib, Deputy Magistrate, Mymensingh, stated that in his understanding child marriage was more prevalent in Bengal than in any other Province. He felt that 'there might be opposition to legislation but no importance need be attached to it as the people would gradually appreciate the improvement.'[136] Nasiruddin Ahmed thought that 'the better policy would be to fix the minimum age of Marriage at 14 and raising the age of Consent to the same age.'[137] Khan Sahib Maulvi Safar Ali, Chairman of Noakhali Municipality, advancing the viewpoint of the Municipality, said that the Municipal Committee was in favour of legislation, fixing a minimum age for Marriage as a more effective remedy than raising the age of Consent, and consider that fixing a minimum age for Marriage would be in consonance with public opinion. And according to the Age of Consent Committee's report, it was understandable from above verifications that Muslim opinion in Bengal was generally in favour of a Law of Marriage and an increase in the age of Consent and according to that opinion neither of the law was against the Muslim scriptures.[138]

The Committee further mentioned that the Hindus of Bengal

observed the custom of child marriage to a larger extent than the Muslims. According to the Report of the Committee, the age of puberty among girls was between eleven and thirteen and generally in the twelfth year. The latest census report reported that the average age of marriage among all communities in Bengal was stated to be twelve and half years and, it might consequently be supposed that twelve was about the average age of marriage among Hindus and 622 girls out of 1,000 were found in a married state between the ages ten to fifteen. Taking the numbers of all religions one may notice that the age of marriage had risen very moderately. It has been stated that 'In 1891, there were 827 unmarried girls between five and ten out of every 1,000 while in 1921 there were 891 showing an increase of 6.4 per cent, for the thirty years. In between the age group of ten to fifteen years, there were 372 unmarried girls in 1891 as against 494 in 1921 showing an advance of 12.2 per cent, for the three decades.' But even this increase did not provide an accurate picture of the number of girls who are unmarried at the critical ages of fifteen and sixteen. The writer of the Census Report of 1921 observed, 'In Bengal 9 out of 10 girls have been married before the age of 16 when none at all have yet been married in England.' A recognition of this considerable reality may aid in a more accurate assessment of the condition by those who believed that an Age of Consent Act of 1891 in marital relations was a unique development in India.[139] The reformers had been very much active in Bengal. The Brahmo Samaj rose up against some of these heinous customs. Other organizations of Bengal within the Hindu community were also working to bring about the much-needed reform.

According to Sekhar Bandyopadhyay, 'as literary and autobiographical evidence of this period suggested, child marriage was the universal norm in high caste *bhadralok* families, where girls were married off by the age of ten or eleven.' According to Ramkrishna Mukherjee's research in the late nineteenth century, '63 per cent of the caste Hindus and 31 per cent of the Scheduled Castes of Bengal practiced child marriage as the preferred form of wedding arrangement for their daughters.' It was no surprise that the Age of Consent Bill of 1891, suggesting to raise the age for the consummation of such marriages to twelve for girls, elicited such vehement opposition in

Bengal. The outcome of the enactment of this bill was equivalent to that of the Widows Remarriage Act of 1856. However, the census statistics of 1911 showed that while the educated upper caste *bhadralok* were steadily disowning this practice, the socially mobile, ambitious lower castes had increasingly begun to adopt it at the turn of the century.[140] The Namasudras, among whom early marriage was so extensively predominant, set on in their conference, 'so early as 1908, that the minimum age of Marriage should be ten years'.[141] But child marriage and widow celibacy instigated to increase in popularity, as in 1911, 22.2 per cent of the Namasudra girls in the age group of 5-12 years were either married or widows, the proportion being much higher than that among the traditional higher castes.[142] Other caste and communal conferences had attempted to abolish the evil through voluntary cooperation, but the progress had been so small and slow that most of the observers who arrived before us had given up hope of any significant modification simply through social reform.[143]

Table 4.7: Percentage of Married Women and Widows among the Females of Different Castes in the Age Group of 5 to 12[144]

Castes	*Percentage of married women and widows among the females of each caste in the age group of 5-12*
Baidya	5.1
Kayastha	8.8
Subarnabanik	11.1
Brahmin	16.0
Gandhabanik	16.3
Jalia Kaibartta	18.3
Namasudra	22.2
Kamar	23.3
Chasi Kaibartta (Mahishya)	25.9
Sundi or Saha	28.2
Sadgop	29.3
Tili and Teli	32.2
Goala	32.7
Pod	35.7

TABLE 4.8: STATEMENT SHOWING NUMBER OF WITNESSES FOR OR AGAINST MARRIAGE AND CONSENT LAWS

Provinces	*Total no. of witnesses*	*Marriage Law*			*Consent Law*			*No. of witnesses who want both the laws*	*No. of those who do not want any law at all*
		Number of witnesses who			*Number of witnesses who*				
		want marriage law	*do not want marriage law*	*have not said either way*	*want consent law*	*do not want consent law*	*have not said either way*		
Bombay	212	153	8	19	102	5	79	44	6
Madras	297	183	56	13	254	27	16	52	43
Assam	37	14	7	8	21	3	5	2	6
Bengal	129	74	39	9	72	25	18	15	24
B&O	64	44	4	8	28	6	26	7	9
UP	228	142	8	36	107	6	79	7	7
CP	80	52	4	13	38	3	29	4	6
Punjab and Shimla	78	50	3	11	17	1	38	8	
NWFP	41	26	2	13	19		22	4	
Ajmer-Merwara	12	3		6	5			3	
Delhi	31	20	3	6	21	1	9		

On the other hand, Jogendra Chakravarthi, Chairman of Dinajpur Municipality, admitted that if puberty was reached before thirteen, cohabitation was not postponed. He was against an alien Government interfering by legislation in religious and social questions and would leave the question to be solved by social reform. Charu Chandra Mitra had presented the Committee with several pamphlets on the subject of child marriage. The main argument, both in his pamphlets as well as in his statement, was that 'there was not a scrap of evidence to show that the present practice of consummation immediately after puberty injured the health of either the mother or the child'.[145]

The questionnaire of the Committee was distributed immediately to approximately 6,000 people and to 1,930 more through numerous local governments, with roughly 1,200 responding. The questionnaire received a broad and overall response (see Table 4.8)[146], demonstrating 'the great interest evinced in the question and the importance attached to it by the public in every Province.'[147] The Committee heard from a large number of lady witnesses from various parts of the country, all of whom had intense understanding of the situations of married life and maternity, allowing them to speak authoritatively about the emotions and opinions of at least the educated section of women in the country.[148] To determine the views of conventional women who were incapable to arrive and give evidence before the Committee, Purdah Parties were organized at some places in which the lady members of the committee attended and meetings of ladies of different shades of opinions were addressed by a lady member of the committee in Peshawar, Karachi, Ahmedabad, Bombay, Poona, Madras, Calicut and Madura and other places to afford occasion for an exchange of views and to create a general interest in the work of the Committee.[149] The Committee toured most of the provinces and recorded evidence at Lahore, Peshawar, Karachi, Delhi, Ahmedabad, Madurai, Vizagapatanam, Dacca, Shillong, Calcutta, Patna, Benaras, Allahabad, Lucknow and Nagpur and surveyed about 400 witnesses of different classes and shades of opinions, including medical men and women, social workers, leading representatives of different classes and communities and exponents of both orthodox and advanced opinions.[150] The evidence of the respondents opposing the proposed legislation was divided into two classes – those who were not in favour of social advancement through legislation, and those who were in favour of raising the age of marriage by social propaganda and not by social legislation. The question was raised as to whether legislation was the real remedy for this social problem. Unlike *sati*, the practice of child marriage was said to be based solely on the most personal and intimate relations between human beings, which were far above legal enforcement, it was claimed. The Assembly, it was argued, could not represent the entire population due to the limited scope of popular franchises. A few representatives from different communities were not capable to enact measures regarding 'social rights' or 'religious customs'.[151] However, the evidence of women doctors examined at different places had been of particular value.[152] The Committee's questions and recommendations, from the initial questionnaire to the final report, emphasized the health consequences not only of early marriages and early maternity, but also of a range of feudal gender traditions, notably the poor state of girls' education, *purdah*, and the confinement of parturient mothers in ill-lit and poorly ventilated *zenanas*. Only Muslim community leaders unanimously opposed the need for a legislative change, claiming that the *Shariat* already protected Muslim girls from early marriages.[153] Eleanor Rathbone has argued that with a number of typical passages, chiefly from the Joshi Report, exemplifying the nature of the sufferings arising from child marriage and finally narrating the conditions under which these sufferings were endured when, as happened in an excessive majority of cases, no medical or any other kind of skilled aid was available. As the 1931 Census Commissioner remarked of the Joshi Report that it is quite impossible to read it, in particular the medical evidence, with any approach to equanimity.[154] According to the Age of Consent Committee, 'The law of the Age of Consent was no doubt originally based on humanitarian considerations regarding the physiological fitness of girls for enduring the strain of early consummation. Circumstances have since changed greatly and various other arguments are now advanced to justify an increase, though the humanitarian ground still predominates.'[155] It had also been shown in the Committee's Report that early maternity was an evil. It made a significant contribution to maternal and infantile mortality in many cases damaged the physical system of the girl and commonly resulted in immorality in the physique of the race.[156] The witnesses recommended an increase in the age, particularly on the grounds of health of the mother and progeny and the appalling maternal and infantile mortality.[157] The issue of child marriage was quite often brought up in the framework of women's health. Apart from localized physical injuries, early cohabitation sometimes was a appalling experience that could severely damage the nervous system, the consequences of which were sensed throughout life, sometimes resulting in noticeable common frailty. In the case of early pregnancy, there was also the high risk of maternal mortality. The death rate, in particular, was very high in the first delivery and in ages less than fifteen. A report published on 1 February 1929 by Dr R. Adiseshan, Assistant Director of Public Health, Madras, showed that 'the proportion of maternal deaths were 51.28 per 1,000 for females less than fifteen years of age compared with 33.04 per 1,000 for those between the ages of fifteen and nineteen years.'[158] In the same way, there was 'a high risk of high neonatal mortality in the case of females below the age of fifteen, the figure being 186.05 per 1,000 as compared to 128.17 per 1,000 for females between the ages of fifteen and nineteen years.'[159]

Some examples of the medical testimony will demonstrate 'both their objectification of the female body and their ability to translate human distress into a fact, which stood in for, yet constituted, the state's real proof of the damaging experiential effects of early marriage.'[160] Some allopathic medical men, Dr S.K. Sen Gupta, Professor of Ophthalmology of National Medical College; Dr J.N. Moitra, Dr Ekendra Nath Ghosh, Professor of Medical College; Dr Nanilal Bhan and Dr J.C. Chatterjee, Teacher of Midwifery of Calcutta Medical School remarked that a girl was physically fit for sexual intercourse when she had reached puberty and that girls in this country attained puberty generally in their twelfth or thirteenth year. Furthermore, they were of the opinion that early maternity was not responsible for high maternal or infantile mortality.[161] At the same time, Sir P. C. Ray refused to lower the marriage age below fifteen, believing that the marriage law was more preferable. Mrinal Kanti Bose favoured the age of fifteen for Marriage legislation and sixteen for consent. Rebati Mohan Sirkar felt that legislation was absolutely necessary to secure the object in view and that fixing the age of marriage was the more effective remedy.[162] Dr Dube, the Health Officer of Lucknow, stated that the mortality of girls from 10 to 15 was nearly double that of boys of the same ages. According to him, two important factors, which contributed to early mortality were early maternity and purdah.[163] Dr Alice L. Ernst, working at Ackerman Hoyt Memorial Hospital in Jhansi, had seen cases too numerous to mention where the health of very young women was ruined through pelvis inflammations, specific and otherwise, by cohabitation with their husbands. Among those, there were traumatic cases that required prolonged treatment in hospital. Early and frequent cohabitation, early motherhood, improper care at the time of delivery, shattered the health of millions of women in India. So reduced have they became in strength (the *purdah* system had contributed to this result, too), that they became easy victims to tuberculosis. Many of the children of these mothers met an early death, and those that survived, had health much below what it should be.[164] Dr Edith Ghosh from Calcutta recounted an incident where a twenty-one-year-old Madrasi girl, after giving birth of her seventh child, said to Dr Ghosh that 'maternity would come on every year, she did not want to live and she died a few months later of inanition.'[165]

The Age of Consent Committee also reported that Rajkumari Das, Principal of Bethune College; Lady Pratima Mitra, Miss Jyotirmoyee Ganguli, Miss Leela Nag, Latika Bose and Mohini Devi were all firmly in favour of Marriage Law at sixteen and proposed eighteen as the minimum.[166] Miss Leela Nag of Deepali Sangha (Deepali Ladies' Association) and one of the organizers of Nari Shiksha Mandir (Women's Education Temple) reported before the Committee that in Bengal 'the health of the girls had been ruined because of cohabitation before physical development'. According to Miss Nag, without child marriage bill, early consummation of marriage could not be stopped. Legislation was the only way to put a stop to the increasing deterioration of the health and mind of a whole nation. She also felt that 'by raising the minimum age of marriage would provide greater facility for the education of girls.'[167] Later, a meeting was convened on 15 September 1929 on behalf of Deepali Sangha to support the Sarda Bill and protest against the comment of K.C. Neogy at the Legislative Assembly. More than three hundred women were present in the meeting, presided by Sarojini Ghosh and Suhasini

Biswas, Sujata Roy, Prabha Roy spoke in support of the Sarda Bill. It was resolved to support the bill.[168] Latika Basu, Secretary of Chittaranjan Seva Sadan (a hospital) of Calcutta, also recommended sixteen, though she would prefer eighteen as minimum age for marriage.[169] Dr M.I. Balfour of Bombay considered that early cohabitation and early maternity were responsible for some part of the high maternal and infant mortality in India and consequently for some part of the poor physique of many of the people. He also thought on medical grounds that cohabitation should not commence before sixteen at the earliest. He wanted to draw the attention of the Committee to the need for more careful investigation of problems connected with child birth and infancy in India.[170] Khan Bahadur Muhammad Akbar Khan, District Judge of Bannu, was adamant that the flaw of early marriage must be remedied through legislation. Khan Sahib Kazi Mir Ahmad Khan, Vice-President of the Peshawar Municipality, was of the same opinion. Khan Bahadur Sadullah Khan, Assistant Commissioner of Hazara; Khan Bahadur Kuli Khan, Assistant Commissioner and Nur Baksh agreed with them. All of them advocated fourteen as the minimum age of marriage and the same age for consent within the marital relation. Khan Bahadur Maulvi Saiduddin, Additional Judicial Commissioner, strongly urged for legislation. Nawabzada Muhammad Nasir Khan, District Judge, Dera Ismail Khan and Khan Bahadur Nawab Wali Mohammad were similarly strong in their opinion that sixteen should be the minimum age for marriage and consent. Khan Sahib Ghulam Sarwar Khan and R. Inayatulla of the Education Service were both for an advance by legislation and suggested fifteen years.[171] Syed Nawab Ali, a resident of Lucknow stated that the law of Islam in such matters was elastic, and judged in the light of the teachings of the Prophet, progressive and he would have no objection if a reasonable minimum age for marriage was fixed by legislation. Syed Wazir Hasan of the Chief Court, Lucknow, stated that he did not think that the fixing of an age of marriage by legislation would be an interference with Islam, but he was opposed to such legislation, because 'it would be treated by the people as an interference with their domestic affairs'.[172] But according to Haji Chaudhury Mohammed Ismail Khan, the present state of illiteracy in India made it imperative not to attempt any further advance on the present law, so far as it relates to married couples as it might lead to disastrous consequences. It was often forgotten that the age of consent was being attempted to be further revised at the instance of a few highly cultured people of the country who represented not more than 5 per cent of the population, but the law, aimed at, would apply not only to those 5 per cent but to 95 per cent of the illiterate mass as well. Ismail Khan argued that 'the law, as it was, had made more than sufficient advance already and no attempt should be made to make a further advance on the present law. The cultured people should look to social reforms for further improving the position.'[173] Mobilization of public opinion was another important suggestion made by some witnesses. They recommended the widespread use of propaganda against the evils of child marriage. For this purpose, the services of paid mullahs and maulvis, in the opinion of Mazhar Uddin, editor of *Alaman*, Delhi, could prove to be a very effective vehicle.[174] It was also suggested that special institutions for women be set up all over the country through which they could become self-reliant, capable of earning an honest living and would, thereby, be prevented from being forced into crime or destitution.[175]

On the other hand, a deputation on behalf of the All India Women's Educational Reform waited on the Committee at 4.15 p.m. on 8 January 1929. It consisted of Kamaladevi Chattopadhyay, Organizing Secretary; Sirirangamma, Mysore; Ishwari Nandan Prasad, Joint Secretary, Bihar; K.P. Jaiswal, Bihar; P.K. Sen, Bihar; S.K.P. Sinha, Bihar; and D.L. Nandeolyer, Bihar. A memorandum was handed over by the deputation of All India Women's Conference (AIWC) on educational reforms while giving evidence at Patna. The AIWC wanted to highlight the fact that it had at each of its three conferences documented its approval of Sir Hari Singh Gour's Age of Consent Bill with the provision that the age within marriage should be sixteen and outside marriage eighteen. It had also heartily supported the Bill to raise the age of marriage, recommending the ages of sixteen and twenty-one for girls and boys, respectively. It was of the obvious estimation that raising the age of consent without raising the age of marriage would be ineffective.[176] The deputation then clarified their opinion on various points. Concerning orthodox men and women who objected the Bill, the deputation members stated that many parents were perhaps afraid of social ostracism, and might welcome the change if it came as a law. In response to the argument that raising the age may lead to immorality, members of the deputation stated that young girls would be looked after as young widows were being looked after. They went on to say that 'child marriage was not sanctioned by the *shastras*. Raising the age of marriage ensured that guardianship of the girl remained in the hands of the parents, which would not be so if only the age of consent was raised.'[177] Jyotirmoyi Ganguli was connected with the educational institution named Vidyasagar Bani Bhavan (Widows' Home) in Calcutta. She informed that those girls who became mothers before fifteen suffered a lot as she came to know this from her mother, Kadambini Ganguly, the first Bengali woman doctor in India. Kadambini told her that it was very difficult for her to manage the delivery. Jyotirmoyi preferred fourteen for the minimum age of marriage for girls.[178] Margaret E. Cousins told the Committee that she had worked much to bring about satisfactory legislation to prevent early marriages and child motherhood, which as they existed in India were a blot on world civilization. She prayed that the investigation of the Committee would bring about a better era for the Brahmin girls. The girls of other castes did not suffer so much, but the millions of Brahmin girls must be saved from the inhumanity of degenerated religious customs. She relied on the power of legislation to remove the evils of child marriage and extramarital excesses just as legislation removed the horrors of *sati*, and she also believed that education and social propaganda had already sufficiently made ready the minds of the Indian people for social reform legislation to be a success, and to become the pivot of a purified and revitalized India.[179]

The journey of the Age of Consent Committee and the evidence they gathered from across India proved how Indians outside the Legislative Assembly considered legislation regarding the age of marriage issue. There was additional support for legislation from the ladies of the city of Lucknow and from the women of various castes and religion of the village Gosainganj, near Lucknow.[180] The ladies of Lucknow were consistently of opinion that a law fixing age of marriage at sixteen was necessary. One Kanyakubj Brahmin demanded marriage age at twenty and stated that she gave her three daughters' marriage at the age of twenty years.[181] In Gosainganj, members of the Kahar caste and Mohammedans said that the practice of child marriage used to be an evil custom and girl married early was put to great trouble in their husband's house. It should be stopped and it would be good if Government made a law.[182] The overall public, though, were not all so sympathetic towards legislation for raising the age of marriage.[183] The Committee visited two villages, Appantirupati and Kallandiri in the Madras Presidency on 28 November 1928, where the women who were present, said that they realized the evil effects of early maternity and consummation and they had no objection to the age of marriage being raised by legislation to fourteen and for consummation to sixteen. However, the men protested and said that it was difficult for them to keep and look after their girls when they had attained puberty.[184] Legislation would force several people to improve and modify their practices making social burden and advocacy less effective, but people could also find their ways around the laws.[185]

Dr (Miss) A.C. Scott, Secretary of Dufferin's Fund, Simla and Chief Medical Officer of the Women's Medical Service in Delhi, admitted that when she was in-charge of a hospital in Delhi, 'the bridegroom being in all cases over thirty years of age, the bride's age was usually about twelve and the most striking factor was that no case was brought to hospital in which there had not been fairly severe haemorrhage.'[186] Another argument that opponents of child marriage employed was that after marriage, young girls were forced to incur the heavy responsibility of a married life for which both their minds and bodies were utterly unprepared. In many ways, as Miss Khadijah Begum Ferozuddin, Professor of College for Women in Lahore stated that it was true that in India, there was no girlhood, they were either children or women.[187] According to Dr (Mrs) Malini B. Sukthankar, Honorary Physician for children at Cama and Albless Hospitals in Bombay,

> a woman is ... not physically fitted for the strain of child bearing, unless she has attained the age of at least seventeen; so that assuming impregnation to take place immediately after her attaining sixteen years, she would be just fit for giving birth to the child at the proper time, without causing lasting injury ... as a result of various circumstances, child-bearing started under that age is found to lead to (I) consumption, anaemia, neurasthenia, lowered vitality, hysteria and various other serious diseases following the premature strain, in

the case of the mother and (II) a very poor breed of children, who either do not live over a year or are sufferers from various diseases during childhood as a result of insufficient resistance and vitality, and die without reaching manhood or womanhood as the case may be.[188]

In Bombay, for instance, the only witnesses discussing the question of age of consent outside marriage were R.P. Masani, Vice-President of the Vigilance Society of Bombay;[189] Miss Katherine Davis, Secretary of the Children's Aid Society[190] and I.S. Haji, Barrister.[191] All of them mentioned the probability of raising the age of consent further in order to suppress prostitution.[192] On 7 August 1928, Kamaladevi Chattopadhyay, Honorary Organizing Secretary of All India Women's Conference on educational reform, stated that 'the age should be raised if the act was to be of any benefit to the girls concerned'. She was strongly of opinion that 'early consummation and early maternity were responsible for the deterioration of the country and she also mentioned that public opinion favoured the fixing of a minimum age of marriage by legislation in preference to the raising of the age of consent, except in the small very orthodox set of people who were in a hopeless minority'.[193] Dr (Mrs) S. Muthulakshmi Reddy, Vice-President of the WIA of Madras, supported wholeheartedly Rai Sahib Harbilas Sarda's efforts and in her opinion, 'legislation fixing the minimum age of marriage was the only effective and sure remedy'.[194]

The Age of Consent Committee's comprehensive survey of the problems under investigation had provided a large amount of valuable and interesting material for the social reformer; moreover, the publication of its report on 26 August 1929 had a more direct and practical significance.[195] The Committee recommended that the age of Consent within the marital relation be raised to 15 years[196] and that sexual intercourse by a husband with his wife below 15 years of age be made an offence and that the said offence be called marital misbehaviour and be included in Chapter XX of the Indian Penal Code dealing with offences relating to marriage[197] and the offence of marital misbehaviour be made punishable with imprisonment of either description for 10 years and fine when the wife is under 12 years of age.[198] The Committee also recommend that the age of Consent for the protection of a girl against rape by a person who was not her husband be raised to 18 years, though Section 361, Indian Penal Code, be amended by substitution of the word 'eighteen' for 'sixteen'[199] and 'in order to deal most effectively with the evil of early marriage and early consummation, a law be enacted fixing the minimum age of marriage of girls at 14 years'.[200] Its conclusion was filled with a strong eugenic sensibility, 'Early maternity is an evil and an evil of great magnitude. It contributes very largely to maternal and infantile mortality, in many cases wrecks the physical system of the girl and generally leads to degeneracy of the physique of the race.'[201] The Committee also reached the conclusion that not only early maternity, but also the frequency of births at short intervals coupled with the conditions under which birth took place had a robust bearing on maternal and infant health.

Following the publication of the Report of the Age of Consent Committee, the Bill was brought before the Legislative Assembly again on 4 September 1929, but was harshly rejected by M.K. Acharya, who raised a number of points.[202] In the first place, the voluminous report of 363 pages was published only a week before the session and, within such a short period, it was neither possible to read the whole of it, nor to scrutinize it in detail. Second, the Committee was not fully representative, and none of the original six members could properly represent the orthodox Hindu opinion. Moreover, the report contained contradictory statements.[203] Acharya stated that the questionnaire was sent out directly to about 6,000 persons and to 1,930 more through the various local governments, of whom about 1,200 responded, which was less than 15 per cent.[204] As regards orthodox ladies' opinions, there was a valuable admission at page six of the Report, 'The Committee has taken care to have the views of this latter class on record; . . . .The Committee, however, notes that, although efforts to get the opinions of orthodox ladies by direct evidence were made, they were not very successful.'[205] Acharya also told that the Committee had not inspired confidence in the minds of the orthodox section and no orthodox ladies would go before them. But there was a telegram from a lady in Kistna, which mentioned that 'on behalf of the women of Kistna, Child Marriage Consent Age Raising Bills condemned strongly interfering religion.' Another telegram from another lady from Kumbakonam, the home of orthodoxy, stated that 'large and influential Brahmin ladies' public meeting at Kumbakonam, held first September, under her presidentship, unanimously protested against Sarda's Marriage Bill pending Assembly and Committee's Report.' The telegram was signed by Valambalammal of Kumbakonam.[206] It was also admitted in the Report that the Moslem representation was very meagre. According to the Report, 'very few Muslim witnesses and theologians had appeared before the Committee.' At the end of the tour, the Committee reconvened at Delhi and a second chance was provided to the witnesses whose statements some of the members measured, was extremely beneficial to attain. But despite this, the reaction was insufficient.[207] But Maulvi Muhammad Yakub, who was on the Committee, expressed a different view and said in his minute that his 'first recommendation is that additional "Moslem" evidence should be brought on the record before the Marriage Bill came up before the House for final disposal.' Thus, according to Acharya, the report was based on 'insufficient evidence and a distorted questionnaire'.[208]

Rai Sahib Harbilas Sarda presented a petition signed by several thousands of opinions in favour of the Bill.[209] Amar Nath Dutt raised his voice against this proposed legislation. He stated that he regretted 'to observe that the Report deserved to be thrown into the waste-paper basket in respect of the evidence recorded'.[210] He reminded the Government how vehemently

> Ishwar Chandra Vidyasagar, late Sir Romesh Chandra Mitra, the first to hold the office of Chief Justice in British India, moved against the Age of Consent Bill; at the height of a movement of marrying girls at not less than fourteen years of age, the late Keshab Chandra Sen, married his own daughter just after twelve; how surreptitiously the polygamy in Bengal fell into disuse, how surely the economic causes were raising the marriageable age of girls, and how modern conditions were doing away with various social evils.[211]

India was the only place 'where marriage law, being diversified in different communities, should be maintained in their existing modes so that the creative thoughts of the youths of India may play freely in criticism and reform', as stated by Amar Nath Dutt.[212] The idea of Hindu child marriage as the epitome of conjugal felicity was imbedded in a patriarchal construction of Hindu society that spoke as if there were only one sex in this world, ignoring the views of women themselves.[213] Although organized Indian women's voices against child marriage did not emerge until the 1920s, signs of women's discontent with the system superseded this. Tanika Sarkar has cited eighteenth century devotional poetry, *Agamani* songs, lullabies and folk songs as depicting the bleakness of the young bride's experience of patrilocal marriage and the joint family system – *the son of a stranger is coming to take me away and I shall never play again*.[214] M.S. Sesha Ayyangar informed that there had been at least half a dozen meetings of ladies, held in Kumbakonam, Triplicane, Madras, Benares and last but not least, there was a meeting held in Cocanada. He said that all these ladies' gatherings were very influential, were well-attended and were thoroughly representative and in every one of these meetings, vehement protests were made against this Bill. Women who attended the meetings, called it 'a most pernicious Bill' and they objected against it on the exclusive basis that it undermined the Hindu religion in this country and they also went to the length of saying that, so far as their own experience was concerned, there was absolutely nothing to justify the demand for a legislation like this.[215] According to K.C. Neogy from Dacca, 'the practice of child marriage was prevalent in the provinces like Madras, Bengal, Punjab and Bihar and Orissa and these provinces were not wholly in favour of legislation'.[216] K.C. Roy was one of the few Bengalis who wholeheartedly supported the Bill. He vehemently protested against K.C. Neogy's arguments attacking the measure and his contention that the Bengal Government really opposed the legislation.[217] Abdul Haye of East Punjab pointed out that 'even the opinions that have been sent to the Government of India did not contain the views of more than half a dozen Muhammadans'.[218] This was what Maulvi Muhammad Yakub said in his minute of dissent, which supported Abdul Haye's contention – the fact remained that 'the Muslim point of view is not sufficiently represented' and Yakub did not think 'it would be proper and safe to introduce a measure of vast social and religious importance, until additional Muslim opinion, especially that of distinguished theologians, was placed on record'.[219]

Dr L.K. Hyder from Agra Division raised to support the Bill and to oppose strongly all amendments, all efforts, which would destroy the little social good that was embodied in that Bill.[220] He examined the answers of students coming from the whole of the United Provinces, Rajputana and the whole of Central India to a question in which they were asked to account for the high rate of mortality among infants. Hyder found that one and all, about 1,200 young men, attempted to answer that question and they said that one of the principal causes of this high mortality was this practice of child marriage.[221] Maulvi Mohammad Shafee Daoodi stated that he came from the Muzaffarpore district and he know how deeprooted the evils of child marriage were in their society, but he was not a believer in the methods adopted by the ardent supporters of the Sarda Bill. According to him, the greatest evil in the country was the illiteracy of the people, so he questioned, regarding 'the steps that the Government and the ardent supporters of this Bill had taken to eradicate that evil from the society'.[222] Shafee Daoodi commented that 'the Mussalmans had got a complete law of their own so far as marriage relationships were concerned'.[223] The Revd J.C. Chatterjee supported the motion that was moved by Harbilas Sarda. He reminded of another piece of legislation, which was enacted many years ago, the legislation for the abolition of *sati* (1929). It was well known that at that time a memorial presented to the Governor-General on which the thumb marks of 50,000 women were placed. These women pleaded that if the law against *sati* was passed, if *sati* was prohibited, then their religion would quiver and that they would commit satyagraha. Those 50,000 women had passed away, and no satyagraha took place. The present Bill was exactly the same kind of legislation. He thought it was very much more important because 'in the case of *sati*, it was one in ten thousand or even one in a million women who became a *sati*, whereas in this case, it was a long-drawn-out *sati*. In the case of millions of child widows, it was worse than *sati*, it was a long-drawn agony'.[224] He also told that Sayid Hassan Nizami appeared before the Committee and had expressed very distinct views favouring this legislation. So also, Saiyid Wazir Hussain strongly supported it. Dr Mufti Muhammad Sadeq of Kadian, a Mohammedan leader, had given strong support to it. He argued if they analysed the evidence and the statistics given in the Age of Consent Committee's Report, they did not find that the majority of Mohammadans had spoken against the Bill.[225] Mian Mohammad Shah Nawaz supported the motion that the Bill to regulate the marriage of children, as reported by the Select Committee, which would make it applicable to all communities, be taken into consideration.[226] He said that Muslim opinion on the whole was in favour of the bill. He also said that the educated women of India rightly said that they had been the victims of the evil custom of early marriage, early consummation and early maternity. The women of India were most vitally affected by this evil custom. They felt rightly that they were 'victimized and tyrannized'.[227] Shah Nawaz pointed out that Khawaja Hasan Nizami said that the present legislation which would penalize marriages of girls below fourteen was most beneficial in the interests of the Mohammedans, and must be passed and the same were the opinions of Maulana Suleman Nadvi and Maulana Mohamed Ali.[228]

D.K. Lahiri Chaudhury from Bengal stated that a reference to the Census Report of 1911 of Bengal, Bihar and Orissa would show that in districts where the percentage of child marriage was the highest, infantile mortality was least although the general mortality was very high. The numbers of married girls between the ages of five and ten were for the district of Darbhanga as high as 565 per 1,000 and for the district of Bhagalpur 435 per 1,000. In both these districts infant mortality was as low as about 13 per cent, although the rate of general mortality was about 35 per cent. In the districts of Balasore, Jalpaiguri and Darjeeling, the numbers of married girls between the ages of five and ten were only 56 per 1,000, 52 per 1,000 and 17 per 1,000 respectively.[229] He objected to this sort of legislation.[230] A.H. Ghuznavi completely opposed the bill and tried to remind that twenty-nine members of the House had written a letter to the Home Member on 13 September 1928, that they were opposed to Sarda's Bill:

> We the undersigned members of the Legislative Assembly are strongly opposed to Rai Sahib Harbilas Sarda's Hindu Child Marriage Bill as it strikes at the root of the most cherished and sacred institutions of Hindus and Muslims and penalizes what is lawful under the personal laws of Hindus and Muslims. We therefore request you to help us in opposing this measure, which affects our law and religion and against which orthodox public opinion has expressed itself or, at least, to maintain the oft-proclaimed neutrality in matters of religion by abstaining from voting on the Bill.[231]

Ghuznavi further informed the report of the Government of Bengal. The report mentioned that three District Judges, 18 recognized

Associations, 7 Bar Associations and the incorporated Law Society of Calcutta were consulted in the matter and copies of the replies received from the Indian Christian Association, the Buddhist Association of Chittagong, the Hillmen's Association of Darjeeling, the Marwari Association, the Jain Swetambari Terapanthi Sabha, the European Association of Calcutta and the Bar Association of the 24-Parganas, Tipperah, Dacca, Midnapore were forwarded for the information of the Government of India. From the replies received, 'it appears that the preponderating majority of opinion is against any legislation on the subject and only a minority of ardent social reformers is in favour of it. The Governor in Council is of the opinion that the Bill may be dropped.'[232] M.A. Jinnah asked whether there was any text, which made 'it obligatory on Mussalmans that they should get their daughters married before the age of 14!' He was not convinced that this Bill in any way militated against the rule of civil laws applicable to marriages amongst Mussalmans.[233] The resistance against this proposed measure was simply the outcome of the misplaced belief that it would interfere with religion. 'It was a fact', M.A. Jinnah noted, that 'people always looked upon these semi-religious usages and practices as the very foundation of their society and any suggestion or reform to change this usage was strongly resisted.' In countries like India, he suggested, where public opinion was not so developed, reforming agencies should not allow themselves to be influenced by public opinion, which could resent social reform in the name of religion. On the other hand, he said, Muslims had to have the courage to say, 'No we are not going to be frightened by that.'[234] Sir Purshotamdas Thakurdas and Lieutenant Colonel H.A.J. Gidney,[235] Pandit Motilal Nehru[236] supported the Bill.

M.K. Acharya argued that the Government had no right to interfere in the religious sacrament of any class of His Majesty's subjects, 'the sacrament might be sane or insane according to the view of some, but in the sacramental portion of it, in the religious portion of it, neither Government nor this House had any right to interfere'.[237] Pandit Nilakantha Das said that whatsoever might be the aim of the reformers in having this penal Act in this form, 'Indians had not come to a stage when the boys and girls would choose their own mates and perform their own marriages and would be themselves responsible for anything happening before and after marriage.'[238]

The Muslim witnesses before the Committee might be divided into three classes – first, those who held that early marriage was not evil and had no effect either on the mother or her progeny, that it was also permitted by Muslim Law and was sanctioned by the practice of the Holy Prophet and other eminent personages and that any legislation fixing a minimum age of marriage would be an interference in Islam. Second, those who held that though early marriage was to a certain extent an evil, as shown by the medical evidence, it was not such a great evil as to justify interference on the part of the government. In their view, the custom would automatically die out with the gradual growth of education, social awareness and better economic conditions. The third category of witnesses comprised those who held early marriage to be a positive evil, ruinous to the health and the progress of the community and against the principles and teachings of Islam. They would not rely merely upon social reform and progress of education but were in favour of taking a bold step by legislation in the best interest of the community. They did not agree with Ulemas and Maulavis who thought that marriage legislation or raising the age of consent would be an interference with the principles and teachings of Islam.[239]

On 19 September 1929, Maulvi Mohammad Shafee Daoodi stated that the Muslim Members of the Assembly were of the opinion that any change in the personal law of Muslims of India should depend on the Muslim votes only of the Legislature.[240] According to Maulvi Muhammad Yakub, 'it was highly objectionable on the part of Muslims to discard and denounce the considered and weighty opinions of the Ulemas and theologians of their faith.' He was really surprised to see that 'some of his friends had lightly brushed aside the weighty and sound pronouncement of Ulemas like Molana Mufti Kifayat-ullah Saheb, President of the Jamiat-ul-Ulema, Maulvi Ahmad Saied Saheb and Molana Moulvi Husain Ahmad Saheb, President of the Theological Academy at Deoband.'[241] Yakub also informed that since this Bill was taken up in this House, they had been receiving a large number of telegrams, letters and proceedings of Muslim meetings denouncing the Bill and asking them to vote against its application to the Mussalmans. He referred to the most important ones. One was from Maulvi Kifayat-ullah, President of the Jamiat-ul-Ulema, in which he said that the present marriage bill was an interference with the Muslim law, and he called upon the Muslim Members of this Assembly to oppose it.[242] A.H. Ghuznavi stated that

> Islam was a self-contained and self-sufficient religion. The treaty by which Shah Alam the Emperor of India, delegated to the East India Company the civil administration of India reserved the right of the Mussulmans to be governed according to the law of their religion, and the British Government as the successor of the East India Company was bound by that treaty and undertakings of the East India Company.[243]

According to Harbilas Sarda, 97 per cent of the population consistently supported the Bill and the opinions of the remaining 3 per cent showed that most of them were in favour of the Bill. 'As regards Bengal', Sarda further mentioned,

> much had been made of the fact that the Provincial Hindu Conference at Dacca refused to accord its support to this Bill. Those who were acquainted with the circumstances of that Conference know the peculiar condition in which this was done. But the Secretary of the Provincial Bengal Hindu Sabha wrote to the Bengal Provincial Hindu Sabha in its general meeting unanimously passed resolution supporting Sarda Bill.[244]

Some members of the Legislative Assembly agreed that early marriage should be abolished, but considered that reform should achieve through other means. K.C. Neogy informed that Justice P.R. Das, despite his legal background, was opposed to the Sarda Bill and clarified on 23 September 1929 that 'social legislation may serve as an eyewash; but it has no effect whatsoever on the people. If the legislation be in advance of the social and moral consciousness of the people, then it will be disobeyed in practice, without any one being the wiser for it. If it be the other way, then legislation is not needed.'[245] M.K. Acharya expressed yet another concern that legislative members like Sir Sivaswamy Aiyar and Diwan Bahadur T. Rangachariar were not religious heads and therefore should not interfere in religious laws: 'They are no more competent to speak on religious matters than I am competent to speak about what is happening in Iceland. I am prepared to admit that among the English educated people of India, 90 per cent are perhaps in favour of the Bill; and I put the blame at the door of the Government, which has enslaved our intellects.'[246] M.K. Acharya was assured that cases of the sexual misbehaviour of girls and boys would raise and contended that early marriage was actually protecting children, preserving their honour. He specified on 23 September 1929 that 'the Government might perhaps prevent three lakhs child widows by this legislation; but at the same time, by this legislation, it would give room within the next ten years, to three million unmarried women wandering about the streets, who would be either victims of abduction and seduction or aggressive parties thereof.'[247] Pandit Madan Mohan Malaviya opposed the Bill. However, the Bill was carried by 67 votes against 14 and the motion was adopted.[248]

A part of the people supported the bill and wrote letters to the editors of newspapers in support of it. It was written in the pages of *Prabasi* that child marriage was prevalent among the lower and poor people in Bengal and there was no doubt that those girls would be benefitted if the marriage age would increase.[249] The Bill became the Child Marriage Restraint Act (XIX of 1929), popularly known as the Sarda Act, on 1 October 1929. The Original Bill applied to Hindus, Jains, Sikhs, Brahmos, Arya Samajists and Buddhists, or people who profess systems of faith, which are offshoots of Hinduism, i.e. persons governed by the Hindu law. The Bill, as redrafted by the Select Committee and passed into law, applied to all classes and communities in British India. Child marriage though common among the Hindus could not be said to be altogether unknown to the other communities. The object of the Act was to restrain child marriages. Therefore, the law should govern the whole people of British India.[250] The Act came into force on 1 April 1930.[251] Section 2 of this Act dealt with the minimum age at which marriage should be solemnized. The age of the boy was fixed at eighteen and the age of the girl at fourteen years. A great deal of debate had fumed round the latter age. Those who characterized conservative Hindu opinions and who sat on the Select Committee articulated the views that it should be lowered to twelve years. Setting an age limit was not an easy task, and there were bound to be differing viewpoints. Having regard to the belief of conventional Hindus that a girl should be married before she attained puberty, the age fourteen set for girls in the Act was high. A statement of the ages of marriage, which obtained in other countries was found in the Report of the Age of Consent Committee.[252]

However, the public press was divided on this issue. Gour's Age of Consent Bill and Sarda's Child Marriage Restraint Bill both took up a lot of newspaper space. *Ananda Bazar Patrika*, *Advance*, *Bengalee*, *The Hindusthan*, *Bangabani* and periodicals like *Modern Review* and *Prabasi* enthusiastically supported these reforms as part of their undertaking to revitalize Hindu society and prevent women from converting to the 'other' faith. Newspapers like *Amrita Bazar Patrika*, *Dainik Basumati*, *Bangabasi*, *Hitavadi* and most Muslim papers like *Soltan* (Daily) and *Masik Mohammadi*, on the other hand, showed 'anti-reform' sentiments as a result of foreign intrusion in their 'domestic affairs'. *Hanifi* (weekly), *Islam Darshan*, *Moajjin*, *Al-Muslim* (weekly), *Bangla Gazette* (weekly), and *Ahle Hadis* (weekly) vehemently opposed the Sarda Act. They published reports of meetings organized by the orthodox ulemas against the bill. The exception was the monthly and weekly *Saogat* and *The Mussalman*. *Hanifi* declared that Child Marriage Restraint Bill was wholly opposed to *Shariat* and termed the Bill as *Abaidha Bibaha Bidhi* (Illegal Marriage Rules),[253] and also as *Pagla Bill* (Crazy Bill).[254] Under the heading, 'Samajik Bishaye Ain' (Law Regarding Social Matter), the editor of *Saogat* wrote that 'the Quran did not stipulate a specific age for marriage or consent. So, it was more appropriate to interpret the silence of the Quran to mean that laws must be enacted according to the need of different countries and societies'.[255] By supporting the Bill, *The Mussalman* wrote that 'We wish to make it clear that we are emphatically against child marriage ... such a law is necessary in the interests of girls.'[256] It was also written in the pages of *The Mussalman* that 'the Bill will be passed in spite of the opposition of the so-called orthodox sections of the Muslims and Hindus in the Legislature and thus a great social evil will be put to an end'.[257]

But protest meetings were held all over Bengal against the Sarda Act. A part of the Hindusthan continued to denounce the Sarda Marriage Act and meetings of Mohammedans for this purpose were held in Calcutta and Chittagong. These protests, however, did not seem to have aroused much interest.[258] Not only Raja Raghunandan

Prasad, but members of the Council of State also tried to repeal the law but failed.[259] There had been a good deal of agitation over the Sarda Act and an attempt was made to have a *hartal* throughout the province on 29 November 1929. The agitation did not appear to have been very successful anywhere. In Malda District, leaders of the Malda Association decided against a *hartal* and in Rangpur, the meeting was captured by some youths mostly belonging to the college, who put in their present President and passed a resolution in favour of the Bill.

> There was a large meeting in Calcutta presided over by Dr A. Suhrawardy, member of the Legislative Assembly at which the usual resolution was passed. There was considerable difference of opinion on the subject of the Act, but it undoubtedly had disturbed a certain section of orthodox opinion and might be used as a means of stirring the Government.[260]

The agitation against this Act continued in certain districts in the province and the commissioner of the Burdwan Division reported that 'marriages had been speeded up in Bankura District and in the Tamluk Subdivision of the Midnapur district.'[261] At the same time, a counter meeting was held in South Calcutta under the Presidentship of Abul Kashem to support the Sarda Act.[262]

There had been a great rush of early marriages throughout the province irrespective of higher and lower caste or class people in anticipation of the Sarda Act coming into force. Wajir Hossein, Judge of Chief Court of Lucknow arranged a marriage ceremony for his four years old daughter with the six-year-old son of the Maharaja of Mahmudabad.[263] *Prabasi* reported that there would be seven thousand such marriages which were performed in Bombay before the enactment of the Sarda Act.[264] Saralabala Sarkar in one of her essays stated that even after the passage of this bill, child marriage was taking place openly in rural and urban areas. But there was not much mention of these incidents in the newspapers, one or two cases of child marriages were hardly reported in the newspapers. According to her, many in our society had no idea how far child marriages were harmful. Child widowhood was the result of this practice; premature motherhood was the reason behind the increase in maternal and child mortality – all these were leading to the decline of the Hindu society. For this, the law should be changed in such a way that the plaintiff did not have to take the risk of depositing money, as recommended by Saralabala Sarkar. Although, the court had such power that a magistrate could stop child marriage if anyone gave notice before the marriage took place.[265] The District Magistrate of Bogra reports that sometimes children of a few months old were being married. But the agitation against the act seems to have died down. A meeting of the Mussalmans of Calcutta and the suburbs was held under the auspices of Jamiat Ulemai Bangla at the *maidan* near the Ochterlony Monument on 17 January 1930 from 2.30 p.m. to 5.30 p.m. to protest against the application of the Child Marriage Act known as the Sarda Act. There was an attendance of 5,000 men. Besides the main meeting, one more meeting was also held and four processions from the Kidderpur, Naziratalab, Panchanantala-Howrah, Kalabagan respectively and one of the Peshwaris joined the meeting. The processions carried black flags as well as other banners. One of them was written *Sarda Bill Gollay jak* (Sarda Bill be damned) and on another was written 'We do not want Sarda Act'. The proceedings commenced at about 2.30 p.m. with recitations from the *Quran*. Sufi Abu Ballav was voted to the chair. He spoke in Urdu. He said that a critical time had arrived. Queen Victoria had proclaimed in 1858 that there would be no interference in religion. The *Quran* did not put any restriction on the age of marriage. The *Hadis* prescribed that marriage should be performed as soon as the girls attend majority. It is foolishness to think that religious question should be decided in any parliament. It should be done by the ulemas only. They would obey all laws but not these, which went against the *Quran* and the *Hadis*. He warned the Government that to give effect to the Act would be disastrous matter. He also warned the Hindus that to annihilate eight crore Mussalmans, 80 crore Hindus would be required. The Mussalmans were not afraid of guns and rifles. He appealed to break the Sarda law. He said it would not be well if he be compelled to oppose Government with three lakh of his disciples. With regard to the present situation, he said that India would then be converted into a *Dar-Ul-Harb* (i.e. a country of the enemy) and *Hadis* even provided that the matter could be set at right by force. He then left the meeting and Maulana Muhammad Nooruddin of Bihar was put on the chair.[266] A volunteer named Syed Ghazi Shah of Afghanistan with Mullajan Mohammad and a few others recited a song in Urdu, 'Give up shedding of tears give up weeping/ If you have the will of martyrdom/ Your heads sacrificed in the cause of truth'. Syed Fazal Shah Afghani said that there was nothing more than the *Quran* in their estimation. Next there was the *Hadis*. They warned the Government that these Muslims who had said in the Assembly that Sarda Act was not interfering with *Shariat* had misled them. He asked them to follow the *Quran*, so that Government might help them and the oppressive Government may be removed from over their heads. The Muslims, their wives and children would not allow the humiliation of the *Quran*. They should be ready to sacrifice their lives. Nooruddin, the President, said that the Government would be compelled to withdraw the Act so long as a single Mussalman lived in India. If by April, Government would not except the Mussalmans from the application of the Sarda Act, they would lay their hands before the Government but would not obey the Act.[267]

The following resolutions were unanimously adopted:

> First, considering the Sarda Act a direct interference with religion, expressing condemnation and calling upon Mussalmans to disobey it for the protection of the *Shariat* and Government to spare any sacrifice whatsoever. Second, declaring the Cattle Protection Bill to be introduced on 22 January 1930 to be a move for stopping cow slaughter and considering it an interference with religion and appealing to the Viceroy to have it withdrawn. Third, forming a local branch of *Majlisi Taha Huz-i-Namus-i Shariat* (Association for the Protection of the Honour of the Shariat) of Delhi with the following office-bearers – Safi Abu Bakar as Patron, Hakim Abdur Rouf as President, Haji Fakir Muhammad as Vice President, H.S. Suhrawardy as Vice President, Amiruddin of Sylhet as Secretary, Khalilur Rahman as Assistant Secretary, Abdul Hakim of Hanafi as Assistant Secretary, Hakim Muhammad Fazil as Treasurer, Azad of Hardoi (the last speaker). There were some enthusiasm displayed at the meeting.[268]

The Chief Secretary to the Government of Bengal wrote to the Commissioners of Dacca, Presidency, Burdwan, Chittagong, Rajshahi that Government had noted in newspapers accounts of various meetings in connection with the Sarda Act. Therefore, the

Commissioners were requested to submit a short report showing the attitude of the Hindus and the Mohammadans in their division towards this Act.[269]

The Commissioner of Burdwan Division, Chinsurah, G. Goode stated that

> I have interviewed in the past 3 months official and non-official but still find it difficult to give any decided opinion as to the seriousness and extent of any agitation, which may follow the enforcement of the Act. As to the Mohammedans, one educated Maulavi at Hooghly, a Khan Saheb says that the Sarda Act is opposed to the Mohammedan religion, since the prophet himself married a girl of 6 years and his example has the force of precept.... I think that very orthodox old-fashioned maulavis dislike the Act (1) on principle because it interferes with socio-religious custom and that if they wished to do so, they could very easily fan the opposition to this measure, which now exists among their illiterate co-religionists to serious heights; (2) because they think the Act is unwise in itself and ignores the social conditions of India; thus they fear that girls who in this country attain maturity rapidly, will go astray before reading the new marriageable age. I think that the illiterate Mohammedans are in the mass opposed to the Bill, they dislike of course change and compulsion, they like to get the problem of marriage solved as early as possible because it is one less anxiety left to vex them, they fear irregular unions with adolescent girls and lastly these is a kind of shame in a girl's menstruation going on without marriage.... Some educated Mohammedans with whom I have discussed the Act, think the people will get used to it but my own impression is that as a community, Mussalmans dislike this legislation. As to Hindus, the educated Bengali who is not conservative and old-fashioned in his religious ideas seems to me to give Act his blessings. Already he has recognized the evils of child marriage and in fact does not require legislation so far as he himself is concerned and naturally he views with anxiety, perhaps even with some complacency, the enforcement of ideas, which he has already voluntarily adopted....Thus Act will make little difference to Bhadralok, but a portion of them may resent the Act.... Generally speaking, I would say that the Act finds supporters from conviction only amongst the progressive and enlightened Bengalis, amongst whom the marriageable age has been voluntarily raised within the last 20 or 30 years that there is a section, which is indifferent to it and the mass of the population of Bengal dislike it. Personally, I think there is ground for anxiety if the Act is strongly enforced. As to propaganda, I think it may do some good but that is unlikely to remove objections, which are deeply rooted.[270]

The Commissioner of Rajshahi Division, Jalpaiguri informed that some meetings were held at Bogra – '13 against the Bill, 3 in favour of the Bill' and 'Little response to *hartal* of 29th. Liberal minded people of both communities are in favour of post puberty marriage.' At Pabna 'On 29th a partial *hartal* – no serious agitation – the agitation will die down. The lower classes of both communities are against the act.' In Malda, 'Local Mohammedans refused a *hartal* on 29th – no agitation here.' Many meetings were held against the Act in the interior in Rangpur. A meeting at Rangpur to denounce the Act was captured by students who adopted a resolution in favour of the Act. No agitation was taken place in Darjeeling. In Dinajpore, meetings against the Act but no *hartal* on the 29th had been reported. No marked interest in the Act in Jalpaiguri. At Rajshahi, no indication of serious discontent had been seen and marriages of minors were being rushed on.[271]

The Commissioner of Ramna (Dacca) wrote that

> Educated Hindus have already raised age of marriage. Some orthodox Hindus are in favour of early marriage. Mohammedans opposed the act as an attack on their religion. Some people like Bahadur Chaudhury Kaziuddin Siddiqui seem to hold the view that the Act is really open to objection from a religious point of view....The fact that marriages are being hurried on before the date on which the Act will come into force however seems to show that there is not at present any general intention to disobey the provisions of the Act.[272]

The District Magistrate of Dacca, C.M. Martin reported that

> Attitude of Hindus towards the Act was divided – orthodox Hindus, educated or not and most of the uneducated Hindus are opposed to the Act. There will be determined opposition among certain classes of Hindus. Basaks of Dacca are determined to defy it. The Mohammedans are divided in their opinion. A very strong class of upper caste Mohammedans is opposed to it. That the bill was introduced by a Hindu was a factor. They are capable of carrying the greater part of Muslim population with them.[273]

The district officer of Mymensingh, G.S. Dutt, ICS said that

> Among the Hindus there is a small section, which warmly welcomes the Act. The majority of the Hindus in rural areas however, while seriously against the Act, are not very particularly enthusiastic about it. The Mohammedans are particularly in a body opposed to the Bill in a more or less violent measure. The educated section of the Mohammedans who know very well that the

Act does not in any way transgress Mohammedan laws have nevertheless fomented discontent with a view to achieving popularity with the mass. A great deal of misrepresentation has been circulated.... Cases of abduction of Hindu and Mohammedan girls by Mohammedans is extremely common in this district. Hindus and Mohammedans fear this Act may increase cases of abduction – so they want repeal and modification of the Act.[274]

The District Magistrate of Faridpur informed that

Only one or two sporadic incidents of little or no importance in connection with the agitation. The meeting on 27th January at Rajbari, was addressed by Dr Pratap Chandra Guha Roy. He said that Swarajists were not responsible for the Act. Bengal members opposed it. Government members supported it. Both Hindus and Muslims view the Act with disfavour as an intervention on their religious and social customs. A large number of marriages took place on the eve of passing of the Act.[275]

The District Magistrate of Barisal stated that

A large public meeting at Barisal – 1,000 Hindus and Muslims attended – there were 5 Mohammedan and Hindu speakers. Only argument against the Act was that it interfered with religion. Rush of marriages suggests that there will no such determined opposition. Among educated Hindus there was no great objection. There is great ignorance among the masses regarding the Act.[276]

The Commissioner of Chittagong said that

It is true that there has been a certain amount of agitators among the Mussalmans and also among the orthodox section of the Hindus against the provisions of the Act, but I do not think the feeling is sufficiently strong or organized to be of any danger to peace or embarrassing to Government. The younger sections of Mohammedans are in favour of the Act and so are educated Hindus.[277]

The District Officer of Chittagong was of opinion that 'Hindus are in favour of the provisions of the Act but apprehensive that the machinery will be used to enforce it. Mohammedans are opposed to this Act on religious ground.'[278] Magistrate's office of Noakhali informed that

Among educated Hindus, there is practically no opposition to the Act – enlightened public opinion of the Hindus is overwhelmingly in favour of the Act. Conservative Brahmins are opposed to the Act. Noakhali Brahmin Sammilani organized a meeting. An unusual number of marriages lately in the district among lower class of illiterate Hindus shows acceptance of the Act … over 85 per cent of the population of this District are Mohammedans of whom less than 5 per cent are literate. From what I have understood of them, these ignorant illiterate masses seem to be an easy prey to the fantastic Maulavis and Mullahs. Whenever they appeal to them in the name of religion, Maulavi Maniruddin Islamabadi of Chittagong came to this District and addressed several meetings during the last 3 or 4 months to create popular Mohammedan opposition against this Act. Maulavi Ibrahim of Feni also did the same. Their efforts have not been in vain. The *hartal* observed here on the 29th was complete and effective.… It would, therefore, to my mind, be a mistake to apply the provisions of the Act stringently and rigorously for some years to come.[279]

It was informed from the Commissioner's office of Presidency Division, Calcutta,

There can, I think, be no doubt that, with the exception of a comparatively few educated and unorthodox Hindus, there is a general undercurrent of dissatisfaction against this Act felt by both communities. Mohammedan opinion is specially opposed to it. The feeling is of course, that legislature should not interfere with the social and religious customs of the people. At the same time, there does not appear to be any widespread or serious agitation against this Act and the fact an unprecedented number of child marriages is now being celebrated through the division would go to show that the people in general have no intention of disobeying the provisions of the Act. The SDO Barrackpore, however, thinks it likely that the upcoming element in his Subdivision will ignore the Act. Nabadwip pandits organized a protest meeting.[280]

Nearly 5,000 Mohammedans were present at Calcutta Maidan Meeting on 17 July 1930, which was already been mentioned. The speeches were all objectionable. The song recited by an Afghan Syed Gazi Shah was also objectionable. Safi Abu Bakr – a *pir* of Hooghly with 30,000 followers – most of the Chandney shopkeepers were under his influence. Syed Gazi Shah and Syed Fazlal Shah were Peshwari volunteers.[281]

A section of Muslims and Brahmins stood firm in their opposition, and at first, some cautious defiance of the law was reinstituted.

Regrettably, the passage of this law coincided with the Civil Disobedience Movement of 1930-1, and the government at that time could not sustain to cause problems for itself by strictly enforcing the law and alienating the 'ultra-conservative' segment of the population on whose assistance it depended. The Government hence slept over the violations of the law and in the odd cases in which 'prosecutions' were initiated, it was acknowledged that 'Government instructions were issued to the magistracy for lenient treatment of the culprits'. As a result, the Act had a disastrous start, and it was widely known that even now it was honoured more in the breach than the observance. In the villages, the illiterate masses were blissfully unaware of the existence of such a law and infant marriages took place every day as a matter of course. In the towns, some flouted the law deliberately, others who were more law-abiding adopted the device of crossing over to neighbouring Indian States or foreign territory where such a law did not exist and thus evaded the Act. However, the vast majority of violations of the law went unnoticed in British India. Nevertheless, this would not mean that the Act was a complete 'dead letter'. Prosecutions under the Act were common, despite accounting for a minor portion of all violations of the law. Cases of certain prosecutions were reported in the press almost every day. Social reformers had organized Sarda Committees to make the law effective in various parts of the country. These Committees carried on their work unostentatiously but had to work against great odds. For the public, 'social conscience was not sufficiently aroused to help them nor did they anywhere have the support of the Government'.[282] Soon after the enactment of the Bill in 1929, the *Jamiat-ul-Ulama-i-Hind* decided to protest against it all over the country. At its ninth annual session held in May 1929 at Amroha the *Jamiat* passed 'a resolution moved by Maulana Hifzur Rahman condemning the Sarda Act as an unjustified interference with Muslim Personal Law and urging the Muslims to overthrow the British administration by cooperating with the Indian National Congress in the independence struggle.'[283] On the other hand, one of the earliest and most vocal social critics, Nausher Ali Khan Yusufazai mentioned with concern the practice of child marriage in his classical work *Bangiya Mussulman* (Bengali Muslims). Sometime later, Mohammad Meherullah Hussein from Sirajganj wrote a reformist tract on child marriage in 1909. In it he stated that 'Muslim society was rampant with ill practices rather than beneficial ones, of which child marriage topped the list.'[284] He suggested twenty and fourteen as the ages when boys and girls should be married off by their parents, thus apprehending the recommendations of the CMRA of 1930. Although, it was not unusual to have daughters married at the age of ten or twelve as late as 1930. One *bhadramahila* writing a short memoir around 1980 mentioned to the age at marriage in her mother's time in the first half of the twentieth century, 'I have heard from mother that girls were married off at the age of ten in her time. She was married at twelve and soon went off clad in a burqa to join her husband in Burdwan where he was posted by the Government'.[285]

On 21 June 1929, *Ananda Bazar Patrika* wrote regarding the Sarda Bill, 'The problems of society of the twentieth century will be solved by the leading minds of the twentieth century; it is foolish to resort to some dead or obsolete *smriti shastra* citations.'[286] Men do not observe the injunctions of Manu, but the unmanly men are always ready to subject women to those injunctions. Even the most traditional household manuals for housewives, for example, *Garhasthya-dharma* [Domestic-Religion (path of rightness or duty)] (1904) by Nagendra Bala Mustafi, *Griha-dharma* [Home-Religion (path of rightness or duty)] (1934) by Priyanath Bose, *Swamee-stree* (Husband-Wife) (1933) by Nandlal Mukherji and so on, rarely depended on the authority of the *shastras*. Though the object might be to defend a traditional institution or practice, the presentation was in terms of social needs in modern times. It is often no more than a garb for a highly conservative message. A series of lessons for the housewife in the form of a conversation between husband and wife by Prafulla Kumar Dhar (1925) ran as follows, 'In our country, a section of our educated persons is eager to bring about the liberation of women (*stree-swadhinata*). But this should be taken into account that how far this will be good for this country lacking independence. Having been encaged like birds, century after century … our women cannot freely fly when you free them from the cage.'[287] While in Ishwar Chandra Vidyasagar's times, 'the case for widow remarriage rested mainly on reinterpretation of the *shastras*', in the late 1920s discussions on the Sarda Bill against child marriage inclined to appeal to such an authority only incidentally.[288] The 1920s or 1930s did not see anything like a women's movement. 'Bengali society', said an editorial in *Ananda Bazar Patrika* in 1923, 'shows great anxiety to point to women's duties, and an equally great disregard for women's rights'.[289] There were so many issues related to women's rights in the 1920s like civil rights, age of consent, and right of succession.[290] There is no doubt that the question of raising the age of consent to eliminate child marriage came to a head in 1929 when Harbilas Sarda proposed in the Indian Legislature his celebrated Bill. This was one issue on which there was a concerted agitation by women's organizations against conservative opinion. Typical of the latter was the Hindu Provincial Conference, which later was merged with the Mahasabha. Meeting at Dhaka in August 1929, the Hindu Provincial Conference of Bengal resolved against the Sarda Bill.[291] Some papers, most prominently the *Basumati*, strongly opposed the Bill. The conservative argument was that to wait till the girls attained the age of sixteen would encourage premarital sex; there was also a section of conservatives opposed to child marriage, but also to legislation because that would allow the state to intervene in matters that ought to be left to Hindu society to take care of. The supporters of the Sarda Bill easily refuted these absurdities; what was interesting in this conflict was the outright rejection of *shastric* authority.[292]

The AIWC began mobilizing support for the passage of the Sarda Bill as soon as it was introduced in the Legislative Assembly. Throughout 1929-30, branches of the AIWC set up small committees to watch and prevent child marriages by persuasion and pressure; by propaganda through press and platform; by means of magic lantern lectures, popular songs and holding protest meetings. When the Sarda Act was passed, women leaders declared it as their victory and sensed that their victory was firm evidence of nationalist support for women's rights. The celebrations, however, proved to be premature. After it was passed, the Act was basically neglected.[293] Anxious about this, the AIWC and other women's organizations petitioned the government to amend the Act to make it easier to prosecute offenders, and established vigilance committees. Sadly, despite their best efforts, there were very few prosecutions. Ironically, the most important lesson of the Sarda Act was to demonstrate the women who endorsed it, how powerless they were when it came to enacting social change through legislation. However, when in 1929, Muslim male legislators were demanding for the exclusion of Muslims from the Act, the AIWC protested against this by sending an appeal to the Viceroy: 'We, speaking on behalf of the Muslim women of India, assert that it is only a small section of Musalmans men who have been approaching your Excellency and demanding exemption from the Act. The Act affects girls and women far more than it affects men and we deny their right to speak on our behalf.'[294] A resolution was passed to keep the Sarda Act intact and applicable to all communities. This was a watershed moment when the issue of Muslim girls was brought into the women's movement of the time, allowing Muslim women to speak for themselves. The striking aspect is how easily women used the 'language of rights' in their demands.[295] A number of dominant members of the Muslim community sent a petition to the Viceroy to oppose the proposal to exempt Muslims from the confines of the Sarda Act. But the battle was far from over. At the same time, the *Times of London* reported that 'the whole Afghan border had been saturated with propaganda about the Sarda Act causing great excitement and resentment among Muslim tribes, and adding to the already endemic instability in that region at the time.'[296]

The AIWC passed a resolution at Lahore on 12 January 1931, 'urging the government to keep the Act intact and to enforce it strictly. It urged all its branches, the youth, women social reform associations and others to educate public opinion and persuade individuals to obey the law and to report cases of violation of the Act.'[297] It had also been mentioned in the Annual Report (1931) of AIWC that 'some protest meetings were held in practically every constituency and telegrams were sent by them to the Viceroy, the Home Member and the Secretary to the Legislative Assembly.'[298] Even after the passing of the Sarda Bill into law, the AIWC continued its efforts to make the law more effective. An important resolution was passed during its twelfth session held at Nagpur in 1937, which condemned 'the unnatural and devitalizing custom of allowing immature girls to become wives and mothers on the grounds that it robbed them of their right to education and freedom and seriously impaired their mental, moral and physical growth.'[299] In the same way, the WIA emphasized the need for women to secure their civil rights through legislation. To eradicate the evil custom of child marriage, the Association passed several resolutions, including one that was passed by the first International Conference held under the auspices of the Association in 1936 at Calcutta.[300] The Calcutta branch of the AIWC organized another meeting at the Albert Hall supporting the Sarda Act and demanding its proper implementation. Sarala Devi Chaudhurani presided over the meeting. The meeting determined that committees would be established all over the country so that suitable action could be taken against those who dishonoured the Act. They requested that 'to prevent child marriage in remote villages, the power of the presidency magistrates and district magistrates to implement the Act should also be given to the sub-divisional judges.'[301] Some resolutions were adopted regarding child marriage at the annual meeting of the Calcutta Branch of the AIWC, held on 9 November 1937, 'We request the new provincial Governments and Legislatures to give evidence in no uncertain terms of their support for so essential a measure.' And the resolution was moved by S.C. Mazumdar and seconded by Mrs Mohini Devi.[302] The Sarda Act was also endorsed by the District Women's Congress, which demanded its proper implementation. Under the presidency of Leelabati Roy, the Bankura District Women's Conference (1939) agreed to lead a movement to amend the Sarda Act to make it more fruitful.[303] In *Prabasi*, it was written that 'as child marriage would be prohibited due to the Sarda Act, girls remained unmarried until they would reach the age of fourteen. As a result of this girls would have enough time to finish their primary education.'[304] Sarala Ray presided over the annual conference of the Calcutta branch of AIWC held at Gokhale Memorial Girls' School, spoke about 'the importance of education and according to her, inadequacy of education was the reason behind child marriage.'[305]

The reaction of the women's movement to Mayo's *Mother India* was perhaps most clearly evident in the attempts to secure the passage of the long-delayed Child Marriage Restraint Bill or Sarda Bill in India. Revisionist explanations of British involvement with the Child Marriage Restraint Act of 1929 strengthened the assumption of colonial conservatism, downplaying any state support and suggesting instead that Government actually sought to block the bill. Mrinalini Sinha resonances the disapproval of Indian women's organizations and nationalist reformers, that 'the Government of India paid lip service to the ideal of social reform while actually employing dilatory tactics to kill the bill'.[306] Mrinalini Sinha stated that the passage of the CMRA in 1929 was rightly seen as a triumph of the fledgling All-India Women's movement. Women's organizations in India had petitioned for child-marriage reform well before the publication of *Mother India*, but support from the government had not been expressive. The women's movement thus exploited the publicity over *Mother India* to gain support for the Sarda Bill both from the colonial government and from male nationalist leaders. The exasperation that women activists felt, especially against the insensitive attitude of the colonial government, was reverberated in Dr (Mrs) Muthulakshmi Reddy's speech, 'Government's Attitude Towards Indian Social Reforms', at the Indian Social Reform Conference held in Madras in December 1927,

> ...we all know what the Government's attitude was when Mr Sarda's Bill was introduced. Even at this stage, in spite of our meetings, in spite of our memorials and petitions, the government member Honorable Crerar brought a dilatory motion to delay such a good and urgent legislation on the plea of religious neutrality. Cannot the enlightened British government follow in the footsteps of the progressive native states even if they do not want to go against the orthodox feelings? Even we women have become discontent and have begun to grumble at the attitude of our government, which is indifferent and unsympathetic to social legislation.[307]

Women activists persuaded Indian politicians in the Assembly to support Sarda's Bill by urging them to neutralize the charges levelled at all Indians in *Mother India*. The representatives of the women's organizations managed to meet with and ensured the support of leaders of all major Indian political parties in the Assembly, including, Motilal Nehru, M.R. Jayakar and Muhammad Ali Jinnah, for the passage of the Sarda Bill.[308] Gandhi, who as a devoted non-cooperationist was boycotting the Assembly, also issued a call to Indians in the Assembly to support the Sarda Bill as a national duty.[309] Mrinalini Sinha wrote that the debates on the Sarda Bill within the Legislative Assembly were some signs of the success of a policy that recognized social reform as the most fitting nationalist rejoinder to *Mother India*, mainly as a result of the efforts of Indian women activists themselves. Even though the women's movement had failed to convince the Viceroy 'to nominate at least two Indian women to the all-male Central Legislative Assembly to participate in the debate over the Sarda Bill, it secured the nomination of one of its members, Rameshwari Nehru, to the Age of Consent

Committee appointed by the government to investigate the effects of premature sexual intercourse and the need to raise the age of consent.'[310] The women of the Arya Samaj in Simla, picketed outside the meetings of the Assembly held in Simla, displaying placards in favour of the Sarda Bill; the endeavours of the women's movement assisted to reveal that 'public opinion, at least among the organized and articulate section of Indian women, opposed child marriage and was in favour of a higher age of consent for girls in India.'[311] By the same token, Malati Patwardhan, the honorary secretary of the WIA, also decided to ensure Bill's passage in admiring tones, 'The passing of this Bill is one of the biggest steps India has ever taken towards her freedom.'[312]

It was thus with the help of the Indian women's movement that one of the most important segments of social reform legislation for women in India, since the Age of Consent Act of 1891, was passed in 1929. The official records of the Indian women's movement, as well as the personal accounts written by Indian women, active in the efforts to secure child-marriage reform, acknowledged no debt to Mayo's *Mother India* for the Sarda Act.[313] However, there was exception regarding the writings of women. Perhaps, one of the most popular autobiographies to be published in this period was *Shikshita Patitar Atmacharit* (Autobiography of an Educated Fallen Woman) (1929). This life story of an educated 'fallen woman' contributes to a conventional defence of girl-child marriage and sharply criticizes the corruption of educated girls. Published at the height of renewed debates about the age of consent for girls, she wrote under the pseudonym Manoda Devi. The narrative has told the story of how an educated high-caste woman fell into the life of a prostitute. In her account, Manoda overtly denounced the Sarda Act, which raised the age of marriage for girls to fourteen years and voiced her anger as social reformers demanded to defend women still 'left young girls outside of marriage at the height of puberty'.[314] In her own words,

> I remembered those thousand instances where virgin girls unable to withstand the first onslaught of youth gave themselves up to illegal satisfaction of their lust and were forced to take shelter in our quarters.... In the natural course of time as the girl attends to puberty, she readily awakens into sex-consciousness. It is necessary that she should be married before that.[315]

It showed what a kind of abhorrence she perceived towards the then contemporary society. Although, there was a debate whether the author of this autobiography was a woman or man!

In her book, Muthulakshmi Reddy, Deputy President of the Madras Legislative Council, wrote that to get the support of the local Council for Sarda's Bill in the Assembly, 'I drafted a resolution, had it signed by a number of Brahmin and Non-Brahmin members.'[316] Later, Reddy, in her presidential address to the Andhra Mahila Maha Sabha held at Bezwada on 3 November 1929, speaking on social and moral legislation, mentioned the Sarda Bill and noted that 'Rai Bahadur Harbilas Sarda, the author of the Child Marriage Restraint Act, will go down to posterity as a great humanitarian and saviour of Indian womanhood because the Child Marriage Restraint Act is nothing but a measure to protect the rights of children.'[317] The third annual session of the Oudh Women's Conference on educational and social reform was held at Lucknow on 23 November 1929 under the presidentship of Iravati Mehta. The Conference was attended by many Muslim and Hindu women, some of whom spoke strongly in favour of the Sarda Act.[318] The Indian women's movement confronted the narrow definition of consent, breaking down nationalist barriers by making visible women's subjective experiences of marriage and indirectly, sexuality. In her message to the Third International Conference on Planned Parenthood, Muthulakshmi argued that the choice of marriage should be left to each individual a girl or a boy, as it was in the West, and that not all men and women needed to marry. Her statement rejected the assumption, common in male nationalists' arguments, that 'choice in marriage was solely a male prerogative and introduced the possibility of not marrying, a theme virtually unheard of even in progressive attacks on child marriage.'[319] An initiative was taken in the Eighth Annual All India Conference of Medical Research Workers that two minor enquiries would be carried out under Major Mallaya, IMS, Police Surgeon, Calcutta, proposed by Colonel Goil, Principal of the Calcutta Medical College. Among the proposals, the first was to collect radiological data with regard to the determination of age in children and minors; the second, to appoint a lady doctor to go round the girls' schools in Calcutta to collect data on the teeth, height, weight, etc., of girls of known age. Under the Sarda Act the determination of the precise age of girls between 12 and 16 years had become very important, and such data should be collected. The Conference agreed to both proposals.[320]

On 16 November 1935, in the pages of *Harijan Patrika*, Gandhi mentioned a useful and instructive bulletin, which had been published by the Anti-Child-Marriage Committee on child marriage. The Census Report for India of 1931 provided the following statistics of the number of girls who are married under the age of 15 by age groups.[321]

TABLE 4.9: PERCENTAGE OF GIRLS WHO ARE MARRIED BETWEEN AGE GROUPS 0 AND 15[322]

Age Group	*Percentage married*
0–1	0.8
1–2	1.2
2–3	2.0
3–4	4.2
4–5	6.6
5–10	19.3
10–15	38.1

The Committee stated that 'Thus nearly one girl in 100 girls of less than one year of age is married and the same horrible fact is repeated in all the other age groups under 15. One consequence of this is the almost unbelievable number of child widows in the country'.

TABLE 4.10: NUMBER OF WIDOWS BETWEEN AGE GROUPS 0 AND 15[323]

Age Group	*Actual Number of Widows*
0–1	1,515
1–2	1,785
2–3	3,485
3–4	9,076
4–5	15,019
5–10	105,482
10–15	185,339

The Committee also reported that another implication of child marriage was the number of young mothers who died in childbirth. There were 2,00,000 deaths the yearly average for India. This worked up to 20 deaths per hour, and a vast number of these deaths occurred to girls in their teens. Sir John Megaw stated that

of every 1,000 young mothers, 100 were destined to die in childbirth before they cease having babies and they had no exact statistics for maternal mortality. It was projected at 24.5 per 1,000 for India whereas it was only 4.5 for England. Finally, the Committee informed that child marriage affected not simply the mother but the child also and, consequently, the race. In India, out of every 1,000 children born, 181 died. This was the average; there were places in India where the average goes up to 400 per 1,000. The very regressive state of India in this context was apparent by a comparison of figures for infant mortality in England and Japan, which were 60 and 124 per mile respectively. The shock was certainly excessive when it was recollected that the evil was a preventable one, and that it was the lack of an educated social conscience, which has allowed the evil to flourish unchecked.[324]

The sex ratio in deaths at the various age periods for 1921 and 1931 given in the UP Census Report was most striking. The very high mortality of females at the reproductive ages was noticeable in the decade 1921-1931.

Table 4.11: Number of Female Deaths per 1,000 Male Deaths in UP[325]

Age	*1921*	*1931*
0–1	877	838
1–5	981	916
5–10	910	871
10–15	865	847
15–20	981	1,000
20–30	1,044	1,070
30–40	935	912
40–50	916	758
50–60	834	784
60 and over	936	877

TABLE 4.12: NUMBER OF MARRIED PER 1,000 OF THOSE AGED 0-15 YEARS[326]

Sex	*1881*	*1891*	*1901*	*1911*	*1921*	*1931*
Males	63	59	59	54	51	77
Females	187	170	162	156	144	181

From the year 1881 to 1921, there has been a decrease of those married under the age of fifteen years. In 1931, the decrease became an increase. One may find that the number of males married under fifteen had risen by 51 per cent and the number of females by 26 per cent since 1921. This was due to the large number of infant marriages that occurred during the six months period between the passage of the Sarda Act and its implementation, but that had to be reckoned as a passing phase. Infant marriage involved infant widowhood and this feature had an implication because widow re-marriage was a 'social ban'. Among Hindus and Jains who place an effective ban on widow re-marriage, there were 221 widows among 1,000 females in the Hindu community and 169 among 1,000 in the latter. These figures, though large in themselves, indicated a decrease since 1921. On the other hand, there had already been a significant rise in the child widows particularly 'under the age of five, which could be attributed to the rush of marriages anticipatory to the Sarda Act'.[327] Laxmibai Rajwade told that 'the Government, humanitarian societies and the people should combine to work a country-wide plan to reduce the enormous waste of precious lives through maternal mortality'. The very moderate provisions of the Sarda Act were not enforced. Through suitable amendments it should be made possible to make the law really effective.[328] It was the interlude between the date when the Act was passed and the date on which it went into effect, which was very chiefly responsible for the massive rise in the numbers of those married below the age of ten years[329] as the Government did not take any action for the implementation of the Act.[330] Gujrat and Bengal appeared to have been particularly energetic in this regard, but other parts of India were not far behind. *Liberty*, a newspaper, described the state of affairs in March 1930, 'A matrimonial wave is just passing over the country. Bride in embryo is being mated to groom in the cradle. The "Sarda Act" is coming into force and ... the poor girl just

TABLE 4.13: NUMBER OF FEMALES (MARRIED) IN THE YEARS 1921 AND 1931 IN INDIA[332]

Age	*1921*	*1931*
0-1	9,066	44,082
1-2	11,595	63,954
2-3	32,197	114,099
3-4	60,755	232,813
4-5	104,850	346,904
5-10	2,016,687	4,200,534
10-15	6,330,207	7,269,208

TABLE 4.14: NUMBER OF WIDOWS IN THE YEARS 1921 AND 1931 IN INDIA[333]

Age	*1921*	*1931*
0-1	759	1,515
1-2	612	1,785
2-3	1,600	3,485
3-4	3,475	9,076
4-5	8,693	15,019
5-10	102,293	105,482
10-15	279,124	185,339

learning to suck the feeding bottle is being carried over to the wedding bower.'[331]

Table 4.13 reveals that there was an incredible increase in the marriage of both sexes at very young ages, so it is understandable that no feasible improvement occurred even after the passage of the Sarda Act. Similarly, Table 4.14 shows that there was indeed a substantial rise in widowhood at very early ages, though 'there was an overall decrease in widows of ten to fifteen years, implying both the clear improvement that preceded the passing of the Sarda Act and the rush of rapid infant marriages that it instigated'.[334] Once the legislation came into effect in April 1930, a number of parents avoided prosecution by leaving British India to perform weddings of their underage daughters and for that in Bengal they went to Chandannagar, which was at that time under French Governance.[335] The *Madras Mail* reported that 90 weddings were performed in Yanam on one day in the month of July in 1934 and that the brides and bridegrooms were the children of people whose homes are in British India territory. Arriving on trains and motor buses ... girls between the ages (of) five and ten were hurriedly married to boys of fifteen and eighteen. Moreover, as the *Madras Mail* noted, 'many parents did not even bother to leave British India, since there had been so few prosecutions for infringement of the Sarda Act.'[336] But

> at the opening of the extraordinary session of the French India Legislative Assembly, M. Crocicchia, the Governor, in the opening speech, made mention of a proposal to fix the marriageable age limit for boys and girls in French India. This was to put an end to the celebration of a number of child marriages in the French settlements in India, especially in Yanam, by British Indian residents who evaded the penalties of the Sarda Act in force in British India.[337]

Public Health Department of Bengal reported that in Nadia district, there was an epidemic of smallpox in village Jatarpur, police station Meherpur, in February 1930 but the fact was described in March 1930 when the epidemic was at its height. It was declared that

> Out of 850 persons in the village 125 were afflicted with smallpox and 17 died. 70 marriages took place in the same village in March to avoid the operations of Sarda Act and a number of bridegrooms were present there at the time. The epidemic subsided quickly after thorough vaccination and revaccination of the remaining population including the bridegrooms present.[338]

It had been reported in the Land Revenue Administration of Bengal for the year 1929-30 that 'the agriculturalists were however affected by the fall in the price of jute and food crops generally, and their indebtedness increased particularly for the reason that the cultivators recklessly borrowed money at a very high rate of interest in order to marry their children before the Sarda Act came into operation'[339] and 'The depressed condition of the jute and the paddy markets and the expenses incidental to the celebration of a large numbers of marriages among the illiterate classes in anticipation of the passing of the Sarda Act account largely for this poor collection.'[340]

Also 'Five districts (Hooghly, Howrah, Nadia, Rajshahi, Malda) reported increase in consumption due to a larger number of marriages held amongst the lower classes of people addicted to the liquor, towards the end of the year, in anticipation of the enforcement of the Sarda Marriage Act from 1 April 1930.'[341] The failure to include a provision for the registration of births and marriages was an obvious flaw in the legislation, making it challenging to prove violations. Prosecutions under the act were occasional; between the act coming into force on 1 April 1930 and 31 August 1932, there were 473 prosecutions and only 167 convictions.[342]

It has been stated that Indian women were organized around the Bill to execute and realize 'a new constituency' in Indian politics, that of women liberated from all religious symbols. However, such a kind could not be sustained for long. As Mrinalini Sinha has showed that the majority of the Hindu members of women's organizations chose to support Congress's calls for a joint electorate, without communal characterization, on the grounds that it would strengthen the new women's constituency as one that functioned without religious differences. Such a stance alienated lower-caste Indians as well as Muslims, who were concerned that such an electorate would lead to Hindu political authoritarianism. However, the subsequent controversies helped in equating the progressive language of women's rights with Hindu-controlled nationalism, while Indian Muslims came to be identified as a community that desired to subjugate women's independence to a religious, collective identity. Sinha traces the traditions in which a colonial liberalism, firmly rooted in a language of universal rights centred on the white man, had given access to a form of Hindu-centric liberalism, concentrated on the upper-caste, elite Hindu man.[343] In the matter of the passage of the CMRA of 1929, or Sarda Act, male leaders strengthened women's rights in ways that accelerated their own advantages and political motivations, with the result that women leaders' claim 'to speak for all-Indian women could be undermined at critical moments'.[344] Geraldine Forbes has emphasized the way in which Indian women's organizations were limited by 'a politics of respectability', which signified that in order to present themselves as national bodies, groups such as the AIWC and the WIA had to follow 'the patriarchal gender norms set out by the politically dominant Congress leadership'. This procedure allowed women leaders to gain more prominence than they would have managed otherwise, but it also placed severe constraints on their ability to secure more gender-equal reforms and reach out to a wider range of Indian women.[345]

The 1930s in colonial India were turbulent years of political mobilization when independence made an appearance with more and more a reality. As several scholars have discovered that Hindu-Muslim tensions and rivalries also played a role in a situation where Muslim personal law came much nearer to British law and provided more rights to women by virtue of its contractual nature, spanning matters of consent, property rights, divorce and maintenance. Hindu laws were indeed far worse for women, offering little to no legal status to wives as individuals or to daughters as heirs, except under matrilineal practices in regions like Kerala. In 1930 it was very real as the agitation against the Sarda Act became entwined with the wider agitations against British rule. The nature of the anti-Sarda Act demonstrations emphasized the range to which social reform had become campaigned within 'the broader discourses of imperialism, nationalism and communalism that dominated the Indian scene in the late 1920s'.[346] However, in the Council of State, on 22 August 1934, Lala Jagadish Prasad moved the first resolution, recommending that steps be taken including a revision of the law to enforce more rigidly the provisions of the CMRA Act, so as to increase the chances of offender being brought to book and minimize the chances of evasion of the law. Nawab Sir Akbar Khan was prepared to support the resolution provided it concerned only Hindus and did not touch Muslims. The Maharaja of Darbhanga strongly opposed the resolution. M.G. Hallet, Home Secretary, said that history had proved in such matters 'more haste means worse speed'; seeing Government's position, Lala Jagadish Prasad withdrew the resolution in view of the Government's attitudes.[347] At about the same time, Rai Bahadur Raghbir Singh moved the Minor Girls' Protection Bill to protect minor girls under fourteen against their being sold by parents or guardians to bridegrooms, be referred to a select committee. Sitaram Raju opposed the Bill on the ground that the Bill was unnecessary as the Sarda Act prevented the marriage of girls below fourteen. Sir Nripen Sircar pointed out certain technical difficulties in suitably drafting the Bill, which was ill-conceived. Sir Henry Craik observed that the object of the Bill might be laudable but it was impracticable.[348] The Government of India Act of 1935 provided an opportunity for nationalist leaders to legislate and regulate family relations. Using this opportunity, 'both the Hindu and Muslim leaders pressed for law reform within their respective personal laws ostensibly to elevate the status of women.'[349] One area to search for the consequent attention on child marriage is in a forward-looking document produced by women leaders on the eve of independence, namely the Report by the Sub-Committee under the Congress leadership of Jawaharlal Nehru, known as Women's Role in a Planned Economy (WRPE), prepared in 1938 by one of twenty-nine sub-committees planning the future nation-state.[350] Section 2 on the 'social status' of women of the Report has two chapters, entitled, 'Marriages and Its Problems' and 'Family Life'.[351] Figures in the WRPE on 'Education' of the Report, that looked at the period between 1931 and 1937 indicated two things – 'large gaps in enrolment between boys and girls, which got worse from primary education onwards but, on the other hand, a much greater rate of increase in schooling for girls than boys over the years'.[352] Child marriage, in the context of education, was called one of Indian society's evils holding back its women. The Report by the Sub-Committee recommended, age of marriage must be progressively raised to the age of majority, i.e. 18 for both parties and the Child Marriage Restraint Act shall be made more effective by making marriages in which either party is of less than twelve years of age, null and void, and by making marriage in contravention of the Act a cognizable offence.[353] 'The mood of the report', as Mary E. John has stated

> was buoyant about what a planned economy would grant its women citizens – with economic and political rights in place, backward customs like child marriage were expected to no longer pose a major challenge and would be dealt with via punitive legal measures. It is unclear, in the terminology and frames employed by this report, whether an age/sex system was centrally at work in the desire to raise the age of marriage to 18 years for both boys and girls.[354]

In 1938, the Child Marriage Restraint (Second Amendment) Act added a new section to the Act, empowering 'the courts to issue an injunction prohibiting the proposed marriage of a child if they came to know that such a marriage was likely to take place'.[355] The abolition of child marriage was undoubtedly a woman's issue, but perhaps more important it was a measure which tested the desire of Indians to modernize. It was propagated as a symbol of a desire to elevate women's social status as independent persons. The movement to raise the age of marriage did not end with the passage of the Sarda Act. The zeal of stirring did not die and the movement continued even after 1929. However, due to the upheaval in the country caused by the challenging political developments arising from the freedom struggle, as well as the onset of the Second World War in the late 1930s and early 1940s, the issue of age of marriage was put on hold. Pandit Thakurdas Bhargava resurrected the issue after India's independence in 1947. Pandit Thakurdas Bhargava introduced three bills to amend the Indian Child Marriage Restraint Act of 1929 on 25 August 1948. The first of these was designed to raise the marriage age of boys and girls from eighteen to twenty in the case of boys and from fourteen to fifteen in the case of girls. A new clause was also sought to be introduced with a view to affording protection to young girls under eighteen against ill-matched marriages. The other bills sought 'to make offences committed under the Child Marriage Restraint Act cognizable'.[356] Renuka Ray welcomed the Bill and hoped when the bills emerged from the Select Committee the provisions would be made more effective. It was a bill whereby it was sought to improve the health of the mothers of the country.[357] The Select Committee submitted a revised Bill, which sought to raise the marriageable age of girls from fourteen to fifteen and of boys from eighteen to twenty stating that the punishment of fine prescribed for offences against this had not be sufficiently deterrent. The Select Committee had suggested that the courts should be bestowed with authority to give simple imprisonment in appropriate cases. In case of severe crimes, mandatory imprisonment had been provided for. Pandit Thakurdas Bhargava said that those who were serious about this law were fully convinced that unless imprisonment was made compulsory it would remain a dead letter.[358]

Despite the Sarda Act, Pandit Bhargava stated, at least 40 per cent of the girls in the country, especially in rural areas, were still being married below the age of 15. This was a serious crime. Referring to the provision in the Bill making offences under the act making cognizable, Pandit Thakurdas said that in free India the police was not corrupt as before. Further, the Select Committee had said that only Inspectors of Police would be authorized to investigate such cases. Dr Pattabhi Sitaramayya said that it was wrong to allow the police to enter into social affairs and he hoped that an interregnum of two years would be allowed before the Act was enforced.[359] Ram Chandra Upadhyaya said that before enforcing any social reform in a particular society, public opinion should be sought. Ananthasayanam Ayyangar welcomed the provisions of the Bill, Tajamul Husain strongly supported the Bill. Naziruddin Ahmed opined that the age limit prescribed for marriage was quite right for upper classes, but it would create a lot of difficulties for lower and poorer classes. In poorer classes girls had to earn their bread by manual labour. It would be dangerous to allow a girl of fourteen to move about without being protected by a husband. On the other hand, N.V. Gadgil said that so far as the Government of India was concerned, they would not agree to raise the marriageable age of either girls or boys. So far as the age limit for marriage was concerned, Gadgil said a legislation in this respect would be much in advance of public opinion. Pandit Thakurdas said that he was 'simply surprised'. However, a compromise was effected and the Bill was passed with certain important amendments. It raised the marriageable age of girl to 15 instead of 16. The marriageable age for boys was however, retained at 18, as provided in the Act. Clause 6 of the Bill making offences under the Act cognizable and vesting power in police officers to investigate an offence was deleted.[360] Thus, a male above eighteen but below twenty-one who contracted a child marriage might be sentenced to simple imprisonment for 15 days or a fine of Rs. 1,000 or both. The punishment for a male above twenty-one who contracted a child marriage was enhanced to simple imprisonment for a period, which might extend to three months and the court might in addition impose a sentence of fine, the amount of which was left to its discretion. In the case of parents, guardians conducting child marriages, the punishment was increased from one month's simple imprisonment or one thousand rupees fine or both, to simple imprisonment, which might extend to three months and an additional liability to fine, the amount of which would be at the discretion of the court.[361] The most radical aspect of Sarda's original bill, as Ishita Pande argues, 'was his (Harbilas Sarda) insistence that child marriages affected both boys and girls and that all marriages contracted below the minimum ages be considered invalid'.[362] Ishita Pande has argued that 'this bill was therefore more genuinely about the childhood of both genders and departed from a prior focus on the girl-child alone'. Nevertheless, going through the *Notes on Infant Marriage* of the 1880s, particularly those of Malabari and Phule, the problem of child marriage for both girls and boys received considerable attention, though not in the final Age of Consent legislation.[363] In contrast with Gour's bill that had targeted girls only, Sarda's revised bill provided a definition of a child as 'a person who, if a male, is under 18 years of age, and if a female, is under 14 years of age'.[364]

In 1978, it was raised further to 18 years for girls and to 21 years for boys. After 1978, the age prescribed for women by CMRA was in conformity with the international norms that were found in the two major conventions; 'The Convention on the Consent to Marriage, Minimum Age for Marriage and Registration of Marriage (the Marriage Convention) of 1962', and the 'Convention on the Elimination of all Forms of Discrimination Against Women (the Women's Convention) of 1979'. Both refer to the age at marriage.[365] CMRA does not provide either for the validity or invalidity of an underage marriage.[366] It is silent about the legal effect of child marriage. The issue of the validity of child marriage was kept out of the scope when CMRA was drafted according to the suggestions of the Joshi Committee. The same policy continues even today. Many accounts today render the history of social reform in somewhat tepid tones, as a very narrowly conceived agenda of social change. The upper caste subject of social reform became invisible within the new nation, and one of the dimensions of this invisibility is that child marriage turned into history for this caste-class of modern womanhood. Stalwarts of the women's movement of the 1970s, like Vina Mazumdar, have frequently spoken about how as 'daughters of independence' they took the equality clauses of the Constitution for granted.[367] This generation effortlessly conceived of themselves as adult daughters of the new India, certainly no longer as child victims of traditional customs. Alongside, as we saw, the newly developing nation and a reborn women's movement signified and marginalized child marriage as the problem of the 'other', contained within agendas to address poverty, fitfully recognized as an ongoing practice in 'backward' regions and groups. None of these advocates of marriage reform have ever interrogated whether raising the age of marriage can advance women's position or not and trigger the social transformation that is assumed to be crucial for the modernizing process. Since the mid-nineteenth century, it assumed that marrying later ensured a higher social standing, yet there had been little evidence of this simple formula working.

NOTES

1. Padma Anagol, 'Age of Consent and Child Marriage in India', The Wiley Blackwell, *Encyclopaedia of Gender and Sexuality Studies*, 21 April 2016, p. 1.
2. Geraldine Forbes, 'Women and Modernity: The Issue of Child Marriage in India', *Women's Studies International Quarterly*, vol. 2, no. 4, 1979, p. 411.
3. Mary E. John, *Child Marriage in an International Frame: A Feminist Review from India*, London and New York: Routledge, 2021, p. 29.
4. Sumita Mukherjee, 'Using the Legislative Assembly for Social Reform: The Sarda Act of 1929', *South Asia Research*, vol. 26, no. 3, 2006, p. 219.
5. Mrinalini Sinha (ed.), *Selections from Mother India: Katherine Mayo*, New Delhi: Kali for Women, 1998, p. 36.
6. Sumit Sarkar, *Modern India 1885-1947*, Madras: McMillan India Ltd., (1983) 1995, p. 165.
7. Mrinalini Sinha (ed.), op. cit., 1998, p. 36.
8. Sumit Sarkar, op. cit., (1983) 1995, p. 167.
9. Mrinalini Sinha (ed.), op. cit., 1998, p. 38.
10. Sabyasachi Bhattacharya, *The Defining Moments in Bengal: 1920-1947*, New Delhi: Oxford University Press, 2014, p. 46.
11. Shahida Lateef, 'Defining Women through Legislation', in Zoya Hasan (ed.), *Forging Identities: Gender, Communities and the State in India*, New Delhi: Kali for Women, 1994, p. 39.
12. Ibid.
13. Ibid., pp. 39-40.
14. *Report of the Age of Consent Committee, 1928-1929*, Calcutta:

Government of India, Central Publication Branch, 1929, p. 12; Azra Asghar Ali, *The Emergence of Feminism Among Indian Muslim Women, 1920-1947*, New York: Oxford University Press, 2000, p. 124.

15. Azra Asghar Ali, op. cit., 2000, p. 125.
16. *Report of the Age of Consent Committee, 1928-1929*, op. cit., p. 23; Azra Asghar Ali, op. cit., 2000, p. 126.
17. *Report of the Age of Consent Committee, 1928-1929*, op. cit., pp. 23-4; Azra Asghar Ali, op. cit., 2000, p. 126.
18. *Report of the Age of Consent Committee, 1928-1929*, op. cit., p. 30; Azra Asghar Ali, op. cit., 2000, p. 126.
19. Ibid.
20. *Report of the Age of Consent Committee, 1928-1929*, op. cit., p. 50.
21. Ibid., p. 33; Azra Asghar Ali, op. cit., 2000, p. 127.
22. Azra Asghar Ali, op. cit., 2000, p. 127.
23. *Report of the Age of Consent Committee, 1928-1929*, op. cit., p. 36; Azra Asghar Ali, op. cit., 2000, p. 127.
24. *Report of the Age of Consent Committee, 1928-1929*, op. cit., p. 65; Azra Asghar Ali, op. cit., 2000, p. 127.
25. Census of India, 1911, vol. 1, part 1 – Report, p. 275.
26. Census of India, 1921, vol. 1, part 1 – Report, chapter VII, p. 153.
27. Ibid., p. 153.
28. Ibid., p. 155.
29. Ibid.
30. Ibid., pp. 157-8.
31. Dagmar Engels, 'The Politics of Childbirth', in *Beyond Purdah? Women in Bengal, 1890–1930*, New Delhi: Oxford University Press, 1996, pp. 123-58.
32. L.S.S. O'Malley, *Census of India (vol. VI): City of Calcutta*, part I, Calcutta: Bengal Secretariat Book Depot, 1913, p. 2, cited in Ambalika Guha, *Colonial Modernities: Midwifery in Bengal, c.1860-1947*, London and New York: Routledge, 2018, p. 114.
33. H.M. Crake, *Report of the Health Officer of Calcutta*, Calcutta: The Corporation Press, 1914, p. 5, cited in Ambalika Guha, op. cit., 2018, p. 114.
34. 'Such articles portraying infant mortality as reflection of the deterioration of race appeared in *Swasthya Samachar* and also in women's magazines such as *Bharati*.' For instance, 'Jatikshoy o Shishu Mrityu' (Racial Deterioration and Infant Mortality), *Bharati*, vol. 43, no. 10, January 1919, cited in Ambalika Guha, op. cit., 2018, p. 116.
35. 'Bengal Legislative Council Interpretations: Mortality of Infants Under One Year in Bengal', *Amrita Bazar Patrika*, 1 April 1919.

36. 'Shishu Marak' ('Infant Mortality'), *Swasthya Samachar*, vol. 8, no. 3, July 1920, 53, cited in Ambalika Guha, op. cit., 2018, p. 115.
37. 'National Health – How Marriage Affects It', (translated) *Swasthya*, January-February 1901, in Pradip Kumar Bose (ed.), *Health and Society in Bengal: A Selection from Late 19th-Century Bengali Periodicals*, New Delhi: Sage, 2006, pp. 134-5.
38. *Report of the Age of Consent Committee, 1928-1929*, op. cit., Appendix V-B, pp. 308-9.
39. Ibid.
40. Sumita Mukherjee, op. cit., 2006, p. 221.
41. J.S. Gupta, 'Children Protection Bill', 1925, *Modern Review*, vol. XXXVIII, pp. 270-73, cited in Geraldine Forbes, op. cit., 1979, p. 411.
42. Mary E. John, op. cit., 2021, p. 30. For knowing Tambe's arguments in detail, Ashwini Tambe, 'The State as Surrogate Parent: Legislating Non-Marital Sex in Colonial India, 1911-1929', *The Journal of the History of Childhood and Youth*, vol. 2, no. 3, 2009, pp. 393–427.
43. L.F. Rushbrook Williams, *India in 1924-25: A Statement prepared for presentation to parliament in accordance with the requirements of the 26th Section of the Government of India Act*, Calcutta: Government of India: Central Publication Branch, 1925, p. 111.
44. The Legislative Assembly Debates, 23 March 1925, Simla: Government of India Press, 1925, p. 2840; Sumita Mukherjee, op. cit., 2006, p. 225.
45. Nripendra Nath Mitra (ed.), *The Indian Quarterly Register, being a Quarterly Journal of Indian Public Affairs, in matters Political, Social and Economic*, July-December 1925, vol. 2, nos. III&IV, Calcutta: The Annual Register Office, p. 170.
46. Ibid.
47. Ibid.
48. Ibid., p. 173.
49. *Young India*, 27 August 1925 cited in M.K. Gandhi, *Women and Social Injustice*, Ahmedabad: Navajivan Press, 1942 (1st edn.), 1958 (repr.), pp. 30-1.
50. *Young India*, 26 August 1926 cited in M.K. Gandhi, op. cit., 1942 (1st edn.), 1958 (repr.), pp. 32-3.
51. *Young India*, 7 October 1926, cited in M.K. Gandhi, op. cit., 1942 (1st edn.), 1958 (repr.), p. 38.
52. *Young India*, 9 September 1926 cited in Monmayee Basu, *Hindu Women and Marriage Law: From Sacrament to Contract*, in Flavia Agnes, Sudhir Chandra and Monmayee Basu (eds.), *Women and Law in India: An*

Omnibus Comprising, New Delhi: Oxford University Press, 2004 (1st edn.), 2016 (Oxford India Paperbacks), pp. 52-3.

53. Nripendra Nath Mitra (ed.), *The Indian Quarterly Register*, July-December, 1925, vol. 2, nos. III&IV, pp. 399-400.
54. *The Statesman*, 20 January 1927. It may be pointed out that Lady Abdul Qadir, Mrs Akhtar Husain, Mrs Kazi Mir Ahmed – these women's names were not mentioned; instead, the names of their husbands were used to identify them.
55. Aparna Basu and Bharati Ray (eds.), op. cit., First Published 1990, 3rd edn. 2018, p. 58.
56. Nripendra Nath Mitra (ed.), *The Indian Quarterly Register: Being a Quarterly Journal of Indian Public Affairs, In matters Political, Social and Economic, Etc.*, January-June, 1927, vol. 1, nos. I&II, Calcutta: The Annual Register Office, pp. 425, 427; Aparna Basu and Bharati Ray (eds.), op. cit., First Published 1990, 3rd edn. 2018, p. 58.
57. 'Child Marriage and Education, Mrs Muthulaxmi Reddy writes in the Social Service Quarterly', *The Modern Review*, September 1927, vol. 42, no. 3, pp. 337-8.
58. *Report of the Age of Consent Committee, 1928-1929*, op. cit., p. 14; *The Legislative Assembly Debates*, vol. 3, 28 March 1927, Delhi: Government of India Press, 1927, p. 2968.
59. *Report of the Age of Consent Committee, 1928-1929*, op. cit., p. 14.
60. Ibid.
61. Ibid., pp. 1-2. Although elsewhere in the report, Rameshwari Nehru's name was mentioned, but when mentioning the names of the members of the Age of Consent Committee, she was identified by her husband's name and mentioned as Mrs Brij Lal Nehru, which undoubtedly indicated a patriarchal mentality.
62. *The Legislative Assembly Debates*, 1 February 1927, Delhi: Government of India Press, p. 368.
63. A.S. Srinivasa Aiyar, *The Child Marriage Restraint Act (Act XIX of 1929), with an Analytical Introduction, Critical Comments, Original Bill, Statement of Objects and Reasons, Reports of the Select Committees (with Minutes of Dissent) and Select Speeches in the Assembly*, Madras: The Law Publishing Company, 1930, pp. 41-2.
64. Harbilas Sarda, *Recollections and Reminiscences: Memoirs*, Ajmer: Shri Bhagwan Swarup Manager, cited in Sumita Mukherjee, op. cit., 2006, pp. 219-20.
65. *The Legislative Assembly Debates*, vol. V, 15 September 1927, Simla: Government of India Press, 1928, pp. 4405-6.

66. Ibid., p. 4407.
67. *Modern Review*, cited in *The Legislative Assembly Debates*, vol. V, 15 September 1927, Simla: Government of India Press, 1928, p. 4409.
68. Azra Asghar Ali, op. cit., 2000, p. 129.
69. Mrinalini Sinha (ed.), op. cit., 1998, p. 1.
70. Sumita Mukherjee, op. cit., 2006, p. 220.
71. Mrinalini Sinha (ed.), op. cit., 1998, p. 1.
72. Katherine Mayo, *Mother India*, New York, 1927, p. 22, cited in Joanna Liddle and Rama Joshi, 'Gender and Imperialism in British India', *South Asia Research*, vol. 5, no. 2, November 1985, p. 147.
73. Joanna Liddle and Rama Joshi, op. cit., November 1985, p. 147.
74. Mrinalini Sinha (ed.), op. cit., 1998, p. 3.
75. Ibid., p. 4.
76. Ibid., pp. 4-5.
77. Manoranjan Jha, *Katherine Mayo and India*, New Delhi: People's Publishing House, 1971.
78. Mrinalini Sinha (ed.), op. cit., 1998, p. 7.
79. Ibid., p. 14.
80. Ibid., p. 19.
81. Ibid., p. 22.
82. Ibid., p. 25.
83. Ibid., p. 27.
84. Joanna Liddle and Rama Joshi, op. cit., 1985, pp. 147-65; Lata Mani, 'Contentious Traditions: The Debate on Sati in Colonial India', *Cultural Critique*, Vol. 7, 1987, pp. 119-56.
85. Mrinalini Sinha (ed.), op. cit., 1998, pp. 32-3.
86. The 1920s were an important period for the history of elite women's involvement in public life in India, *Annual Reports of the Women's India Association*, especially for the years 1920 to 1930, National Archives of India, Fawcett Library, and Adyar Library and Research Centre in Madras. M.E. Cousins, *What Women Have Gained by the Reforms*, Madras: Besant Tress, n.d.; M.E. Cousins, *The Awakening of Asian Womanhood*, Madras: Ganesh and Co., 1922, pp. 1-26, 50-83; and K. Chattopadhyay, Margaret E. Cousins and Sakuntala Thampi (eds.), *The Awakening of Indian Women*, Madras: Everymans Press, 1939, pp. 1-20.
87. S. Muthulakshmi Reddy, *My Experience as a Legislator*, Madras: Current Thought Press, 1930, pp. 3-4.; Mrs Reddy, *Autobiography of Dr (Mrs) S. Muthulakshmi Reddy: A Pioneer Woman Legislator*, Madras: M.L.J. Press, 1964, pp. 1-2; Dr Aparna Basu (ed.), *The Pathfinder: Dr*

Muthulakshmi Reddy, Delhi: AIWC Publication, 1986, pp. 1-8.

88. For the WIA's involvement in child marriage reform even before *'Mother India'*, *Stri Dharma*, vol. 8, no. 9, July 1925, pp. 132-3 and *Stri Dharma*, vol. 8, no. 11, September 1925, p. 163; *Annual Reports of the WIA*, especially for the years 1924-5 and 1925-6; and 'Social Welfare Measures', 1921-8, File no. 7, *Muthulakshmi Reddy Papers*, New Delhi: Nehru Memorial Museum and Library, cited in Mrinalini Sinha (ed.), op. cit., 1998, p. 40.
89. Geraldine H. Forbes, *Women in Modern India*, Cambridge: Cambridge University Press, 1996, pp. 83-90.
90. Madras Legislative Council Debates, vol. 42, no. 1, 17 March 1919, p. 37.
91. Aparna Basu and Bharati Ray (eds.), op. cit., First Published 1990, 3rd edn. 2018, pp. 57-8.
92. Mrinalini Sinha (ed.), op. cit., 1998, p. 41.
93. *All India Women's Conference, Annual Report*, 1928, pp. 37-40, cited in Aparna Basu and Bharati Ray (eds.), op. cit., First Published 1990, 3rd edn. 2018, p. 58.
94. *Salana Report: All India Muslim Ladies Conference*, held at Hyderabad on February 1929, Muslim Educational Conference Report, not dated, pp. 1-70.
95. Mrinalini Sinha, *Specters of Mother India: The Global Restructuring of an Empire*, Durham/Delhi: Duke University Press/Zubaan, 2006, pp. 152-96.
96. Mrinalini Sinha, 'Reading Mother India: Empire, Nation and the Female Voice', *Journal of Women's History*, vol. 6, no. 2, Summer 1994, p. 24.
97. Mrinalini Sinha, op. cit., 1994, p. 24; Rameshwari Nehru, 'Early Marriage', in Shyam Kumari Nehru (ed.), *Our Cause: A Symposium by Indian Women*, Allahabad: Kitabistan, 1938, pp. 256-7. Rameshwari Nehru, *Gandhi is My Star: Speeches and Writings of Shrimati Rameshwari Nehru*, edited by Professor Somnath Dhar, Patna: Pustak Bhandar, 1950, pp. 72-80.
98. Aparna Basu and Bharati Ray (eds.), op. cit., First Published 1990, 3rd edn. 2018, pp. 60-1.
99. Kamaladevi Chattopadhyay discusses her contribution in her autobiography, *Inner Recesses, Outer Spaces: Memoirs*, New Delhi: Navrang, 1986, pp. 113-17; Jamila Brijbhusan, *Kamaladevi Chattopadhyay, Portrait of a Rebel*, New Delhi: Abhinav, 1976, pp. 40-1. Dhanvanthi Rama Rau discusses her role in her autobiography, *An*

Inheritance: The Memoirs of Dhanvanthi Rama Rau, London: Harper and Row, 1977, pp. 41, 43, 83, 151-8.

100. *The Indian Ladies Magazine*, News and Notes Section, vol. III, no. 3, October 1929, p. 145.
101. Aparna Basu and Bharati Ray (eds.), op. cit., First Published 1990, 3rd edn. 2018, p. 59.
102. 'Report on Meetings and Speeches at Albert Hall, College Street, Calcutta', *Ananda Bazar Patrika*, 12 January 1929; Sabyasachi Bhattacharya, *The Defining Moments in Bengal: 1920-1947*, New Delhi: Oxford University Press, 2014, pp. 54, 60-1.
103. *Ananda Bazar Patrika*, 7 September 1929.
104. *Ananda Bazar Patrika*, editorial on 'The Swadeshi Spirit and the Women of Bengal', 5 March 1928.
105. *Ananda Bazar Patrika*, editorial on 'The Women's Cell', 10 January 1924, cited in Sabyasachi Bhattacharya, op. cit., 2014, pp. 61-2.
106. *All India Women's Conference, Annual Report*, 1932, p. 74.
107. Aparna Basu and Bharati Ray (eds.), op. cit., First Published 1990, 3rd edn. 2018, p. 60.
108. 'Sarada Bill Sambandhe Mahilader Mat' (Women's Opinion about Sarda Bill), *Prabasi*, Ashwin (September-October), 1336 (1929), vol. 1, part 29, p. 962.
109. Dagmar Engels, op. cit., 1996, p. 45.
110. *Jayasree*, Agrahayan (November-December), 1340 BS/1933, cited in Bhaswati Chatterjee, 'The Second Social Reform Movement: Gender and Society in Bengal, 1930s-1950s', unpublished Ph.D. thesis, Department of History, Calcutta University, 2016, p. 147. https://shodhganga.inflibnet.ac.in/handle/10603/211610, accessed on 31 January 2021.
111. Sumita Mukherjee, op. cit., 2006, p. 224.
112. Census of India, 1921, vol. 1, part 1, p. 154; Sumita Mukherjee, op. cit., 2006, p. 224.
113. *The Legislative Assembly Debates*, vol. II, 26 March 1928, Delhi: Government of India Press, 1928, pp. 1970-2.
114. Ibid., p. 1976; Sumita Mukherjee, op. cit., 2006, p. 224.
115. *The Legislative Assembly Debates*, vol. III, 8 September 1928, Simla: Government of India Press, 1929, p. 349.
116. Nripendra Nath Mitra (ed.), *The Indian Quarterly Register: Being a Quarterly Journal of Indian Public Affairs in matters Political, Social and Economic*, July-December 1928, vol. 2, nos. III&IV, pp. 168-9.
117. Nripendra Nath Mitra (ed.), *The Indian Quarterly Register: Being a*

Quarterly Journal of Indian Public Affairs in matters Political, Social and Economic, 1928, vol. 2, p. 3; Monmayee Basu, op. cit., 2004 (1st edn.), 2016 (Oxford India Paperbacks), pp. 53-4.

118. Monmayee Basu, op. cit., 2004 (1st edn.), 2016 (Oxford India Paperbacks), p. 54.
119. *The Legislative Assembly Debates,* vol. 1, no. 2, 29 January 1929, Delhi: Government of India Press, p. 190.
120. Ibid., pp. 190-1.
121. Ibid., p. 191.
122. Ibid., p. 192.
123. Ibid.
124. Ibid., p. 195.
125. Ibid.
126. Ibid., pp. 197-8.
127. Ibid., p. 201.
128. Ibid., p. 204; Monmayee Basu, op. cit., 2004 (1st edn.), 2016 (Oxford India Paperbacks), p. 54; 'Sarda's Child Marriage Bill Postponed' (Notes), *The Modern Review,* February, 1929, vol. XLV, nos. 1-6, January to June, 1929, p. 284.
129. 'The Hindu Child Marriage Bill' (Notes), *The Modern Review,* March 1929, vol. XLV, nos. 1-6, January to June, 1929, pp. 397-8.
130. *Report of the Age of Consent Committee, 1928-1929,* op. cit., Appendix V-D, pp. 311-14.
131. *Report of the Age of Consent Committee, 1928-1929,* op. cit., pp. 66-7.
132. Ibid., p. 67.
133. Ibid., pp. 67-8.
134. Ibid., p. 68.
135. Ibid., p. 68.
136. Ibid., p. 70.
137. Ibid.
138. Ibid., p. 71.
139. Ibid., pp. 71-2.
140. Sekhar Bandyopadhyay, *Caste, Culture and Hegemony: Social Domination in Colonial Bengal,* New Delhi: Sage Publications, 2004, p. 155.
141. *Report of the Age of Consent Committee, 1928-1929,* op. cit., p. 72.
142. Sekhar Bandyopadhyay, op. cit., 2004, p. 49.
143. *Report of the Age of Consent Committee, 1928-1929,* op. cit., p. 72.
144. Census of India, 1911, vol. V, part 1, Table V, pp. 351-5, cited in Sekhar Bandyopadhyay, op. cit., 2004, p. 156.
145. *Report of the Age of Consent Committee, 1928-1929,* op. cit., p. 74.

146. Ibid., Appendix III-A, p. 302.
147. *Report of the Age of Consent Committee, 1928-1929*, op. cit., p. 2.
148. Ibid., p. 3.
149. Nripendra Nath Mitra (ed.), *The Indian Quarterly Register: Being a Quarterly Journal of Indian Public Affairs, in matters Political, Social and Economic*, vol. II, July-December 1929, nos. III&IV, Calcutta: The Annual Register Office, pp. 225-6.
150. Ibid., p. 225; *Report of the Age of Consent Committee, 1928-1929*, op. cit., p. 3.
151. Azra Asghar Ali, op. cit., 2000, p. 135.
152. Nripendra Nath Mitra (ed.), *The Indian Quarterly Register: Being a Quarterly Journal of Indian Public Affairs, in matters Political, Social and Economic*, vol. II, July-December 1929, nos. III&IV, Calcutta: The Annual Register Office, p. 226.
153. Judy Whitehead, 'Modernising the motherhood archetype: Public health models and the Child Marriage Restraint Act of 1929', *Contributions to Indian Sociology*, vol. 29, nos. 1-2, 1 January 1995, p. 201.
154. Eleanor Rathbone, *Child Marriage: The Indian Minotaur, An Object-Lesson from the Past to the Future*, London: George Allen & Unwin Ltd., 1934, pp. 25-6.
155. *Report of the Age of Consent Committee, 1928-1929*, op. cit., pp. 156-7.
156. Ibid., p. 102.
157. Ibid., p. 49.
158. Ibid., pp. 320, 325.
159. Ibid., p. 327.
160. Judy Whitehead, op. cit., 1 January 1995, p. 202.
161. *Report of the Age of Consent Committee, 1928-1929*, op. cit., pp. 74-5.
162. Ibid., p. 75.
163. Oral evidence of Dr Dube, Health Officer, Lucknow, 18 January 1929, in *Age of Consent Committee Evidence, 1928-1929: Oral Evidence and Written Statements of Witnesses from (United Provinces Contd.) Lucknow and Ajmer-Merwara*, vol. IX, Calcutta: Government of India Central Publication Branch, 1929, pp. 94-5.
164. Written Statement of Dr Alice L. Ernst, M.D., Women's Union Missionary Society of America, Ackerman-Hoyt Memorial Hospital, Jhansi, 14 August 1928, in *Age of Consent Committee Evidence, 1928-1929: Oral Evidence and Written Statements of Witnesses from (United Provinces Contd.) Lucknow and Ajmer-Merwara*, vol. IX, Calcutta:

Government of India Central Publication Branch, 1929, pp. 218-23.

165. Oral Evidence of Dr (Mrs) Edith Ghosh, representative of Bengal Presidency Council of Women, 19 December 1928, in *Age of Consent Committee Evidence, 1928-1929: Oral Evidence and Written Statements of Witnesses from Bengal Presidency,* vol. VI, Calcutta: Government of India Central Publication Branch, 1929, p. 40.
166. *Report of the Age of Consent Committee, 1928-1929,* op. cit., p. 76.
167. Written Statement, dated 14 November 1928, of Miss Leela Nag, M.A., Deepali Ladies' Association, Organizer, 'Nari Shiksha Mandir' (Women's Educational Institute), 3 Bakshi Bazar Road, Dacca, in *Age of Consent Committee Evidence, 1928-1929: Oral Evidence and Written Statements of Witnesses from Bengal Presidency,* vol. VI, Calcutta: Government of India Central Publication Branch, 1929, pp. 376-7.
168. *Jayashree,* Jyaistha (May-June), 1337 BS/1930.
169. Oral Evidence of Mrs Latika Basu, Secretary, Chittaranjan Seva Sadan, 148, Russa Road, South Calcutta, 19 December 1928, in *Age of Consent Committee Evidence, 1928-1929: Oral Evidence and Written Statements of Witnesses from Bengal Presidency,* vol. VI, Calcutta: Government of India Central Publication Branch, 1929, p. 68.
170. Written statement of Dr M.I. Balfour, Bombay, in *Age of Consent Committee Evidence, 1928-1929: Oral Evidence and Written Statements of Witnesses from the Bombay Presidency (Continued – Bombay and Poona) and the Central Provinces and Berar,* vol. III, Calcutta: Government of India Central Publication Branch, 1929, pp. 27-9.
171. *Report of the Age of Consent Committee, 1928-1929,* op. cit., p. 31.
172. Ibid., pp. 219-20.
173. Written statement dated 20 December 1928 of Haji Chaudhury Mohammed Ismail Khan, MLA, Barishal, Bengal, in *Age of Consent Committee Evidence, 1928-1929: Oral Evidence and Written Statements of Witnesses from Bengal Presidency,* vol. VI, Calcutta: Government of India Central Publication Branch, 1929, p. 104.
174. Oral Evidence of Maulana Mazhar Uddin, Editor, *Alaman,* Delhi, in *Age of Consent Committee Evidence, 1928-1929: Oral Evidence and Written Statements of Witnesses from the Punjab, NWFP and Delhi,* vol. I, Calcutta: Government of India Central Publication Branch, 1929, p. 505.
175. Written statement dated 10 August 1928, of Atiya Begum Sahiba, Malabar Hill, Bombay, in *Age of Consent Committee Evidence, 1928-1929: Oral Evidence and Written Statements of Witnesses from the Bombay*

Presidency (Continued – Bombay and Poona) and the Central Provinces and Berar, vol. III, Calcutta: Government of India Central Publication Branch, 1929, pp. 272-3.

176. On behalf of All India Women's Educational Reform, Patna, 8 January 1929, in *Age of Consent Committee Evidence, 1928-1929: Oral Evidence and Written Statements of Witnesses from Bihar and Orissa, Assam and Burma*, vol. VII, Calcutta: Government of India Central Publication Branch, 1929, p. 126.
177. Aparna Basu and Bharati Ray (eds.), op. cit., First Published 1990, 3rd edn. 2018, pp. 59-60.
178. Oral evidence of Miss Jyotirmoyi Ganguli, M.A., 6, Guru Prasad Chaudhuri Lane, Calcutta, 18 December 1928, in *Age of Consent Committee Evidence, 1928-1929: Oral Evidence and Written Statements of Witnesses from Bengal Presidency*, vol. VI, Calcutta: Government of India Central Publication Branch, 1929, pp. 12-18.
179. Written statement dated 25 December 1928, of Margaret E. Cousins, Ex-Secretary of the Women's Indian Association, in *Age of Consent Committee Evidence, 1928-1929: Oral Evidence and Written Statements of Witnesses from the Madras Presidency*, vol. IV, Calcutta: Government of India Central Publication Branch, 1929, pp. 570-1.
180. *Age of Consent Committee Evidence, 1928-1929: Oral Evidence and Written Statements of Witnesses from (United Provinces Contd.) Lucknow and Ajmer-Merwara*, vol. IX, Calcutta: Government of India Central Publication Branch, 1929, pp. 433-4.
181. Ibid., p. 434.
182. Ibid.
183. Sumita Mukherjee, op. cit., 2006, p. 229.
184. Notes on a Visit to Villages by the Age of Consent Committee, Madura, in *Age of Consent Committee Evidence, 1928-1929: Oral Evidence and Written Statements of Witnesses from the Madras Presidency (Ootacamund, Calicut, Madura and Vizagapatam) and Coorg*, vol. V, Calcutta: Government of India Central Publication Branch, 1929, p. 358.
185. Sumita Mukherjee, op. cit., 2006, p. 229.
186. Written statement, 3 August 1928 of Dr (Miss) A.C. Scott, Chief Medical Officer, Women's Medical Service, Secretary, Countess of Dufferin's Fund, Simla, in *Age of Consent Committee Evidence, 1928-1929: Oral Evidence and Written Statements of Witnesses from the Punjab, N.W.F.P. and Delhi*, vol. I, Calcutta: Government of India Central Publication Branch, 1929, p. 26.
187. Written statement dated 23 August 1928 of Miss Khadijah Begum

Ferozuddin, Professor of History and Oriental Languages, College for Women, Lahore, in *Age of Consent Committee Evidence, 1928-1929: Oral Evidence and Written Statements of Witnesses from the Punjab, N.W.F.P. and Delhi*, vol. I, Calcutta: Government of India Central Publication Branch, 1929, pp. 255-8.

188. Written statement dated 11 August 1928 of Dr (Mrs) Malini B. Sukthankar, Honorary Physician for children, Cama and Albless Hospitals, Bombay, in *Age of Consent Committee Evidence, 1928-1929: Oral Evidence and Written Statements of Witnesses from the Bombay Presidency (Continued – Bombay and Poona) and the Central Provinces and Berar*, vol. III, Calcutta: Government of India Central Publication Branch, 1929, p. 158.
189. Written statement, 18 August 1928 of R.P. Masani, Vice-President, Vigilance Society, Bombay, in *Age of Consent Committee Evidence, 1928-1929: Oral Evidence and Written Statements of Witnesses from the Bombay Presidency (Continued – Bombay and Poona) and the Central Provinces and Berar*, vol. III, Calcutta: Government of India Central Publication Branch, 1929, pp. 212-14.
190. Written statement, 11 August 1928 of Miss Katherine Davis, Secretary, The Children's Aid Society, Children's Home, Umarkhadi, in *Age of Consent Committee Evidence, 1928-1929: Oral Evidence and Written Statements of Witnesses from the Bombay Presidency (Continued – Bombay and Poona) and the Central Provinces and Berar*, vol. III, Calcutta: Government of India Central Publication Branch, 1929, pp. 176-82.
191. Written statement of I.S. Haji, Bar-at-Law, Chowpatty Sea Face, Bombay, no. 7, in *Age of Consent Committee Evidence*, vol. III, op. cit., pp. 125-30.
192. Judy Whitehead, op. cit., 1 January 1995, p. 203.
193. Written statement, 7 August 1928, of Kamaladevi Chattopadhyay, Honorary Organizing Secretary, All India Women's Conference on Educational Reform, Dhareshwar Gardens, Bangalore, in *Age of Consent Committee Evidence, 1928-1929: Oral Evidence and Written Statements of Witnesses from the Madras Presidency*, vol. IV, Calcutta: Government of India Central Publication Branch, 1929, pp. 8-13. Kamaladevi Chattopadhyay, *Indian Women's Battle for Freedom*, New Delhi: Abhinav Publications, pp. 56-9, 61-3.
194. Written Statement, 10 August 1928 Dr (Mrs) S. Muthulakshmi Reddy, Vice President of the Women's Indian Association, Madras, Vice

President of the Women Graduates' Union, Madras and Secretary to the Indian Ladies' Samaj, Madras, Vice President of Sri Sarada Ladies' Union, Madras, in *Age of Consent Committee Evidence*, vol. IV, op. cit., p. 362.

195. India in 1929-30: A statement prepared for presentation to Parliament in accordance with the requirements of the 26th Section of the Government of India Act (5 & 6 Geo. V, Chap. 61), Calcutta: Government of India Central Publication Branch, 1931, p. 7.
196. *Report of the Age of Consent Committee, 1928-1929*, op. cit., pp. 184, 196.
197. Ibid., pp. 123, 196.
198. Ibid., p. 124.
199. Ibid., p. 200.
200. Ibid., pp. 178, 196.
201. Cited in Laxmibai Rajwade, 'The Indian Mother and Her Problems', in Shyam Kumari Nehru (ed.), *Our Cause: A Symposium by Indian Women*, Allahabad: Kitabistan, 1938, p. 80.
202. *The Legislative Assembly Debates*, vol. IV, 4 September 1929, Simla: Government of India Press, 1930, p. 240.
203. Paragraph 362 of the Report, under the heading, 'Relation between early marriage and maternal and infantile mortality', stated that 'From the figures of 1921 census quoted in Appendices VI-C and VII-C, in some provinces of India it appears that where more girls under 15 are married, greater infantile mortality exists.' On the other hand, in other Provinces, as the Report specified, 'This is in Burma where the girls are married hardly below 15...'. *The Legislative Assembly Debates*, vol. IV, 4 September 1929, Simla: Government of India Press, 1930, pp. 244-5.
204. *The Legislative Assembly Debates*, vol. IV, 4 September 1929, Simla: Government of India Press, 1930, p. 254.
205. Ibid.
206. Ibid., p. 255.
207. Ibid., p. 256.
208. Ibid.
209. Ibid.
210. Ibid., p. 259.
211. Ibid., p. 261. There has been a lot of controversy among scholars about Vidyasagar's position regarding the Age of Consent Bill. Vidyasagar was as proactive about the Consent Bill as the government wanted it

to be. Many think that the situation could have been different if it had been his own proposal. So, there was no question of his retreat or self-contradiction.

212. Ibid.
213. *The Legislative Assembly Debates*, vol. II, 26 March 1928, Delhi: Government of India Press, 1928, p. 1974.
214. Tanika Sarkar, *Hindu Wife, Hindu Nation: Community, Religion, and Cultural Nationalism*, Bloomington and Indianapolis: Indiana University Press, p. 45.
215. *The Legislative Assembly Debates*, vol. IV, 4 September 1929, Simla: Government of India Press, 1930, p. 262.
216. Ibid., p. 275.
217. *The Legislative Assembly Debates*, vol. IV, 5 September 1929, Simla: Government of India Press, 1930, pp. 348-50.
218. *The Legislative Assembly Debates*, vol. IV, 4 September 1929, Simla: Government of India Press, 1930, p. 279.
219. Note by Maulvi Muhammad Yakub, *Report of the Age of Consent Committee, 1928-1929*, op. cit., p. 282.
220. *The Legislative Assembly Debates*, vol. IV, 5 September 1929, Simla: Government of India Press, 1930, p. 343.
221. Ibid., p. 345.
222. Ibid., p. 358.
223. Ibid., p. 360.
224. Ibid., pp. 362-3.
225. Ibid., p. 366.
226. Ibid., pp. 373-4.
227. Ibid., p. 375.
228. Ibid., p. 376.
229. *The Legislative Assembly Debates*, vol. IV, 11 September 1929, Simla: Government of India Press, 1930, p. 651.
230. Ibid., p. 652.
231. Ibid., p. 655.
232. Ibid., pp. 657-8.
233. Ibid., p. 667.
234. Ibid.
235. Ibid., p. 674.
236. Ibid., p. 680.
237. *The Legislative Assembly Debates*, vol. V, 18 September 1929, Simla: Government of India Press, 1930, p. 1056.
238. Ibid., p. 1088.

239. *Report of the Age of Consent Committee, 1928-1929*, op. cit., p. 6.
240. *The Legislative Assembly Debates*, vol. IV, 19 September 1929, Simla: Government of India Press, 1930, p. 1140.
241. Ibid., p. 1142.
242. Ibid., p. 1143.
243. Ibid., p. 1156.
244. *The Legislative Assembly Debates*, vol. V, 23 September 1929, Simla: Government of India Press, 1930, p. 1248.
245. Ibid., pp. 1277-8.
246. Ibid., p. 1283.
247. A.S. Srinivasa Aiyar, *The Child Marriage Restraint Act (Act XIX of 1929), with an Analytical Introduction, Critical Comments, Original Bill, Statement of Objects and Reasons, Reports of the Select Committees (with Minutes of Dissent) and Select Speeches in the Assembly*, Appendix D (1), Legislative Assembly Debates, Madras: The Law Publishing Company, 1930, p. 133.
248. Nripendra Nath Mitra (ed.), *The Indian Quarterly Register: Being a Quarterly Journal of Indian Public Affairs, in matters Political, Social and Economic*, vol. II, July-December 1929, nos. III&IV, Calcutta: The Annual Register Office, p. 150.
249. 'Balyabibaha Nishedhak Ain' (The Law Prohibiting Child Marriage), *Prabasi*, Kartik (October-November), 1336 (1929), vol. 2, part 29, p. 166.
250. A.S. Srinivasa Aiyar, *The Child Marriage Restraint Act (Act XIX of 1929), with an Analytical Introduction, Critical Comments, Original Bill, Statement of Objects and Reasons, Reports of the Select Committees (with Minutes of Dissent) and Select Speeches in the Assembly*, Madras: The Law Publishing Company, 1930, p. 4.
251. Ibid., p. 5.
252. Ibid., p. 8; *Report of the Age of Consent Committee, 1928-1929*, Appendix X-B, Calcutta: Government of India Central Publication Branch, 1929, p. 343.
253. Sunil Kanti De, 'Sarda Bill O Muslim Sambad-Samayik Patra' (Sarda Bill and Muslim Newspapers-Periodicals), in *Itihas Anusandhan*, Kolkata: Paschimbanga Itihas Samsad, vol. 9, p. 370.
254. *Hanifi*, 23 September 1929, cited in Sunil Kanti De, op. cit., p. 372.
255. *Weekly Saogat*, 6 September 1929, p. 1.
256. *The Mussalman*, 27 September 1929, p. 4.
257. *The Mussalman*, 20 September 1929, p. 8.
258. Intelligence Report – Second Half of October 1929, Home Political,

File no. 73/1930 (1-8), West Bengal State Archives (hereafter WBSA).

259. 'Sarada Ain Batil Koribar Byartha Chesta' (Unsuccessful Attempts to Repeal the Sarda Act), *Prabasi*, Chaitra (March-April), 1338 (1931), vol. 2, part 31, p. 899; 'Balyabibaha Punarprabartaner Byartha Chesta' (Unsuccessful Attempts to Reintroduce Child Marriage), *Prabasi*, Kartik (October-November), 1339 (1932), vol. 2, part 32, p. 152.
260. Intelligence Report – 18 December 1929, Sarda Act, Home Political, File no. 73/1930 (1-8), WBSA.
261. Intelligence Report – Second Half of December 1929, Home Political, File no. 73/1930 (1-8), WBSA.
262. *Weekly Saogat*, 6 December 1929, p. 10.
263. 'Balyabibaha Nirodh Aainer Phal' (The Result of Child Marriage Prohibition Act), *Prabasi*, Baishakh (April-May), 1337 (1930), vol. 1, part 30, pp. 172-3.
264. 'Balyabibaha Nirodh Aain' (Child Marriage Prohibition Act), *Prabasi*, Poush (December-January), 1336 (1929), vol. 2, part 29, pp. 457-8.
265. Saralabala Sarkar, 'Sarda Aainer Akarjakarita' (Ineffectiveness of Sarda Act), in Chitra Deb (ed.), *Saralabala Rachanasangraha* (Collection of Essays of Saralabala), vol. 2, Calcutta: Ananda Publishers, pp. 604-5.
266. Intelligence Report – first half of March, 1930, Home Political, File no. 73/1930 (1-8), WBSA.
267. Ibid.
268. Ibid.
269. Bengal Secretariat, 1 February 1930, Confidential D.C. no. 640-44, Home Political, File no. 73/1930 (1-8), WBSA.
270. *Letter from the Commissioner of Burdwan Division, Chinsurah, G. Goode, dated 20th February 1930, to the Chief Secretary to the Government of Bengal, W.D.R. Prentice*, Home Political, File no. 73/1930 (1-8), WBSA.
271. *Letter from the Commissioner of Rajshahi Division, Jalpaiguri, dated 1 March 1930, to the Chief Secretary to the Government of Bengal, W.D.R. Prentice*, Home Political, File no. 73/1930 (1-8), WBSA.
272. *Letter from the Commissioner of Ramna (Dacca) Division, dated 5th March 1930, to the Chief Secretary to the Government of Bengal, W.D.R. Prentice*, Home Political, File no. 73/1930 (1-8), WBSA.
273. *Report of C.M. Martin, District Magistrate of Dacca, dated 17 February 1930, to the Chief Secretary to the Government of Bengal, W.D.R. Prentice*, Home Political, File no. 73/1930 (1-8), WBSA.

274. *Letter from G.S. Dutt, I.C.S., District Officer, Mymensingh, dated 26 February 1930, to the Chief Secretary to the Government of Bengal, W.D.R. Prentice*, Home Political, File no. 73/1930 (1-8), WBSA.
275. *Letter from the District Magistrate of Faridpur, dated 21st February 1930, to the Chief Secretary to the Government of Bengal, W.D.R. Prentice*, Home Political, File no. 73/1930 (1-8), WBSA.
276. *Letter from the District Magistrate of Barisal, dated 27 February 1930, to the Chief Secretary to the Government of Bengal, W.D.R. Prentice*, Home Political, File no. 73/1930 (1-8), WBSA.
277. *Letter from the Commissioner of Chittagong, dated 10 March 1930, to the Chief Secretary to the Government of Bengal, W.D.R. Prentice*, Home Political, File no. 73/1930 (1-8), WBSA.
278. *Letter from the District Officer of Chittagong, dated 19 February 1930, to the Chief Secretary to the Government of Bengal, W.D.R. Prentice*, Home Political, File no. 73/1930 (1-8), WBSA.
279. *Letter from the Magistrate's Office of Noakhali, dated 1 March 1930, to the Chief Secretary to the Government of Bengal, W.D.R. Prentice*, Home Political, File no. 73/1930 (1-8), WBSA.
280. *Letter from the Commissioner Office of Presidency Division, dated 26 March 1930, to the Chief Secretary to the Government of Bengal, W.D.R. Prentice*, Home Political, File no. 73/1930 (1-8), WBSA.
281. Home Political, File no. 73/1930 (1-8), WBSA.
282. Rameshwari Nehru, 'Early Marriage', in Shyam Kumari Nehru (ed.), *Our Cause: A Symposium by Indian Women*, pp. 262-3.
283. Tahir Mahmood, *Muslim Personal Law: Role of State in the Subcontinent*, New Delhi: Vikas Publishing House, 1977, p. 53.
284. Mohammad Meherullah Hussein, *Balya Bibaher Bishmay Phal* (The Poisonous Fruit/Result of Child Marriage), Sirajganj: Author, 1909, cited in Sonia Amin, *The World of Muslim Women in Colonial Bengal, 1876-1939, Social, Economic and Political Studies of the Middle East and Asia*, vol. 55, New York: Brill, 1996, p. 56.
285. Moslema Khatun, 'Amar Jibaner Galpakatha' (The Story of My Life), in Nurunnahar Faizunnessa (ed.), *Kaler Samukh Bhela* (The Raft Ahead of Time), Dhaka: Muktadhara, 1988, cited in Sonia Amin, op. cit., pp. 56-7.
286. *Ananda Bazar Patrika*, 21 June 1929, editorial 'Apatti Keno' (Why Object); *Ananda Bazar Patrika*, 3 September 1929, editorial, 'Balya Bibaha Birodh' (Child Marriage Protest).
287. Prafulla Kumar Dhar, *Strir Sahit Kathopakathan* (Conversations with Wife), Calcutta, 1332 BS, 1925 CE, p. 138.

288. Sabyasachi Bhattacharya, *The Defining Moments in Bengal: 1920-1947*, New Delhi: Oxford University Press, 2014, p. 49.
289. *Ananda Bazar Patrika*, editorial, 'Janani O Jaya' (Mother and Wife), 12 January 1923.
290. Sabyasachi Bhattacharya, op. cit., p. 59.
291. *Ananda Bazar Patrika*, 3 September 1929.
292. *Ananda Bazar Patrika*, editorials on prevention of child marriage and resistance to it, 18 August 1929, 3 September 1929, cited in Sabyasachi Bhattacharya, op. cit., p. 60.
293. Aparna Basu and Bharati Ray (eds.), op. cit., First Published 1990, 3rd edn. 2018, p. 61.
294. Ibid.
295. Mary E. John, op. cit., 2021, p. 32.
296. *Times of London*, 19 May 1930, p. 13.
297. Nripendra Nath Mitra (ed.), *The Indian Annual Register*, vol. 1, January-June 1931, p. 373; All India Women's Conference, Annual Report, 1931, p. 60, cited in Aparna Basu and Bharati Ray (eds.), op. cit., First Published 1990, 3rd edn. 2018, p. 62.
298. Aparna Basu and Bharati Ray (eds.), op. cit., First Published 1990, 3rd edn. 2018, p. 62.
299. *Proceedings of the Annual Meeting of the All India Women's Conference*, Nagpur Session, 1937. Q/I/FC/49, pp. 168-70, India Office Library and Records, London, cited in Azra Asghar Ali, op. cit., 2000, p. 145.
300. Mona Hensman, 'Report of the First International Conference of Women in India', *Stri Dharma*, vol. XIX, no. 4, May 1939, pp. 126-7, cited in Azra Asghar Ali, op. cit., 2000, p. 145.
301. 'Sarada Aainer Samarthan O Sanshodhoner Dabi' (Demand for Support and Amendment of the Sarda Act), *Prabasi*, Baishakh (April-May), 1340 (1933), vol. 1, part 33, p. 155.
302. *The Modern Review*, December 1937, p. 716.
303. 'Bankura Zilla Mahila Sammelan' (Women's Conference of Bankura District), *Prabasi*, Ashar (June-July), 1346 (1939), vol. 1, part 39, pp. 410-11.
304. 'Balyabibaha Nirodh Aain O Strishiksha' (Child Marriage Prohibition Act and Women's Education), *Prabasi*, Agrahayan (November-December), 1336 (1929), vol. 2, part 29, pp. 316-19; 'Sarada Aain O Balikadiger Shiksha' (Sarda Act and Girl's Education), *Prabasi*, Chaitra (March-April), 1337 (1930), vol. 2, part 30, p. 1002; Sri Charuchandra Bandyopadhyay, 'Samajer Bartaman Abastha O Mahilader Kartabya'

(The Current State of Society and the Duties of Women), *Prabasi*, Magh (January-February), 1338 (1931), vol. 2, part 31, pp. 485-90.

305. 'Nikhil Bharat Mahila Sammelaner Kolikata Sakhar Adhibeshan' (Session of the Calcutta Branch of the All India Women's Conference), *Prabasi*, Poush (December-January), 1348 (1941), vol. 2, part 41, p. 352.
306. Mrinalini Sinha, op. cit., 2006.
307. 'Speeches and Writings', vol. 2, part 2, *Muthulakshmi Reddy Papers*, cited in Mrinalini Sinha (ed.), op. cit., 1998, pp. 45-6.
308. Mrinalini Sinha (ed.), op. cit., 1998, pp. 46-7.
309. Mrinalini Sinha, op. cit., 2006, p. 153; For Gandhi's wire to members of the Legislative Assembly, the speech by Mukhtiar Singh, extract from Legislative Assembly Debates, 16 September 1929, Home, Judicial, 570/29, 1929. For Gandhi's initial lack of faith in legislation, Rameshwari Nehru's recollection of her first encounter with Gandhi as a member of the Government of India's Age of Consent Committee. Nehru, 'Gandhiji and Women', in Chandrashankar Shukla (ed.), *Incidents of Gandhiji's Life*, Bombay: Vora, 1949, pp. 209-14. Gandhi's attitude toward the relationship between state and society was more complex than the popular perception of his simple repudiation of the state. Ronald J. Terchek, *Gandhi: Struggling for Autonomy*, London: Rowman and Littlefield, 1999, pp. 166-7; and Bhiku Parkeh, *Gandhi's Political Philosophy: A Critical Examination*, Basingstoke: Macmillan, 1989, pp. 113-21.
310. Legislative Department 3-II/28.A, 1928; and Home Judicial File no. 382/27, 1927, cited in Mrinalini Sinha (ed.), op. cit., 1998, p. 47.
311. Mrinalini Sinha (ed.), op. cit., 1998, p. 47.
312. Mrinalini Sinha, op. cit., 2006, p. 153.
313. For reconstructions of the women's campaign in India for the passage of the Sarda Bill, Kamaladevi Chattopadhyay, *Inner Recesses, Outer Spaces: Memoirs*, New Delhi: Navrang, 1986, pp. 113-17; Dhanvanthi Rama Rau, *An Inheritance: The Memoirs of Dhanvanthi Rama Rau*, London: Harper and Row, 1977, p. 151; Jahanara Shahnawaz, *Father and Daughter: A Political Autobiography*, Lahore: Nigarishat, 1971, pp. 97-8; Hansa Mehta, *Indian Women*, Delhi: Butala and Co., 1981, p. 63; and Amrit Kaur, *Challenge to Women*, Allahabad: New Literature, 1946, p. 5. File nos. 7, 8, 12, AIWC Files; and 'Social Welfare Measures', File nos. 8, 9 and 10, *Muthulakshmi Reddy Papers*, cited in Mrinalini Sinha (ed.), op. cit., New Delhi: Kali for Women, 1998, p. 49.

314. Durba Mitra, *Indian Sex Life: Sexuality and the Colonial Origins of Modern Social Thought*, New Jersey: Princeton University Press, 2020, pp. 197-8.
315. Manoda Devi, 'Shikshita Patitar Atmacharit' (Autobiography of an Educated Fallen Woman), in Bijit Ghosh (ed.), *Promila Smritikatha Samgraha* (Collection of Promila Memoirs), Kolkata: Punascha, 2014, pp. 333-402.
316. Dr (Mrs) S. Muthulakshmi Reddy, *My Experience as a Legislator*, Madras: Current Thought Press, 1930, p. 98.
317. 'The Andhra Mahila Maha Sabha', in Nripendra Nath Mitra (ed.), *The Indian Quarterly Register, Being a Quarterly Journal of Indian Public Affairs in Matters Political, Social and Economic*, vol. II, July-Dec. 1929, nos. III&IV, Calcutta: The Annual Register Office, pp. 396-7.
318. 'The Oudh Women's Conference', in Nripendra Nath Mitra (ed.), *The Indian Quarterly Register, Being a Quarterly Journal of Indian Public Affairs in Matters Political, Social and Economic*, vol. II, July-December 1929, nos. III&IV., Calcutta: The Annual Register Office, p. 398.
319. Mytheli Sreenivas, *Wives, Widows, and Concubines: The Conjugal Family Ideal in Colonial India*, Bloomington and Indianapolis: Indiana University Press, pp. 78-9.
320. *The Indian Medical Gazette*, vol. 66, June 1931, p. 342. *The Indian Medical Gazette*, vol. 66, May 1931, p. 270; *The Indian Medical Gazette*, vol. 66, August 1931, p. 451.
321. *Harijan*, 16 November 1935, cited in M.K. Gandhi, op. cit., 1942 (1st edn.), 1958 (repr.), p. 40.
322. Ibid.
323. Ibid.
324. Ibid., pp. 40-1.
325. Cited in Laxmibai Rajwade, 'The Indian Mother and Her Problems', op. cit., 1938, p. 77.
326. Ibid.
327. Laxmibai Rajwade, 'The Indian Mother and Her Problems', op. cit., 1938, p. 79.
328. Ibid., p. 84.
329. Census of India, 1931, vol. 1, part 1, Delhi: Manager of Publications, 1933, p. 229.
330. 'Balyabibaha-Nirodh Aainer Proyog' (Enforcement of Child Marriage Prohibition Act), *Prabasi*, Bhadra (August-September), 1338 (1931), vol. 1, Part 31, p. 726.
331. Census of India, 1931, vol. 1, part 1, p. 230.

332. Census of India, 1931, vol. 1, part 1, Report, Chapter VI. – Civil Condition, p. 224.
333. Ibid.
334. Ibid.
335. 'Sarada Aainke Fanki Deoa' (Evading the Sarda Act), *Prabasi*, Shraban (July-August), 1341 (1934), vol. 1, part 34, p. 623.
336. *Madras Mail*, 3 July 1934. Reprinted in Government of Madras Order no. 2454 (Law General), 28 August 1934 cited in Mytheli Sreenivas, op. cit., 2008, pp. 80-1. The report added that, 'owing to the large number of marriages that took place, the accommodation in Yanam was found insufficient during the last marriage season'. 'Sarada Aainke Fanki Deoa' (Evading the Sarda Act), *Prabasi*, Shraban (July-August), 1341 (1934), vol. 1, part 34, p. 623.
337. 'Child Marriage Restraint Act in French India', *Modern Review*, May 1937, p. 598.
338. Dr R.B. Khambata (ed.), *Bengal Public Health Report: Reports of the Bengal Sanitary Board and the Chief Engineer Public Health Department, For the Year 1930*, Calcutta: Bengal Secretariat Book Depot, 1932, p. 99.
339. Government of Bengal, Revenue Department, *Report of the Administration of Bengal, 1929-1930*, Calcutta: Bengal Secretariat Book Depot, 1931, p. 5.
340. Ibid., p. 70.
341. Ibid., p. 152.
342. Home Department, Judicial, National Archives of India, 563/33, cited in Andrea Major, 'Mediating Modernity: Colonial State, Indian Nationalism and the Renegotiation of the "Civilizing Mission" in the Indian Child Marriage Debate of 1927-1932', Carey A. Watt and Michael Mann (eds.), *Civilizing Missions in Colonial and Postcolonial South Asia: From Improvement to Development*, London/New York/Delhi: Anthem Press, 2011, p. 183.
343. Mrinalini Sinha, op. cit., 2006.
344. Ibid.
345. Geraldine Forbes, 'The politics of respectability: Indian women and the Indian National Congress', in D.A. Low (ed.), *The Indian National Congress: Centenary Highlights*, Oxford: Oxford University Press, 1988, pp. 54-67; Tanika Sarkar, 'Politics and Women in Bengal – The Conditions and Meaning of Participation', *Indian Economic and Social History Review*, vol. 21, no. 1, 1984, pp. 91-101.
346. Andrea Major, op. cit., 2011, p. 185.

347. Nripendra Nath Mitra (ed.), *The Indian Annual Register: An Annual Digest of Public Affairs of India, Recording the Nation's Activities each year in matters Political, Economic, Industrial, Educational, Social, Etc.*, vol. II, July-December 1934, Calcutta: The Annual Register Office, pp. 88 (c)-88 (d).
348. Ibid., p. 111.
349. Flavia Agnes, *Law and Gender Inequality: The Politics of Women's Rights in India*, Delhi: Oxford University Press, 2001 (Oxford India Paperbacks), p. 68.
350. K.T. Shah (ed.), *Women's Role in Planned Economy: Report of the Sub-Committee*, Bombay: Vora & Co. Publishers Ltd., 1956; Maitrayee Chaudhuri, 'Citizens, Workers and Emblems of Culture: An Analysis of the First Plan Document on Women', *Contributions to Indian Sociology*, (n.s.) vol. 29, nos. 1&2, 1995, pp. 211-35.
351. Maitrayee Chaudhuri, 'Citizens, Workers and Emblems of Culture: An Analysis of the First Plan Document on Women', *Contributions to Indian Sociology*, (n.s.) vol. 29, nos. 1&2, 1995, p. 214.
352. K.T. Shah, (ed.), op. cit., 1956, p. 131.
353. Ibid., p. 220.
354. Mary E. John, op. cit., 2021, pp. 35-6.
355. For details, Nripendra Nath Mitra (ed.), *The Indian Annual Register: An Annual Digest of Public Affairs of India, Recording the Nation's Activities each year in matters Political, Economic, Industrial, Educational, Social*, vol. I, January-June, 1938, Calcutta: The Annual Register Office, pp. 86-7, 89; Nripendra Nath Mitra (ed.), *The Indian Annual Register: An Annual Digest of Public Affairs of India, Recording the Nation's Activities each year in matters Political, Economic, Industrial, Educational, Social*, vol. II, July-December 1938, Calcutta: The Annual Register Office, p. 69.
356. 'Restraining Child Marriage', *Amrita Bazar Patrika*, 26 August 1948, p. 5.
357. Ibid.
358. *Amrita Bazar Patrika*, 5 April 1949, p. 1.
359. Ibid.
360. *Amrita Bazar Patrika*, 5 April 1949, p. 8.
361. *Amrita Bazar Patrika*, 25 June 1949, p. 5.
362. Home, Judicial, File: 534/25 (NAI, 1925), cited in Ishita Pande, 'Sorting Boys and Men: Unlawful Intercourse, Boy-Protection, and the Child Marriage Restraint Act in Colonial India', *The Journal of the History of Childhood and Youth*, vol. 6, no. 2, 2013, p. 342.

363. Mary E. John, op. cit., 2021, p. 33.
364. The law that came into operation in April 1930 resonated with a secular nationalist vision because it applied to all communities.
365. Jaya Sagade, *Child Marriage in India: Socio-legal and Human Rights Dimensions*, New Delhi: Oxford University Press, p. 44.
366. Sara Hossain, 'Chapter 20. Equality in the Home: Women's Rights and Personal Laws in South Asia', in Rebecca J. Cook (ed.), *Human Rights of Women: National and International Perspective*, Philadelphia: University of Pennsylvania Press, 2012, pp. 465-94.
367. Vina Mazumdar, 'Introduction', in Vina Mazumdar (ed.), *Symbols of Power: Studies on the Political Status of Women in India*, New Delhi: Allied Publishers, 1979, pp. xi-xxiv.

CHAPTER 5

Contemporary Concerns on the Age of Marriage

The Child Marriage Restraint Act of 1929 (CMRA) failed to achieve its goal of eradicating child marriages from India. It is also true that the CMRA has been haunted by the spectre of failure since its inception. The occurrence of child marriages increased dramatically between the time the law was passed in September 1929 and when it took effect on 1 April 1930, in anticipation of its application. In her book on child marriage, the British politician Eleanor Rathbone projected from the census statistics that 'the number of children hustled into matrimony in the fatal six months (between the passage of the bill and its becoming law) was probably not less than three million girls and two million boys.'[1] Few cases were reported in British India; fewer still ended in convictions. This was not astonishing, given the colonial state had covertly ordered provincial governments to avoid controversy by limiting prosecutions to a minimum.[2] It is also possible, of course, to regard the CMRA as a success, as a bill that was passed into law despite the fact that other similar bills controlling child marriage were rejected in their time and downgraded to the 'ash heap of history', and as a bill that had at least some functional effect in reducing child marriages and that has, moreover, gone through over time.[3]

The CMRA lived on in the statute book in postcolonial India with minor adjustments. In 1949, the minimum ages of marriage were amended to fifteen years for females and eighteen years for males in India. In 1978, the 'child was redefined yet again as a person who, if a male, has not completed 21 years of age, and if a female, has not completed 18 years of age'.[4] In 2000, the United Nation's Population

Division confirmed that '35.7 per cent of females in India and 9.5 per cent of males in these age ranges were married'. The 2001 Census of India showed that '300,000 girls under fifteen years of age had already given birth'. International organizations, including the United Nations, continue to generate frantic appeals to curb underage marriages, warning that India has 'the largest number of child brides in the world, one-third of the global total'.[5]

In 2006, the CMRA was finally repealed and replaced by the Prohibition of Child Marriage Act (PCMA), which preserved the minimum ages of marriage as set by the CMRA but made underage marriages voidable upon the wife's option. The PCMA of 2006 came into effect to address what is regarded to be a social problem. For the very first time, the legislative body endeavoured to give a new dimension into such social legislation. Nonetheless, legislators have been cautious about imposing a radical divergence between law and custom. The PCMA does not make child marriage unlawful. Furthermore, its effectiveness is dependent on determining the age, both to validate the marriage and to develop proficiency for annulment. In rural society, however, age is a matter of conjecture. There is a significant misalignment between the legal emphasis on digital age and the social perspective of age and willingness for marriage. According to this calculation, the majority of girls are married between the ages of 16 and 17, followed by 14 and 15, as 13 is the average age for girls to reach puberty. In social understanding, a girl is ready for marriage when she reaches puberty.

In the 2021 Winter Session of Parliament, the government introduced a bill to raise the minimum age of marriage for women from 18 to 21, making it the same as the age for men. This came almost two years after a surprise announcement in the budget speech of February 2020, that the government was contemplating such a move. In July 2020, a task force was set up by the Niti Aayog to examine the issue, which requested concerned parties to share their opinions. Although the task force's report is yet to be made public, the government outlined the amendment bill to the Prohibition of Child Marriage Act of 2006 (PCMA), which was then referred to a parliamentary committee. According to Mary E. John,

To understand what is at stake here we must begin by noting that the new law intends to redefine any person who has not yet reached the age of 21 as a 'child'. This is necessary in order to ensure that marriages below the age of 21 are prohibited with legal force, in other words, treated as 'criminalizable'. The government's rationale for doing this is listed in the unusually lengthy 'objects and reasons' section of the new bill (PCMA of 2021). The list of ills that the proposed amendment intends to remedy includes everything from a woman's physical, mental and reproductive health, to her disadvantages in higher education, employment opportunities, skill training and entry into the work force. No bill in recent times has claimed to address such a wide range of conditions.[6]

She also added,

Though the average age at marriage is now above 20, a very large proportion of women in the age group 20-24 years married before the age of 21-56 per cent in all, as per NFHS 4 (2015-16) data, and 70 per cent of the poorest fifth. The new law will bring large numbers of young people and their families into zones of illegality, robbing women of the legal protection that marriage provides.[7]

It can be argued that the law is an ineffective tool for bringing about change in areas such as the marriage system. Particularly given that such laws do not, or cannot, address underlying issues such as a social convergence on 'universal' and 'compulsory marriage'. Furthermore, in child or underage marriage, the agency is moving from the parents to the child. We need to figure out why this occurrence is on the rise and how strategy, rather than law, can address the problem. Most of the social activists and feminists oppose this new legislation by focusing on a few issues. They have argued that there is no point in raising the age of marriage without providing education, security and self-reliance for girls. Second, legislation alone will not do anything, but if this law is introduced, various misdeeds like, false allegations of abduction, trafficking of girls will increase through its gaps. They also questioned who would take care of the safety of poor unmarried girls in rural areas. There is no denying that these fears are not false. But there is no reason to think that only legislation will be enacted and the government will not take the expected action to make it effective. The fact that laws have not been enforced in the past does not mean that they will not succeed in the future. The overall development of education, health, and the economy is inextricably linked with the issue of raising the age of marriage for girls. Therefore, the Government should try to implement the law step by step according to the plan. But as long as that 'adequate arrangement' is not in place, what solutions do we have for girls? In a word, 'getting married'! This arrangement is not only for the girls of low-income families in the villages or for those who do not have much education or employment opportunities. But even in affluent families in urban areas, the thought of marriage revolves around the head of the guardian at the age of eighteen.

The issue of giving the daughter in marriage is really like fulfilling a responsibility – *Kanyadan* (burden of a daughter) on the part of the guardian, the responsibility of which has to be taken by the girl at the end. Not all of these girls would have become self-sufficient or survived if they had gotten married after 21 years, but they would have been given a chance to make their lives a little better. The rules of society did not change in one day, nor will they change in one day. But any change starts with the law; although it has some misapplications, gradually the benefits match. The government announcement has spoken of gender equality. The thought of the government is that the age of marriage of boys is 21, so, the marriage age of girls should also 21. However, not just raising the age of marriage, but at the same time, some more thinking is needed to change this trend. For example, the girl who has not done any studies also needed some education. Handicrafts, sewing, computers, bridal decorating, mobile repair, spice business – she can do anything. But if the marriage is done, then how will the girls enjoy the benefits?[8] On the contrary, if they know that they cannot get married now, their parents will be interested in teaching them to work without leaving them behind. Even if all the girls do not start earning a lot, the education will remain in them. Some self-confidence, self-reliance will be created, which will work in the future.

Marriage is fundamentally different from adulthood, suffrage, and sexual rights. It is not only a right, but also a collective responsibility; therefore, it is pointless to confuse marriage with anything else. From 18 to 21, graduating from high school is not just three years of life, but several steps towards becoming. Marriage means more than just consenting to sex, it means being prepared to take on the responsibility of having children. Study or not, 18 years is not enough time to learn something, to develop good and bad feelings and opinions, and to reduce the age difference between husband and wife. If the age of marriage of girls is increased from 18 to 21, then positivity can be noticed in some cases, like, the maturity of body and mind of a girl, the ability to take decisions to protect herself, the scope to gain education; malnutrition, infant and maternal mortality will lessen. Parents also need to be told not to shove their daughters into danger for the rest of their lives. But before that, we have to realize for ourselves that getting married at the age of 18 is never good for girls. We are obstructing passing the law because we cannot protect the law and we are forgetting our real responsibility by raising the question of safety and the rights of girls. Otherwise, it was our responsibility to make it clear that the age of marriage for girls should be raised and necessary arrangements should be made for it.

NOTES

1. Eleanor F. Rathbone, *Child Marriage: The Indian Minotaur: An Object-Lesson from the Past to the Future*, London: George Allen & Unwin, 1934, p. 47.
2. Ishita Pande, *Sex, Law, and the Politics of Age: Child Marriage in India, 1891-1937*, Cambridge: Cambridge University Press, 2020, pp. 20-1.
3. For instance, Neeraj Hatekar, Rajni Mathur, and Pallavi Rege, '"Legislating" Social Change: Strange Case of the Sarda Act,' *Economic and Political Weekly*, vol. 42, no. 2, 13-19 January 2007, pp. 145–53.
4. Ishita Pande, op. cit., p. 21.
5. UNICEF, Ending Child Marriage in India, www.unicef.org/rosa/media/691/file, accessed on 28 April 2022.
6. Mary E. John, 'A Suitable Girl? Marriage, Age and Equality', https://www.theindiaforum.in/article/suitable-girl, accessed on 28 April 2022.
7. Ibid. 'According to a survey by Partners for Law in Development, 65 per cent of the cases under the existing child marriage law were in response to elopement (not necessarily involving marriage) and were filed by disapproving parents or families. These cases would be wrongfully filed to harass the couple, their age or legality of the marriage notwithstanding.

Increasing the age to 21 will bring more consenting adults who choose to marry under the threat of such harassment, and could become a tool for people to oppose interreligious and intercaste marriages. The current socio-economic system makes people want to marry their daughters as soon as they can or choose not to have a daughter at all. Increasing the legal marriage age without changing patriarchal social norms can result in parents feeling even more "burdened" by what they view as an additional responsibility of the girl child, which in turn could lead to an increase in sex-selective practices.' Poonam Muttreja, Alok Yajpeyi and Martand Kaushik, 'Instead of raising women's marriage age, here are six things India should do to curb child marriage', https://scroll.in/article/1020697/instead-of-raising-womens-marriage-age-here-are-six-things-india-should-do-to-curb-child-marriage, accessed on 28 April 2022.

8. 'Adhikar Chai Ekusher' (Want the rights of twenty-one), *Ananda Bazar Patrika*, 3 January 2021, p. 4.

Conclusion

During the first three decades of the twentieth century, social reformers and women's rights activists around the world, particularly in India, struggled hard to raise the marriage age. The subject did not elicit the equivalent fervour for the remaining of the twentieth century as it was carried out in the late 1920s. As activists in the realm of health and law, work to prevent child marriage throughout the world, it is necessary to consider the correlation between two crucial conceptual aspirations that have moulded the path of legal reforms in the age of marriage – 'feminism' and 'population control'. As soon as the Indian Parliament raised the age of marriage to 18 years for girls and 21 years for boys in 1978, this course of action hardly made a wave. Despite the fact that the marriage age for girls had already been laid down at 15 years for approximately thirty years, a small number of lawmakers regarded the event as significant. As an article in *The Times of India* remarked, 'Even though the measure (was) of vital social significance, the attendance in the chamber was poor, the debate was lackadaisical, and a bell had to be rung to draw in enough members to fulfil a quorum for passage.'[1] Indian feminist historians may even agree that the heated controversies preceding the Child Marriage Restraint Act of 1929 (CMRA or Sarda Act) and the contrasted stances connected with the Age of Consent debates of 1891 are one of the most widely researched developments in their ground. However, according to Rajani Bhatia and Ashwini Tambe, 'feminist historians and activists are relatively less enthusiastic regarding the legal change in the 1970s'.[2] While earlier generations of reformers were worried regarding women's education or the 'health of future generations', initiatives to raise the age of marriage in the 1970s reveal an apprehension about birth control and women's rights. The issue of birth control through legislation requiring a advanced age of marriage is a hotly debated topic.

The Department of Social Welfare of the Government of India published *Towards Equality: Report of the Committee on the Status of Women in India* in 1974. It was undoubtedly profoundly transformative for its authors, who saw themselves as 'nationalists and beneficiaries of the Constitution's equality clauses'.[3] In the middle of discussions on culture, family and law, population and fertility (some of which took quite conservative positions), child marriage – or, more accurately, age at marriage – did not hold a prominent position for the Committee on the Status of Women in India (CSWI). In the 'demographic chapter', there were two small tables on child marriage, where the authors do mention that 'the 1971 Census was the first census to directly ask ever – married women their age at marriage, although the results were not available in time for the Report'. Commenting on trends from 1901 to 1971 for both men and women, based on estimations computed from age distribution and marital status, they noted that 'while average age at marriage for men remained higher, the rate of increase for women had been considerably greater; male ages rose from 20.2 to 22.2 years, while in the case of women, the comparable figures were 13.2 and 17.2'. So, it may be said that, 'the average age at marriage had gone up by two years in the case of males and by four years in the case of females over these seventy years'.[4]

TABLE C.1: AVERAGE AGE AT MARRIAGE, INDIA, 1901-1971[5]

Decade	*Males*	*Females*
1901–11	20.2	13.2
1911–21	20.5	13.6
1921–31	18.4	12.6
1931–41	20.2	15.0
1941–51	19.8	15.4
1951–61	21.4	16.1
1961–71	22.2	17.2

TABLE C.2: AVERAGE AGE AT MARRIAGE, INDIA, 1961-1971[6]

Area	*Males*	*Females*
Rural	21.6	16.7
Urban	24.3	19.2
TOTAL	22.2	17.2

In rural sectors, the mean age at marriage for males was higher than that of females by 4.9 years. The disparity was even greater in urban areas, namely, '5.1 years, though the rural-urban differences were small'.[7]

In the fifty-page chapter 'On the Socio-cultural Setting of Women's Status' in *Towards Equality*, only two pages were devoted to age at marriage, which provided a fascinating blend of viewpoints, assessment, and suggestions. It is worth noting that the CSWI makes no mention of child marriage being a problem of the past that had been effectively determined. Recognizing that it was a severe problem, particularly in rural areas where their statistics displayed that 13.8 per cent of women were married between the ages of 10 and 14, they went on to explain that 'one redeeming feature of child marriage in India was that customarily consummation takes place only after puberty'. The Status report stated that the low age of marriage was connected to the near-acceptance of marriage in India was predominantly significant, making this an issue to be considered from their birth or early childhood. Early marriage is followed by what appear to be simple solutions to a variety of problems.[8] The Report briefly noted that low age of marriage was responsible for population growth, low standards of health for women and high mortality in the child-bearing age. In the chapter on 'law', the report stated that 'they would not advocate annulling early marriages because it would cause more problems than it would solve. Instead, the report proposed for girls' right to reject a marriage upon reaching majority, whether or not it had been consummated, and suggested that courts would not grant any relief if a marriage was entered into in violation of age requirements. Marriage registration was another appropriate verification (including bigamous marriages), but failure to do so cannot invalidate a marriage.'[9]

In October 1978, the course of legal reform that had previously been articulated in the Special Marriages Act of 1954 became the law of the land for all marriages – 18 for girls and 21 for boys – and this has not altered since then. This action was under deliberation for a certain period and under the Government of Indira Gandhi in 1974 legislation had been projected. According to Geraldine Forbes, whereas 'the Age of Consent controversy of 1891 had more to do with whether the British government had a right to interfere in Hindu social customs and the CMRA of 1929 was used as proof that Indians and women's organizations more specifically were deeply concerned with changing certain social practices, the 1978 law was related to population policies.'[10] Women demographers like Malini Karkal and Kumudini Dandekar appeared to be the only opposing voices arguing that simply raising the legal age of marriage to decrease births was unlikely to produce results – rather, women's educational and occupational position required to be strengthened.[11] Raising the marriage age to 18 for girls and 21 for boys had found its way into governmental discussions by 1974, and it was declared in 1976 as part of the new National Population Policy, halfway during the National Emergency of 1975-7.[12] Age at marriage emerged as a relatively reliable apparatus for population control after the Emergency was lifted in 1977, when the repercussion of the enforced decontaminate measures of those years led to the decline of the Congress government under Indira Gandhi, leading to its passage in 1978 with little public debate[13] and little negative fallout.

The current apprehension with child marriage can only be understood as a result of the government's anxiety about the population problem and disapproval of Indian women's 'real' (as opposed to legal) status. The adversaries of those who favoured an increased age of marriage are not from the orthodox Hindu section anymore; but moderately people of both groups share a common class background and commitment to modernity. The former group, on the other hand, condemns the new laws for their efficacy and practicability. A variety of certain aspects will determine whether or not raising the age of marriage can achieve the twofold objectives of population control and boosting the status of women. However, just like in the past, there is the issue of imposing this kind of law while several birth information remain unregistered. Possibly among of the most major obstacles to get recognition for this rising marriage age is the issue of safeguarding women till they attain this age. In a society that keeps insisting on women being protected by a male, whether it is a father, husband, or son, the responsibility of lengthening this security enhances many more complications the longer women remain single. As educational organizations can communicate this hardship, some reformers argue that what India requires first and foremost is schools for girls and at time of marriage the 'adult age' will obviously maintain.[14] It is essential to recollect who was at the heart of social reform initiatives from the beginning of the nineteenth century. This still suggested that upper caste girls were the essential focus of social reform. In ways that have not been necessarily observed, the intervening century, particularly after independence, wrought underlying transformations in the existence of this now modernizing girls, notably if they were urban and middle class, whose very modernity guaranteed that their upper-caste position became progressively unnoticeable. The report of *Towards Equality* documented not only increases in literacy rates and educational access, but also a reduction of gender gaps in higher education for this group of women or girls. Whereas their mothers were likely married off in premature condition and grandmothers even before adolescence, urban middle-class girls in the 1970s would almost certainly complete high school as part of present-day social and cultural norms and expectations, with a significant proportion going on to college for graduation.[15] In upper-caste middle-class society, a quiet social alteration in perceptions of 'childhood' and 'girlhood' was thus achieved, symbolic of their separate class location, one that anticipates further investigation from the worldwide research.[16] This is not to say that child marriage did not occur in subsequent decades. Child marriage had become a public issue as the twentieth century came to an end; at a time when countries like India were undertaking on a new economic doctrine and principles noticeable by varying preferences of the state in progress, broadening world markets, and what is now simply defined as 'neoliberalism' in the twenty-first century.[17]

The statistics on marriage in different newspaper reports proposed that the CMRA of 1929 was a disaster. The number of wives under fifteen increased from 8.5 million to 12 million and husbands under the age of fifteen also rose from 3 million to more than 5 million and the number of wives under the age of five had quadrupled. Historians have ascribed this dramatic rise to parents attempting to marry off their young children before the CMRA came into effect.[18] The CMRA had no visible influence on marital attitude and behaviour until it was amended in 1978. The perseverance of child marriage in India demonstrated that neither law nor advancement was particularly effective in raising the age of marriage. It was realized, gradually, that more collective state action was necessary; additionally, a number of social evils were attributed to child marriage. For example, the gender gap in health and education was thought to be caused by child marriage. There was a need for a much powerful law, so in 2006, a new law was passed that sought to prohibit child marriages rather than simply restrain them. The Prohibition of Child Marriage Act of 2006 (PCMA) went into effect on 11 January 2007 and was implemented in West Bengal in December 2008. The characteristics of this law:

(a) 'The minimum age for marriage for men and women continues to be 21 and 18, respectively.'
(b) 'The Act has for the first time declared child marriage voidable. Despite subsequent changes, a child marriage is not void by default. A contracting party who was a child at the time of the marriage has the option to nullify the marriage within 2 years of attaining majority. There is a provision for the return of all valuables, money, ornaments, and gifts made in marriage upon nullity. According to Section 12, a marriage is null and void if there is force or deceit or trafficking involved in the marriage.'
(c) 'The Act allows for maintenance from the husband or his parents for the girl till her remarriage. The court may also make suitable provision for her residence until her remarriage. As all children born from the marriage are declared legitimate, the Act further allows for appropriate orders for custody of children from such marriages.'
(d) 'All the punishments for contracting a child marriage have been enhanced. The punishment for a man over 18 years of age is rigorous imprisonment up to two years or with a fine of up to 100,000 or both. A similar punishment is prescribed for anyone who performs, conducts, directs, or abets any child marriage. The same punishment is also prescribed for anyone who solemnizes or promotes such a marriage. No woman can however be punished with imprisonment. The Act also makes all offences cognizable and non-bailable.'
(e) 'The Act further allows for injunctions to prohibit child marriage,

including ex parte interim injunctions. It states that any child marriage solemnized in contravention of an injunction will be void and whoever disobeys such injunction shall be punished with imprisonment.'

(f) 'The Act lays emphasis on the prohibition of child marriage by providing for the appointment of Child Marriage Prohibition Officers (CMPO) by the state governments and gives powers to these officers to prevent such marriages.'[19]

The PCMA is extensively reliant on ascertaining the petitioners' ages at the time of marriage. Nevertheless, it should be noted that the age issue is convoluted by a spectrum of laws that oppose and express in a different way to each other. The incompatible character of personal laws causes confusion about the legal age for marriage. Despite the fact that the Hindu Marriage Act of 1955 states that a girl must be 18 years old and a boy must be 21 years old before they are married, the concern for age is excluded from the list of conditions that render a marriage null and void. As a result, such marriages are not void under the Hindu Marriage Act, though they are punishable under the PCMA. According to Muslim Personal Law (*Shariat*) of 1937, puberty, presumed at 15 years, is considered the minimum age for marriage. In the Christian Marriage Act of 1872, marriages of minors were not measured illegal as long as consent of the minor's guardian has been acquired. It is only under the Special Marriage Act 1954, that all marriages are declared void when either of the parties to the marriage has not attained the requisite age. Discrepancies in the suitable age for marriage between the personal laws and the PCMA have precipitated difficulties and resulted in varying court decisions. This hampers the implementation of PCMA.

We have argued that girls were married at a young age often by forcing them to drop out of school, for a variety of economic and social reasons. According to popular belief, a daughter's labour is devoted to the 'marital household', so her working life starts with marriage. Daughters and their bodies are regarded as storehouses of 'honour' in rural families. Parents are concerned about teenage sexuality and are also anxious regarding the probability of elopement, which would bring embarrassment to the family. Besides this, a lack

Table c.3: International Conventions and National Legislations Addressing Child Marriage[20]

Year	*Policies and Acts*	*Brief Outline*
1927	Sharda Bill (Sarda Bill)	Bill to restraint the solemnization of child marriages
1929	Child Marriage Restraint Act (CMRA)	Minimum age was set at 14 years for girls
1949	Amendment of the CMRA	Minimum age of girls was increased from 14 to 15
1955	Hindu Marriage Act	Regulate marriages for Indians and Jains
1969	Registration of Births and Deaths Act	Need for Registration of all births and deaths within 21 days or one year
1978	Amendment of the Child Marriage Restraint Act	Minimum age was increased to 18 for girls and 21 for boys (from 15 and 18 respectively)
1992	GOI signs UN CRC (1989)	
1993	GOI signs UN CEDAW (1979)	Adds limitation for civil registrations
1998	Maharasthra Registration of Marriage Act 1998	Following the Goa Registration of Marriages Act, 1961, registrations were made compulsory (State Level only)
2004	Prevention of Child Marriage Bill	Revised the CMRA of 1929, punishments substantially increased, institutional reform (Child Marriage Prevention Officers)
2006	Prohobition of Child Marriage Act	Repealed Child Marriage Restraint Act (CMRA) 1929-78
2013	National Policy for Children	Including Child Marriage
2013	Registration of Births, Deaths and Marriages Act	Amendment of the 1969 Act, including the registration of marriages

of job opportunities, homelessness, and general impoverishment – parents are forced to withdraw their daughters from school and they are compelled to organize their daughter's early marriage. The number of elopements appears to be increasing.[21] Elopement marriage is becoming more popular. In most of the cases, one may hardly find any example of parents criminalizing the act of elopement and discrediting the marriage. Parents have not used violence or pursued government intervention to separate couples who have made their own marriage decisions.

The indetermination of age, on which law so heavily relies, is one of the least effective parts of the process. However, expecting each section of legislation, particularly social legislation, to have a reasonably instant and recognizable result, appears simple. In this respect, I believe that the attempts to raise the marriageable age should be viewed as 'symbolic reform' and as a result, significant factors of what individuals with 'political authority' consider as valuable. But, during nineteenth and twentieth centuries, in most of the cases, ordinary girls have made these demand; the leaders of the women's movement and those who work with the law have built this movement and after much of these efforts, the proposals have been tabled in Parliament. Then the law was passed through a long process. But nothing happened overnight at the Government's own initiatives, so the question is that what happened today that the Government of India has started thinking about raising the age of marriage for girls. The Government has mainly considered the opportunities regarding higher education, physical and mental condition of girls.[22] But the fact that there are so many differences between law-making and its implementation, is evidenced by the previous Acts enacted earlier. The overall picture of the age at which girls get married is not the same in every state of India, because of the diverse socio-economic situation and the caste system. So, it is high time to rethink about this matter, considering all the positive and negative aspects and needless to say that it demands new research in the coming days. The issue of women's empowerment through raising the age of marriage of girls from 18 to 21 is really controversial. However, it is never reasonable to assume that all initiatives for this legal action will be negative. Looking back at history, it is clear that no solution can be found by enacting laws alone. It is desirable to take necessary steps to make that law effective in practice. We learn from history. So we have to think anew by learning from the past. In addition to raising the legal age of marriage for girls, education for girls, their health issues should also be brought into the overall discussion by judging them from a new perspective; realizing that those issues complement each other, so appropriate measures need to be taken to make the law a reality.

NOTES

1. 'Bill to raise age of marriage okayed', *The Times of India*, 22 February 1978, p. 9.
2. Rajani Bhatia and Ashwini Tambe, 'Raising the Age of Marriage in 1970s India: Demographers, Despots, and Feminists', *Women's Studies International Forum*, 2013, pp. 1-12.
3. Vina Mazumdar, 'Introduction', in Vina Mazumdar (ed.), *Symbols of Power: Studies on the Political Status of Women in India*, New Delhi: Allied Publishers, 1979, pp. xi-xxiv.
4. *Towards Equality: Report of the Committee on the Status of Women in India*, New Delhi: Government of India, 1974, p. 23.
5. Ibid.
6. Ibid.
7. Ibid.
8. Kumud Sharma and C.P. Sujaya (eds.), *Towards Equality: Report of the Committee on the Status of Women in India*, New Delhi: Pearson Education, 2012 (1974), p. 60, cited in Mary E. John, *Child Marriage in an International Frame: A Feminist Review from India*, London and New York: Routledge, 2021, p. 38.
9. Kumud Sharma and C.P. Sujaya (eds.), *Towards Equality: Report of the Committee on the Status of Women in India*, New Delhi: Pearson Education, 2012 (1974), p. 86, cited in Mary E. John, op. cit., 2021, p. 38.
10. Geraldine H. Forbes, 'Women and Modernity: The Issues of Child Marriage in India', *Women's Studies International Quarterly*, vol. 2, 1979, pp. 407-19.
11. Rajani Bhatia and Ashwini Tambe, op. cit., p. 5.
12. Jaya Sagade, *Child Marriage in India: Socio-legal and Human Rights Dimensions*, New Delhi: Oxford University Press, 2005, pp. 43-59.
13. Brinder Pal Singh Sehgal, *Population Control and the Law: Problems, Policies, Remedial Measures*, New Delhi: Deep and Deep Publications, 1989, p. 124; Kuttan Mahadevan and M. Sumangala, 'Population Policy in India: Perspectives for the Future', *Indian Journal of Public Administration*, vol. 38, no. 3, 1 July 1992, pp. 227-40.

14. Bal Paril, 15 June 1976, 'Raising Marriageable Age: Demographic Impact', *The Economic Times*, pp. 5, 7, cited in Geraldine H. Forbes, op. cit., p. 417.
15. Mary E. John, op. cit., p. 40.
16. Ibid.
17. Ibid., pp. 41-2.
18. Biswajit Ghosh, 'Child Marriage, Society and the Law: A Study in a Rural Context in West Bengal, India', *International Journal of Law, Policy and the Family*, vol. 25, no. 2, 2011, pp. 199-219.
19. Ishita Chowdhury and Utsarjana Mutsuddi, 'Love and Law: Understanding Child Marriage in Rural West Bengal', in Samita Sen and Anindita Ghosh (eds.), *Love, Labour and Law: Early and Child Marriage in India*, New Delhi: Sage/Stree, 2021, pp. 109-10.
20. Elvira Graner, 'Governing Child Marriage in India: The Protracted Reform Process', in Samita Sen and Anindita Ghosh (eds.), *Love, Labour and Law: Early and Child Marriage in India*, p. 73.
21. Ishita Chowdhury and Utsarjana Mutsuddi, op. cit., pp. 105-38.
22. 'Adhikar Chai Ekusher' (Want the rights of twenty-one), *Ananda Bazar Patrika*, 3 January 2021, p. 4.

Glossary

Arghopradan	Offerings to the Lord
Bahir	World; Public Sphere
Balyavivaha/ Balyabibaha	Early Marriage/Child Marriage
Bhadralok	Prosperous, well-educated people, typically Bengalis, regarded as members of a social class; a social group whose gentility was defined by their upper-caste status and abstention from manual labour; respectable people and culturally refined gentlemen
Brahmos	Relating to *'Brahma'*, the supreme being, Hindu God of Creation; a small but influential progressive Bengali community, emerged in nineteenth century. They were the first social reformers, and the first to grant their women equal rights. They were the pioneers of liberal political awareness and Indian nationalism, and familiarized ethical and professional ideals into Indian law, medicine, natural sciences, teaching, journalism, and civil administration. Initially known as the Calcutta Unitarian Committee in 1823, the Brahmo Sabha in 1829, and finally the Brahmo Samaj in 1843, this community was instrumental in the origin and advancement of every significant religious, social, and political

	movement in India from 1820 to 1930. Although the Brahmo Samaj was established at the house of Firingi Kamal Basu at Jorasanko in August 1828 on the initiative of Rammohan Roy, it was only the beginning. The real triumph of the Brahmo Samaj began after the establishment of the Tattvabodhini Sabha in 1839 and was accelerated on 21 December 1843 by Devendranath Tagore's conversion to Brahmo Dharma by Ramchandra Vidyabagish along with twenty other members of the Brahmo Samaj
Brahmacharya	Austere abstinence
Dayabhaga	Bengal School of Hindu Law of inheritance
Garbhadhan	Ritual, consummation of marriage straight after the first menstrual flow
Ghar	Home; Private sphere
Ginni	Eldest female member or head of the household among female members
Gouridan	Offering of daughters for marriage at the age of eight to ensure pre-menstrual marriage
Karewa	Levirate marriage, in which the widow was accepted as the bride by one of the brothers of the deceased husband
Karta	Eldest male member or head of the household
Kulin	Highest grades of the Brahman, Kayastha and Baidya castes supposedly constituted by the early medieval ruler Ballal Sen (1160-1179) on the basis of certain virtues
Mitakshara	Other than Bengal, rest of India followed this Hindu Law of inheritance
Nirishwar Bibaha	Non-deist marriage

Niskama karma	A detached way; selfless deed or dispassionate action free from worldly desires
Palki	A palanquin
Parashara Samhita	Anthology of Parashara
Proja	Procreation (related to Hindu Marriage)
Puranas	A vast genre of Indian literature about a wide range of topics, particularly about legends and other traditional lore
Purdah	Custom of secluding women
Rati	Conjugal love (related to Hindu Marriage)
Sati	Virtuous and chaste woman; the practice in Hinduism of a wife burning herself with the body of her dead husband
Satidaha	Burning of wives of dead husbands
Sahamarana or Sahagamana	Concremation ritual; actually, the widow burnt with her husband's corpse
Sakam karma	The fruits of one's action
Shastras	In Hinduism, a work of sacred scripture
Shastric achara	Scriptural services
Striachar	Women's rituals
Sampradan	The gift of the daughter or bride
Shariat	Islamic canonical law based on the teachings of the Quran and the traditions of the Prophet (Hadith and Sunna), prescribing both religious and secular duties and sometimes retributive penalties for law-breaking
Zenana	Female quarters of the house

Bibliography

PRIMARY SOURCES

Archival Records (West Bengal State Archives)

Intelligence Report – Second Half of October 1929, Home Political, File No. 73/1930 (1-8), West Bengal State Archives (hereafter WBSA).

Intelligence Report – 18 December 1929, Sarda Act, Home Political, File No. 73/1930 (1-8), WBSA.

Intelligence Report – Second Half of December 1929, Home Political, File No. 73/1930 (1-8), WBSA.

Intelligence Report – first half of March 1930, Home Political, File No. 73/1930 (1-8), WBSA.

Intelligence Report – first half of March 1930, Home Political, File No. 73/1930 (1-8), WBSA.

Bengal Secretariat, 1 February 1930, Confidential D.C. Nos. 640-44, Home Political, File No. 73/1930 (1-8), WBSA.

Letter from the Commissioner of Burdwan Division, Chinsurah, G. Goode, dated 20 February 1930, to the Chief Secretary to the Government of Bengal, W.D.R. Prentice, Home Political, File No. 73/1930 (1-8), WBSA.

Letter from the Commissioner of Rajshahi Division, Jalpaiguri, dated 1 March 1930, to the Chief Secretary to the Government of Bengal, W.D.R. Prentice, Home Political, File No. 73/1930 (1-8), WBSA.

Letter from the Commissioner of Ramna (Dacca) Division, dated 5 March 1930, to the Chief Secretary to the Government of Bengal, W.D.R. Prentice, Home Political, File No. 73/1930 (1-8), WBSA.

Report of C.M. Martin, District Magistrate of Dacca, dated 17 February 1930, to the Chief Secretary to the Government of Bengal, W.D.R. Prentice, Home Political, File No. 73/1930 (1-8), WBSA.

Letter from G.S. Dutt, I.C.S., District Officer, Mymensingh, dated 26 February

1930, to the Chief Secretary to the Government of Bengal, W.D.R. Prentice, Home Political, File No. 73/1930 (1-8), WBSA.

Letter from the District Magistrate of Faridpur, dated 21 February 1930, to the Chief Secretary to the Government of Bengal, W.D.R. Prentice, Home Political, File No. 73/1930 (1-8), WBSA.

Letter from the District Magistrate of Barisal, dated 27 February 1930, to the Chief Secretary to the Government of Bengal, W.D.R. Prentice, Home Political, File No. 73/1930 (1-8), WBSA.

Letter from the Commissioner of Chittagong, dated 10 March 1930, to the Chief Secretary to the Government of Bengal, W.D.R. Prentice, Home Political, File No. 73/1930 (1-8), WBSA.

Letter from the District Officer of Chittagong, dated 19 February 1930, to the Chief Secretary to the Government of Bengal, W.D.R. Prentice, Home Political, File No. 73/1930 (1-8), WBSA.

Letter from the Magistrate's office of Noakhali, dated 1 March 1930, to the Chief Secretary to the Government of Bengal, W.D.R. Prentice, Home Political, File No. 73/1930 (1-8), WBSA.

Letter from the Commissioner office of Presidency Division, dated 26 March 1930, to the Chief Secretary to the Government of Bengal, W.D.R. Prentice, Home Political, File No. 73/1930 (1-8), WBSA.

Assembly and Council Proceedings and Assembly Debates

1855. Legislative Council Proceedings: The Hindoo Widows' Remarriage Bill. November.

1872. Proceedings of the Council of the Governor-General of India, 1872.

1891. Abstract of the Proceedings of the Council of the Governor-General of India, assembled for the Purpose of Making Laws and Regulations, 1891.

1919. *Madras Legislative Council Debates.* Vol. 42, No. 1.

1925. *The Legislative Assembly Debates.* Simla: Government of India Press.

1927. *The Legislative Assembly Debates.* Vol. 3.

1927. *The Legislative Assembly Debates.* Vol. 5.

1928. *The Legislative Assembly Debates.* Vol. 2.

1928. *The Legislative Assembly Debates.* Vol. 3.

1929. *The Legislative Assembly Debates.* Vol. 1, No. 2.

1929. *The Legislative Assembly Debates.* Vol. 4.

1929. *The Legislative Assembly Debates.* Vol. 5.

Government Records & Reports

1929. *Age of Consent Committee Evidence, 1928-1929: Oral Evidence and Written Statements of Witnesses from (United Provinces Contd.) Lucknow and Ajmer-Merwara.* Vol. IX. Calcutta: Government of India, Central Publication Branch.

1929. *Age of Consent Committee Evidence, 1928-1929: Oral Evidence and Written Statements of Witnesses from Bengal Presidency.* Vol. VI. Calcutta: Government of India, Central Publication Branch.

1929. *Age of Consent Committee Evidence, 1928-1929: Oral Evidence and Written Statements of Witnesses from Bihar and Orissa, Assam and Burma.* Vol. VII. Calcutta: Government of India, Central Publication Branch.

1929. *Age of Consent Committee Evidence, 1928-1929: Oral Evidence and Written Statements of Witnesses from the Bombay Presidency (Continued - Bombay and Poona) and the Central Provinces and Berar.* Vol. III. Calcutta: Government of India, Central Publication Branch.

1929. *Age of Consent Committee Evidence, 1928-1929: Oral Evidence and Written Statements of Witnesses from the Madras Presidency (Ootacamund, Calicut, Madura and Vizagapatam) and Coorg.* Vol. V. Calcutta: Government of India, Central Publication Branch.

1929. *Age of Consent Committee Evidence, 1928-1929: Oral Evidence and Written Statements of Witnesses from the Madras Presidency.* Vol. IV. Calcutta: Government of India, Central Publication Branch.

1929. *Age of Consent Committee Evidence, 1928-1929: Oral Evidence and Written Statements of Witnesses from the Punjab, N.W.F.P. and Delhi.* Vol. I. Calcutta: Government of India, Central Publication Branch.

Crake, H.M. 1914. *Report of the Health Officer of Calcutta.* Calcutta: The Corporation Press.

1893. *McLeod's Medical Report on Child Wives NF J C/17 Proceedings 104-17.* Government of Bengal, Judicial Department.

Mitra, Nripendra Nath. 1931. *The Indian Annual Register, January-June.* Vol. 1. Calcutta: The Annual Register Office.

———. 1938. *The Indian Annual Register, January-June.* Vol. I. Calcutta: The Annual Register Office.

———. 1934. *The Indian Annual Register, July -December.* Vol. II. Calcutta: The Annual Register Office.

———. 1938. *The Indian Annual Register, July-December.* Vol. II. Calcutta: The Annual Register Office.

———. 1927. *The Indian Quarterly Register, being a Quarterly Journal of Indian*

Public Affairs, in matters Political, Social and Economic, January-June. Vol. 1, Nos. I & II. Calcutta: The Annual Register Office.

______. 1925. *The Indian Quarterly Register, being a Quarterly Journal of Indian Public Affairs, in matters Political, Social and Economic, July-December.* Vol. 2, Nos. III & IV. Calcutta: The Annual Register Office.

______. 1928. *The Indian Quarterly Register, being a Quarterly Journal of Indian Public Affairs, in matters Political, Social and Economic, July-December.* Vol. 2, Nos. III & IV. Calcutta: The Annual Register Office.

______. 1929. *The Indian Quarterly Register, being a Quarterly Journal of Indian Public Affairs, in matters Political, Social and Economic, July-December.* Vol. 2, Nos. III & IV. Calcutta: The Annual Register Office.

1893. Proceedings Files nos. 105-6, File J C/172. Government of Bengal, Judicial Department, June.

n.d. *Progress of Education in India, 1937-1947, 2 Vols.* New Delhi: Government of India.

1931. *Report of the Administration of Bengal, 1929-1930.* Calcutta: Bengal Secretariat Book Depot.

1929. *Report of the Age of Consent Committee, 1928-1929.* Calcutta: Government of India, Central Publication Branch.

1890. Report of the Fourth Annual Session of the Indian National Social Conference.

1889. Report of the Third Annual Session of the Indian National Social Conference.

1884. Report on Native Papers (Bengal). (Available Online)

1886. Report on Native Papers (Bengal). (Available Online)

1887. Report on Native Papers (Bengal). (Available Online)

1891. Report on Native Papers (Bengal). (Available Online)

1974. *Towards Equality: Report of the Committee on the Status of Women in India.* New Delhi: Government of India, Ministry of Education & Social Welfare.

Census Publications

Baines, J.A. 1893. *General Report on the Census of India, 1891.* London: HMSO.

Bourdillon, J.A. 1883. *Report on the Census of Bengal 1881.* Calcutta: Bengal Secretariat Press.

n.d. *Census of India, 1901, Volume 6, Part 1.*

n.d. *Census of India, 1911, Volume 1, Part 1.*

n.d. *Census of India, 1911, Volume 5, Part 1.*

n.d. *Census of India, 1921, Volume 1, Part 1.*
n.d. *Census of India, 1931, Volume 1, Part 1.*
n.d. *Census of India, 1931, Volume 5, Part 1.*
n.d. *Census Report of Bengal, 1901.*
n.d. *Census of India, 1941, Volume 4.*
Gait, E.A. n.d. *Report on the Census of Lower Provinces of Bengal and their Feudatories, 1901.* Calcutta: Bengal Secretariat Press.
O'Donnell, C.J. 1893. *Report on the Census of Lower Provinces of Bengal and their Feudatories 1891.* Calcutta: Bengal Secretariat Press.
O'Malley, L.S.S. 1913. *Census of India (Vol.VI): City of Calcutta, Part I.* Calcutta: Bengal Scretariat Book Depot.
Porter, A.E. 1933. *Census Report of Bengal and Sikkim, 1931, Census of India, Volume V, Part I, Chapter IV.* Calcutta: Central Publication Branch.
Porter, A.E. 1932. *Report on the Census of Bengal,* 1931. Calcutta.
Risley, H.H., and E.A. Gait. 1903. *Report on the Census of India, 1901.* Calcutta: Office of the Superintendent of Government Printing.

Other Government Publications

Aiyar, A.S. Srinivasa. 1930. *The Child Marriage Restraint Act (Act xix of 1929): with an Analytical Introduction, Critical Comments, Original Bill, Statement of Objects and Reasons, Reports of the Select Committees (with Minutes of Dissent) and Select Speeches in the Assembly.* Madras: The Law Publishing Company.
1868. *Gazette of India, Supplement.* 19 September.
1931. *India in 1929-30: A Statement Prepared for Presentation to Parliament in accordance with the requirements of the 26th Section of the Government of India Act (5 & 6 Geo. V, Chap. 61).* Calcutta: Government of India, Central Publication Branch.
1931. *The Indian Medical Gazette. Vol. 66.* May.
1931. *The Indian Medical Gazette. Vol. 66.* June.
1931. *The Indian Medical Gazette. Vol. 66.* August.
Williams, L.F. Rushbrook. 1925. *India in 1924-25: A Statement Prepared for Presentation to Parliament in accordance with the requirements of the 26th Section of the Government of India Act.* Calcutta: Government of India, Central Publication Branch.

Organizational Reports of Non-Governmental Organizations

1928. *All India Women's Conference, Annual Report.*

1932. *All India Women's Conference, Annual Report.*
n.d. *All India Women's Conference, Annual Report, 1931.*
n.d. *Annual Reports of the Women's Indian Association, 1924-25; 1925-26.*
1929. *Salana Report: All India Muslim Ladies Conference.* Hyderabad.

Newspapers, Periodicals and Journals (English)

American Ethnologist
Amrita Bazar Patrika
Bengal Past and Present
Canadian Journal of Women and the Law
Comparative Studies in Society and History
Contributions to Indian Sociology
Cultural Critique
Economic and Political Weekly
Feminist Legal Studies
Feminist Studies
Gender & History
Harijan Patrika
Hindoo Patriot
History Compass
Indian Economic and Social History Review
Indian Journal of Development Research and Social Action
Indian Journal of Gender Studies
Indian Messenger
Indian Mirror
International Journal of Law, Policy and Family
Journal of British Studies
Journal of History, Jadavpur University
Journal of Indian History, The University of Kerala
Journal of Indian Law Institute
Journal of National Law University, Delhi
Journal of Women's History
Law and History Review
Legal Theory
Madras Mail
Modern Asian Studies
National Law School Journal
Oxford Literary Review
Pioneer

Signs: Journal of Women in Culture and Society
Social Change
Social Scientist
Sociological Bulletin
South Asia Research
South Asian History and Culture
Stri Dharma
Studies in History
The American Historical Review
The Calcutta Christian Observer
The Economic Times
The Friend of India
The Indian Ladies Magazine
The Journal of Asian Studies
The Journal of the History of Childhood and Youth
The Lawyers
The Mahratta
The Modern Review
The Mussalman
The Statesman
The Times (London)
The Times of India
Times of London
Women's History Review
Women's Studies Int. Quart.
Women's Studies International Forum
Young India

Newspapers, Periodicals and Journals (Bengali)

Ahmadi
Aalochana
Amrita Bazar Patrika
Ananda Bazar Patrika
Anusandhan
Anustup
Bamabodhini Patrika
Bandhab
Bangabasi
Bangadarshan

Bharatbarsha
Bharati
Burdwan Sanjivani
Dacca Prakash
Dainik O Samachar Chandrika
Desh
Hanifi
Hitakari
Jayasree
Nabyabharat
Prabasi
Sahachar
Shakti
Samachar Darpan
Sambad Prabhakar
Sanjivani
Saogat
Somprakash
Sudhakar
Sulabh Samachar O Kusdaha
Swasthya
Swasthya Samachar
Tattvabodhini Patrika

Unpublished Thesis

Chakravarti, Bhaswati. n.d. The Second Social Reform Movement: Gender and Society in Bengal, 1930s-1950s. unpublished Ph.D thesis, Department of History, University of Calcutta. https://shodhganga.inflibnet.ac.in/handle/10603/211610, accessed on 31 January 2021.

E-Resources

https://archive.org
http://nationalarchives.nic.in/
https://indianculture.gov.in
http://thewire.in/women/india-new-law-age-at-marriage-women
https://lawandhistoryreview.org/article/aparna-bandyopadhyay

https://scroll.in/article/1020697/instead-of-raising-womens-marriage-age-here-are-six-things-india-should-do-to-curb-child-marriage
www.unicef.org/rosa/media/691/file
https://dspace.gipe.ac.in
https://www.theindiaforum.in/article/suitable-girl
https://eparlib.nic.in
https://ndl.iitkgp.ac.in
https://www.jstor.org/site/south-asia-open-archives/saoa/report-native-papers-1876-1916
https://www.ncbi.nlm.nih.gov
https://www.cssscal.org
https://doi.org/10.11588/xarep.00000434
https://doi.org/10.11588/xarep.00000435
https://doi.org/10.11588/xarep.00000499
https://doi.org/10.11588/xarep.00000500
https://doi.org/10.11588/xarep.00000501
https://doi.org/10.11588/xarep.00000987
https://doi.org/10.11588/xarep.00000988
https://doi.org/10.11588/xarep.00000989
https://doi.org/10.11588/xarep.00000990
https://doi.org/10.11588/xarep.00000991
https://doi.org/10.11588/xarep.00000992
https://doi.org/10.11588/xarep.00000993
https://doi.org/10.11588/xarep.00000994

SECONDARY SOURCES

Books, Chapters in Edited Volumes and Articles (English)

Agarwal, Bina. 1994. *A Field of One's Own: Gender and Land Rights in South Asia.* Cambridge: University of Cambridge.

Agarwala, S.N. 1962. *Age at Marriage in India.* Bombay: Kitab Mahal Publishing Ltd.

Agnes, Flavia. 2013. 'Controversy over Age of Consent.' *Economic and Political Weekly* XLVIII (29): 10-13 July 20.

_____. 2011. *Family Law Volume 1: Family Laws and Constitutional Claims.* New Delhi: Oxford University Press.

_____. 2011. *Family Law Volume 2: Marriage, Divirce, and Matrimonial Litigation.* New Delhi: Oxford University Press.

______. 1999 (ninth impression, 2012). *Law and Gender Inequality: The Politics of Women's Rights in India.* New Delhi: Oxford University Press.

______. 1996. 'Redefinig the Agenda of the Women's Movement Within a Secular Framework.' In *Women and the Hindu Right: A Collection of Essays*, edited by Tanika Sarkar and Urvashi Butalia. New Delhi: Kali for Women.

______. 1994. 'Triple Talaq Judgement: Do Women Really Benefit?'. *Economic and Political Weekly*, 14 May.

______. 1992. *Give Us this Day Our Daily Bread: Procedures and Case Law on Maintenance.* Bombay: Majlis.

______. 1992. 'Protecting Women against Violence? Review of a Decade of Legislation, 1980-89.' *Economic and Political Weekly* Vol. 27, No. 17, pp. WS19-WS33, 25 April.

______. 1990. 'Fighting Rape - Has Amending the Law Helped?' *The Lawyers*, February.

Agnes, Flavia, Sudhir Chandra, and Monmayee Basu, 2004 (2016). *Women and Law in India.* New Delhi: Oxford University Press (Oxford India Paperbacks).

Ali, Azra Asghar. 2000. *The Emergence of Feminism Among Indian Muslim Women 1920-1947.* Oxford: Oxford University Press.

Amin, Sonia. 1996. *The World of Muslim Women in Colonial Bengal, 1876-1939.* New York: Brill.

Amrita Bazar Patrika. 1919. 'Bengal Legislative Council Interpretations: Mortality of Infants Under One Year in Bengal.' 1 April.

Amrita Bazar Patrika. 1948. 'Restraining Child Marriage', 26 August.

Anagol, Padma. 2016. 'Age of Consent and Child Marriage in India.' In *The Wiley Blackwell Encyclopedia of Gender and Sexuality Studies*, by Nancy A. Naples. John Wiley & Sons, 21 April.

______. 2010. 'Feminist Inheritances and Foremothers: the beginnings of Feminism in Modern India.' *Women's History Review*, Vol. 19, No. 4, pp. 523-46, September.

______. 2007. 'Rebellious Wives and Dysfunctional Marriages: Indian Women's Discourses and Participation in the Debates over Restitution of Conjugal Rights and the Child Marriage Controversy in the 1880s and 1890s.' In *Women and Social Reform in Modern India*, edited by Sumit Sarkar and Tanika Sarkar. New Delhi: Permanent Black.

______. 2005 (2016). *The Emergence of Feminism in India, 1850-1920.* New Delhi: Ashgate Publishing/Routledge.

Anagol-McGinn, Padma. 1992. 'The Age of Consent Act (1891) Reconsidered:

Women's Perspectives and Participation in the Child-Marriage Controversy in India.' *South Asia Research*, Vol. 12, No. 2, pp. 100-18, November.

Ananda Bazar Patrika. 1929. 'Report on Meeting and Speeches at Albert Hall, College Street, Calcutta.' 12 January.

Ananda Bazar Patrika. 1928. 'The Swadeshi Spirit and the Women of Bengal.' 5 March.

Ananda Bazar Patrika. 1924. 'The Women's Cell.' 10 January.

Aries, Philippe. 1962 (1960). *Centuries of Childhood: A Social History of Family Life*. New York: Alfrd A. Knopf.

Balasubrahmanyan, Vimal. 1990. *In Search of Justice: Women, Law, Landmark Judgements, and Media*. Pune: Shubhada Saraswat Prakashan for publisher not identified D.T. Research Centre for Women's Studies.

Bandyopadhyay, Aparna. 2020. 'Muslim Voices and Historiographical Silences: The Age of Consent Controversy in Colonial Bengal.' *The Docket, Law and History Review*, Vol. 3, No. 2, June.

______. 2015. 'Revisiting the Women's Question in Late Colonial Bengal.' In *The Other Universe: An Anthology of Women's Studies*, edited by Aparna Bandyopadhyay and Krishna Dasgupta. Kolkata: Setu Prakashani.

Bandyopadhyay, Sekhar. 2007. 'Caste, Widow-Remarriage, and the Reform of Popular Culture in Colonial Bengal.' In *Women and Social Reform in Modern India*, edited by Sumit Sarkar and Tanika Sarkar. New Delhi: Permanent Black.

______. 2004. *Caste, Culture and Hegemony: Social Domination in Colonial Bengal*. New Delhi: Sage Publications.

______. 2004 (2016). *From Plassey to Partition and After: A History of Modern India*. New Delhi: Orient BlackSwan.

Banerjee, Gooroodass. 1879. *Tagore Law Lectures-1878: The Hindu Law of Marriage and Stridhan*. Calcutta: Thacker Spink & Co.

Banerjee, Shyamananda. 1968. *National Awakening and the Bangabasi*, Calcutta: Amitava-Kalyan Publishers.

Banerjee-Dube, Ishita. 2014. *A History of Modern India*. Delhi: Cambridge University Press.

Bannerji, Himani. 2001. *Inventing Subjects: Studies in Hegemony, Patriarchy and Colonialism*. New Delhi: Tulika.

______. 2000. 'Projects of Hegemony: Towards a Critique of Subaltern Studies' "Resolution of the Women's Question".' *Economic and Political Weekly*, Vol. 35, No. 11, pp. 902-20, 11-17 March.

Basu, Aparna. 1998. 'From Child Bride to "Hindoo Lady": Rukhmabai and the Debate on Sexual Respectability in Imperial Britain.' *The American Historical Review*, Vol. 103, No. 4, pp. 1119-46, October.

_____. 1991 (1992). 'Women's History in India: An Historiographical Survey.' In *Writing Women's History: International Perspectives*, edited by Karen Offen, Ruth Roach Pierson and Jane Rendall. London: Macmillan Press.

_____. 1986. *The Pathfinder: Dr. Muthulakshmi Reddi.* Delhi: AIWC Publication.

Basu, Aparna, and Bharati Ray. 1990 (2018). *Women's Struggle: A History of All India Women's Conference, 1927-1990.* New Delhi: Manohar.

Basu, Monmayee. 2004 (2016). 'Hindu Women and Marriage Law: From Sacrament to Contract.' In *Women & Law in India*, by Flavia Agnes, Sudhir Chandra and Monmayee Basu. New Delhi: Oxford University Press (Oxford India Paperbacks).

Basu, Srimati. 1999. 'Review Essay of Women and Law in Colonial India: A Social History by Janaki Nair.' *Gender & History*, Vol. 11, No. 1, pp. 173-6, April.

Bhatia, Rajani, and Ashwini Tambe. 2013. 'Raising the age of marriage in 1970s India: Demographers, Despots, and Feminists.' *Women's Studies International Forum*, pp. 1-12.

Bhattacharya, Sabyasachi (ed.). 2020. *A Comprehensive History of Modern Bengal, 1700-1950, Volume II.* Kolkata: The Asiatic Society, in association with Primus Books.

_____. 2020. *A Comprehensive History of Modern Bengal, 1700-1950, Volume III.* Kolkata: The Asiatic Society, in association with Primus Books.

_____. 2014. *The Defining Moments in Bengal, 1920-1947.* New Delhi: Oxford University Press.

Bhavan, S. 1995. 'Demographic Profile and Future Strategies for Development of the Girl Child in India.' *Social Change*, Vol. 25, Nos. 2-3, June-September.

Borthwick, Meredith. 1984. *The Changing Role of Women in Bengal, 1849-1905.* New Jersey: Princeton University Press.

_____. 1982. 'The Bhadramahila and Changing Conjugal Relations in Bengal.' In *Women in India and Nepal*, edited by Michael Allen and S.N. Mukherjee. Canberra: South Asian History Section of the Australian National University.

Bose, Pradip Kumar. 2006. *Health and Society in Bengal: A Selection from Late 19th-Century Bengali Periodicals.* New Delhi: Sage.

_____. 1878. *Brahmo Public Opinion*, Calcutta: Published for the proprietors by K.N. Dutt.

Bridenthal, Renate, and Claudia Koonz. 1977. *Becoming Visible: Women in European History.* Boston: Houghton-Mifflin.

Brijbhusan, Jamila. 1976. *Kamaladevi Chattopadhyay, Portrait of a Rebel.* New Delhi: Abhinav.

Burton, Antoinette. 1999. 'Conjugality on Trial: the Rukhmabai Case and the Debate on Indian Child-Marriage in Late-Victorian Britain.' In *Disorder in the Court: Trials and Sexual Conflict at the Turn of the Century*, edited by George Robb and Nancy Erber. London: Macmillan.

Carroll, Berenice A. 1976. *Liberating Women's History: Theoretical and Critical Essays.* Urbana: University of Illinois Press.

Carroll, Lucy. 2007. 'Law, Custom, and Statutory Social Reform: The Hindu Widows' Remarriage Act of 1856.' In *Women and Social Reform in Modern India: A Reader, Volume 1*, edited by Sumit Sarkar and Tanika Sarkar. New Delhi: Permanent Black.

———. 1983. 'Law, Custom, and Statutory Social Reform: The Hindu Widows' Remarriage Act of 1856.' *Indian Economic and Social History Review*, Vol. 20, No. 4, pp. 363-88.

Chakrabarti, Sambuddha. 1995. 'Changing Notions of Conjugal Relations in Nineteenth-Century Bengal.' In *Mind, Body and Society: Life and Mentality in Colonial Bengal*, edited by Rajat Kanta Ray. Oxford: Oxford University Press.

Chakraborty, Aishika. 2008-9. 'Contract, Consent and Ceremony: The Brahmo Marriage Reform (1860-1930).' *Journal of History* (Department of History, Jadavpur University), Vol. 26.

Chakraborty, Rachana. 2009. 'Women's Education and Empowerment in Colonial Bengal.' In *Responding to the West: Essays on Colonial Domination and Asian Agency*, edited by Hans Hagerdal. Amsterdam: Amsterdam University Press.

Chakravarti, Uma. 2003 (1989). 'Whatever Happened to the Vedic Dasi? Orientalism, Nationalism, and a Script for the Past.' In *Recasting Women: Essays in Colonial History*, edited by Kumkum Sangari and Sudesh Vaid. New Delhi: Zubaan Publishers/Kali for Women.

———. 1999. 'Beyond the Altekarian Paradigm: Towards a New Understanding of Gender Relations in Early Indian History.' In *Women in Early Indian Societies*, edited by Kumkum Roy. New Delhi: Manohar.

———. 1993. 'Conceptualizing Brahmanical Patriarchy in Early India: Gender, Caste, Class and State.' *Economic and Political Weekly*, pp. 579-85, April 3.

———. 1990. 'Whatever Happened to the Vedic Dasi? Orientalism, Nationalism, and a Script for the Past.' In *Recasting Women: Essays in*

Indian Colonial History, edited by Kumkum Sangari and Sudesh Vaid. New Brunswick: Rutgers University Press.

_____. 1988. 'In Search of Our Past: A Review of the Limitations and Possibilities of the Historiography of Women in Early India'. *Economic and Political Weekly*, Vol. 23, No. 18.

Chakravarti, Uma, and Kumkum Roy. 1988. 'Breaking Out of Invisibility: Rewriting the History of Women in Ancient India.' In *Retrieving Women's History*, edited by S.J. Kleinberg. Oxford: Berge, UNESCO.

Chanda, Ipshita. 2014. 'Introduction: Women Writing Gender.' In *Shaping the Discourse: Women's Writings in Bengali Periodicals, 1865-1947*, edited by Ipshita Chanda and Jayeeta Bagchi. Kolkata: Stree, School of Women's Studies, Jadavpur University.

Chandra, Sudhir. 2004 (2016). 'Enslaved Daughters: Colonialism, Law and Women's Rights.' In *Women & Law in India*, by Flavia Agnes, Sudhir Chandra and Monmayee Basu. New Delhi: Oxford University Press (Oxford India Paperbacks).

_____. 1998. *Enslaved Daughters: Colonialism, Law and Women's Rights*. New Delhi: Oxford University Press.

_____. 1996. 'Rukhmabai: Debate Over Woman's Right to Her Person.' *Economic and Political Weekly*, pp. 2937-47, 2 November.

_____. 1992. 'Whose Laws? Notes on a Legitimizing Myth of the Colonial Indian State.' *Studies in History*, Vol. 8, No. 2, pp. 187-211.

Chatterjee, Bhaswati. 2021. 'Child Marriage and the Second Social Reform Movement.' In *Love, Labour and Law: Early and Child Marriage in India*, edited by Samita Sen and Anindita Ghosh. New Delhi/Kolkata: Sage Publications/Stree.

Chatterjee, Nandini. 2010. 'English Law, Brahmo Marriage and the Problem of Religious Difference: Civil Marriage Laws in Britain and India.' *Comparative Studies in Society and History*, Vol. 52, No. 3, pp. 10-52.

Chatterjee, Partha. 2003 (1989). 'The Nationalist Resolution of the Women's Question.' In *Recasting Women: Essays in Colonial History*, edited by Kumkum Sangari and Sudesh Vaid. New Delhi: Zubaan Publishers Pvt. Ltd/Kali for Women.

_____. 1993. *The Nation and Its Fragments: Colonial and Postcolonial Histories*. New Jersey: Princeton University Press.

_____. 1990. 'The Nationalist Resolution of the Women's Question.' In *Recasting Women: Essays in Indian Colonial History*, edited by Kumkum Sangari and Sudesh Vaid. New Brunswick: Rutgers University Press.

_____. 1989. 'Colonialism, Nationalism and Colonized Women: The

Contest in India.' *American Ethnologist* (Wiley), Vol. 16, No. 4, pp. 622-33, November.

Chatterji, Ramananda. 1890. 'Frequent Cases of Suicide among Young men and Women.' *Indian Messenger*, Vol. VII.

Chattopadhyay, Kamaladevi. 1986. *Inner Recesses, Outer Spaces: Memoirs*. New Delhi: Navrang.

______. 1983. *Indian Women's Battle for Freedom*. New Delhi: Abhinav Publications.

Chattopadhyay, Kamaladevi, and others. 1939. *The Awakening of Indian Women*. Madras: Everyman's Press.

Chaudhuri, Maitrayee. 1995. 'Citizens, Workers and Emblems of Culture: An Analysis of the First Plan Document on Women.' *Contributions to Indian Sociology*, Vol. 29, Nos. 1&2, pp. 211-35.

Chintamani, C. Yajnesvara. 1901. *Indian Social Reform, in four parts, Being a Collection of Essays, Addresses, Speeches, etc., with an Appendix*. Madras: Minerva Press/Thompson & Co.

Chowdhry, Prem. 1996. 'Contesting Claims and Counter-Claims: Questions of the Inheritance and Sexuality of Widows in a Colonial State.' In *Social Reform, Sexuality and the State*, edited by Patricia Uberoi. London: Sage Publications.

______. 1995. 'Popular Perceptions of Widow-remarriage in Haryana: Past and Present.' In *From the Seams of History: Essays on Indian Women*, edited by Bharti Ray. Delhi: Oxford University Press.

______. 1994. *The Veiled Women: Shifting Gender Equations in Rural Haryana, 1880-1990*. New Delhi: Oxford University Press.

______. 1993. 'Conjugality, Law and State: Inheritance Rights as Pivot of Control in Northern India.' *National Law School Journal*, Vol. 5, Issue 1.

Chowdhury, Ishita, and Utsarjana Mutsuddi. 2021. 'Love and Law: Understanding Child Marriage in Rural West Bengal.' In *Love, Labour and Law: Early and Child Marriage in India*, edited by Samita Sen and Anindita Ghosh. New Delhi: Sage/Stree.

Cousins, M.E. 1922. *The Awakening of Asian Womanhood*. Madras: Ganesh and Co.

______. n.d. *What Women Have Gained by the Reforms*. Madras: Besant Tress.

Das, Veena. 1995. *Critical Events: An Anthropological Perspective on Contemporary India*. New Delhi: Oxford India Paperbacks.

Deb, Mahesh Chundra. 1956. 'A Sketch of the Condition of the Hindoo Women.' In *Awakening in Bengal in Early Nineteenth Century (Selected*

Documents): Volume One, edited by Goutam Chattopadhyay. Calcutta: Progressive Publishers.

Derrett, J. Duncan M. 1968. *Religion, Law and the State in India.* London: Faber and Faber.

Desai, Neera, and Usha Thakkar. 2001 (1st edn.). *Women in Indian Society.* India: National Book Trust.

Dutt, Paramananda. 1935. *Memoirs of Motilal Ghose.* Calcutta: Amrita Bazar Patrika Office.

Engels, Dagmar. 1996. *Beyond Purdah? Women in Bengal 1890-1939.* Delhi: Oxford University Press.

_____. 1985. 'The Age of Consent Act of 1891: Colonial Ideology in Bengal.' *South Asia Research* Vol. 3, No. 2, pp. 107-34.

Fernandes, Leela. 2003. 'Review of Tanika Sarkar's Hindu Wife, Hindu Nation: Community, Religion, and Cultural Nationalism.' *The Journal of Asian Studies*, Vol. 62, No. 2, pp. 683-85, May.

Forbes, Geraldine Hancock. 1996 (2015). *The New Cambridge History of India IV. 2: Women in Modern India.* New Delhi: Cambridge University Press.

_____. 1988. 'The Politics of Respectability: Indian Women and the Indian National Congress.' In *The Indian National Congress: Centenary Highlights*, edited by D. A. Low. Oxford: Oxford University Press.

_____. 1979. 'Women and Modernity: The Issue of Child Marriage in India.' *Women's Studies International Quarterly*, Vol. 2, 407-19.

_____. 1975. *Positivism in Bengal: A Case Study in the Transmission and Assimilation of an Ideology.* India: Minerva Associates Private Limited.

Gandhi, M.K. 1942 (1958). *Women and Social Injustice.* Ahmedabad: Navajivan Press.

Ghose, Benoy. 1981. *Selections from English Periodicals of 19th Century Bengal, Vol. 6, 1861-1874.* Calcutta: Papyrus.

_____. 1980. *Selections from English Periodicals of 19th Century Bengal, Vol. 3, 1849-56.* Calcutta: Papyrus.

Ghosh, Biswajit. 2011. 'Child Marriage, Community, and Adolescent Girls: The Salience of Tradition and Modernity in the Malda District of West Bengal.' *Sociological Bulletin* (Indian Sociological Society), Vol. 60, No. 2, pp. 307-26, May-August.

_____. 2011. 'Child Marriage, Society and the Law: A Study in a Rural Context in West Bengal, India.' *International Journal of Law, Policy and Family*, Vol. 25, No. 2, pp. 199-219.

_____. 2011. 'Early Marriage of Girls in Contemporary Bengal: A Field View.' *Social Change* (Sage), Vol. 41, No. 1, pp. 41-61.

Ghosh, Biswajit, and Ananda Mohan Kar. 2010. 'Child Marriage in Rural West Bengal: Status and Challenges.' *Indian Journal of Development Research and Social Action*, Vol. 6, Nos. 1-2, pp. 1-23, January-December.

Ghosh, Durba. 2007. 'Review of Mrinalini Sinha's Specters of Mother India: The Global Restructuring of an Empre.' *Journal of British Studies* Vol. 46, No. 3, July.

Ghosh, J.C. 1891. *Age of Consent: Remarks on the Bill of 1891.* Calcutta.

Ghosh, Subhasri. 2014. 'Coming of Age in Colonial India: The Discourse and Debate over the Age of Consummation in the Nineteenth Century.' In *Colonial Girlhood in Literature, Culture and History, 1840-1950*, edited by Kristine Moruzi and Michelle J. UK: Palgrave Macmillan.

Gidumal, Dayaram. 1889. *The Status of Woman in India, or A Handbook for Hindu Social Reformers.* Bombay: Fort Printing Press.

______. 1888. *The Life and Life-Work of Behramji M. Malabari.* Bombay: Education Society's Press.

Graner, Elvira. 2021. 'Governing Child Marriage in India: The Protected Reform Process.' In *Love, Labour and Law: Early and Child Marriage in India*, edited by Samita Sen and Anindita Ghosh. New Delhi: Sage/Stree.

Guha, Ambalika. 2018. *Colonial Modernities: Midwifery in Bengal, c.1860-1947.* London and New York: Routledge.

Gupta, J.S. n.d. 'Children Protection Bill.' *Modern Review.*

Hartman, Mary S., and Lois Banner. 1973. *Clio's Consciousness Raised: New Perspectives on the History of Women.* London: Pluto Press.

Hatekar, Neeraj, Rajni Mathur, and Pallavi Rege. 2007. '"Legislating" Social Change: Strange Case of the Sarda Act.' *Economic and Political Weekly*, Vol. 42, No. 2, pp. 145-53.

Heimsath, Charles H. 1962. 'The Origin and Enactment of the Indian Age of Consent Bill, 1891.' *The Journal of Asian Studies*, Vol. 21, No. 4, pp. 491-504, August.

Heimsath, Charles. 1964. *Indian Nationalism and Hindu Social Reform.* Princeton: Princeton University Press.

Hossain, Sara. 2012. 'Chapter 20. Equality in the Home: Women's Rights and Personal Laws in South Asia.' In *Human Rights of Women: National and International Perspective*, edited by Rebecca J. Cook. Philadelphia: University of Pennsylvania.

Jabbi, M.K. 1986. 'Child Marriages in Rajasthan.' *Social Change*, Vol. 16, No. 1, pp. 3-9.

Jain, M.P. 1952. *Outlines of Indian Legal History.* Bombay: N.M. Tripathi Private Ltd.

Jayawardena, Kumari. 1995. *The White Woman's Other Burden: Western Women and South Asia During British Colonial Rule.* London and New York: Routledge.

Jha, Manoranjan. 1971. *Katherine Mayo and India.* New Delhi: People's Publishing House.

John, Mary E. 2022. 'A Suitable Girl? Marriage, Age and Equality'. https://www.theindiaforum.in/article/suitable-girl.

______. 2021. *Child Marriage in an International Frame: A Feminist Review from India.* New York: Routledge.

______. 2021. 'Some Historiographical Challenges in Approaching Child Marriage in India.' In *Love, Labour and Law: Early and Child Marriage in India*, edited by Samita Sen and Anindita Ghosh, pp. 1-28. New Delhi/Kolkata: Sage Publications/Stree.

Kapadia, K.M. 1966. *Marriage and Family in India.* New Delhi: Oxford University Press.

Kapur, Ratna. 2020 (1996). *Feminist Terrains in Legal Domains: Interdisciplinary Essays on Women and Law in India.* New Delhi: Zubaan Publishers/Kali for Women.

Kapur, Ratna, and Brenda Cossman. 1996. *Subversive Sites: Feminist Engagements with Law in India.* New Delhi/Thousand Oaks/London in association with The Book Review Literary Trust: Sage Publications.

Karlekar, Malavika. 2005. *Re-visioning the Past: Early Photography in Bengal, 1875-1915.* New Delhi: Oxford University Press.

Karve, Irawati. 1968. *Kinship Organisation in India.* Bombay: Asia Publishing House.

Kaur, Amrit. 1946. *Challenge to Women.* Allahabad: New Literature.

Kopf, David. 1979. *The Brahmo Samaj and the Shaping of the Modern Indian Mind.* New Jersey: Princeton University Press.

Kosambi, Meera. 2007 (First Paperback Printing 2011). 'Child Brides and Child Mothers: The Age of Consent Bill (1891).' In *Crossing Thresholds: Feminist Essays in Social History*, by Meera Kosambi. New Delhi: Permanent Black.

______. 2007 (First Paperback Printing 2011). 'Resisting Conjugality: Rakhmabai's Protest.' In *Crossing Thresholds: Feminist Essays in Social History*, by Meera Kosambi. New Delhi: Permanent Black.

______. 2007 (2011). *Crossing Thresholds: Feminist Essays in Social History.* Ranikhet: Permanent Black.

______. 1995. 'Gender reform and competing state controls over women:

The Rakhmabai case (1884-1888).' *Contributions to Indian Sociology*, Vol. 29, Nos. 1&2, pp. 265-90.

———. 1991. 'Girl Brides and Socio-Legal Change: Age of Consent Bill (1891) Controversy.' *Economic and Political Weekly*, Vol. 26, No. 31/32, pp. 1857-68, 3-10 August.

———. 1988. 'Women, Emancipation and Equality: Pandita Ramabai's Contribution to Women's Cause.' *Economic and Political Weekly*, Vol. 23, No. 44, pp. WS38-WS49, 29 October.

Kumar, Radha. 1993. *The History of Doing: An Illustrated Account of Movements for Women's Rights and Feminism in India, 1800-1990.* London/New Delhi: Verso/Kali for Women.

———. 1983. 'Family and Factory: Women in the Bombay Cotton Textile Industry, 1919-1939.' *Indian Economic and Social History Review*, Vol. 20, No. 1, pp. 81-110.

Lal, Ruby. 2013. *Coming of Age in Nineteenth-Century India: The Girl-Child and the Art of Playfulness.* Cambridge: Cambridge University Press.

Lateef, Shahida. 1994. 'Defining Women through Legislation.' In *Forging Identities: Gender, Communities and the State in India*, edited by Zoya Hasan. New Delhi: Kali for Women.

———. 1990. *Muslim Women in India: Political & Private Realities: 1890s - 1980s.* New Jersey: Zed Books Ltd.

Liddle, Joanna, and Rama Joshi. 1985. 'Gender and Imperialism in British India.' *South Asia Research*, Vol. 5, No. 2, November.

Mahadevan, Kuttan, and M. Sumangala. 1992. 'Population Policy in India: Perspectives for the Future.' *Indian Journal of Public Administration*, Vol. 38, No. 3, pp. 227-40.

Mahmood, Tahir. 1980. 'Marriage-Age in India and Abroad - A Comparative Conspectus.' *Journal of Indian Law Institute*, Vol. 22, No. 1, pp. 38-80.

———. 1978. *Civil Marriage Law: Perspectives and Prospects.* New Delhi: Indian Law Institute.

———. 1977. *Muslim Personal Law: Role of State in the Subcontinent.* Delhi: Vikas Publishing House.

Major, Andrea. 2011. 'Mediating Modernity: Colonial State, Indian Nationalism and the Renegotiations of the "Civilizing Mission" in the Indian Child Marriage Debate of 1927-1932.' In *Civilizing Missions in Colonial and Postcolonial South Asia: From Improvement to Development*, edited by Carey A. Watt and Michael Mann. London: Anthem Press.

Majumdar, Rochona. 2009. *Marriage and Modernity: Family Values in Colonial Bengal.* Durham and London: Duke University Press.

Majumdar, Vina. 1979. 'Introduction.' In *Symbols of Power: Studies on the Political Status of Women in India*, edited by Vina Mazumdar. New Delhi: Allied Publishers.

Mani, Lata. 2003 (1989). 'Contentious Traditions: The Debate on Sati in Colonial India.' In *Recasting Women: Essays in Colonial History*, edited by Kumkum Sangari and Sudesh Vaid. New Delhi: Zubaan Publishers/ Kali for Women.

______. 1998. *Contentious Traditions: The Debate on Sati in Colonial India.* Berkeley: University of California Press.

______. 1987. 'Contentious Traditions: The Debate on Sati in Colonial India.' *Cultural Critique*, Vol. 7, pp. 119-56.

Masselos, Jim. 1992. 'Sexual Property/Sexual Violence: Wives in nineteenth-Century Bombay.' *South Asia Research*, Vol. 12, No. 2, November.

Mayo, Katherine. 1927. *Mother India.* New York.

Menon, Nivedita. 1999 (2001). *Gender and Politics in India.* New Delhi: Oxford University Press.

______. 1993. 'Abortion and the Law: Questions for Feminism.' *Canadian Journal of Women and the Law*, Vol. 6, No. 1, pp. 103-18.

Menski, Werner F. 2003. *Hindu Law: Beyond Tradition and Modernity.* New Delhi: Oxford University Press.

Mill, James. 1840. *The History of British of India, with notes by H.H. Wilson.* London: James Madden.

Mitra, Durba. 2020. *Indian Sex Life: Sexuality and the Colonial Origins of Modern Social Thought.* New Jersey: Princeton University Press.

Mitra, Samarpita. 2020. *Periodicals, Readers and the Making of a Modern Literary Culture: Bengal at the Turn of the Twentieth Century.* Leiden/ Boston: Brill.

Mody, Perveez. 2002. 'Love and the Law: Love Marriage in Delhi.' *Modern Asian Studies*, Vol. 36, No. 1, pp. 223-56.

______. 2008. *The Intimate State: Love-Marriage and the Law in Delhi.* New Delhi: Routledge.

Mozoomdar, P.C. 1887. *The Life and Teachings of Keshub Chunder Sen.* Calcutta: Baptist Mission Press.

Mukherjee, Sumita. 2006. 'Using the Legislative Assembly for Social Reform: The Sarda Act of 1929.' *South Asia Research*, Vol. 26, No. 3, pp. 219-33.

Mukhopadhyay, Amitabha. 1957. 'Sati as a Social Institution in Bengal.' *Bengal Past and Present*, Vol. 76.

Murmu, Maroona. 2020. *Words of Her Own: Women Authors in Nineteenth-Century Bengal.* New Delhi: Oxford University Press.

Murshid, Ghulam. 1983. *Reluctant Debutante: Response of Bengali Women to Modernization, 1849-1905.* Rajshahi: Rajshahi University Press.

Muttreja, Poonam, Alok Vajpeyi, and Martand Kaushik. 2022. 'Instead of Raising Women's Marriage Age, here are Six Things India Should do to Curb Child Marriage.' https://scroll.in/article/1020697/instead-of-raising-womens-marriage-age-here-are-six-things-india-should-do-to-curb-child-marriage.

Nair, Janaki. 1996. *Women and Law in India: A Social History.* New Delhi/Bangalore: Kali for Women/National Law School of India University.

Nandy, Ashis. 1994. 'Sati as Profit Versus Sati as Spectacle.' In *Sati, the Blessing and the Curse*, edited by J.S. Hawley. New York: Oxford University Press.

______. 1980. *At The Edge of Psychology: Essays in Politics and Culture.* Delhi: Oxford University Press.

______. 1980. 'Sati: A Nineteenth Century Tale of Women, Violence and Protest.' In *Rammohun Roy and the Process of Modernization in India*, edited by V.C. Joshi. Delhi: Vikas Publishing House.

Natarajan, S. 1959. *A Century of Social Reform in India.* Bombay: Asia Publishing House.

Nehru. 1949. 'Gandhiji and Women'. *Incidents of Gandhiji's Life*, edited by Chandrashankar Shukla. Bombay: Vora.

Nehru, Rameshwari. 1950. In *Gandhi is My Star: Speeches and Writings of Shrimati Rameshwari Nehru*, edited by Somnath Dhar. Patna: Pustak Bhandar.

______. 1938. 'Early Marriage.' In *Our Cause: A Symposium by Indian Women*, edited by Shyam Kumari Nehru. Allahabad: Kitabstan.

Pal, Bipin Chandra. 1932. *Memoirs of My Life and Times, in the Days of My Youth (1857-1884).* Calcutta: Modern Book Agency.

Pande, Ishita. . 2020. 'Power, Knowledge, and the Epistemic Contract on Age: The Case of Colonial India.' *American Historical Review*, Vols. 407-17, April.

______. 2020. *Sex, Law and the Politics of Age: Child Marriage in India, 1891-1937.* Cambridge: Cambridge University Press.

______. 2013. '"Listen to the Child": Law, Sex, and the Child Wife in Indian Historiography.' *History Compass*, Vol. 11, No. 9, pp. 687-701.

______. 2013. 'Phulmoni's Body: the Autopsy, the Inquest and the Humanitarian Narrative on Child Rape in India.' *South Asian History and Culture*, Vol. 4, No. 1, pp. 9-30.

______. 2013. 'Sorting Boys and Men: Unlawful Intercourse, Boy-Protection, and the Child Marriage Restraint Act in Colonial India.' *The Journal of the History of Childhood and Youth*, Vol. 6, No. 2, pp. 332-58.

______. 2012. 'Coming of Age: Law, Sex and Childhood in Late Colonial India.' *Gender & History*, Vol. 24, No. 1, pp. 205-30, April.

Panjabi, Kavita, and Paromita Chakravarti. 2012. *Women Contesting Culture: Changing Frames of Gender Politics in India.* Kolkata: Stree, School of Women's Studies, Jadavpur University.

Paranjape, Makarand. 1996. *Sarojini Naidu, Selected Letters, 1890s to 1940s.* New Delhi: Kali for Women.

Parashar, Archana. 1992. *Women and Family Law Reform in India: Uniform Civil Code and Gender Equality.* New Delhi: Sage.

Parekh, Bhiku. 1989. *Gandhi's Political Philosophy: A Critical Examination.* Basingstoke: Macmillan.

Paril, Bal. 1976. 'Raising Marriageable Age: Demographic Impact.' *The Economic Times*, 15 June.

Patel, Reena. 2005. 'Review of Flavia Agnes, Sudhir Chandra and Monmayee Basu's Women & Law in India.' *Feminist Legal Studies*, Vol. 13, pp. 259-61.

Pathak, Zakia, and Rajeswari Sunder Rajan. 1992. 'Shahbano.' In *Feminists Theorize the Political*, edited by Judith Butler and Jean W. Scott. New York: Routledge.

______. 1989. 'Shahbano.' *Signs: Journal of Women in Culture and Society* (The University of Chicago Press), Vol. 14, No. 3, pp. 558-82.

Rajwade, Laxmibai. 1938. 'The Indian Mother and Her Problems.' In *Our Cause: A Symposium by Indian Women*, edited by Shyam Kumari Nehru. Allahabad: Kitabstan.

Raman, Sita Anantha. 2009. *Women in India: A Social and Cultural History*, Volume 2. California: ABC CLIO.

Ramusack, Barbara. 1981. 'Women's Organizations and Social Change.' In *Women and World Change: Equity Issues in Development*, edited by N. Black and A.C. Cottrell. London: Sage Publications.

Rao, Anupama. 1999. 'Review of Sudhir Chandra's book, Enslaved Daughters: Colonialism, Law and Women's Rights.' *The Journal of Asian Studies*, Vol. 58, No. 2, pp. 543-4, May.

Rappaport, Helen. 2003. *Queen Victoria: A Biographical Companion.* California: ABC-CLIO.

Rathbone, Eleanor. 1934. *Child Marriage: The Indian Minotaur, An Object-Lesson from the Past to the Future.* London: George Allen & Unwin Ltd.

Rau, Dhanvanthi Rama. 1977. *An Inheritance: The Memoirs of Dhanvanthi Rama Rau.* London: Harper and Row.

Ray, Bharati. 1995. 'The Three Generations: Female Rivalries and the Joint Family in Bengal, 1900-1947.' In *Mind, Body and Society: Life and Mentality in Colonial Bengal,* edited by Rajat Kanta Ray. Oxford: Oxford University Press.

______. 1991. 'Women of Bengal: Transformation in Ideas and Ideals, 1900-1947.' *Social Scientist,* Vol. 19, Nos. 5/6, pp. 3-23, May-June.

______. 1991. 'Bengali Women and Politics of Joint Family, 1900-47.' *Economic and Political Weekly,* Vol. 26, No. 52, 28 December.

______. 1988. 'Beyond the Domestic/Public Dichotomy: Women's History in Bengal, 1905-1947.' In *Modern Bengal: A Socio-Economic Survey,* edited by S.P. Sen and N.R. Ray. Calcutta.

Ray, Bharati, and Aparna Basu. 1999. *From Independence Towards Freedom: Indian Women Since 1947.* New Delhi: Oxford University Press.

Ray, Utsa. 2019. 'How to be a Good Wife? Some Thoughts on "New" Domesticity in Nineteenth Century Bengal.' In *Writing Women in History: Glimpses from India's Colonial Past,* edited by Suparna Gooptu. Kolkata: K.P. Bagchi & Company.

Raychaudhuri, Tapan. 2000. 'Love in a Colonial Climate: Marriage, Sex and Romance in Nineteenth-Century Bengal.' *Modern Asian Studies,* Vol. 34, No. 2, May.

______. 1988. *Europe Reconsidered: Perceptions of the West in Nineteenth Century Bengal.* Delhi: Oxford University Press.

Reaume, Denise. 1996. 'What is Distinctive about Feminist Analysis of Law.' *Legal Theory,* Vol. 2.

Reddy, Mrs. 1964. *Autobiography of Dr (Mrs) S. Muthulakshmi Reddy: A Pioneer Woman Legislator.* Madras.

Reddy, S. Muthulakshmi. 1930. *My Experience as a Legislator.* Madras: Current Thought Press.

Rowbotham, Sheila. 1975. *Hidden from History: 300 Years of Women's Oppression and the Fight Against It.* New York: Pantheon Press.

Sagade, Jaya. 2005. *Child Marriage in India: Socio-legal and Human Rights Dimensions.* Delhi: Oxford University Press.

Sangari, Kumkum, and Sudesh Vaid. 2003 (1989). *Recasting Women: Essays in Colonial History.* New Delhi: Zubaan/Kali for Women.

Sanyal, Rajat. 1980. *Voluntary Associations and the Urban Public Life in Bengal (1815-1876): An Aspect of Social History.* India: Riddhi.

Sarasvati, Ramabai. 1888. *The High-Caste Hindu Women.* Philadelphia: J.B. Rodgers Printing Company.

Sarkar, Mahua. 2020. 'The Idea of Justice and Evolution of the Calcutta High Court, 1862-1915.' In *A Comprehensive History of Modern Bengal, 1700-1950,* Vol. II, by Sabyasachi Bhattacharya. Kolkata: The Asiatic Society, in association with Primus Book.

______. 1997. *Justice in a Gothic Edifice: The Calcutta High Court & Colonial Rule in Bengal.* Calcutta: Firma KLM Private Limited.

Sarkar, Sumit. 2007. 'Vidyasagar and Brahmanical Society.' In *Women and Social Reform in Modern India,* edited by Sumit Sarkar and Tanika Sarkar. New Delhi: Permanent Black.

______. 2003. 'The Controlled Emancipation of Wives.' In *Social and Religious Reform: The Hindus of British India,* edited by Amiya P. Sen. New Delhi: Oxford University Press.

______. 1983. *Modern India: 1885-1947.* Madras: MacMillan India Ltd.

Sarkar, Sumit, and Tanika Sarkar. 2007. *Women and Social Reform in Modern India, Volume 1 & 2.* New Delhi: Permanent Black.

Sarkar, Tanika. 2020. 'Changing Hindu Women: Bengal in the Long Nineteenth Century.' In *A Comprehensive History of Modern Bengal, 1700-1950, Volume II,* edited by Sabyasachi Bhattacharya. Kolkata: The Asiatic Society, in association with Primus Books.

______. 2020. 'Intimate Violence in Colonial Bengal: A Death, a Trial and a Law, 1889-1891.' *Law and History Review,* Vol. 38, No. 1, pp. 177-200, February.

______. 2008. 'Wicked Widows: Law and Faith in Nineteenth-century Public Sphere Debates.' In *Behind the Veil: Resistance, Women and the Everyday in Colonial South Asia,* edited by Anindita Ghosh. London: Palgrave Macmillan.

______. 2007. 'Conjugality and Hindu Nationalism: Resisting Colonial Reason and the Death of a Child-Wife.' In *Women and Social Reform in Modern India: A Reader, Volume I,* edited by Sumit Sarkar and Tanika Sarkar. Ranikhet: Permanent Black.

______. 2001. 'Enfranchised Selves: Women, Culture and Rights in Nineteenth-Century Bengal.' *Gender & History,* Vol. 13, No. 3, pp. 546-65, November.

______. 2001. *Hindu Wife, Hindu Nation: Community, Religion, and Cultural Nationalism.* Bloomington and Indianapolis: Indiana University Press.

______. 2000. 'A Prehistory of Rights: The Age of Consent Debate in Colonial Bengal.' *Feminist Studies,* Vol. 26, No. 3, pp. 601-22.

______. 1999. *Words to Win: The Making of Amar Jiban: A Modern Autobiography.* New Delhi: Kali for Women.

______. 1996 (2020). 'Colonial Law-making and Lives/Deaths of Indian

Women: Different Reading of Law and Community.' In *Feminist Terrains in Legal Domains*, edited by Ratna Kapur. New Delhi: Kali for Women/Zubaan.

———. 1995. 'Hindu Conjugality and Nationalism: in Late Nineteenth Century Bengal.' In *Indian Women: Myth and Reality*, by Jasodhara Bagchi. India: Sangam Books.

———. 1994. 'Bankimchandra and the Impossibility of a Political Agenda.' *Oxford Literary Review*, Vol. 16.

———. 1993. 'Rhetoric Against Age of Consent: Recasting Colonial Reason and Death of a Child-Wife.' *Economic and Political Weekly*, Vol. 28, No. 36, pp. 1869-79.

———. 1992. 'The Hindu Wife and the Hindu Nation: Domesticity and Nationalism in Nineteenth-Century Bengal.' *Studies in History*, Vol. 8, No. 2, pp. 213-35.

———. 1984. 'Politics and Women in Bengal - the Conditions and Meaning of Participation.' *Indian Economic and Social History Review*, Vol. 21, No. 1, pp. 91-101.

Sastri, Sivanath. 1974 (2nd edn.). *History of the Brahmo Samaj, Volume 1 (1911), Volume 2 (1912).* Calcutta: Sadharan Brahmo Samaj.

———. 1912. *History of the Brahmo Samaj: Volume II.* Calcutta: Brahmo Mission Press.

———. 1911. *History of the Brahmo Samaj, Volume I.* Calcutta: R. Chatterji.

Sathe, S.P. 1993. *Towards Gender Justice.* Bombay: S. N. D. T. Women's University.

Sehgal, Brinder Pal Singh. 1989. *Population Control and the Law: Problems, Policies, Remedial Measures.* New Delhi: Deep and Deep Publications.

Sen, Amiya P. 2003. 'Introduction.' In *Social and Religious Reform: The Hindus of British India*, edited by Amiya P. Sen. New Delhi: Oxford University Press.

———. 2003. *Social and Religious Reform: The Hindus of British India.* Delhi: Oxford University Press.

———. 1993. *Hindu Revivalism in Bengal, 1872-1905: Some Essays in Interpretation.* Delhi: Oxford University Press.

Sen, Asoke. 1977. *Iswar Chandra Vidyasagar and His Elusive Milestones.* Calcutta: Riddhi-India.

Sen, Samita. 2012. 'Crossing Communities: Religious Conversion, Rights in Marriage, and Personal Law.' In *Negotiating Spaces: Legal Domains, Gender Concerns and Community Constructs*, by Flavia Agnes and Shoba Venkatesh Ghosh. New Delhi: Oxford University Press.

———. 2009. 'Religious Conversion, Infant Marriage and Polygamy:

Regulating Marriage in India in the Late Nineteenth Century.' *Journal of History*, Vol. 26, pp. 99-145.

_____. 1997. 'Book Review of Jasodhara Bagchi's Indian Women: Myth and Reality.' *Indian Journal of Gender Studies* (Sage Publications), Vol. 4, No. 2, pp. 277-80.

Sen, Samita, and Anindita Ghosh. 2021. *Love, Labour and Law: Early and Child Marriage in India.* New Delhi/Kolkata: Sage Publications India Pvt Ltd/Stree.

Shah, K.T. 1956. *Women's Role in Planned Economy: Report of the Sub-Committee.* Bombay: Vora & Co. Publishers Ltd.

Shahnawaz, Jahan Ara. 1971. *Father and Daughter: A Political Autobiography.* Lahore: Nigarishat.

Sharma, Kumud, and C.P. Sujaya. 2012 (1974). *Towards Equality: Report of the Committee on the Status of Women in India.* New Delhi: Pearson Education.

Singh, Indu Prakash. 1989. *Women, Law and Social Change in India.* New Delhi: Radiant Publishers.

Singha, Radhika. 2003. 'Colonial Law and Infrastructural Power: Reconstructing Community, Locating the Female Subjects.' *Studies in History*, Vol. 19, No. 1, pp. 87-126, January-June.

_____. 1998. *A Despotism of Law: Crime and Justice in Early Colonial India.* New Delhi: Oxford University Press.

Sinha, Mrinalini. 2012. 'Potent Protests: The Age of Consent Controversy, 1891.' In *Handbook of Gender*, edited by Raka Ray. New Delhi: Oxford University Press.

_____. 2006. *Specters of Mother India: The Global Restructuring of an Empre.* Durham and London: Duke University Press.

_____. 1999. 'The Lineage of the "Indian" Modern: Rhetoric, Agency and the Sarda Act in Late Colonial India." In *Gender, Sexuality and Colonial Modernities*, edited by Antoinette Burton. London and New York: Routledge.

_____. 1998. *Selections from Mother India: Katherine Mayo.* New Delhi: Kali for Women.

_____. 1995. *Colonial Masculinity: The 'Manly Englishman' and the 'Effeminate Bengali' in the Late Nineteenth Century.* New York: Manchester University Press.

_____. 1994. 'Reading Mother India: Empire, Nation and the Female Voice.' *Journal of Women's History*, Vol. 6, No. 2.

_____. 1989. 'The Age of Consent Act: The Ideal of Masculinity and Colonial Ideology in Nineteenth-Century Bengal.' In *Shaping Bengali Worlds,*

Public and Private, edited by T.K. Stewart. Michigan: Michigan State University.

———. 1954. *Knocking at the Door (Lectures and Other Writings).* Calcutta: Living Age Press.

Sinha, Pradip. 1965. *Nineteenth Century Bengal: Aspects of Social History.* Kolkata: Firma KL Mukhopadhyay.

Southard, Barbara. 1995. *The Women's Movement and Colonial Politics in Bengal.* Delhi: Manohar.

Sreenivas, Mytheli. 2008. *Wives, Widows, and Concubines: The Conjugal Family Ideal in Colonial India.* Bloomington and Indianapolis: Indiana University Press.

Swasthya. 1901. 'National Health - How Marriage Affects It (Translated).' January-February.

Tahmankar, D.V. 1956. *Lokamanya Tilak: Father of Indian Unrest and Maker of Modern India.* London: John Murray Publishers.

Tambe, Ashwini. 2019. *Defining Girlhood in India: A Transnational History of Sexual Maturity Laws.* Urbana: University of Illinois Press.

———. 2009. *Codes of Misconduct: Regulating Prostitution in Late Colonial Bombay.* Minneapolis: University of Minnesota Press.

———. 2009. 'The State as Surrogate Parent: Legislating Nonmarital Sex in Colonial India, 1911-1929.' *The Journal of the History of Childhood and Youth*, Vol. 2, No. 3, pp. 393-427.

Tattvabodhini Patrika. 1872 (June). 'The Civil Marriage Bill.'

Telang, K.T. 1916. *Selected Writing and Speeches.* Bombay: K.R. Mitra.

Terchek, Ronald J. 1999. *Gandhi: Struggling for Autonomy.* London: Rowman and Littlefield.

Tharu, Susie, and Tejaswini Niranjana. 1996. 'Problems for a Contemporary Theory of Gender.' In *Subaltern Studies IX*, edited by Dipesh Chakrabarty. New Delhi: Oxford University Press.

———. 1915. *The Miscellaneous Writings of the Late Hon'ble Mr. Justice M. G. Ranade.* Bombay: The Manoranjan Press.

The Modern Review. 1937. 'Child Marriage Restraint Act in French India.' May.

———. 1929. 'Sarda's Child Marriage Bill Postponed.' February.

———. 1929. 'The Hindu Child Marriage Bill.' March.

———. 1927. 'Child Marriage and Education, Mrs Muthulaxmi Reddy writes in the Social Service Quarterly', September. pp. 337-8.

The Times of India. 1978. 'Bill to Raise Age of Marriage Okayed.' 22 February.

Tyagi, Anju. 2018. 'Review of Flavia Agnes's Family Law and Constitutional

Claims; Marriage, Divorce and Matrimonial Litigation.' *Journal of National Law University Delhi*, pp. 130-4.

Vidyasagar, Ishwarchandra. 1864. *Marriage of Hindu Widows*. Calcutta: The Sanskrit Press.

Viswanathan, Gauri. 1998. *Outside the Fold: Conversion, Modernity and Belief*. New Jersey: Princeton University Press.

Walsh, Judith E. 2004. *Domesticity in Colonial India: What Women Learned When Men Gave Them Advice*. USA: Rowman and Littlefield Publishers.

Whitehead, Judy. 1995. 'Modernising the Motherhood Archetype: Public Health Models and the Child Marriage Restraint Act of 1929.' *Contributions to Indian Sociology*, pp. 187-209.

Yang, Anand A. 2007. 'Whose Sati? Widow Burning in Early-Nineteenth-Century India.' In *Women and Social Reform in Modern India: A Reader*, Volume 1, edited by Sumit Sarkar and Tanika Sarkar. New Delhi: Permanent Black.

Bengali Language Sources

BOOKS, CHAPTERS IN EDITED VOLUMES AND ARTICLES

Ananda Bazar Patrika, 3 January 2021. 'Adhikar Chai Ekusher' (Want the rights of twenty-one).

_____, 21 June 1929. 'Apatti Keno' (Why Object).

_____, 3 September 1929. 'Balya Bibaha Birodh' (Child Marriage Controversy.)

_____, 12 January 1923. 'Janani O Jaya' (Mother and Wife).

Anusandhan. 1891 (1298). 'Bibidha Prasanga' (Miscellaneous Context), 32 Ashar (June-July), Vol. 4, 23 Issue.

_____. 1891 (1298). 'Sammatir Bill O Brahmo Samaj' (Consent Bill and Brahmo Samaj), 31 Baishakh (April-May), Vol. 4, No. 19, pp. 456-8.

Bandhab. 1291 Bangabda. 'Balyabibaha Sambandhe Malabarir Mantabya' (Malabari's Comments on Child Marriage), Vol. 8, No. 8.

Bandyopadhyay, Aparna. 2014. 'Tin Aain Sambandhe Dui Char Katha' (Two or Four Words about the Act III). In *Nari: Andare Bahire* (Woman: Inside and Outside), edited by Shubhrakumar Mukhopadhyay, Pratapkumar Sen and Eeshita Chattopadhyay. Kolkata: Hooghly Mohsin College.

Bandyopadhyay, Sri Charuchandra. 1931 (1338). 'Samajer Bartaman Abastha

O Mahilader Kartabya.' (The Current State of Society and the Duties of Women). *Prabasi*, Magh (January-February), Volume 2, Part 31.

Basu, Amrit Lal. 1367BS. 'Sammati Sankat.' (Consent Dilemma). In *Samajchitre Unabingsha Shatabdir Bangla Prahasan* (Bengali Farce of Nineteenth Century in Social Representation), edited by Dr. Jayanta Goswami. Kolkata: Sahityashree.

Basu, Chandranath. 1880. 'Bibaher Bayas O Uddeshya' (Age and Purpose of Marriage). *Bangadarshan.*

Basu, Ishan Chandra. 1884. *Nari Neeti* (Principle of Women). Calcutta: Gurudas Chattopadhyay.

______. 1884. *Streediger Prati Upadesh* (Advice to the Wives/Advice for Women). Calcutta: Victoria Press.

Basu, Swapan. 2003. *Sambad-Samayik Patre Unish Shatake Bangali Samaj,* Vol. 2 (Bengali Society of Nineteenth Century in Newspapers and Periodicals: Vol. 2). Calcutta: Paschimbanga Bangla Academi.

Bharati. 1919. 'Jatikshoy o Shishu Mrityu' (Racial Deterioration and Infant Mortality). Vol. 43, No. 10, January.

Bose, Priyanath. 1934. *Griha-dharma* (Household duties). Calcutta.

Chakrabarty, Ajit Kumar. 1958. *Maharshi Devendranath Thakur.* Calcutta: Jijnasa.

Chakraborty, Sambuddha. 1995. *Andare Antare: Unish Satake Bangali Bhadramahila* (Domestic and Mental Spaces: Elite Women in Nineteenth Century). Calcutta: Stree.

Chanda, Rani. 1384. *Amar Ma'r Baper Bari* (My Mother's Father's House). Kolkata: Visva-Bharati Granthan Bibhag.

Chandra, Srinath. 1969 (1913). *Brahmo Samaje Challis Bathsar* (Forty Years in Brahmo Samaj). Kolkata: Brahmo Mission Press.

Chaudhurani, Sarat Kumari. 1357 Shraban. 'Didima' (Grandmother). In *Sarat Kumari Chaudhuranir Rachanabali* (Writings of Sarat Kumari Chaudhurani), edited by Sri Brajendranath Bandyopadhyay and Sri Sajanikanta Das. Kolkata: Bangiya Sahitya Parishat.

Das, Jibanananda. 1954. 'Amar Ma, Baba' (My Mother and Father). Uttar Suri.

De, Sunil Kanti. 1994. 'Sarada Bill O Muslim Sambad-Samayik Patra' (Sarda Bill and Muslim Newspapers-Periodicals). Vol. 9, in *Itihas Anusandhan.* Kolkata: Paschimbanga Itihas Samsad.

Deb, Chitra. 1980 (1982). *Thakurbarir Andarmahal* (Inner Space of Tagore Household). Kolkata: Ananda Publishers.

Debi, Saradasundari. 2013 (2016). 'Atmakatha' (Autobiography). In *Andarer Itihas: Narir Jabanbandi*, Volume 2 (Inner History: Women's

Testimony), edited by Ahana Biswas and Prasun Ghosh. Kolkata: Gangchil.

Devi, Ashapurna. 1966. *Subarnalata.* Kolkata: Mitra O Ghosh Publishers Private Limited.

Devi, Giribala. 1957. 'Raybari'. In *Giribala Devir Rachanabali,* by Bani Roy. Kolkata: Ramayani Prakash Bhaban.

Devi, Jyotirmoyee. 1331 BS. 'Narir Pratibha' (Women's Talent). *Bharati,* Vol. 48, Nos. 1-6.

Devi, Manoda. 2014. *Shikshita Patitar Atmacharit* (Autobiography of an Educated Fallen Woman). Vol. 2, in *Promila Smritikatha Samgraha* (Collection of Promila Memoirs), edited by Bijit Ghosh. Kolkata: Punascha.

Dhar, Prafulla Kumar. 1925. *Strir Sahit Kathopakathan* (Conversations with Wife). Calcutta.

Gangopadhyay, Prabhat Chandra. 1946. *Banglar Nari Jagaran* (Women's Awakening in Bengal). Kolkata: Sadharan Brahmo Samaj.

Ghosh, Benoy. 2020 (1963). *Samayikpatre Banglar Samajchitra,* Vol. 5 (Social Life in Bengal as Depicted in Bengali Periodicals). Calcutta: Deep Prakashan (Revised Edition).

_____. 1963. *Samayikpatre Banglar Samajchitra,* Vol. 2 (Social Life in Bengal as Depicted in Bengali Periodicals). Calcutta: Bikkhan Prakashak.

_____. 1960. *Samayikpatre Banglar Samajchitra, 1840-1905, Vol. 2, Tattvabodhini Patrikar Rachana Sankalan* (Social Representation of Bengal in Periodicals, Volume 2: Compilation of Essays of Tattvabodhini Patrika). Kolkata: Bikkhan Bhaban, Bengal Publishers Private Ltd.

Hussein, Mohammad Meherullah. 1909. *Balya Bibaher Bishmay Fal* (The Poisonous Fruit/Result of Child Marriage). Sirajganj: Author.

Kar, Bankubihari. 2003. *Purba Banglar Brahmo Samajer Itibritta* (History of the Brahmo Samaj of East Bengal). Kolkata: Sadharan Brahmo Samaj.

Khatun, Moslema. 1988. 'Amar Jibaner Galpakatha' (The Story of My Life). In *Kaler Samukh Bhela* (The Raft Ahead of Time), edited by Nurunnahar Faizunnessa. Dhaka: Muktadhara.

Mahalanabish, Gurucharan. 1982 (1974). 'Atmakatha' (Autobiography). In *Atmakatha,* 2 edited by Naresh Jana, Manu Jana and Kamal Kumar Sanyal. Calcutta: Ananya Prakashan.

Mahalanobis, Monika. 1941. *Brahmananda Keshubchandrera Patrabali* (Letters of Brahmananda Keshubchandrera). Calcutta: Navabidhan Press.

Majumdar, Leela. 1986 (2010). *Pakdandi* (A Circuitous or Spiral Route that Leads to The Top of a Mountain). Kolkara: Ananda Publishers.

Mitra, Bimal. 1961. *Kari Diye Kinlam.* Kolkata: Mitra O Ghosh Publishers Private Limited.

Mitra, Harendralal. 1367BS. 'Aain Bibhrat' (Legal Breaches). In *Samajchitre Unabingsha Shatabdir Bangla Prahasan* (Bengali Farce of Nineteenth Century in Social Representation), edited by Dr. Jayanta Goswami. Kolkata: Sahityashree.

Mitra, Krishna Kumar. 1974 (1937). *Atmacharit* (Autobiography). Calcutta: Bashanti Chakraborty.

Mukhopadhyay, Bhudev. 1882. *Paribarik Prabandha* (Essays on Family Matters). 9th edn. (1919), Chinsurah: Published by Shri Kumardev Mukhopadhyay in Budhoday Press.

______. 1892. *Samajik Prabandha* (Eassays on Social Matters). Chinsurah: Bishwanath Trust Fund.

Mukhopadhyay, Biswanath. 1986. 'Sahabas Sammati Bill (1891) Sediner Samajik Andolon' (Age of Consent Bill (1891) The Social Movement of that Day). *Desh*, Vol. 53, No. 30.

Mukhopadhyay, Shaktisadhan. 2020. 'Sahabas Sammati Bill O Vidyasagar/ Raay: Bekasur Khalas' (Age of Consent Bill and the Judgement of Vidyasagar: Acquitted). *Anustup*, Vol. 54, Nos. 3-4.

Mustafi, Sreemati Nagendra Bala. 1904. *Garhasthya-dharma* ('Domestic duties'). Burdwan: Shri Khagendranath Mustafi.

Nabyabharat. 1890. 'Hari Mohan Maiteer Danda o Samaj' (Penalty of Hari Mohan Maitee and Society). Vol. 8, No. 4, 1297 Shraban (July-August).

______. 1890. 'Sammatir Bayas O Swadeshiyadiger Nikat Abedan' (Age of Consent and Appeal to the Natives). Vol. 8, No. 4, Poush (December-January).

Nasrin, Taslima. 1993. *Lajja* (Shame). Dhaka: Pearl.

______. 1992 (2012). *Nirbachita Column* (Selected Column). Kolkata: Ananda Publishers Private Limited.

Nath, Shankar Kumar. 2019. *Unish Shataker Kayekjon Bangali-Gabeshak Chikitsak: Ramendrasundar Trivedi Smriti Pustakmala: 14* (Some Bengali-Researcher Doctors of the Nineteenth Century: Ramendrasundar Trivedi Memorial Books: 14). Kolkata: Bangiya Bigyan Parishad.

Pal, Sri Bipin Chandra. 1884 (1806 Shakabda). 'Bangalir Balyakrira O Tahar Bishomoy Fal (Pratham Prastab)' (Childhood Sports of Bengali and Its Poisonous Results: First Proposal). *Aalochana*, Vol. 1.

______. 1884 (1806 Shakabda). 'Bangalir Balyakrira O Tahar Bishomoy Fal (Dwitiya Prastab).' (Childhood Sports of Bengali and Its Poisonous Results: Second Proposal). *Aalochana*, Vol. 1.

Prabasi. 1929 (1336). 'Balyabibaha Nirodh Aain' (Child Marriage Prohibition Act), Poush (December-January), Vol. 2, No. 29.

______. 1929 (1336). 'Balyabibaha Nirodh Aain O Strishiksha' (Child Marriage Prohibition Act and Women's Education). Agrahayan (November-December), Vol. 2, No. 29.

______. 1930 (1337). 'Balyabibaha Nirodh Ainer Fal' (The Result of Child Marriage Prohibition Act). Baishakh (April-May), Vol. 1, No. 30.

______. 1929 (1336). 'Balyabibaha Nishedhak Aain.' (The Law Prohibiting Child Marriage.), Kartik (October-November), Vol. 2, No. 29.

______. 1932 (1339). 'Balyabibaha Punarprabartaner Byartha Chesta' (Unsuccessful Attempts to Reintroduce Child Marriage). Kartik (October-November), Vol. 2, No. 32.

______. 1931 (1338). 'Balyabibaha-Nirodh Aainer Proyog' (Enforcement of Child Marriage Prohibition Act). Bhadra (August-September), Vol. 1, No. 31.

______. 1939 (1346). 'Bankura Zilla Mahila Sammelan' (Women's Conference of Bankura District). Ashadhr (June-July), Vol. 1, No. 39.

______. 1941 (1348). 'Nikhil Bharat Mahila Sammelaner Kolikata Sakhar Adhibeshan' (Session of the Calcutta Branch of the All-India Women's Conference). Poush (December-January), Vol. 2, No. 41.

______. 1931 (1338). 'Sarada Aain Batil Koribar Byartha Chesta' (Unsuccessful Attempts to Repeal the Sarda Act). Chaitra (March-April), Vol. 2, No. 31.

______. 1930 (1337). 'Sarada Aain O Balikadiger Shiksha' (Sarda Act and Girl's Education). Chaitra (March-April), Vol. 2, No. 30.

______. 1933 (1340). 'Sarada Aainer Samarthan O Sanshodhoner Dabi' (Demand for Support and Amendment of the Sarda Act). Baishakh (April-May), Vol. 1, No. 33.

______. 1934 (1341). 'Sarada Aainke Fanki Deoa' (Evading the Sarda Act). Shraban (July-August), Vol. 1, No. 34.

______. 1929 (1336). 'Sarada Bill Sambandhe Mahilader Mat' (Women's Opinion about Sarda Bill). Ashwin (September-October), Vol. 1, No. 29.

Ray, Bharati. 2002 (2014). *Nari O Paribar: Bamabodhini Patrika* (Women and Family: Bamabodhini Patrika). Kolkata: Ananda Publishers.

Roy, Kamini. 1918. *Balikasikshar Adarsha* (The Ideal of Girls' Education). Calcutta: Sudhir Kumar Sen.

Roy, Rammohan. 1973. 'Sahamaran Visaye Pravartak O Nivartaker Sambad' (News of promoters and deterrents on dying together or burning oneself to death on one's husband's funeral pyre). In *Rammohan Rachanavali* (Writings of Rammohan), edited by Ajit Kumar Ghosh. Calcutta: Haraf Prakashani.

Sarkar, Akshaychandra. n.d. 'Hindu Parinay Pratha' (Hindu Marriage Custom). *Bharatbarsha.*

Sarkar, Saralabala. 1989 (2015). 'Sarda Aainer Akarjakarita' (Ineffectiveness of Sarda Act). Vol. 2, in *Saralabala Rachanasangraha* (Collection of Essays of Saralabala), edited by Chitra Deb. Calcutta: Ananda Publishers.

Sastri, Sivanath. 1918 (rpt. 2000). *Atmacharit* (Autobiography). Kolkata: Sadharan Brahmo Samaj.

_____. 1878. *Ei Ki Brahmo Bibaha* (Is this Brahmo form of Marriage?). Kolkata: Albert Press.

_____. 1903 (1983). *Ramtanu Lahiri O Tatkalin Banga Samaj* (Ramtanu Lahiri and The Then Bengal Society). Calcutta: New Age Publishers.

Sen, Keshub Chandra. 1910. *Acharya Keshub Chandrer Baktrita* (Speeches of Acharya Keshub Chandra). Calcutta.

_____. 1885. *Brahmikadiger Prati Srimadacharya Keshub Chandra Sener Upadesh* (Srimadacharya Keshub Chandra Sen's Advice to the women of Brahmo Samaj). Calcutta: Bidhan Yantra.

Sen, Sri Maheshchandra. 1892. 'Sahabas Sammati O Samaj' (Consent to Sexual Intercourse and Society). *Nabyabharat*, Vol. 10, No. 12, Chaitra (March-April).

_____. 1892. 'Sahabas Sammati O Samaj' (Consent to Sexual Intercourse and Society). *Nabyabharat*, Vol. 10, No. 8, Agrahayan (November-December).

_____. 1892. 'Sahabas Sammati O Samaj' (Consent to Sexual Intercourse and Society). *Nabyabharat*, Vol. 10, No. 2, Jyaistha (May-June).

Swasthya Samachar. 1920. 'Shishu Marak' (Infant Mortality). July.

Tagore, Rabindranath. 1369. 'Dena Paona' (Assets and Liabilities). In *Galpaguccha*, by Rabindranath Tagore. Kolkata: Visva Bharati Granthanbibhag, Ashwin.

Vidyasagar, Ishwar Chandra. 1972. 'Bidhababibaha Prachalita Haoya Uchit Kina Etadbisayak Prastab' (A Suggestion on whether Widow Remarriage is to be Practiced). In *Vidyasagar Rachana Samgraha, Vol. 2* (Collection of Writings of Vidyasagar: Volume 2), edited by Ishwar Chandra Vidyasagar. Calcutta: Vidyasagar Smarak Jatiya Samiti.

_____. 1972. 'Bidhababibaha Prachalita Haoya Uchit Kina Etadbisayak

Prastab: Dwitiya Prastab' (A Suggestion on whether Widow Remarriage is to be Practiced: Second Proposal). In *Vidyasagar Rachana Samgraha, Vol. 2* (Collection of Writings of Vidyasagar: Volume 2), edited by Ishwar Chandra Vidyasagar. Calcutta: Vidyasagar Smarak Jatiya Samiti.

Index

Printed and bound by CPI Group (UK) Ltd, Croydon, CR0 4YY

13/09/2026

14961005-0001